DATE DUE

NOV 0 6 1989			

CONRAD: THE CRITICAL HERITAGE

THE CRITICAL HERITAGE SERIES

GENERAL EDITOR: B. C. SOUTHAM, M.A., B.LITT. (OXON.)
Formerly Department of English, Westfield College, University of London

For a list of books in the series see the back end paper

CONRAD

THE CRITICAL HERITAGE

Edited by
NORMAN SHERRY
Professor of English, University of Lancaster

ROUTLEDGE & KEGAN PAUL LONDON AND BOSTON

First published 1973
by Routledge & Kegan Paul Ltd
Broadway House, 68–74 Carter Lane,
London EC4V 5EL and
9 Park Street,
Boston, Mass. 02108, U.S.A.
© Norman Sherry 1973
No part of this book may be reproduced in
any form without permission from the
publisher, except for the quotation of brief
passages in criticism
ISBN 0 7100 7388 7
Library of Congress Catalog Card Number 73-75945

Printed in Great Britain by
Butler and Tanner Ltd,
Frome and London

To Edward Shils

General Editor's Preface

The reception given to a writer by his contemporaries and near-contemporaries is evidence of considerable value to the student of literature. On one side we learn a great deal about the state of criticism at large and in particular about the development of critical attitudes towards a single writer; at the same time, through private comments in letters, journals or marginalia, we gain an insight upon the tastes and literary thought of individual readers of the period. Evidence of this kind helps us to understand the writer's historical situation, the nature of his immediate reading-public, and his response to these pressures.

The separate volumes in the *Critical Heritage Series* present a record of this early criticism. Clearly, for many of the highly productive and lengthily reviewed nineteenth- and twentieth-century writers, there exists an enormous body of material; and in these cases the volume editors have made a selection of the most important views, significant for their intrinsic critical worth or for their representative quality— perhaps even registering incomprehension!

For earlier writers, notably pre-eighteenth century, the materials are much scarcer and the historical period has been extended, sometimes far beyond the writer's lifetime, in order to show the inception and growth of critical views which were initially slow to appear.

In each volume the documents are headed by an Introduction, discussing the material assembled and relating the early stages of the author's reception to what we have come to identify as the critical tradition. The volumes will make available much material which would otherwise be difficult of access and it is hoped that the modern reader will be thereby helped towards an informed understanding of the ways in which literature has been read and judged.

B.C.S.

Contents

ACKNOWLEDGMENTS   *page* xv
ABBREVIATIONS   xvii
INTRODUCTION   1
NOTE ON THE TEXT   45

Almayer's Folly (1895)

1   Unsigned notice, *Daily News*, April 1895   47
2   Unsigned review, *Scotsman*, April 1895   48
3   Unsigned review, *Daily Chronicle*, May 1895   49
4   ARTHUR WAUGH, notice, *Critic*, May 1895   50
5   Unsigned review, *World*, May 1895   51
6   Unsigned review, *Athenaeum*, May 1895   52
7   H. G. WELLS, unsigned review, *Saturday Review*, June 1895   53
8   JAMES ASHCROFT NOBLE, review, *Academy*, June 1895   54
9   Unsigned review, *Speaker*, June 1895   55
10   Unsigned review, *Guardian*, July 1895   57
11   Unsigned review, *Bookman*, September 1895   58
12   Unsigned review, *Literary News*, September 1895   59
13   Unsigned review, *Nation* (U.S.A.), October 1895   60
14   Unsigned review, *Spectator*, October 1895   61

An Outcast of the Islands (1896)

15   Conrad on the literary profession, March 1896   62
16   Unsigned review, *Daily Chronicle*, March 1896   63
17   Extracts from notices in two Scottish papers, March 1896   65
18   JAMES PAYN, review, *Illustrated London News*, April 1896   66
19   Unsigned review, *Daily News*, April 1896   68
20   Unsigned review, *National Observer*, April 1896   69
21   Unsigned review, *Sketch*, May 1896   70
22   Unsigned article, *Bookman*, May 1896   72
23   H. G. WELLS, unsigned review, *Saturday Review*, May 1896   73
24   Unsigned review, *Manchester Guardian*, May 1896   77

CONTENTS

25 Unsigned review, *Spectator*, May 1896   78
26 Unsigned review, *Athenaeum*, July 1896   79
27 Unsigned review, *Nation* (U.S.A.), April 1897   80

The Nigger of the 'Narcissus' (1897)

28 ARNOLD BENNETT on Conrad and Kipling, December 1897   82
29 Unsigned notice, *Daily Mail*, December 1897   83
30 W. L. COURTNEY, review, *Daily Telegraph*, December 1897   85
31 Unsigned review, *Glasgow Herald*, December 1897   88
32 Unsigned review, *Daily Chronicle*, December 1897   89
33 Unsigned review, *Spectator*, December 1897   92
34 I. ZANGWILL, unsigned review, *Academy*, January 1898   94
35 ARTHUR SYMONS on Kipling and Conrad, *Saturday Review*,
    January 1898   97
36 HAROLD FREDERIC, unsigned review, *Saturday Review*,
    February 1898   98

Tales of Unrest (1898)

37 Unsigned review, *Daily Telegraph*, April 1898   101
38 Unsigned review, *Daily Mail*, April 1898   103
39 EDWARD GARNETT, unsigned article, *Academy*, October 1898   104
40 Unsigned article, *Academy*, January 1899   109

Lord Jim (1900)

41 Unsigned review, *Manchester Guardian*, October 1900   111
42 W. L. COURTNEY, review, *Daily Telegraph*, November 1900   114
43 Unsigned review, *Academy*, November 1900   115
44 Unsigned notice, *Sketch*, November 1900   118
45 Unsigned review, *Spectator*, November 1900   119
46 Unsigned review, *Speaker*, November 1900   120
47 Unsigned review, *Pall Mall Gazette*, December 1900   122
48 Unsigned review, *Daily News*, December 1900   124
49 Unsigned review, *Bookman*, February 1901   126
50 Unsigned review, *Critic* (U.S.A.), May 1901   127

Youth: A Narrative and Two Other Stories (1902)

51 CONRAD on 'Heart of Darkness', 1898 and 1899   129

CONTENTS

52 EDWARD GARNETT, unsigned review, *Academy and Literature*,
December 1902   131
53 Unsigned review, *Manchester Guardian*, December 1902   134
54 Unsigned review, *The Times Literary Supplement*, December
1902   136
55 Unsigned review, *Athenaeum*, December 1902   137
56 GEORGE GISSING on Conrad, 1902   140
57 JOHN MASEFIELD, review, *Speaker*, January 1903   141

Typhoon, and other stories (1903)

58 Unsigned review, *Morning Post*, April 1903   143
59 Unsigned review, *Daily Mail*, April 1903   145
60 Unsigned review, *Glasgow Evening News*, April 1903   148
61 Unsigned notice, *Academy*, April 1903   151
62 Unsigned review, *Academy*, May 1903   152
63 A. T. QUILLER-COUCH, review, *Bookman*, June 1903   155
64 Unsigned review, *Speaker*, June 1903   157

Nostromo (1904)

65 CONRAD on writing *Nostromo*, 1903–17   159
66 ARNOLD BENNETT on *Nostromo*, 1912   161
67 CONRAD as a personality in modern literature, 1904   162
68 Unsigned review, *The Times Literary Supplement*, October
1904   164
69 Unsigned notice, *Review of Reviews*, November 1904   166
70 Unsigned notice, *Black and White*, November 1904   166
71 Unsigned review, *Daily Telegraph*, November 1904   167
72 C. D. O. BARRIE, review, *British Weekly*, November 1904   169
73 Unsigned review, *Manchester Guardian*, November 1904   171
74 EDWARD GARNETT, review, *Speaker*, November 1904   174
75 JOHN BUCHAN, unsigned review, *Spectator*, November 1904   177
76 Unsigned notice, *Illustrated London News*, November 1904   180

The Secret Agent (1907)

77 A. N. MONKHOUSE, review, *Manchester Guardian*, September
1907   181
78 Unsigned review, *The Times Literary Supplement*, September
1907   184

CONTENTS

79 Unsigned review, *Country Life*, September 1907   186
80 ARNOLD BENNETT on *The Secret Agent*, 1907   190
81 EDWARD GARNETT, unsigned review, *Nation*, September 1907   191
82 Unsigned notice, *Truth*, October 1907   194
83 Unsigned review, *Glasgow News*, October 1907   195
84 Conrad's reply to the Garnett review, October 1907   197
85 Unsigned notice, *Star*, October 1907   198
86 STEWART EDWARD WHITE, review, *Bookman* (U.S.A.),
       January 1908   199
87 Unsigned article, *Edinburgh Review*, April 1908   201
88 JOHN GALSWORTHY on Conrad, 1908   203

A Set of Six (1908)

89 ROBERT LYND, review, *Daily News*, August 1908   210
90 W. L. COURTNEY, review, *Daily Telegraph*, August 1908   213
91 Unsigned review, *Country Life*, August 1908   217
92 Conrad's response to the reviews, August 1908   219
93 EDWARD GARNETT, unsigned review, *Nation*, August 1908   221
94 CONRAD on Garnett's review in *Nation*, August 1908   224
95 EDWARD THOMAS, review, *Bookman*, October 1908   225

Under Western Eyes (1911)

96 Unsigned review, *Pall Mall Gazette*, October 1911   227
97 RICHARD CURLE, review, *Manchester Guardian*, October 1911   228
98 Unsigned review, *Morning Post*, October 1911   231
99 Unsigned review, *Westminster Gazette*, October 1911   233
100 Conrad's defence of *Under Western Eyes*, October 1911   236
101 EDWARD GARNETT, unsigned review, *Nation*, October 1911   237
102 FORD MADOX HUEFFER, signed article, *English Review*,
        December 1911–March 1912   240

'Twixt Land and Sea (1912)

103 ROBERT LYND, review, *Daily News*, October 1912   251
104 JOHN MASEFIELD, review, *Manchester Guardian*, October 1912   254
105 Unsigned review, *Standard*, October 1912   256
106 Extract from *Spectator*, November 1912   258

Chance (1914)

107 CONRAD, letter to J. B. Pinker, June 1913   259

108 CONRAD on selling his work in America, July 1913   260
109 HENRY JAMES's *Criticism*, 1914   263
110 ROBERT LYND, review, *Daily News*, January 1914   271
111 C. E. MONTAGUE, review, *Manchester Guardian*, January 1914   273
112 ARNOLD BENNETT's opinion, 1914   276
113 EDWARD GARNETT, unsigned review, *Nation*, January 1914   277
114 Some opinions of *Chance*, 1914   281
115 Unsigned review, *Glasgow News*, February 1914   283

Victory (1915)

116 ROBERT LYND, review, *Daily News*, September 1915   285
117 Unsigned review, *Scotsman*, September 1915   287
118 WALTER DE LA MARE, unsigned review, *The Times Literary Supplement*, September 1915   289
119 WALTER DE LA MARE, review, *Westminster Gazette*, October 1915   292
120 Unsigned review, *Nation*, October 1915   295
121 Unsigned review, *Atlantic Monthly*, October 1915   298
122 GERALD GOULD, review, *New Statesman*, October 1915   299
123 Unsigned review, *Glasgow Evening News*, October 1915   301
124 WILLIAM LYON PHELPS on *Victory*, 1917   303

The Shadow-Line (1917)

125 Unsigned review, *Nation*, March 1917   304
126 Extract from an unsigned review, *Morning Post*, March 1917   308
127 Extract from a review, *Bookman*, June 1917   309
128 GERALD GOULD, review, *New Statesman*, March 1917   310

Arrow of Gold (1919)

129 Extract from a review, *New Republic*, May 1919   313
130 Unsigned review, *Morning Post*, August 1919   314
131 WALTER DE LA MARE, unsigned review, *The Times Literary Supplement*, August 1919   316
132 Unsigned review, *New Statesman*, August 1919   321
133 W. L. COURTNEY on Conrad's admirers and detractors, August 1919   324
134 Unsigned review, *Nation*, September 1919   325

The Rescue (1920)

135 CONRAD on completing *The Rescue*, 1919   328
136 Unsigned review, *Morning Post*, June 1920   329
137 VIRGINIA WOOLF, unsigned review, *The Times Literary Supplement*, July 1920   332
138 Unsigned review, *Punch*, July 1920   336
139 Unsigned review, *Nation*, July 1920   337
140 W. DOUGLAS NEWTON, review, *Sketch*, July 1920   341
141 Unsigned review, *London Mercury*, August 1920   342
142 E. M. FORSTER's criticism of Conrad, 1920   345

The Rover (1923)

143 Unsigned review, *Manchester Guardian*, December 1923   349
144 FREDERIC F. VAN DE WATER, review, *New York Tribune*, December 1923   351
145 Unsigned review, *The Times Literary Supplement*, December 1923   354
146 Unsigned review, *Glasgow Evening News*, December 1923   356
147 RAYMOND MORTIMER, review, *New Statesman*, December 1923   358
148 CONRAD, letter to John Galsworthy, February 1924   360
149 DESMOND MACCARTHY on the quality of *The Rover*, 1931   361

Suspense (1925)

150 CONRAD on the reception of *The Rover* and *Suspense*, February 1924   363
151 J. C. SQUIRE on the death of Conrad, *London Mercury*, September 1924   364
152 P. C. KENNEDY, review, *New Statesman*, September 1925   365
153 LEONARD WOOLF, review, *Nation and Athenaeum*, October 1925   366
154 GARNETT's answer to Kennedy's review, 1925   369
155 Unsigned review, *Spectator*, October 1925   372
156 MILTON WALDMAN, review, *London Mercury*, November 1925   375
157 W. SOMERSET MAUGHAM on Conrad's Bornean novels, 1933   377

SELECT BIBLIOGRAPHY   379

INDEX   381

Acknowledgments

The author and publishers would like to thank the following for kind permission to reproduce copyright material. All possible care has been taken to trace ownership of the selections included and to make full acknowledgment for their use.

The Trustees of the Joseph Conrad Estate and J. M. Dent & Sons Ltd for extracts from *Joseph Conrad: Life and Letters* by G. Jean-Aubry, *Conrad's Polish Background*, ed. Z. Najder and *Joseph Conrad's Letters to R. B. Cunninghame Graham*, ed. C. T. Watts; David Garnett, the trustees of the Joseph Conrad Estate and J. M. Dent and Sons Ltd for extracts from *Letters from Joseph Conrad*, ed. Edward Garnett; David Garnett for articles, reviews and letters by Edward Garnett, Duke University Press, the Trustees of the Joseph Conrad Estate and J. M. Dent and Sons Ltd for extracts from *Joseph Conrad: Letters to William Blackwood and David S. Meldrum*, ed. William Blackburn; the *New Statesman* for reviews by Raymond Mortimer and P. C. Kennedy; the Literary Trustees of Walter de la Mare, and the Society of Authors as their representative, for reviews by Walter de la Mare; the Society of Authors as the literary representative of the Estate of John Galsworthy for an article by John Galsworthy; the Society of Authors as the literary representative of the Estate of John Masefield for reviews by John Masefield; the *Daily Telegraph* for reviews by W. L. Courtney; the Estate of Arnold Bennett for extracts from *The Letters of Arnold Bennett*, ed. James Hepburn and *The Journals of Arnold Bennett*, ed. Newman Flower; the Literary Executor of W. Somerset Maugham, William Heinemann Ltd and Doubleday & Company Inc. for extracts from 'Neil Macadam' from *The Complete Short Stories of W. Somerset Maugham*; Edward Arnold Ltd and Harcourt Brace Jovanovich Inc. for 'Joseph Conrad: A Note' in *Abinger Harvest*, copyright 1936, 1964 by E. M. Forster; David Higham Associates Ltd for article on Conrad in *English Review* by Ford Madox Hueffer; the Author's Literary Estate and the Hogarth Press for extract from a review by Leonard Woolf in *Nation and Athenaeum*, 1925; the Executors of H. G. Wells for reviews by H. G. Wells; MacGibbon and Kee Ltd for extract from *Portraits* by Desmond MacCarthy; Charles Scribner's Sons for extract from *Notes on Novelists with Some Other Notes* by Henry James, copyright 1914 Charles Scribner's Sons, renewal copyright 1942 Henry James.

The author would also like to acknowledge the help of Mr Singleton, of the *Manchester Guardian* Library; the staff of the National Library of Scotland and of the Colindale Newspaper Library of the British Museum. Dr C. T. Watts was of great assistance in reading the book at proof stage.

Abbreviations

The following abbreviations are used in the headnotes and elsewhere:

CPB   *Conrad's Polish Background: Letters to and from Polish Friends*, ed. Z. Najder, trans. Halina Carroll, 1964.

L&L   *Joseph Conrad: Life and Letters*, G. Jean-Aubry, 1927.

LCG   *Joseph Conrad's Letters to R. B. Cunninghame Graham*, ed. C. T. Watts, 1969.

LEG   *Letters from Joseph Conrad, 1895–1924*, ed. Edward Garnett, Charter Books, New York, 1962.

LWB   *Joseph Conrad: Letters to William Blackwood and David S. Meldrum*, ed. William Blackburn, 1958.

JAB   *The Journals of Arnold Bennett*, ed. Newman Flower, 1932.

LAB   *Letters of Arnold Bennett*, ed. James Hepburn, 1968.

BJC   *A Bibliography of Joseph Conrad*, Theodore G. Ehrsam, 1969.

References to the works of Joseph Conrad are to the Collected Edition, Dent, 1950.

Introduction

In an unsigned review of *The Rescue* in the *London Mercury*, August 1920 (No. 141), the writer commented that 'the growth of Mr. Conrad's reputation, a plant now a quarter of a century old, has been throughout a curious and impressive subject of study'. This reputation, as reflected in the critical commentary of the time, was indeed impressive in its immediately resting on the originality and genius of Conrad's work. It would be true to say that, on the whole, Conrad fared extremely well at the hands of contemporary reviewers. But from the beginning there was recognition also of those characteristics which would prevent Conrad's becoming a 'popular' writer. The curious aspect of his reputation may be said to lie largely in an extraordinary and late flowering of his popularity with the general reader on the publication of *Chance* when, it is generally agreed, his greatest work was done, an aspect with an ironic slant that Conrad would have appreciated. Minor and more curious aspects of his reputation lay in the puzzlement of reviewers initially as to how to 'place' him which resulted in his being consigned to the island of Borneo as his proper oeuvre and to a series of comparisons with other contemporary writers which irked Conrad, understandably.

Not the least interesting aspect of his reputation with the critics is Conrad's reaction to it, and his constant attempts, increasing in later years, to take a hand in moulding it. Most frequently, he affected to ignore the commentary published on his work. Writing in 1903, to Kazimierz Waliszewski, eight years after the publication of *Almayer's Folly*, his first novel, Conrad, wishing to give Waliszewski some notion of his progress in the world of letters, wrote: 'Herewith some reviews of my books . . . I wished to give you an idea of what they say here about me. The newspapers are stupid.'[1] In 1899 he wrote to Blackwood: '. . . the blind distribution of praise or blame . . . which is the very essence of "periodical" criticism seems to me to be a work less useful than skirt-dancing and not quite as honourable as pocket-picking.'[2] And in 1919, he wrote to a Mr Cumberland, 'I must confess that, in truth, I never did care what anybody said. It may appear a most brutal and ungrateful thing to come from a man who has been so well understood.' This comment, of course, was made late in his career when he had achieved a large reading public. Soon after the publication of *Almayer's Folly*, he complained rather perversely of being over-rated: 'I consider it [*Almayer's Folly*] honestly a miserable failure. Every critic (but two or three) overrated the book.' But the greatest possible caution has to be exercised over Conrad's statements about his own work and its reception. Edward Garnett rightly stresses this strange aspect of Conrad: 'When Conrad was particularly pleased with his work he pooh-poohed it in his letters—"This is the sort of rot I am writing now" . . . and again, "I send you the second installment of 'Jim'—which is too wretched for words".'[3]

It must be remembered, also, that Conrad's pretence at indifference to commentary masked a deep concern with his works' reception which sprang from his constant concern that his 'art' should be properly understood but also that he should make money out of it. Financial difficulties were continuous and, although he contrived to live reason-ably well always, he was given at intervals to despair over his situation and to unlikely schemes for improving it. The two sources of irritation crop up at intervals throughout his life.

The recognition of Conrad's genius coupled with his lack of popu-larity with the general reader influenced not only Conrad's reaction to the contemporary response to his work but also his relationship with publishers. Underlying all was his need to earn a living. It was Edward Garnett, reader for Fisher Unwin, who, with his talent for discovering genius, recognized the quality of *Almayer's Folly* and this, and *An Out-cast of the Islands*, were published by his firm. Conrad was paid £20 for the copyright of the first, and £50 plus a 12½ per cent royalty for the second.[4] It should be remembered that Conrad was thirty-eight when his first novel was published, that to continue writing he gave up a career as a seaman, and that he had no other regular income, save what he could earn as a writer. Soon after the publication of *An Outcast of the Islands*, he married and thereafter had a wife and family to support. His outburst to Garnett when Garnett first visited him at his lodgings in Gillingham Street—'But I *won't* live in an attic. I'm past that, you understand? I *won't* live in an attic!'—is understandable, particularly since it followed Garnett's declaration about a writer's need to follow his own path and disregard the public's taste. The note of Conrad's future dilemma sounded ominously at the very beginning of his second career.

He fell out with Fisher Unwin when, after the publication of *An*

Outcast of the Islands, he was offered a low royalty and an advance of £50 on a book of short stories. Unwin had lost on Conrad's books—the first edition of *Almayer's Folly* had been of 2,000 copies, and a third impression was not needed for seven years. Fisher Unwin's 'town traveller', David Rice, had prevailed on the booksellers at Edward Garnett's instigation to subscribe most of the edition. Garnett tells us that the result was 'that the title *Almayer's Folly* long remained a jest in "the trade"' at Rice's own expense. Garnett, who was for many years to advise and assist Conrad, now was instrumental in bringing *The Nigger of the 'Narcissus'* to the notice of Sidney Pawling of Heinemann, and indirectly to the notice of the influential W. E. Henley, editor of the *New Review*, who subsequently published the novel as a serial prior to book publication. It was Garnett also who brought Conrad into contact with *Blackwood's Magazine* which accepted 'Karain'. *Maga*, as the magazine was known, was held in great esteem: 'It was ... the ambition of all young writers in my day to find themselves in *Blackwood*,' wrote Sir Hugh Clifford, and William Blackwood was sympathetic and helpful and patient with young talent.

In his need to make a living, however, Conrad became entangled in promises to various sources for material, seeking advances on unfinished scripts and finding that the pressure of then having to complete a work or of being involved in a serialization of a work he was engaged on, a great strain. 'If one only could do without serial publication,' he exclaimed.

William Blackwood, however, having signed a contract with Conrad for a volume of three tales in 1898, and having been pleased with 'Youth' and 'Heart of Darkness', waited until 1902 for the third story, 'The End of the Tether'. This was partly due to the unexpected expansion of *Lord Jim*, which was to have completed the trilogy, from a short story into a novel. On the other hand, Blackwood increased the pressure on Conrad by beginning the publication of *Lord Jim* as a serial with only four instalments ready.

By 1902, Conrad's affairs were in some disorder. In 1900, he had borrowed £50 from Blackwood and was to take out an insurance policy on which to borrow money to pay an outstanding debt. Blackwood stood as surety for part of the insurance loan. Conrad was also involved in fulfilling agreements with Heinemann, Blackwood and Ford Madox Hueffer. It was at this point that he allowed his agent, J. B. Pinker, who had been handling his affairs since 1900, to take over also his dealings with Blackwood, which until then he had insisted on handling himself. Pinker constantly assisted Conrad with loans but his intrusion here seems to have, in part, helped to break the relationship with Blackwood, whose tradition was to form personal relationships with his authors. However, the break outwardly came with Blackwood's refusal to give a further loan on the copyright of *Lord Jim* and some other stories. At an interview, he spoke directly to Conrad: 'He was very kind but told me plainly that I was a loss to the Firm.' Conrad was to reflect wistfully on his association with William Blackwood who 'looked upon the writing of fiction as something not to be bounded altogether by time or space'. But at the time of the break he stoutly refused to compromise his art, even in face of his lack of general popularity. 'However unfavourably it may affect the business in hand', he insisted to William Blackwood, after the interview, 'I shall not depart from my method . . . All my endeavours shall be directed to understand it better, to develop its great possibilities, to acquire greater skill in the handling—to mastery in short.'

After the break with Blackwood, Conrad depended to a great extent upon Pinker to place his material and give him financial aid. In 1902 he wrote to Pinker: 'I am nearly going mad with worry . . . death would be the best thing. It would pay off all my debts.' The previous November Conrad had received £240 from Pinker, part of it for work still unplaced. In 1908 he wrote to Galsworthy: 'Ah! my dear, you don't know what an inspiration-killing anxiety it is to think: "Is it saleable?" There's nothing more cruel than to be caught between one's impulse, one's act, and that question, which for me simply is a question of life and death.' He worked out that he had written eleven novels and had lived on an average of £650 per year, and apart from other debts owed Pinker £1,572. In 1899 Conrad shared an *Academy* award which brought him £50, and in 1905 he was given a grant of £500, and a Civil List pension of £100 per annum in 1910. In the same year he sold some of his manuscripts at not very high prices to John Quinn who in 1924 was to sell the manuscript of *Victory* alone for $8,100. Yet, while writing *Under Western Eyes*, Conrad was desperately upset over Pinker's refusal to advance more money unless the novel was finished in a fortnight: 'Does he think I am the sort of man who wouldn't finish the story in a week if he could? . . . he talks of *regular supplies of manuscript* to a man who in these conditions . . . sends him MS at the rate of 7,600 words a month; and he actually writes as if I were a swindler from whom nothing can be got unless he's pinched.' But he also wrote: 'The fact remains that Pinker was the

4

only man who backed his opinion with his money, and that in no grudging manner . . .'

It is not surprising that his money troubles together with the intense emotion he put into his writing should have brought on a breakdown after the writing of *Under Western Eyes*.

Conrad's success as a writer in popular terms came through the agency of Hugh Clifford, who in 1909 persuaded Gordon Bennett, proprietor of the *New York Herald*, to take an interest in Conrad's work. He serialized *Chance* in 1912, and as a result Alfred Knopf of Doubleday persuaded his firm to promote *'Twixt Land and Sea*. Conrad suddenly became a best-seller. In England, *Chance* sold 13,200 copies in two years, where *Under Western Eyes* had sold 4,112. By 1923, when Conrad paid his visit to the United States, he was a successful author, famous both in England and across the Atlantic.

'A WRITER OF GENIUS'

Almayer's Folly (1895) and *An Outcast of the Islands* (1896)

'In the 'nineties *Almayer's Folly* was an immense and exhilarating surprise to those who cared for good letters' (*London Mercury*, No. 141). The surprise lay in the uniqueness and originality of the work. The *Literary News* (U.S.A.) in a highly appreciative review (No. 12) stressed that 'a new vein [had] been struck in fiction' and the *Guardian* (this is not the *Manchester Guardian*) used the same metaphor: '[Conrad's] is evidently not the hand of a novice, and we can only hope that he will give us more of such pure ore from the virgin mine which he has struck' (No. 10). Many found the book haunting and unexpected: '. . . we have been struck with the book, and know nothing quite like it of recent years', wrote the reviewer in the *Daily Chronicle* (No. 3), and the *Speaker* (No. 9) found it was 'impossible to forget the book'. This quality of uniqueness had been instrumental in leading to Fisher Unwin's acceptance of the novel for publication. Edward Garnett, reader for Unwin's, spoke of his reaction to the manuscript: 'The strangeness of the tropical atmosphere . . . excited my curiosity about the author, who I fancied might have Eastern blood in his veins.' [5] W. H. Chesson, who originally drew Garnett's attention to the novel, recalled many years later in his review of *Under Western Eyes* (*Daily Chronicle*, 13 October 1911): '*Almayer's Folly* was then under my eyes as Mr. Unwin's receiver and weeder of MSS; and I remember how the magical melancholy of that masterpiece submerged me and how its note of haunted loneliness called me into isolation, while I read it in the clamorous heart of London.'

For many critics, the novel secured Conrad a place among contemporary authors. The *Daily Chronicle* (No. 3) concluded: 'Mr. Conrad may go on, and with confidence; he will find his public, and he deserves his place.' The reviewer in the *Saturday Review* (No. 7), probably H. G. Wells, prophesied that *Almayer's Folly* would 'certainly secure Mr. Conrad a high place among contemporary story-tellers', and the *Speaker* (No. 9) told its readers: 'If Mr. Conrad can give us another story as striking and life-like as this, his place in our literature ought to be an assured one.' The obvious point was made that Conrad had, as the *Daily News* (No. 1) put it, 'annexed the island of Borneo', and Arthur Waugh in the *Critic* (No. 4) echoed this: 'The "parochial" spirit in fiction has extended to Borneo, a tract hitherto untouched by the novelist, but now annexed by Mr. Joseph Conrad, a new writer.'

Conrad's reactions to the reviews can be traced in his letters. The *Scotsman* (No. 2) had called the novel 'a remarkable book', and Conrad wrote to Marguerite Poradowska, his cousin in Belgium (whom he addressed as 'aunt'): 'The Scottish papers (dailies) have begun to review my *Folly*. Short, journalistic, but highly laudatory! Above all, the *Scotsman*, a big Edinburgh paper, gets almost enthusiastic.'[6] The *World* (No. 5) classed the novel as 'a dreary record of the still more dreary existence of a solitary Dutchman doomed to vegetate in a small village in Borneo', and Conrad, in a letter of 18 May 1895 to his publisher, responded with relish: 'But the poor old *World* kicks at me ... like a vicious donkey ... no criticism in the true sense of the word.'[7] But writing to Marguerite Poradowska, 11 June 1895, Conrad says: 'have gone back to writing, much encouraged by *seven columns and a half* in the *Weekly Sun*, in which T. P. O'Connor buried me under an avalanche of compliments.'[8] It is in this review that the term 'genius' is for the first (but certainly not the last) time applied to Conrad: 'But under the magic of the writer of genius who has told its story—and he is a writer of genius—I learned almost the entire mystery and heart of this strange, far-off region.'

On the whole, there is a sense of fairness about the reviews though some critics were puzzled. Granted that the novel 'stands far apart from the common run of novels', as *Bookman* (No. 11) stated, 'Why it does not take its place among those of first-rate power and excellence is difficult to say with any precision.' And the *Bookman*'s criticism is one which I think Conrad took to heart but which he found difficult to apply: 'In bits it [the novel] is excellent and earns instant admiration. As a whole it is a little wearisome . . . The action drags.'

The *Nation* (U.S.A.) (No. 13) surely shamed itself with the remark: '*Almayer's Folly* offers a good opportunity for protest. Borneo is a fine field for the study of monkeys, not men. The only interesting native of Borneo got away and was long ago introduced to an astonished civilisation as "The old man from Borneo/Who's just come to town."'

Undoubtedly, then, Conrad had much to be satisfied with in the response of reviewers to this 'new' writer, and a writer who was by certain leading reviewers recognized as having arrived fully grown on the literary scene. It is quite impossible to speak of Conrad's 'prentice work. Though the reviews are a mixed bag, Conrad's impact was distinct and forceful.

Conrad credited his continued career as a novelist to the encouragement of Garnett who persuaded him he could write another novel, but it seems unlikely that Conrad required such persuasion. As early as the creation of *Almayer's Folly* he was a dedicated writer: 'I am in the midst of struggling with Chap. XI; a struggle to the death, you know! If I let up, I am lost! I am writing you just before going out. I must go out sometimes, alas! I begrudge each minute I spend away from paper.'9 And by August 1894 he had established the outline of the plot for, and begun writing, his second novel, then called *Two Vagabonds*, as a letter to his cousin shows.10 This novel was also to be set in Borneo, earlier in time than *Almayer's Folly* but with the return of characters such as Babalatchi, the one-eyed statesman (who had so touched Garnett's heart11), already well-established in his first novel: 'You see that I can't get away from Malays. I am devoted to Borneo', continued Conrad in his letter to his cousin of August 1894.12 No doubt this emotion was strengthened by those reviewers who spoke of his annexing this area for novel writing. He was reassured by the *Guardian's* call to give more of the pure ore from his virgin mine. And he had no reason to be disappointed with the reception of his second novel, for the same points of originality and genius were made about it. In a letter to Edward Garnett of 24 May 1896, Conrad shows his pleasure in the notice the book attracted, and particularly in a review by H. G. Wells: 'Any amount of reviews! Heaps! It's distracting if one could take it all in. But one does not—fortunately. You are the best of invalids to send me the commented *Sat. Rev.* I had seen it! I was puzzled by it but I felt confusedly what you say in your letter. Something brings the impression off—makes its effect. What? It can be nothing but the expression

—the arrangement of words, the style—Ergo: the style is not dishonourable. I wrote to the reviewer. I did! And he wrote to me. He did!! And who do you think it is?—He lives in Woking. Guess. Can't tell? I will tell you. It is H. G. Wells. May I be cremated alive like a miserable moth if I suspected it! Anyway he descended from his "Time-Machine" to be kind as he knew how. It explains the review.'[13] Conrad had a right to be pleased. Wells did after all in the same review (No. 23) write: '*An Outcast of the Islands* is, perhaps, the finest piece of fiction that has been published this year, as *Almayer's Folly* was one of the finest that was published in 1895.' The *Daily Chronicle* (No. 16) spoke of 'an intense art' and many were agreed that they had in their midst 'a writer of singular power' (*Scotsman*, No. 17a), or a book of 'singular and indefinable power' (*Glasgow Herald*, No. 17b), or an author with 'the marvellous power of depicting a painful situation' (*Black and White*, 2 May 1896). The *Citizen*, 2 May 1896, again used that overworked term 'genius'. 'What is genius? In the abstract it is perhaps impossible to say; in the concrete possible but hazardous. Yet we dare say that there is something very like genius in Mr. Joseph Conrad's second novel . . . We have no space for futile adjectives; we simply urge again the one short word we gave at the outset—our opinion may be wrong—as the fit one.' Even the *Spectator* (No. 25) felt, with reservation, that this 'short word' could be applied: '. . . much is forgiven to genius, and there is genius in this novel.'

Again, Conrad's originality is suggested by the reviewers' difficulty in slotting him into an easily recognizable place. 'This is a book apart and not at all easy to classify', said the *Tablet*, 25 April 1896. The *Guardian*, 10 June 1896, granted that 'the story is fantastically unlike anything that would occur to European ideas'. One characteristic of contemporary criticism, that of assessing an author by comparing him with established writers, which showed in reviews of *Almayer's Folly*, was present again, and more strongly, in the reviews of *An Outcast of the Islands*, in attempts to place Conrad. The *Athenaeum* had earlier compared him with Louis Becke (see No. 6, p. 51) and had also suggested, 'Conrad has, we imagine, studied Zola to some purpose'. The *Weekly Sun*, more prone to the use of superlatives, spoke of Conrad in the same breath as Balzac and Turgenev: 'Turgenieff has created "The Lear of the Steppes"; Balzac, the Lear of the Boulevards, "Pere Goriot". Almayer is the Lear of the Malay Archipelago.' The *Spectator* (No. 14) ended its review of *Almayer's Folly* with the prophecy: 'Joseph Conrad . . . might become the Kipling of the Malay Archipel-

ago.' Sixteen years later in a review of *Under Western Eyes*, W. H.
Chesson recalled this early placing of Conrad and gave his reply to it:
'Someone coined the absurd phrase "Kipling of the Malay Archipelago"
as a description of a Conrad promised or portended by his first book,
forgetting that the essence and ambition of each of these artists suffice
not only to separate them, but to place them on different planes. For
Mr. Conrad represents the genius of negation as surely as Mr. Kipling
represents the genius of affirmation' (*Daily Chronicle*, 13 October 1911).
And yet the Kipling comparison was understandable, though it was
often used as a stick to beat Conrad. Referring to the *Spectator*'s account
of Conrad as a future 'Kipling of the Malay Archipelago', the review in
National Observer (No. 20), unsigned but probably by W. E. Henley
(see headnote to No. 20), adds: '. . . we fear that this prophecy has not
been fulfilled. Mr. Kipling is a master of rapid delineation of character,
of vivid directness of style . . . Mr. Conrad, on the contrary, is diffuse.'
And not content with placing Conrad as Kipling's inferior, the reviewer
saw him as Stevenson's inferior: 'It is like one of Mr. Stevenson's South
Sea Stories, grown miraculously long and miraculously tedious.' Even
the *Sketch* (No. 21), though full of praise for *An Outcast of the Islands*,
comments: 'He lacks, though he will not lack it long, the master's
[Stevenson] reserve and reticence.' The *Manchester Guardian*'s comparison with Kipling (No. 24) was a much sounder one: '. . . as masculine as Kipling, but without that parade of masculinity which Kipling
loves.' The *Daily Chronicle* (No. 16) saw that 'Excepting in Melville,
perhaps, we know nothing to match his scenic descriptions of tropical
islands', and James Payn, himself a popular novelist of the time, saw
Conrad as a disciple of Victor Hugo (*Illustrated London News*, No. 18).

And the attempt to place his novels led to further criticism. The
World, 1 April 1896, defines the novel as a 'romance' and complains
that as such it should have a different hero: 'The worst faults of the
romance are its redundancy and the absence of greatness of any kind
in the persons concerned. A mere rogue does very well for a novel, but
for a romance we want at least one "archangel of the pit".' James Payn,
in the *Illustrated London News* (No. 18), says of Willems: '. . . never did
so mean a skunk figure as the hero of a novel.' The repulsive character
of the hero troubled many of Conrad's critics. The general charge
against his early novels then, as now, was that they were diffuse. The
National Observer (No. 20) spoke of the 'besetting sin of wordiness'.
H. G. Wells, in the *Saturday Review* (No. 23), though full of praise,
made much of this weakness of Conrad: 'One fault it has, and a glaring

fault . . . Mr. Conrad is wordy: his story is not so much told as seen intermittently through a haze of sentences. His style is like river-mist.' The *Daily Chronicle* (No. 16) found it necessary to speak of a tendency 'towards superfluity . . . touches are added to what is already complete, and the surplusage weakens the whole picture.' The *Weekly Sun*, extravagantly in Conrad's favour, admitted that 'faults of overladen and exaggerated epithet which defaced the first book are even more noticeable in the second'. Conrad had his own answer in a letter to his publisher, Fisher Unwin, on 28 May 1896 when he wrote: 'My style may be atrocious—but it produces its effect—is as unalterable as . . . the size of my feet—and I will never disguise it in boots of Wells's (or anybody else's) making. . . . I shall make my own boots or perish.'[14]

After such a reception, Conrad might have been expected to go on to further success, but the next part of his life is marked by unsettlement and two false starts. He began a novel called *The Sisters*, about a young Russian living in a studio in Paris. On Garnett's—sound—advice, he abandoned this and began *The Rescuer: A Tale of Narrow Waters*, returning to the Malayan archipelago and that Captain Tom Lingard of *Almayer's Folly* who had been praised in the *Spectator* (No. 25): 'There is, however, one grand character in the book—that of the old seaman, Tom Lingard. This personage, who is conceived on the colossal scale of primitive romance, looms through the lurid atmosphere of crime and sensuality like a legendary type of rugged, incorruptible manhood.' On 24 March 1896 Conrad married Miss Jessie George, and continued work on *The Rescuer* while on honeymoon and living in Brittany, but by August he had laid *The Rescuer* aside.

The *Literary World*, 24 April 1896, had commented: 'In *An Outcast of the Islands* Mr. Joseph Conrad clings on to the success he scored by his *Almayer's Folly*. Having made a hit he has gone on shooting through the old hole. . . . We hope Mr. Conrad will drop Sambir and its villains and *vauriens* when he makes his next effort, and delight his readers with—to use theatrical language—entirely new characters, new scenery, and new dresses.' The influence of this comment may, perhaps, be seen in the novel Conrad began before returning to England—*The Nigger of the 'Narcissus'*, originally entitled, *The Fore-castle: A Tale of Ships and Men*. Like *The Rescuer* this was a tale of the sea, but left Malayan waters to deal with the journey of the *Narcissus* from Bombay to London.

'NO PLOT AND NO PETTICOATS'

The Nigger of the 'Narcissus' (1897) and *Tales of Unrest* (1898)

With the publication of *The Nigger of the 'Narcissus'* (1897), Conrad gained, if not a wider reading public, at least a strengthening of his reputation among those who appreciated his work. The period following, up to the publication of *A Set of Six* (1908), shows, in terms of critical reception, an increasing admiration on the part of reviewers. This is paralleled on Conrad's part by an increasing sense of strain which came from his continuous concern about the reception of his work, but also from his method of personal absorption in his fiction which made writing an exhausting occupation. The measure of his personal involvement, the imaginative re-living of his experiences and events, can be judged from his way of writing about his novels. To Garnett on 10 January 1897 (seven days before he completed the novel), he wrote: 'Nigger died on the 7th at 6 p.m.; but the ship is not home yet. Expected to arrive tonight and be paid off tomorrow. And the end! I can't eat—I dream—nightmares—and scare my wife. I wish it was over! But I think it will do! . . . Mind I only think—not sure.'[15] Arnold Bennett certainly thought it would do. The novel appeared first in Henley's journal, the *New Review* (August to December 1897), and in December it was published in book form. On 6 December, Arnold Bennett wrote in his journal: 'This afternoon, reading in the *New Review* (which this month ceases to exist) the conclusion of Joseph Conrad's superb book *The Nigger of the 'Narcissus'*, I had a mind to go on at once with my Staffordshire novel,[16] treating it in the Conrad manner, which after all is my own, on a grander scale.'[17]

Conrad was certainly cock-a-hoop at the reception of this book. To Garnett (7 January 1898) he exclaims: 'I had 23 reviews. One indifferent (*The Standard*) and one bad (*The Academy*). Two or three of a hesitating kind in prov. papers. The rest unexpectedly appreciative. Did I tell you I had a warm letter from Quiller Couch? He is going to say something about the book in *Pall Mall Magazine* for Febry.—';[18] and on 15 January: 'Sinjohn [John Galsworthy] writes me that the *N.* is in great request at his club—Junior Carlton. Great Guns!'[19] and 'Chesson wrote me a splendid letter about the *Nigger*. It quite cheered me.'[20] And Garnett speaks of 'a general blast of eulogy from a dozen impressive sources, including James Payn, A. T. Quiller-Couch, W. L. Courtney. . . .'[21]

There is no doubt that the novel was well and impressively received, and its unusual nature in comparison with the 'usual' batch of books particularly struck reviewers. Its originality also caused some of the more intelligent to reconsider the formulas they usually applied. Particularly noticeable was the fact that it had no plot and no romantic interest. The 'something about the book' that Quiller-Couch wrote was merely table-talk, but he did raise these two issues: 'As folks usually understand the term, it has no "plot". It is just the narrative of the homeward voyage of a sailing-ship from Bombay to London Dock. There is no love-making—no word of it. The *Narcissus* carried no woman on board. . . .'[22] The points he makes had already been brought out. The *Daily Mail* (No. 29) most closely mirrors Q: 'The tale is no tale, but merely an account of the uneventful voyage of the *Narcissus* from Bombay to the Thames', and 'the only female in the book is the ship herself'. 'What is the plot of this volume?' asks the reviewer in the *Standard*, 24 December 1897, 'It has not one.' And the *Academy* (No. 34), in a sensible review which raised the right questions and tried to answer them honestly, states tersely: 'The tale has no plot and no petticoats.' It was clearly a novel to puzzle. Conrad was dispensing 'with the love of women and the love of money, those hackneyed themes of the common novelist'. James Payn returned to the extraordinary fact that there were 'no women in it at all', and he promptly compared Conrad with the then famous Clark Russell: 'When Mr. Clark Russell writes his stories of the sea, he is so far complaisant to his readers as to admit a petticoat on board, even at the risk of contravening the Queen's Regulations' (*Illustrated London News*, 5 February 1898). It thus seemed to the *Pall Mall Gazette*, 20 December 1897, that it was 'difficult to appraise Mr. Conrad's work by comparison with other writers about the sea and the burning East, or by an estimate based upon any canons of literary criticism'. The *Daily Chronicle* (No. 32) catches the accent of puzzlement with its first sentence: 'There may be better tales of the sea than this, but we have never read anything in the least like it.' Deprived of 'true' heroes and heroines, the *Speaker*, 15 January 1898, made the point: 'That which gives its character to the book is the account of the great storm. . . . We have had many descriptions of storms at sea before, but none like this.' Conrad was acclaimed as a writer of the sea by a number of journals and magazines: '. . . gives us the sea as no other story-teller of our generation has been able to render it' (*Saturday Review*, No. 36); 'No finer or more vivid description of a storm at sea has been written' (*Pall Mall Gazette*, 20 December 1897).

But some found it possible to 'place' the novel by seeing it as part of a particular 'fashion in modern fiction': 'The psychology of the primitive passions of man (as opposed to the opposite sex) is a fashion in modern fiction which has created the fame of some strong writers,' commented the *Illustrated London News*, 8 January 1898, and linked the novel with those of Louis Becke and Morley Roberts. Courtney's comparison of the *Nigger* with Stephen Crane's *The Red Badge of Courage* (No. 30) is part of this desire to find a source for Conrad's undoubted power and originality. The *Speaker*, 15 January 1898, seems to be following Courtney's review very closely: ' "The Red Badge of Courage" has much to answer for. That remarkable feat of the imagination has inspired a whole school of descriptive writers of a new class, who aspire to make visible to us the inside of great scenes—battlefields, shipwrecks, moving incidents of every kind. Mr. Conrad . . . has now followed in the footsteps of Mr. Stephen Crane, and . . . in its vividness, its emphasis, and its extraordinary fulness of detail, [the picture of life on the *Narcissus*] is a worthy pendant to the battle-picture presented to us in "The Red Badge of Courage".' 'Many critics will call this story but an "episode", and compare the book with Mr. Crane's "Red Badge of Courage", ' wrote Q.

Conrad's own concern with reviews at this time, and indeed with any titbit of information about the reception of the *Nigger*, reflects, I think, his personal belief that he had achieved something fresh and original here. To Miss Watson, later to be the wife of his friend E. L. Sanderson, immediately upon the completion of his novel, he wrote carefully: 'I think it has certain qualities of art that make it a thing apart. I tried to get through the veil of details at the essence of life.'[23] It is this view which received endorsement and extension by himself twenty-seven years later. It also acts as a continuous and final broadside to the opinion (which he came to find abhorrent) that he was a mere writer of sea stories. To Henry S. Canby, on 7 April 1924, he wrote:[24]

Well, I won't bore you with a discussion of fundamentals. But surely those stories of mine where the sea enters can be looked at from another angle. In the *Nigger* I give the psychology of a group of men and render certain aspects of nature. But the problem that faces them is not a problem of the sea, it is merely a problem that has arisen on board a ship where the conditions of complete isolation from all land entanglements make it stand out with a particular force and colouring.

The reputation he had established with a certain readership does not seem, however, to have made Conrad feel secure in his new profession, and he still heard the call of the sea. Writing to Cunninghame Graham about Symons's linking him with Kipling as a writer of distinction but without an idea (No. 35), Conrad ended: 'Last night a heavy gale was blowing and I lay awake thinking that I would give ever so much (the most flattering criticism) for being at sea, the soul of some patient faithful ship standing up to it under lower topsails and no land anywhere within a thousand miles. Wouldn't I jump at a command if some literary shipowner suddenly offered it to me!'[25] 1898 was a year of 'struggling anxiety', and a year of 'unavailing labour over The Rescue'[26] but no berth turned up. His attempt to escape from the life of a writer arose from one of his recurring crises of confidence in himself, but with the publication in April 1898 of his first collection of short stories, Tales of Unrest, a tangible acknowledgment of his ability came. He shared the Academy award, which brought him fifty guineas, with Sidney Lee (Life of Shakespeare) and Maurice Hewlett (The Forest Lovers). 'When I opened the letter I thought it was a mistake,' Conrad wrote to Garnett on 13 January 1899,[27] but it was not, and the Academy's account of Conrad's work came at an appropriate moment, for though Tales of Unrest was praised many reviewers pointed to the depressing nature of the tales. The Spectator (No. 33) had sounded a similar note in reviewing The Nigger of the 'Narcissus': '. . . we own to having found [it] . . . almost unbearingly depressing', and now the Daily Telegraph (No. 37) saw in the short story 'The Idiots' 'sheer morbid horror'. Other reviewers followed this line: 'grey, grim and pitiless as Fate' (Black and White, 23 April 1898); 'To print all these miserable and tragic episodes on end in a single volume is artistically a mistake' (Westminster Gazette, 4 May 1898); 'he revels in the sombre, the doleful, and in tragedy unrelieved' (World, 11 May 1898).

Surely Garnett answers these remarks in the first general assessment of Conrad's work to appear (see No. 39). Nevertheless, there is something bizarre about Conrad's short stories, at least those published as late as 1908. And one has sympathy for the reviewer of Tales of Unrest in the Daily Telegraph (No. 37) who, when speaking of the conclusion of 'An Outpost of Progress' (where Kayerts has hanged himself and is described as having 'one purple cheek playfully posed on the shoulder . . . he was putting out a swollen tongue at his Managing Director'), argues: 'This is vivid, but assuredly it is ghastly.'

Conrad was living at this time at Ivy Walls, Stanford-le-Hope, in Essex, but, as a result of his meeting with Ford Madox Hueffer (later Ford) in September 1898, he took over Pent Farm in Kent. It was here that he collaborated with Ford on *The Inheritors* (1901) and *Romance* (1903). Pent Farm was silent witness to the creation of most of his great work, for it was there that *Lord Jim, Youth, Typhoon* and *Nostromo* were written.

With the publication of *Lord Jim* (1900), *Youth* (1902), and *Typhoon and other stories* (1903), Conrad's critical reception reached a high point of approval. *Lord Jim*, begun as a short story for the *Youth* volume but growing into a novel, appeared first as a serial in *Blackwood's*. Its creation was accompanied by many moments of doubt: 'I fear I have not the capacity and the power to go on' (letter to Sanderson, 12 October 1899),[28] but also by moments of elation: 'I am old and sick and in debt—but lately I've found I can still write—*it* comes!—*it* comes!—and I am young and healthy and rich' (26 March 1900).[29] And it was finished in a rush of creative power; as he told Galsworthy:[30]

The end of *L.J.* has been pulled off with a steady drag of 21 hours. I sent wife and child out of the house (to London) and sat down at 9 A.M. with a desperate resolve to be done with it. Now and then I took a walk round the house, out at one door in at the other. Ten-minute meals. A great hush. Cigarette ends growing into a mound similar to a cairn over a dead hero. Moon rose over the barn, looked in at the window and climbed out of sight. Dawn broke, brightened. I put the lamp out and went on, with the morning breeze blowing the sheets of MS. all over the room. Sun rose. I wrote the last word and went into the dining-room. Six o'clock I shared a piece of cold chicken with Escamillo (who was very miserable and in want of sympathy, having missed the child dreadfully all day). Felt very well, only sleepy: had a bath at seven and at 1.30 was on my way to London.

David Meldrum, Blackwood's literary adviser, recalls Conrad's visit to Blackwood's: 'Fortunately I was in the office this morning when Conrad called with the conclusion of *Jim*, which went off to the typewriter *instanter*. He was, of course, in great spirits at being finished, and goes to Bruges on Wednesday I think. . . .'[31]

'THE SPOILED CHILD OF THE CRITICS'

Lord Jim (1900), *Youth* (1902), and *Typhoon* (1903)

'The *Outcast* is a heap of sand, the *Nigger* a splash of water, *Jim* a lump of clay. A stone, I suppose will be my next gift to the impatient mankind'—oddly enough, in writing in this way to Garnett, [32] Conrad is at his most confident. *Lord Jim* was so well received that he was not even disturbed by the unfavourable response in *Literature*. He wrote to

Blackwood: ' "Literature" went for me heavily—otherwise I am the spoiled child of the critics.'[33] Meldrum, writing of the excellent notices in the *Daily Chronicle* and *Manchester Guardian* (No. 41), said that he had sent them to Conrad 'who lives in need of these encouragements . . .' (letter to Blackwood, 26 October 1900),[34] but by 27 November 1900 Conrad was referring to the *Spectator* (No. 45) and the *Speaker* (No. 46) in delight at having satisfied in 'the same week—Whig and Tory'.[35]

The novel was hailed as being original and his best work: 'may rank as a memorable event', 'remarkable originality', 'written . . . with a concentration of purpose, a grasp of material, a deep energy which make it a great performance' (*Manchester Guardian*, No. 41); 'a book of great originality . . . exerts a spell such as is rarely encountered in modern fiction' (*New York Daily Tribune*, 3 November 1900). 'Remarkable' was the term used by the *Spectator* (No. 45), *Morning Post*, 26 December 1900, *Sketch* (No. 44) and *Speaker* (No. 46). For the *Manchester Guardian* (No. 41), *British Weekly*, 29 November 1900, *Athenaeum*, 3 November 1900, and *Literary World*, 23 November 1900, it was his best work, for the *Spectator* (No. 45) his 'latest and greatest'. The *Speaker* (No. 46) declared: '[*Lord Jim*] brings Mr. Conrad at once into the front rank of living novelists.' To Meldrum, 27 November 1900, Conrad wrote: 'Henry James wrote me an absolutely enthusiastic letter about the book',[36] and though we have no extracts from the letter, it is obvious from Conrad's remarks that James was fulsome in his praise: 'Wouldn't you think a boy had written it? Such enthusiasm! Wonderful old man, with his record of wonderful work!'[37] There is a clear connection between James's praise of *Lord Jim* and the fact that, for the first time, critics began to link Conrad's name with that of James (see *Pall Mall Gazette*, No. 47), while the *Bookman* (No. 49) in a none too enthusiastic review put the relation in this way: 'If Mr. Henry James had a consummate knowledge of life at sea and in the Pacific Coast towns and settlements, he would write a novel very like *Lord Jim*.' Many critics stressed the method of narration, some praising (see the *Speaker*, No. 46), and the *Critic* (U.S.A., No. 50) described Conrad's method in terms of a 'spider' metaphor: 'Imagine a fat, furry spider with green head and shining points for eyes, busily at work . . . on a marvellous web,—and you have the plot of *Lord Jim*.' But the method of narration was for many a weakness. *Literature* (15 December 1900) would have it that Conrad 'cannot write what is commonly understood as a novel . . . it is the method of telling this history of a soul that appears to us mistaken.' And the *Graphic*, 22 December 1900, speaks of the novel being damaged by '328 consecutive pages . . . occupied by a merchant captain's after-dinner story. It must have occupied, at the very least eleven consecutive hours.' Though full of praise for the novel the *Academy*, 10 November 1900 (No. 43), also spoke of these fatal eleven hours and no doubt the *Graphic* was following the *Academy* in this matter. '[The reader] feels as though wandering in a morass of wonderful language and incomprehensible events', wrote the *Daily News* (No. 48). Courtney of the *Daily Telegraph* reveals what he and many critics then felt was a quality which Conrad lacked—economy of language (No. 42).

The response to the volume *Youth*, published by Blackwood on 13 November 1902, is interesting because of the obvious influence of an unsigned review by Edward Garnett in *Academy and Literature* (No. 52) upon the notices which followed. Initially, it was the title story that received attention—' "Youth" is by far the most striking' (*Sketch*, 3 December 1902), 'Everyone must read "Youth"' (*Sphere*, 3 January 1903, and cf. also the *Daily Telegraph*, 26 November 1902). Then came Garnett's substantial and intelligent account of the three stories. He spoke of *Youth* as 'a modern English epic of the Sea' and of *Heart of Darkness* as 'the high-water mark of the author's talent'. Later that month, on 20 December 1902, the *Daily Chronicle* and the *Athenaeum* (No. 55) likewise saw *Youth* as an epic, while the *Manchester Guardian* (No. 53), in an otherwise penetrating review, took up Garnett's phrase with only slight modification—'high-water mark of English fiction'. Conrad himself noticed this follow-your-leader criticism and referred to it in a letter to Garnett on 22 December 1902:[38]

. . . The ruck takes its tone from you. You know how to serve a friend! I notice the reviews as they come in since your article. Youth is an epic; that's settled. And the H. of D. is this and that and the other thing—they aren't so positive because in this case they aren't intelligent enough to catch on to your indications. But anyhow it's a high water mark. If it hadn't been for you it would have been, dreary bosh—an incoherent bogie tale. Yes. That note too was sounded only you came just in time. . . .

However the *Manchester Guardian* was fairly intelligent—and, I suppose, you have seen the thawing of great snows on the hoary summits of the Athenaeum? I am still shaking at the august phenomenon.

Conrad is a little unfair to the *Athenaeum*. That 'august' periodical had given qualified praise to *Almayer's Folly*, *An Outcast of the Islands*, and *Lord Jim*. Their reviewer had simply become more fulsome in his praise: 'The art of Mr. Conrad is exquisite and very subtle. He uses the tools of his craft with the fine, thoughtful delicacy of a mediaeval clockmaker. . . . Mr. Conrad is something of a law unto himself, and creates his own forms, as he certainly has created his own methods.'

Typhoon and other stories which collected, apart from the title story, 'Amy Foster', 'Falk', and 'To-morrow' was published in London on 22 April 1903. The response to this collection, in particular to 'Typhoon', was overwhelming, and reading the notices today one has the feeling that Conrad was on the verge of being overestimated. Certainly there was great praise, the impression of which must have remained with Conrad since he refers to it in his Author's Note to *Typhoon* written sixteen years later. It is true that the *Standard*, 6 June 1903, and *Graphic*, 9 May 1903, thought between them that the story of 'Typhoon' didn't amount to much, but they were alone in this view. More typical was the comment of the *Illustrated London News*, 9 May 1903, which had earlier serialized 'Amy Foster': ' "Typhoon" is a book of magnificent originality.' Indeed, criticism was beginning to be replaced by admiration in face of Conrad's growing reputation. To its account of 'To-morrow', a story which we would not today rate very highly, the *Morning Post* (No. 58), troubled by the cruelty of the conclusion, adds the following rider: 'But what would you have? With such an imagination Mr. Conrad must do as he chooses, and we can only admire him.' And the distinguished periodical *Academy* (No. 62) embraced him: 'before such distinct achievement criticism may well lay down its arms.' That the *Academy* should speak in this way is in itself very interesting since two weeks earlier than this review it had carried an extract from an article on Conrad which appeared in the *New York American* and had pointed to the extravagance of the writer's superlatives on Conrad (see No. 61).

And also, at last, those two popular writers of the time, Kipling and Stevenson, with whom Conrad had been particularly compared to his detriment, were seen to be level-pegging. For the *Morning Post* (No. 58), if Kipling was supreme on land, Conrad had no equal on the seas. And *The Times Literary Supplement*, 24 April 1903, seemed willing to give pride of place to Conrad: '. . . not even Mr. Kipling . . . has quite the same power of intense vividness.'[39] The *Speaker* (No. 64) spoke of Conrad in the same breath as Stevenson in the following tender and curious manner: 'There are times in reading his work when we think that Stevenson with new experiences has taken up his work when it broke off in his noble fragment *Weir of Hermiston*.' Never before had the treachery of the sea been so ably described: 'the most amazing description of the utter madness of the sea . . . we have ever read', *Morning Post* (No. 58); 'the most elaborate storm piece that one can recall in English literature', *Daily Mail* (No. 59); and the term 'storm piece' is taken up by Conrad sixteen years later in his preface to the novel. The *Manchester Guardian*, 23 April 1903, made a point which we today still endorse: 'It is only a few months since we had the "Youth" volume. . . . We may well believe . . . that Mr. Conrad is now writing in the fulness of his power and rejoice in a period of fecundity.' And even in disappointing reviews—the *Saturday Review*, 23 May 1903, for example,—we are told that Conrad was 'not repeating successes, not working by a publisher's rule'.

'UNSYMPATHETIC TO THE GENERAL PUBLIC'

Nostromo (1904), *The Secret Agent* (1907), and *Under Western Eyes* (1911).

The three major works which followed—*Nostromo*, *The Secret Agent*, and *Under Western Eyes*—have in common the fact that Conrad considered them all to have been, in terms of critical response, failures, and yet in truth all of them—even *Nostromo*—received a good deal of commendation. It may be that Conrad expended so much creative energy and hope on them that any response was likely to be a disappointment. The extent of his creative effort is seen in his collapse after completing *Under Western Eyes*. It may be also that he saw his fullest efforts at obtaining general popularity failing, and tended to discount mere critical acclaim. It is certain that the response to each of these novels involved a misunderstanding of himself and his intentions which must have been irritating.

While *Typhoon* was being reviewed, Conrad was hard at work on *Nostromo*, 'the most anxiously meditated of the longer novels', as he wrote in his Author's Note to the novel: 'It took the best part of the years 1903-4 to [write it] with many intervals of renewed hesitation, lest I should lose myself in the ever-enlarging vistas opening before me as I progressed deeper in my knowledge of the country.'[40] Both his friend Richard Curle and his wife Jessie, like Conrad, held the belief that *Nostromo* was ill received. 'As a book it aroused little enthusiasm . . . and as a serial (in *T.P.'s Weekly*) it provoked numerous bewildered and indignant protests from readers who, in Conrad's words, "wrote many letters complaining of so much space being taken by utterly unreadable stuff"',' wrote Richard Curle;[41] and Jessie Conrad said: '. . . its reception was perhaps the greatest disappointment—literary disappointment—Conrad ever had. He used to say it was "a dead frost".'[42] And in reply to Arnold Bennett's letter in praise of *Nostromo* (No. 66) Conrad wrote: 'The joy your praise of that novel has given me is immense. With the public it was the blackest possible frost.'[43] This was on 25 November 1912 and Conrad may well have forgotten details of the reviews by that time. They are tedious; they are myopic; they underrate *Nostromo* as surely as they overrated *Typhoon*; but they are not all condemnatory. Conrad was misunderstood, even attacked, but he was also praised.

The first sentence of the review in the *Illustrated London News* (No. 76) is as good an example of the praise as any: 'To say that *Nostromo* is the great achievement in fiction of the year is to state altogether imperfectly our appreciation of Mr. Conrad's latest novel.' It must have been disturbing to be as misunderstood as Conrad was by *Black and White* (No. 70), but intelligence is evident in most of the *Manchester Guardian's* (No. 73) review. In particular, Garnett's highly sensitive and understanding account is so slanted as to answer many earlier criticisms of the novel (No. 74).

The *Scotsman* (1 November 1904) was put out by the change in background: 'Mr. Conrad generally sails in Eastern Seas', but it was again the form of the novel which caused dismay. *Nostromo* did not follow 'with a single mind the spiritual history of an individual', it lacked something of the intensity and concentration of previous novels according to the *Manchester Guardian* (No. 73). And it showed, as the *Athenaeum* stated (5 November 1904), 'a magnificent disregard for the dangers of digression and retrospection'. Ultimately, one comes to feel that Conrad forgot the praise but remembered the criticism and certainly the criticism in *TLS* (No. 68) must have pained: '. . . the publication of this book as it stands is an artistic mistake.'

For Conrad, *The Secret Agent* was a fresh experiment. To R. B. Cunninghame Graham, on 7 October 1907, he wrote that this novel 'had some importance for me as a new departure in *genre* and as a sustained effort in ironical treatment of a melodramatic subject'.[44] Conrad describes in his Author's Note the inception of *The Secret Agent* following his absorption in writing *Nostromo* and he makes vivid the jump he took from one novel to the other: 'One fell to musing before the phenomenon—even of the past: of South America, a continent of crude sunshine and brutal revolutions, of the sea . . . the reflector of the world's light. Then the vision of an enormous town presented itself, of a monstrous town more populous than some continents and in its man-made might as if indifferent to heaven's frowns and smiles; a cruel devourer of the world's light.'[45] The subject came to him as the result of 'a few words uttered by a friend in a casual conversation' about anarchists. There is no doubt that Ford Madox Hueffer was the friend mentioned here, and no doubt either that Hueffer provided the subject. But Conrad was beginning to look for a larger audience, a more popular appeal, and he saw that in writing about anarchists in Soho he was at least treating a 'widely discussed subject', but treating it on his own terms. Writing to his literary agent, J. B. Pinker, on 18 May 1907, while working on the final form of *The Secret Agent*, Conrad spoke of 'an element of popularity in it . . . my mind runs much on popularity now. I would try to reach it not by sensationalism but by means of taking a widely discussed subject for the *text* of my novel',[46] and further evidence of his desire to gain popularity appears in another letter to Pinker written two and a half months later. There Conrad speaks of *The Secret Agent* as a book 'to produce some sensation'.[47] Recognizing that it would not be written 'on popular lines', he yet recorded, rather naïvely, the reasons for possible success:[48]

Of course it will not be on popular lines. Nothing of mine can be, I fear. But even Meredith ended by getting his sales. Now, I haven't Meredith's delicacy, and that's a point in my favour. I reckon I may make certain of the support of the Press for the next few years. The young men who are coming in to write criticisms are in my favour so far. At least all of whom I've heard are. I don't get in the way of established reputations. One may read everybody and yet in the end want to read me—for a change if for nothing else. For I don't resemble anybody; and yet I am not specialized enough to call up imitators as to matter or style. There is nothing in me but a turn of mind which, whether valuable or worthless, cannot be imitated.

What Conrad did not foresee was that his novel might be attacked on the grounds of the 'sordid surroundings and the moral squalor of the tale'. He wrote in his Author's Note to the novel: 'I must conclude that I had still preserved much of my pristine innocence in the year 1907.'[49] His recollection of the novel's being criticized on these grounds was certainly accurate as we see from reviews in the *Daily News*, 12 September 1907, *Truth* (No. 82), the *Weekly Sun*, 21 September 1907, *Daily Mail*, 14 September 1907. The *Morning Post*, 19 September 1907, described it as 'too sordid to be tragic and too repulsive to be pathetic; yet it has some of both these elements in it. It grips the imagination fiercely and insistently. It is a comedy of the Inferno, perhaps too terrible to have been written, at least without some compensating glimpse of Paradise.' What probably hurt Conrad most was that it was chosen by the *Edinburgh Review* (No. 87) as an example of modern ugliness in fiction, though a stout defender, Arnold Bennett, took up his cause on this issue (see headnote to No. 87).

Certainly the more sensational aspect of the story, the portrayal of the Soho anarchists, caught the eye of the press. Whether or not it is true that a visitor from America informed Conrad 'that all sorts of revolutionary refugees in New York would have it that the book was written by somebody who knew a lot about them',[50] certainly the British press (and the *New York Daily Tribune*, 14 September 1907, also) thought it was. The *Morning Post*, 19 September 1907, entitling its review 'The Real Anarchist', felt that 'the incidental portraits and the sidelights on the problem of Anarchism are . . . even more valuable than the central story' and that 'it is a study of real value for the student of contemporary politics', a book of instruction, in fact. Indeed, though many critics would have endorsed the view expressed by the *Spectator*, 21 September 1907—'There is something about his genius that ill accords with the amenities and actualities of a normal humdrum home-keeping existence'—on the whole they felt able to add that, nevertheless, 'it was a sure instinct that guided him in the present instance to choose for his *milieu* the colony of Anarchists and revolutionists who find asylum in our midst, and the result is a psychological romance of terrorism at once so subtle and yet so engrossing as to maintain, and even advance, his reputation as a literary sorcerer of the first rank'. The *Spectator* stressed Mr. Conrad's 'penetrating insight into the psychology of the monstrous brood of enigmatical persons' which London 'harbours'. The *Observer*, 15 September 1907, saw it as a 'masterly study of the inner workings of the disordered minds whose aim is destruction, violence, and the overturning of law and order by means of bombs'; and the *Scotsman*, 16 September 1907, remarked on 'an unusually intimate knowledge of the characteristics and devices of anarchist conspiracy in London'. Garnett, in his review (No. 81), made the point that, though Conrad's character sketches supply us 'with a working analysis of anarchism that is profoundly true . . philosophical anarchism of certain creative minds is . . . out of the range of the author's survey'. R. B. Cunninghame Graham also felt it necessary to criticize Conrad's treatment of the anarchists, and Conrad replied: 'But

I don't think that I've been satirizing the revolutionary world. All these people are not revolutionaries—they are shams.'[51]

A few critics, notably R. A. Scott-James in the *Daily News*, 12 September 1907, recognized that Conrad was presenting a new genre to us: 'Mr. Conrad has written a detective story. Not such a detective story as we are accustomed to in England, but one in which the most fearful and, as a rule, unintelligible crimes, such as bomb-throwing, seem to be the only natural acts of people not very bad, not very clever, not, in fact, much different from other law-abiding citizens', and the *Sunday Times*, 20 October 1907, recognized that in other hands the story 'would have resulted in nothing but the wildest sensationalism'. By January 1908, Conrad felt able to give his verdict on *The Secret Agent* to John Galsworthy: '*The Secret Agent* may be pronounced by now an honourable failure. It brought me neither love nor promise of literary success. I own that I am cast down. I suppose I am a fool to have expected anything else. I suppose there is something in me that is unsympathetic to the general public. . . . Foreignness, I suppose.'[52] Again though, if we look at the reviews, the novel can in no wise be pronounced a failure. For one thing, *TLS* (No. 78), which had so lamentably failed to understand and appreciate *Nostromo*, accepted this novel, seeing the work as an advance on *Nostromo*: '. . . [it] increases Mr. Conrad's reputation, already of the highest.'

The reviews I have included of *A Set of Six* tend to be critical—Lynd in the *Daily News* (No. 89), Courtney in the *Daily Telegraph* (No. 90), and Anderson Graham in *Country Life* (No. 91), but the collection of stories was praised, perhaps over-praised, by the *Observer*, 16 August 1908: 'There is not a story of the six . . . that is not a consummate work of art.' Indeed, the tendency to over-praise Conrad's work which began with *Typhoon* and received a set-back with the publication of *Nostromo* and *The Secret Agent*, gained strength now. Criticism of Conrad at this stage in his career was becoming no easy task. The *Sunday Times* best indicates the growth of Conrad's reputation. The reviewer, speaking of how he had for a fortnight tried to forget the existence of books and had left all behind, goes on to say 'there was one book the reading of which I could not bring myself to postpone, for it bore the name of Mr. Joseph Conrad'. Arnold Bennett catches the flavour of the beginnings of author worship when he writes in *New Age*, 19 September 1908: 'The *Athenaeum* is obsequious. In common with every paper in this country, it has learnt that the proper thing is to praise Mr. Conrad's work. Not to appreciate Mr. Conrad's work at this time of day would amount to bad form' (p. 412). And while Edward Thomas's review of *A Set of Six* is depressingly ordinary (see No. 95), his speaking of Conrad as 'lord of language' is a further indication of the way the tide was turning in Conrad's favour.

There is no doubt that Conrad's next novel, *Under Western Eyes*, was again for Conrad a failure. In his Author's Note to '*Twixt Land and Sea*, he assures us that 'there is no denying the fact that "Under Western Eyes" found no favour in the public eye'.[53] If by this he means that the generality of reviews were against his work then he was totally wrong. Of course, the notion of Conrad as a foreigner became more widespread. The *Athenaeum*, 21 October 1911, felt bound to say that 'the book reads like a translation from some other tongue', and R. A. Scott-James took up Garnett's term 'slavonic': 'all he has written is rather Slavonic than English . . . Mr. Conrad, though he writes in English, has the blood of Eastern Europe in him' (*Daily News*, 13 October 1911). Indeed, this 'foreignness' was what led to such praise of the novel. Conrad was seen as an instructor in things Russian which had confused the Western mind. The *Sphere*, 11 November 1911, speaks of *Under Western Eyes* as being 'hailed everywhere as his greatest achievement'. *TLS*, 12 October 1911, and the *Daily Telegraph*, 25 October 1911, were representative of many reviewers—the *Westminster Gazette* (No. 99), the *Morning Post* (No. 98), for example. The *Daily Telegraph*, stated: 'It will endure, because it is a human document, interpreting the spirit of modern Russia to the lands of the West', and *TLS*: 'Most English readers of Russian fiction . . . find themselves constantly baffled by a kind of strangeness which persists through all their efforts at thorough comprehension.' There is a barrier and 'Mr. Joseph Conrad, who has unique qualifications for the task, tries to show what that barrier is'.

In Garnett's review of the book (see No. 101) there is no evidence of a serious charge against Conrad, though the phrase 'vindictive art' placed in front of us and then denied by Garnett is perhaps evidence of how he felt. There is no doubt that Garnett was angered by the account of the Russian revolutionaries in the novel, the originals of whom, Garnett no doubt felt, Conrad was guying rather shamelessly, originals whom Garnett looked upon as friends. In a letter to Conrad which has not survived, Garnett attacked him on the grounds of putting 'hatred' into the novel and Conrad's reply (No. 100) is an important one. In 1936, 12 years after the death of Conrad and just a few days before his own death, Garnett wrote an Introduction to a collection of

Conrad's Prefaces and with typical honesty retracted his original charge: 'I unjustly charged Conrad with putting hatred into the book and after re-reading the story twenty-five years later, I own I was wrong.'[54] But Conrad was not unprejudiced, as his letter to Garnett on receipt of Constance Garnett's translation of Dostoevsky's *The Brothers Karamazov* shows: 'I don't know what D. stand for or reveals, but I do know that he is too Russian for me. It sounds to me like some fierce mouthings from prehistoric ages.'[55]

'AN AMAZING BLOODY FOREIGNER'

Apart from Conrad's insistence on the 'failure' of his work from *Nostromo* onwards, there was a new strain in the commentary on his novels which disturbed him, perhaps because he saw it as a danger to his reputation and possible success as a 'selling' novelist. He had been criticized for morbidness of subject-matter (*Tales of Unrest*); unduly complicated methods of narration (*Lord Jim* and *Nostromo*); failing to introduce the necessary ingredients of the love story into the novel (*The Nigger of the 'Narcissus'*); excessive diffuseness of style (*Almayer's Folly* and *An Outcast of the Islands*). All of these criticisms Conrad accepted without too much difficulty, but the charge of Slavonism was one which disturbed him deeply, the more so since the most ardent exponent of this view was his friend Edward Garnett. When Garnett reviewed *The Secret Agent* in the *Nation* (No. 81), he seemed to be following up a comment made in an earlier review in *TLS* (No. 78) that Conrad as an 'alien of genius, casting about for a medium in which to express his sympathy and his knowledge, hit upon our own tongue'. Garnett took up the very term 'alien spirit of those distant people [Polish race]'. Moreover, he added the term 'Slav' which was to haunt Conrad and ultimately to call forth a reply in the Author's Note to *A Personal Record* (1912). Garnett follows *TLS* very closely: 'It is good for us English to have Mr. Conrad in our midst visualising for us aspects of life we are constitutionally unable to perceive, for by his astonishing mastery of our tongue he makes clear to his English audience those secrets of Slav thought and feeling which seem so strange and inaccessible in their native language'; and 'It [the novel] has the profound and ruthless sincerity of the great Slav writers mingled with the haunting charm that reminds us so often of his compatriot Chopin.'

The *Glasgow News* (No. 83) took up Garnett's remarks: Conrad 'has imported into English literature a quality, a mood, a temperament which has never appeared in it before—something perhaps entirely alien to our national genius . . . so new that one does not feel it British at all; it is Slavonic.' No wonder Conrad wrote to Garnett: 'I've been so cried up of late as a sort of freak, an amazing bloody foreigner writing in English (every blessed review of *S.A.* had it so—and even yours) that anything I say will be discounted on that ground by the public.'[56] And a few days later Conrad stressed to Garnett: 'You seem to forget that I am a Pole.'[57] This does not seem to have dissuaded Garnett from sticking to his term 'Slav' for we find him using it again in his review of Conrad's next publication *A Set of Six* (1908) (see No. 93), seeing these stories as 'essentially Slav in [their] ironic acceptance of the pathetic futility of human nature . . . Slav in their psychological insight'. Conrad recognized the danger of this line of approach and quite clearly it is for this reason that he laid the 'failure' of *The Secret Agent* with the general public to 'foreignness' (see p. 23 above). After *Under Western Eyes* (when their political disagreement grew) Garnett was never again on quite such good terms with Conrad, and Conrad moved on to younger men such as Richard Curle for support. The emotional pressure is very great as we can see in Conrad's reply to Garnett's review of *A Set of Six* when he offers the peculiar but moving answer: 'I had to work like a coal miner in his pit quarrying all my English sentences out of a black night.'[58] As late as 1924, only six months before his death, Conrad was still defending himself. In a letter to Charles Chassé, he refutes the racial charge on the grounds that what was seen as racial was in fact personal: 'I have asked myself more than once whether if I had preserved the secret of my origins under the neutral pseudonym of "Joseph Conrad" that temperamental similitude would have been put forward at all. As to myself, I have no doubt. I believe that, here at any rate, what is personal has been put to the account of racial affinities. The critics detected in me a new note and as, just when I began to write, they had discovered the existence of Russian authors, they stuck that label on me under the name of Slavonism.'[59]

The next charge was an extension of this, that Conrad was a man without a country or language (see No. 89), which led to fierce retorts from Conrad.

Conrad suffered a breakdown after completing *Under Western Eyes*. His wife, writing to David Meldrum on 6 February 1910, says: 'Poor Conrad is very ill and Dr. Hackney says it will be a long time before he is fit for anything requiring mental exertion. . . . There is the M.S. complete but uncorrected and his fierce refusal to let even I touch it. It lays on a table at the foot of his bed and he lives mixed up in the scenes and holds converse with the characters.'[60] The nature of that novel may well be one reason for the collapse. The *Standard*, 20 October 1911, began its review: 'One wakes from the reading of Mr. Conrad's new novel as . . . from . . . a nightmare. The pursuit of the unhappy Razumov, pursuit by agents human and divine, has all the fatalistic inhumanity of a dream.' The strain of writing of Razumov's own mental strain, seems to have affected Conrad. To look again so intimately at 'the sustained psychology of a mood having its origin in a crime' appears to have been too much for him. All the novels that follow *Under Western Eyes* are less intense, or so it seems to me. Richard Curle speaks of a change taking place in Conrad's work with *A Set of Six* which 'marked so distinct a change in his technique' (see No. 97). Curle saw the change in terms of a less exuberant vocabulary and of 'psychology . . . swallowing romance'. Certainly the style is simpler, less imaginative, more a parody of certain obvious Conradian qualities, and perhaps it is due to a desire for popular success. But much rather I see it as a growing refusal to engage himself too deeply in the tragic emotions of his characters. The detachment becomes more real, the interest more pretended. It is, ironically enough, at this point that Conrad became a popular success, a best-seller not merely the best reviewed. Popular success was suggested with the publication of *'Twixt Land and Sea* (1912) and became a reality with *Chance* in 1913. It had thus taken eighteen years for Conrad to make a breakthrough.

'STIFF READING'

The reasons for his lack of popularity had been noted from the beginning. Even those reviewers who were most impressed by him admitted that he could not easily attain success and popularity, and this must clearly have had its effect on the reading public. The *Spectator* (No. 33), writing of *The Nigger of the 'Narcissus'*, whilst speaking of Conrad as a genius, nevertheless saw fit to add the following caveat: 'but his choice of themes, and the uncompromising nature of his methods, debar him from attaining a wide popularity'. In reviewing *An Outcast of the Islands*, the *Academy*, 27 June 1896, speaking of the 'ordinary man' felt able to legislate for his reading habits: 'To such novel readers

. . . Mr. Joseph Conrad's extremely able story . . . is not to be recommended. The book would bore them; they would find it dull.' At the same time 'it falls little, if at all, short of being a masterpiece'. The same journal two years later, in speaking of Conrad as a 'writer's writer', advised readers 'who want brisk dialogue and breathless action' to go elsewhere. Again, on the publication of *Lord Jim* (his most popular novel before the success of *Chance*) many friendly reviewers seemed at pains to warn off readers: 'It is not to be accepted easily, it cannot be read in a half doze, and by the great public . . . it may remain neglected or unknown' (*Manchester Guardian*, No. 41); 'The obstructions set in the way of the reader are many' (*Daily News*, No. 48); 'Let not the tired reader . . . approach *Lord Jim*' (*Bookman*, No. 49); 'If he keeps on writing the same sort, he may arrive at the unique distinction of having few readers in his own generation' (the *Critic*, No. 50). And this seeming conspiracy among even friendly critics continued with the 'popular' *Youth* volume: 'It would be useless to pretend that [it] can be very widely read' (*Manchester Guardian*, No. 53). His great friend Hugh Clifford in his unsigned review of *Youth* in the *Spectator*, 29 November 1902 (reprinted in *Littell's Living Age*, 10 January 1903 under Clifford's name), wrote: 'the very refinements and subtleties inseparable from his habit of thought and literary method have caused his books to make but a faint appeal to the general public. Give a dog a bad name, and hang him; call a book "stiff reading" and let it go by the board . . . "Youth", it must be confessed, furnishes as much "stiff reading" as any of its predecessors.' The *Sketch*, 29 April 1903, does not hesitate to state of *Typhoon* that 'this is no book for the superficial reader' and this view was echoed by the *Glasgow Herald*, the *Athenaeum*, and the *Standard*.[61]

And if Conrad failed to reach a wide public with his volumes of short stories, how much could he expect from the complexities of *Nostromo*? It was, after all, *TLS* (No. 68) that suggested that, because of Conrad's movement 'backwards and forwards, through such a labyrinth of South American politics and into the careers of so many persons', because of 'Mr. Conrad's retrospective habit', 'there are moments when it is impossible to feel sure whether the past or the present is being described' and 'many readers will never survive' the novel. The attempt at treating a popular subject with *The Secret Agent* failed. Conrad's method, his refusal to allow a chronological unfolding of his plot, came under continued censure: 'This book absolutely defies all laws of construction: it races backwards and forwards with lordly disregard of time. It stops at an exciting moment of the plot for a long examination of motives or for a historical retrospect. Not content with such wilfulnesses of treatment, Mr. Conrad encourages himself in obscurities of style. His book is almost as stiff reading as a dissertation on metaphysics' (*Sunday Times*, 20 October 1907). The *Athenaeum*'s review of *The Secret Agent* on 28 September 1907 discussed the cleavage between Conrad, the reviewer's favourite, and the great general public. The true cause of the division was the temperament and mind of Conrad:

The subtlety of his mental processes, the keenness of the artistic senses, have placed him further away from the great reading public—if infinitely nearer to the select few who have trained faculties of literary appreciation—than many a writer of far less worth. For the most part the reviewer finds it impossible to regret this, for the reason that the very mental attributes which may hedge Mr. Conrad about with barriers where the crowd is concerned, are the qualities which make his work a permanent delight to the few, and a real addition to literature.

'ONE OF THE MARVELS OF OUR LITERATURE'

'Twixt Land and Sea (1912), *Chance* (1914), *Victory* (1915), *The Shadow-Line* (1917), *The Arrow of Gold* (1919), *The Rescue* (1920)

Yet, after eighteen years of writing, Conrad still had hopes of popular success. To Alfred Knopf, who persuaded Doubleday to promote *Chance*, he wrote:[62]

When it comes to popularity I stand much nearer the public mind than Stevenson, who was super-literary, a conscious virtuoso of style; whereas the average mind does not care much for virtuosity. My point of view, which is purely human, my subjects, which are not too specialized as to the class of people or kind of events, my style, which may be clumsy here and there, but is perfectly straightforward and tending towards the colloquial, cannot possibly stand in the way of a large public.

In a letter to the publisher Doubleday, 21 December 1918, Conrad again returned to his desire for a wide readership: 'I am sufficient of a democrat to detest the idea of being a writer of any "coterie" of some small self-appointed aristocracy in the vast domain of art or letters. . . . I want to be read by many eyes and by all kinds of them, at that.'[63] And in his Author's Note to *Chance*, he commented: 'What I always feared most was drifting unconsciously into the position of a writer for a limited coterie; a position which would have been odious to me as throwing a doubt on the soundness of my belief in the solidarity of all mankind in simple ideas and in sincere emotions.'[64] There is a strong feeling here that Conrad was now deliberately seeking popularity, that, after *Under Western Eyes* and his long years of dedicated resolve and artistic honesty, he was greatly in need of success, almost at any price. And popular success was achieved. *Chance* sold 13,200 copies in two years. Clearly, publicity was an important factor in overcoming the resistance of the reading public. Edward Garnett's view was that probably 'the figure of the lady on the "jacket" of *Chance* did more to bring the novel into popular favour than the long review by Sir Sidney Colvin in the *Observer*'.

But one has to take into account also that Conrad now returned to the East for the setting for several works and to his 'earlier' manner, which may have encouraged a greater popularity. Apart from *The Arrow of Gold*, the works of the next seven years are set in the East— *Victory*, two of the four tales in *Within the Tides*, *The Shadow-Line*, and *The Rescue*. The other exception, *Chance*, brings back the narrator, Marlow. Certainly this pleased the critics. The *Spectator* (No. 106), reviewing '*Twixt Land and Sea*, reflected: 'It is with deep satisfaction therefore that we see that in his new book he has once more shaken himself free [of changes in matter and style]. He has returned with fresh vigour to his earlier course.' Richard Curle in *Everyman*, 24 December 1912, saw a return to the earlier manner but a retaining of 'the finish of his later period'.

Leaving aside a wider popularity, the critics now seem incapable of finding anything wrong with his work. Evaluation is being replaced by adoration. For *TLS*, the three stories, 'A Smile of Fortune', 'The Secret Sharer' and 'Freya of the Seven Isles', are 'each a masterpiece'; by the *Standard* (No. 105) Conrad is acclaimed 'first king of a new country' and the *Observer*, 20 October 1912, speaks of 'the divine accident (with all that it means of life and beauty) [that] has happened in these three stories. . . . They are as good as anything Conrad has ever written, tales as good as any man might hope to write.' Conrad had become 'a great architect of novels' and *Chance* was 'wonderfully and ingeniously planned' (*Standard*, 16 January 1916); for *Punch* 'the whole thing is much nearer wizardry than workmanship' (No. 114f); 'Joseph Conrad is one of the marvels of our literature' (*Daily Telegraph*, No. 114e); there is 'magically vital description' (*Observer*, No. 114d); and the *Daily Chronicle* (No. 114a) speaks of 'spell' and 'entrancement'. H. M. Tomlinson in the *Star*, 19 January 1914, wrote about Conrad's other works but refused to review *Chance* because 'it is a work of genius easily recognised'.

The undertow to all this was there, but not strong. Garnett in the *Nation* (No. 113) gave a critical assessment of the novel; the *Literary World*, 5 February 1914, saw faults in the method: 'The device of telling a story at second or third hand, which Mr. Conrad here uses, has its advantages but the disadvantages seem to us much greater . . . the characters . . . are apt to become faint and shadowy'; and *Public Opinion*, 23 January 1914, was honest: 'The critics have been puzzling themselves what to say about Mr. Conrad's new story, "Chance". . . . Most of them do not understand it or know what to say.' It had been a long hard slog and Conrad's letter to John Galsworthy, 19 March 1914, seems to indicate that recognition had come too late: '*Chance* had a tremendous press. How I would have felt about it ten or eight years ago I can't say. Now I can't even pretend I am elated. If I had *Nostromo*, *The Nigger*, *Lord Jim*, in my desk or only in my head, I would feel differently no doubt.'[65]

For *Victory* there was another chorus of praise. Conrad is a 'past-master of literary magic' and 'he projects a spell so powerfully that the reader emerges from perusal of the story with a numbing sense of being no less bewitched than the Enchanted Heyst', *Nation*, U.S.A., 15 April 1915. The *Spectator*, 2 October 1915, speaks of 'enchantment' and the American journal, *Bookman*, May 1915, of 'the fascination' of being held 'spellbound'.

Many reviewers recognized, however, that *Victory* differed radically from Conrad's other works in its allegorical nature, and for many this also was cause for congratulation. The *Scotsman* (No. 117), recognizing that Jones and his crew are mere figures of melodrama, begins at the end of the review to see the struggle in symbolic terms, 'we appear to be witnessing not a murderous contest between men, but a struggle between the spiritual powers of the universe temporarily incarnate in a little group of human beings on a lonely Pacific island'. And the *Nation*'s remarks (No. 120) support this view of looking at the matter: 'The issue in *Victory* is as clear as in a Mystery play—the conflict between the forces of darkness and of light', and the real justification for melodramatic characters is there: they are 'extravagant, grotesque, as the author meant them to be . . . it gives it a curiously symbolic force'. According to the *Standard*, 24 September 1915, Jones and Pedro are 'a sort of evil Prospero and his Caliban'. On the other hand, the *Glasgow Evening News* (No. 123), a consistent champion of the early

Conrad, now felt it necessary to state that Mr Jones and Ricardo, '—an emaciated, gentlemanly blackguard and his follower, a human jaguar—are stock types of villainy in the lower regions of literary and dramatic art'. The *New Statesman* (No. 122) followed by the *Morning Post*, 4 October 1915, raised serious doubts. Lip-service is paid and then the *Statesman*'s reviewer, Gerald Gould, makes the following statement: 'there is . . . a rather fatigued air of delicacy, an evasion, a reticence in manner.' A. N. Monkhouse of the *Manchester Guardian*, 24 September 1915, says that Mr Jones 'a sinister, bloodless creature, smacks of the stage; Stevenson might have produced him in an uninspired mood'. Stevenson at this stage in Conrad's career was still being thrown at his head.

The titles of the reviews of *The Shadow-Line* (1917) are in themselves instructive: 'The Great Conrad' (*Nation*); 'Mr. Conrad's Parable' (*Morning Post*); 'Mr. Conrad's "Ancient Mariner"' (*Saturday Review*), and each of these headings reflects the general direction the critics took in their account of *The Shadow-Line*. The *Nation* wrote a remarkable paean of praise: 'one of the great ones, not of the present, but of the world' (No. 125), and for the *Spectator*, 31 March 1917, 'The genius of Mr. Conrad disarms criticism'. Conrad, in his Author's Note, went out of his way to deny that the work was 'intended to touch on the supernatural. Yet more than one critic has been inclined to take it in that way.'[66] And this was certainly so of *Truth*, 28 March 1917, which spoke of a haunted ship, as did the *Spectator*, 31 March 1917, and the *Daily News*, 19 March 1917. The *Manchester Guardian*, 19 March 1917, referred to 'occult suggestion' and the *Nation* (No. 125) to Conrad's 'elfin power of mingling the natural with the supernatural'. Perhaps inevitably, many critics compared the novel with Coleridge's 'Ancient Mariner'. For the *Scotsman* it was a 'prose version of "The Ancient Mariner" so far as general effect and to some extent treatment are concerned'; the *Spectator* saw it as 'a Conradian version of "The Ancient Mariner"'. On the whole the view held of *The Shadow-Line* was that it was 'scarcely one of Mr. Conrad's big achievements' (*Bookman*, No. 127), and Clement Shorter (his Literary Letter in the *Sphere* was always signed C.K.S.), surely has his hand on the pulse of the reading public when he speaks of the 'reading elect' and 'reading many' coming together here (14 April 1917):

A new book by Mr. Joseph Conrad is a literary event to many of us, and so it has been for nearly a quarter of a century. Since Mr. George Meredith died and Mr. Thomas Hardy ceased to write novels no novelist other than Mr. Conrad has appeared who has been able to give me that particular thrill—the thrill which came to an earlier generation as each of the novels of Dickens and Thackeray came from their publishers. And it was gratifying to find that with his eighteenth book, *Victory*, Mr. Conrad became not only one of the favourite novelists of the elect but one of the favourite novelists of the many.

I suspect that the story exceeded any one of the others, even *The Nigger of the 'Narcissus'*, in its immediate popularity. Mr. Conrad's new story, *The Shadow Line*, is of slighter material, but it is a great and never-to-be-forgotten book all the same.

With the publication of *The Arrow of Gold*, Conrad became the grand old man of letters, taking over the mantle of Thomas Hardy (*New Statesman*. No. 132). To his friend, Sir Sidney Colvin, writing in the *Observer*, 24 August 1919 (reprinted in September in *Littell's Living Age*), Conrad was 'the master': 'But all intelligent readers alike must agree in any case . . . in thanking the master for a study of a woman's heart and mystery scarcely to be surpassed in literature.' There was evidence of this excessive respect in the opening remarks in the *Saturday Review*, 23 August 1919, remarks which border on the comic but are serious for all that: 'Mr. Conrad is in the rare and happy position of being recognised by his contemporaries as belonging less to them than to the future'—alas, we don't have Conrad's ironic response to this! And later in the same review, it is argued that the critic is in the position of a lecturer 'explaining to an already initiated audience not that his subject is a classic, but how this particular classic affects him individually'.

But such praise did not prevent legitimate criticism of the novel. Conrad wrote to Colvin on 7 August: 'the first notices . . . in *Mg. Post*, *Dly. Mail*, *Dly. News* are very poor, puzzle-headed, hesitating pro-nouncements; yet not inimical.'[67] Reluctant criticism is represented by the review in *Everyman*, 9 August 1919, by the novelist J. D. Beresford: 'I must admit that I find a just perceptible falling away from the abilities of the artist, who gave us, say, *Lord Jim*', to which Conrad responded in a letter to his agent Pinker on 14 August: 'Beresford . . . finds I am growing old, a rather sudden conclusion to arrive at on the evidence of only one book; because . . . nobody found traces of senile decay in *Victory* or *Shadow Line*.'[68]

But perhaps Conrad himself recognized that a decline was setting in. He becomes increasingly concerned with reviews and increasingly concerned that at least his friends Curle, Colvin, etc. should review him.

Granted the danger of reading Conrad's own words about his work straight and ignoring his habit of depreciating his own work, perhaps his remarks to his old friends, the Sandersons, during his writing of *The Arrow of Gold* best reflect his concern: 'I have been working every morning. You can imagine what sort of stuff that is. No colour, no relief, no tonality; the thinnest possible squeaky bubble. And when I've finished with it, I shall go out and sell it in the market place for 20 times the money I had for the *Nigger*, 30 times the money I had for the *Mirror of the Sea*.'[69] Whatever had gone wrong with Conrad was perhaps best put by the reviewer in the *Morning Post* (No. 130), 'how carefully and completely the author obscures in it the "story" elements as these are popularly conceived and contrived'.

Although Conrad denied that he was getting old he nevertheless in the last five years of his life speaks as if he saw the end coming (see his letter to Edward Garnett on *The Rescue* (No. 135), and something of the same note appears in a letter written fourteen months later, the more nautical colouring determined by the fact that he was writing to Admiral Goodenough: 'That thing [*The Rescue*] has been on the stocks for something like twenty years. . . . It struck me . . . that my time was running out and I wanted the deck cleared before going below. As to leaving any loose ends hanging over the side, I couldn't bear the thought of it'[70]).

But if Conrad had an uncertain press for *The Arrow of Gold*, he was very much back in favour with *The Rescue*. Richard Curle comments judiciously in the *New Statesman* on 'His wider reputation, long delayed, but now in the full flood of recognition that is not alone literary' (3 July 1920). We can see W. Douglas Newton in the *Sketch* (No. 140) trying to criticize the novel in the last sentence of his review and then giving up in face of a work which he says is 'so massive, so profound, so beautiful'. *Punch* (No. 138) and the *Westminster Gazette*, 25 June 1920, rhapsodize, and the *Glasgow Evening News*, 5 August 1920, speaks of the novel in the same breath as *King Lear*, 'Lycidas' and the 'Ode to a Nightingale' and is in no doubt that it is 'Mr. Conrad's masterpiece'. More tentatively the reviewer in the *London Mercury* (No. 141), having asked the important question 'whether the wider reputation had not come . . . to a writer whose best work was already done', answers that 'the finest of living English novelists (in succession to Mr. Hardy, retired) . . . has produced his finest work'.

One new aspect of Conrad was commented upon, and not entirely favourably. We have come a long way from *The Nigger of the 'Nar-*

cissus', and Conrad had become as 'complaisant' as Clark Russell in admitting 'a petticoat on board' (see above, p. 12). The reviewer in the *Nation* (No. 139) was not sure that he liked Conrad as 'a novelist of love', but it was the paralysing effect of love on Lingard's initiative that troubled the critic in the *Spectator*, 10 July 1920, and this paralysing effect is present also in *Arrow of Gold*. And in common with many other reviewers, Rose Macaulay stated: 'Mr. Conrad's sure touch on men always a little fails him with women' (*Time and Tide*, 9 July 1920).

After *Under Western Eyes* (1911), Conrad's work also became much less complex in terms of character and conflict. Captain Anthony in *Chance* is essentially a 'good' man; *Victory* can be seen in allegorical terms; *The Arrow of Gold* and *The Rescue* are essentially tales of love-bewitched men; and the simplifying process is continued in *The Rover* (1923). In some ways it was a conscious process. In a letter to Edward Garnett, 4 December 1923, Conrad speaks of his 'secret desire to achieve a feat of artistic brevity, once at least' before he died,[71] and certainly this brevity was achieved in *The Rover* and was generally commented upon. For the *Manchester Guardian* (No. 143) 'the narrative is as fast and as bare as the wind', and for *TLS* (No. 145) the new story is 'straightforward Conrad'.

The Times, 3 December 1923, spoke for the general reader in insisting that 'everyone will read [*The Rover*] with an enjoyment unmitigated by any necessity for intellectual strivings'. And Martin Armstrong in the *Spectator*, 15 December 1923, perhaps put his finger on the nature of *The Rover*, well done though the book is, when he wrote that Conrad 'writes in a familiar convention and is true to type, the type being the adventure novel beloved of boys, which G. A. Henty turned out regularly every year and Stevenson raised to a classic in *Treasure Island*'. Now Garnett tells us that Conrad stigmatized Rider Haggard, who was in the Henty tradition, as being 'too horrible for words'.[72] The critics might well be gushing, but not for reasons that would satisfy Conrad.

'HE HAD NOTHING TO SAY'

The wave of reaction to Conrad began with some delicately expressed criticism in *TLS* (No. 137) of *The Rescue*: 'Mr. Conrad has never striven harder to heap up beauty of scene and romance of circumstance ... beauty seems to be sought with effort, as though to bolster up some deficiency in the central idea ... as if Mr. Conrad's belief in romance had suddenly flagged and he had tried to revive it by artificial stimulants.' No less imaginatively critical, but more devastatingly, E. M. Forster followed this in his review of *Notes on Life and Letters* (No. 142), which appeared in the following year, where 'the deficiency in the central idea' becomes a 'central obscurity'— 'the secret casket of his genius contains a vapour rather than a jewel' and also 'we need not try to write him down philosophically, because there is, in this particular direction, nothing to write. No creed, in fact.' Leonard Woolf, *Nation and Athenaeum*, 8 December 1923, in taking up this line, seemed also to be mapping out future re-assessment immediately after Conrad's death. Remarking that between *The Secret Sharer* and *The Rover* 'in essentials, in his vision, his thoughts, and his feelings, and in the form and power of their presentation to his reader, no writer . . . has ever changed less than Mr. Conrad', he goes on with 'the younger or youngest generation see only this eternal sameness in him so that they tend to see nothing in him'. Courtney confirmed this: 'Conrad is no longer popular with the younger school of writers' (*Daily Telegraph*, 14 December 1923), and Raymond Mortimer, in the *New Statesman* (No. 147), attacked the novel as 'downright bad'.

Conrad died before completing *Suspense*, though we see from his letter to Eric Pinker (No. 150) that he still had hopes of a better response for this novel, but Mortimer's criticism of *The Rover* was echoed in P. C. Kennedy's review of *Suspense* in the *New Statesman* (No. 152): 'I am frankly convinced that, if *Suspense* had been the work of an unknown man, it would not have suggested to most people that it was by an author of genius at all.' We have come full circle from the critical reception of *Almayer's Folly*.

E. M. Forster's criticism was followed up by the *Spectator* (No. 155): 'He had stories to tell. And oddly enough he had nothing to say', and by Leonard Woolf (No. 153): 'I had the feeling which one gets on cracking a fine, shining, new walnut . . . only to find that it has nothing inside it.' Conrad was not alive by then to answer this charge, though he had had something to say in the essay 'Books' in *Notes on Life and Letters* about those who try 'to discover the fettering dogmas of some romantic, realistic, or naturalistic creed in the free work of its own inspiration'[73] and in a letter to Garnett of 20 July 1905, he appears to be endorsing Forster's view of him, though he is, of course, being ironic: 'to say it [the essay] contains all my philosophy of life is a severe hit . . . for myself I don't know what my philosophy is. I wasn't even aware I had it. . . . Shall I die of it do you think?'[74] Perhaps the best reply to this charge of emptiness is made in *Heart of Darkness* where Woolf's very image is rather differently explored: seamen's yarns, the narrator tells us, have 'the whole meaning . . . within the shell of a cracked nut', but with Marlow's story 'the meaning of an episode was not inside like a kernel but outside, enveloping the tale' (p. 48).

Clearly, for a less biased judgment, smacking less of a conspiracy of the 'young writers', we have to turn to Garnett's dispassionate review in the *Weekly Westminster* (No. 154), and anyway, the old genius was gone from the earth. He would have been ironically amused. Perhaps the last word should be left to those reviewers who had no artistic axe to grind but responded to Conrad's achievement. Monkhouse, who had reviewed Conrad over many years for the *Manchester Guardian*, ended his review of *Suspense* with the following sentence: 'And so comes to an end the reviewing of Conrad's novels; here is the last of that great series that has brought deep experiences to so many of us.'

CRITICISM, PAST, PRESENT, AND FUTURE

It has generally been assumed that Conrad did not receive substantial critical attention until recent years; in 1952, Douglas Hewitt commented that 'his true significance is now beginning to be appreciated'. But Conrad gained marked recognition with his first novel and was given serious consideration by certain critics very early in his career. This came initially from friends: there was Edward Garnett's *Academy* article of 15 October 1898 (see No. 39); Hugh Clifford's 'The Genius of Mr. Joseph Conrad' in the *North American Review*, June 1904, pp. 842–52; John Galsworthy's 'Joseph Conrad: A Disquisition' in the *Fortnightly Review* of April 1908 (No. 88), in which he stated that the ten novels then published were probably 'the only writing of the last twelve years that will enrich the English language to any great extent'; and Arthur Symons's article in *Forum* of April 1915, entitled simply 'Conrad'. At this stage, examination of Conrad's work is mingled with accounts of the man, his origins and 'exotic' background, but more scholarly scrutiny of Conrad's work was taking place. Stephen Reynolds's 'Joseph Conrad and Sea Fiction' appeared in *Quarterly Review*, July 1912; Richard Curle's *Joseph Conrad: A Study* was published in England and America in 1914; and Wilson Follett's book, with its detailed title, *Joseph Conrad: a short study of his intellectual and emotional attitude toward his work and of the chief characteristics of his novels,* followed in 1915. During the next year there was Hugh Walpole's *Joseph Conrad,* and John Freeman in his *The Moderns: Essays in Literary Criticism* (pp. 243-64) and William Lyon Phelps in his *The Advance of the English Novel* (pp. 192-217; No. 124) both gave a chapter to Conrad.

Before the First World War ended, F. W. Cutler's article 'Why Marlow?' appeared in *Sewanee Review,* January 1918, and in April 1925 in the same journal, Donald Davidson's 'Directed Indirections', both pieces still worthy of our attention. Even before the twenties, Conrad was treated as a writer of classics. We have some indication of the strength of feeling he engendered when we recall that the reviewer in the *Times Literary Supplement,* 26 July 1917, speaking of the new edition of *Lord Jim* (Dent, 1917), felt it necessary to insist: 'It is not a question of luxury, but of necessity: we have to buy Mr. Conrad; all our friends have to buy Mr. Conrad.'

During the last years of his life he had many distinguished visitors, several of whom published a record of the occasion—Virginia Woolf, 'Mr. Conrad: A Conversation' in the *Nation and Athenaeum,* 1 September 1923, Desmond McCarthy in the *New Statesman,* 9 August 1924 (just after Conrad's death); Lady Ottoline Morrell, 'Joseph Conrad: An Impression' in *Nation and Athenaeum,* 30 August 1924, and R. L. Mégroz, who first met Conrad in 1922, in his book dealing principally with Conrad's conversation, *A Talk with Joseph Conrad* (1926). After Conrad's death, the reminiscences began to appear. Ford Madox Ford brought out his eccentric but lively *Joseph Conrad: A Personal Remembrance* (1924), which Ford himself characterized as 'a novel, not a monograph; a portrait, not a narration . . . a work of art, not a compilation'. Conrad's wife published her memoirs, *Joseph Conrad as I Knew Him* (1926), and a year later there was John Galsworthy's 'Reminiscences of Conrad' in *Castles in Spain and other Screeds.* There was an account in E. V. Lucas's *The Colvins and their Friends* (1928), and a splendid one—'Genius at the Turn of the Century'—by the artist William Rothenstein in the *Atlantic Monthly* of February 1932. Sir Henry Newbolt's record of his meeting with Conrad in *My World as in my Time* (1932) is perhaps the most revealing we have, and H. G. Wells, in his *Experiment in Autobiography* (1934), told us that Conrad 'reminded people of Du Maurier's Svengali and . . . Cutliffe Hyne's Captain Kettle'.

In 1935, Jessie Conrad published a more substantial account of her husband, *Joseph Conrad and His Circle.* Apart from reminiscences, excellent and seminal work was also being produced at this time. There was Gustave Morf's *The Polish Heritage of Joseph Conrad* (1930), perhaps to be seen today as the first of the psychological studies of Conrad and his background, and Edward Crankshaw's *Joseph Conrad: Some Aspects of the Art of the Novel* (1936). In 1927, Conrad's friend and first biographer, G. Jean-Aubry, had brought out his two volumes *Joseph Conrad: Life and Letters*. It might have been assumed that, with the storehouse of information that Jean-Aubry provided on the one hand, and the works by Morf and Crankshaw on the other, the two directions that future scholarship might take had been suggested, but the thirties were not to see any further work of importance, and indeed there was a decline of interest in Conrad on the part of the public. The novelist Elizabeth Bowen, reviewing Crankshaw's book in the *Spectator*, 24 April 1936, commented: 'Conrad is in abeyance. We are not clear yet how to rank him; there is an uncertain pause.'

But once out of the thirties, evidence of a revival began to appear in the shape of important contributions to Conrad studies on both sides of the Atlantic. Conrad, as a major novelist of our time along with Joyce and Lawrence, became a subject for scholarly study and research. Undoubtedly, the most influential volume in Conrad studies has been John Dozier Gordan's *Joseph Conrad: The Making of a Novelist* (1940). It is a book that does four things remarkably well: it pioneers source study (Gordan made a short visit to Borneo to seek out the Olmeijer family who were the source for *Almayer's Folly*); it traces the evolution of plot and character through manuscript and typescript; it studies the elaborate changes which Conrad made in the journey from manuscript to final text; and finally it makes a start (which I hope this present work completes) on the assessment of contemporary criticism of Conrad's novels as they were published.

Work of a more directly literary kind appeared in a critical assessment by F. R. Leavis in *Scrutiny*, June and October 1941 (reprinted in *The Great Tradition*, 1948), which claimed: 'Conrad is among the very greatest novelists in the language—or any language.' Miss Bradbrook's short but pertinent account, *Joseph Conrad: Poland's English Genius*, was also published in 1941. During the forties there were, in addition, two important contributions from America: M. D. Zabel's 'Chance and Recognition' in *Sewanee Review*, winter 1945, and A. J. Guerard's *Conrad* (1947), a preliminary study from one of the most perceptive critics in the field.

The fifties contributed two further critical studies of value—Douglas

Hewitt's brief work, *Conrad: A Reassessment*, 1952 (still, set alongside Frederick Karl's *A Reader's Guide to Joseph Conrad*, 1960, the best introduction we have), and Guerard's *Conrad the Novelist* (1958). But the fifties also saw some new directions being taken. Thomas Moser's book, *Joseph Conrad: Achievement and Decline* (1957), placed Conrad on the psychiatrist's couch, as well as pointing in a particularly convincing way to the decline of his work after 1913. The psychological approach reached its apotheosis in Bernard Meyer's *Joseph Conrad: A Psychoanalytical Biography* (1967). Irving Howe, with a commitment to the left, gave an account of Conrad as a political novelist, which is both idiosyncratic and original, in *Politics and the Novel* (1957). This has been followed in the sixties by Eloise Knapp Hay, *The Political Novels of Joseph Conrad* (1963) and Avrom Fleishman, *Conrad's Politics* (1967). The publication of valuable biographical material began with a cache of letters from Conrad to his publisher, Blackwood, *Joseph Conrad: Letters to William Blackwood and David S. Meldrum*, ed. W. Blackburn (1958), and was followed by the letters from Tadeusz Bobrowski, Conrad's uncle and guardian, scrupulously edited by Zdzisław Najder (*Conrad's Polish Background*, 1964), and from Conrad to his friend, R. B. Cunninghame Graham, meticulously edited by C. T. Watts (*Joseph Conrad's Letters to R. B. Cunninghame Graham*, 1969). Whereas the fifties had seen G. Jean-Aubry's *The Sea-Dreamer* (1957) which he subtitled *A Definitive Biography*, Jocelyn Baines's *Joseph Conrad: A Critical Biography* (1960) must certainly remain the definitive account of Conrad's life, and we now have Conrad's son Borys's recollections in *My Father: Joseph Conrad* (1970). The Polish influence on Conrad, still not sufficiently documented, has been recently explored by Andrzej Busza, and his work 'Conrad's Polish Literary background and some illustrations of the influence of Polish Literature on his work', *Antemurale* 10 (1966), 109–255, should be made more easily available. My own two volumes on Conrad's life and sources, *Conrad's Eastern World* and *Conrad's Western World* appeared in 1966 and 1971.

As for critical studies in the sixties, there is *The Art of Joseph Conrad: a Critical Symposium* (1960), edited by R. W. Stallman, which gathers together a wide-ranging collection of articles; John Palmer's *Joseph Conrad's Fiction* (1968), which among other things sets out to disprove the decline in Conrad's later work; Paul Kirschner's *Conrad: the Psychologist as Artist* (1968), which has valuable things to say about the influence of Turgenev, Maupassant, and Anatole France; J. I. M.

Stewart's *Joseph Conrad* (1968), a critical survey which takes into account previous studies and is as urbane and perceptive as only this author can be; and Lawrence Graver's *Conrad's Short Fiction* (1969), which because it concentrates on Conrad's short stories provides us with a valuable new perspective. Three articles should be noted, R. P. Warren's 'Nostromo', *Sewanee Review*, summer 1951; Tony Tanner's 'Butterflies and Beetles—Conrad's Two Truths', *Chicago Review*, winter 1963, and Ian Watt's 'Story and Idea in Conrad's *The Shadow-Line*', *Critical Quarterly*, summer 1960.

In recent years, attention has been paid increasingly to Conrad's symbolism and imagery—James Guetti's *The Limits of Metaphor* (1967); Donald Yelton's *Mimesis and Metaphor* (1967); and to mythic patterns —Claire Rosenfield's *Paradise of Snakes: An Archetypal Analysis of Conrad's Political Novels* (1967). Interesting new approaches are found in E. W. Said's *Joseph Conrad and the Fiction of Autobiography* (1966) and Bruce Johnson's *Conrad's Models of Mind* (1971).

Perhaps the soundest approaches today, and those for which we should be eternally grateful, are to be found in the careful attempt on the part of Bruce Harkness to establish Conrad's text—*Conrad's Heart of Darkness and the Critics* (1960) and *Conrad's Secret Sharer and the Critics* (1962), and the Norton edition of *Lord Jim* in which Moser has produced the most authoritative text at present possible.

Apart from the predominantly British and American contributions to Conrad studies, valuable work has and is being done in other parts of the world; Hans van Marle in Holland, Ivo Vidan in Yugoslavia, René Rapin in Switzerland, Ugo Mursia in Italy, G. J. Resink in Indonesia, and certainly not least, the clutch of Polish scholars— Wit Tarnawski, Przemysław Mroczkowski, Róza Jabłkowska, Stefan Zabierowski, Jozef Miłobedzki, Barbara Koc and Witold Chwalewik.

Conrad has, politically, been both condemned and claimed by the left and by the right, but one of Conrad's greatest irritations—the comparison with writers such as Stevenson—has ceased, and another—his being ranked as a writer of sea stories—has lost its credence.

An interesting aspect of Conrad's reputation is the number of films that have been made from his novels and short stories—*An Outcast of the Islands* (1951), *Lord Jim* (1925 and 1965), *Romance* (1927), *Nostromo* (1926), *The Secret Agent* (1956), 'The Secret Sharer' (1952), *Under Western Eyes* (1937), *Victory* (1920, 1930, and 1941), and *The Rescue* (1929). Given the static and involuted quality of Conrad's writing, and his own failure to make a play of *The Secret Agent*, this has its own irony.

One would not like to be too dogmatic on such a topic, but it does seem possible that Conrad might be on the verge of a renaissance with a wider reading public who will find in him a great deal that is significant to the present state of mankind, a 'popular' appeal which Conrad could hardly have envisaged but which would have given him great satisfaction. His fascination for writers, popular and scholarly alike, is not in question. Theodore Ehrsam, *A Bibliography of Joseph Conrad* (1969), in listing articles and books about Conrad reaches a grand total of 2043.[75] And few writers have had a quarterly journal given over completely to them as is *Conradiana*, edited by Edward Bojarski and Marion C. Michael.

What work lies in the future? This is difficult to prophesy. At a literary critical level work needs to be done on Conrad's use of rhetoric. There is still no complete edition of Conrad's letters, though it is known that Frederick Karl and Zdzisław Najder have this mammoth task well in hand. There is still no definitive text. Perhaps this is the next step.

NOTES

1 Letter of December 1903, *CPB*, p. 241.
2 Letter of 8 November 1899, *LWB*, p. 72.
3 *LEG*, p. 27.
4 There is some doubt about the royalty. Garnett recalls the royalty as 10 per cent. Conrad's own words are a little vague, 'about $12\frac{1}{2}$ per cent royalty'.
5 *LEG*, p. 2.
6 Letter of 2 May 1895, *Letters of Joseph Conrad to Marguerite Poradowska (1890–1920)*, trans. and ed. John A. Gee and Paul J. Sturm (Yale University Press, 1940), p. 95.
7 Jessie Conrad, *Joseph Conrad and His Circle* (New York, 1964), p. 52.
8 *Letters to Marguerite Poradowska*, p. 98.
9 Letter of 29 March or 5 April 1894, *Letters to Marguerite Poradowska*, p. 64.
10 Letter of 18(?) August 1894, ibid., pp. 76–7.
11 *LEG*, p. 2.
12 *Letters to Marguerite Poradowska*, p. 77.
13 *LEG*, p. 53.
14 Jocelyn Baines, *Joseph Conrad: A Critical Biography* (London, 1960), p. 167.
15 *LEG*, p. 83.

16 Probably *A Man from the North* (1898).

17 *JAB*, i, 64.

18 *LEG*, pp. 125-6.

19 Ibid., p. 128.

20 Ibid., p. 127.

21 Ibid., p. 16.

22 *Pall Mall Magazine*, March 1898, p. 428.

23 *L&L*, i, 200.

24 Ibid., ii, 342.

25 Letter of 31 January 1898, *LCG*, p. 72.

26 *LEG*, p. 2.

27 Ibid., p. 150.

28 *L&L*, i, 282.

29 *LEG*, p. 169.

30 *L&L*, i, 295.

31 Letter of 14 July 1900, *LWB*, p. 104.

32 *LEG*, p. 172.

33 Letter of 19 December 1900, *LWB*, p. 122.

34 *LWB*, p. 113.

35 Ibid., p. 115.

36 *LWB*, p. 116.

37 *LEG*, pp. 172-3.

38 Ibid., p. 184.

39 *TLS* began its review with the sentence, '[Conrad] has written little that is finer than the purple patches in *Typhoon*'.

40 Author's Note to *Nostromo*, pp. xvii and xx.

41 Introduction to *Nostromo*, p. viii.

42 *Joseph Conrad as I Knew Him* (London, 1926), p. 120.

43 *L&L*, ii, 143.

44 *LCG*, p. 169.

45 Author's Note to *The Secret Agent*, p. xii.

46 *L&L*, ii, 49.

47 Ibid., ii, 54.

48 Loc. cit.

49 Author's Note to *The Secret Agent*, p. vii.

50 Ibid., p. xiv.

51 Letter of 7 October 1907, *LCG*, p. 170.

52 *L&L*, ii, 65.

53 Author's Note to *'Twixt Land and Sea*, p. vii.

54 *Conrad's Prefaces to his Works* (Dent, 1965), pp. 267.

55 Letter of 27 May 1912, *LEG*, p. 240.

56 Letter of October 1907, *LEG*, p. 205.

57 Letter of October 1907, *LEG*, p. 209.

58 Letter of 28 August 1908, *LEG*, pp. 214.

59 Letter of 31 January 1924, *L&L*, ii, 336.

60 *LWB*, p. 192.

61 The *Critic* (U.S.A.), September 1903, p. 280, had his own idea why Conrad had failed: '*Typhoon* has been outstripped in popularity by many inferior books. The cause is not far to seek. Mr. Conrad has failed to avail himself of a very puissant form of advertising, and one which would cost him nothing. He has neglected to court the interviewer.'

62 Letter of 20 July 1913, *L&L*, ii, 147.

63 Ibid., ii, 214.

64 Author's Note to *Chance*, pp. viii–ix.

65 *L&L*, ii, 152.

66 Author's Note to *The Shadow-Line*, p. v.

67 *L&L*, ii, 224.

68 Ibid., ii, 226.

69 Ibid., ii, 198.

70 Letter of 25 September 1920, *L&L*, ii, 249.

71 *LEG*, p. 300.

72 *LEG*, p. 9.

73 (London, 1921, p. 8), first published in the *Speaker* (1905).

74 *LEG*, p. 193.

75 See also the most recent and voluminous bibliographical contribution, Bruce E. Teets and Helmut E. Gerber, eds. *Joseph Conrad, An Annotated Bibliography of Writings About Him.*

Note on the Text

In order to keep the book within reasonable limits, I have not included reviews of *The Inheritors* (1901) and *Romance* (1903), both written in collaboration with Ford Madox Hueffer (later Ford). Conrad's two books of reminiscences, *The Mirror of the Sea* (1906) and *A Personal Record* (1912), and his essay collections *Notes on Life and Letters* (1921) and *Last Essays* (1926), also two short-story collections, *Within the Tides* (1915) and *Tales of Hearsay* (1925), have not found a place. Conrad the dramatist is of such little significance that I have also excluded reviews of *One Day More* (1905), which is based on his short story 'Tomorrow', and of the play, *The Secret Agent* (1922).

The material is in general arranged chronologically. Where a reviewer has given a lengthy outline of plot which is not in any way a comment on the work in question I have omitted the outline and indicated this; where a particularly long quotation is given from the text, I have omitted this and given the reference to the passage quoted. Except in the case of obvious typographical errors, I have left the texts as they were published.

Headnotes indicate whether an extract or a complete review is printed, and I have identified reviewers where possible and given explanatory references to people and publications where I think they would be helpful. The numbered footnotes are mine.

ALMAYER'S FOLLY

29 April 1895

1. Unsigned notice, *Daily News*

25 April 1895, 6

No novelist has yet annexed the island of Borneo—in itself almost a continent. But Mr. Joseph Conrad, a new writer, is about to make the attempt in a novel entitled *Almayer's Folly*, which Mr. Unwin will publish. Mr. Conrad says that he combines 'the psychological study of a sensitive European living alone among semi-hostile Arabs and Malays with the vivid incidents attaching to the life of pirates and smugglers.' A merely 'sensitive' European has no business among the semi-savages of Borneo. What you want is an unbounded, reckless hospitality to all sorts of impressions. However the story is praised by those who have seen it in manuscript. The author is intimately acquainted with Borneo and its people. The physical setting of his story is as picturesque as the world offers. The European's closest friend is an ex-pirate, and the reassertion of the old savage instinct in the pirate's lovely daughter—an atavistic fit, if that be not too rude an expression—is one of the chief incidents of the tale. The book is to be included in Mr. Unwin's Library of Six Shilling Fiction.

2. Unsigned review, *Scotsman*

29 April 1895, 3

This is the only occasion on which Conrad was referred to as 'Dr'.

Dr Joseph Conrad's story, *Almayer's Folly*, is a remarkable book, which will probably attract all the more attention because its author's name is new to readers of novels, and because its scene of action lies in regions as yet little, if at all, visited by novelists. It follows the career of a man —a Dutchman—who had gone out young to Macassar to trade.

[a summary of the plot is given]

. . . The story is powerfully imagined, and wrought out with a fine unity of effect which colours the whole book with pathos; while the pictures of Malay life, and of the characters of slave, trader, and Rajah, are done with a skill drawn, if not from an intimate experience of life in Borneo, then from a great gift of imagination. The story is a sad one; but it has nothing depressing in its sombreness. It will be read by many with interest and admiration for its own merits; and every one who reads it will look with hopeful anticipations for the future productions of its author's pen.

3. Unsigned review, *Daily Chronicle*

11 May 1895, 3

Review entitled 'White Man and Brown'.

Let us begin by acknowledging Mr. Conrad's main triumph before proceeding to criticism: he has written a short novel, with scene pitched in a far foreign land, with foreign characters, about which the majority of people have only the vaguest ideas, and he has not for one moment caused us to wish that his pictures and his plot had been nearer home. He is a man who can write of Borneo and never bore, if so frivolous a phrase, used in honest and deserved compliment, do not offend him. The few Malay words sprinkled about his pages set up none of the feeble irritation that most foreign tongues, used as local colour, are apt to do; they have the piquancy of capsicums in a curry. Mr. Conrad, like many another novelist, is content with an idea rather than a plot, and he is well advised. His idea is of one white man, a Dutchman, with the sensitive, nervous temperament of the West, a dreamy lack of initiative and will-power, condemned by circumstances to dwell in a native settlement upon a Bornean river, his only companions, besides his native wife and his half-caste daughter, the strange Eastern beings realised, with one exception (Babalatchi, the Comic Opera Minister) very perfectly and with great apparent ease. The ever-failing fortune of this man, Almayer; the savage hatred for him of his Malay wife; the half-hearted affection of his daughter; and the consistent treachery of every other creature towards him, save the hero, a Rajah's son, Dain Maroola, form the thread of the story. Dain and Nina, the daughter, are lovers, and the author rises to scenes of considerable power and passion in telling their story; a story which makes one feel that the old notion of hero and heroine may still have some excuse, that there are still novelists who can breathe life into the old ideals of love and bravery. But Mr. Conrad's claims to be read rest not only upon his finely conceived and simply executed love-scenes; he essays and succeeds in a subtler task when he shows the emasculating and despair-breeding effect of the tired but scheming East upon a weak neurotic

49

Western organisation. This is done in no set piece of description, but the knowledge of it is built up in the reader's mind by a hundred touches, small in themselves. Mr. Conrad has also the art of creating an atmosphere, poetic, romantic. He tells, as only one who has seen it can, of the creeping decay of house and boat, stage, balcony, and building; he makes one know the warm moisture that slowly rots, as readily as he makes one feel the inertia that fails ever to repair or reconstruct.

The scenery does not appear behind the characters like the 'back cloth' at a theatre—it mingles with them to the end that one may know they would not have been what they were had the white fogs not risen nightly from the river. The lush green backgrounds of poisonous jungle; the broad waters, slapped with tropic rain or gleaming in miasmic moonlit mist; the swift dark canoes, shooting noiselessly on errands of love and hatred; the 'slump' of the sullen alligator seeking the stream—all this is not a setting of the story, it is as much the story as the human interest. To say this is to say much; but we have been struck with the book, and know nothing quite like it of recent years. It is slight and short enough, but gives evidence of abundant stores of material in the author's possession. Mr. Conrad may go on, and with confidence; he will find his public, and he deserves his place.

4. Arthur Waugh, notice, *Critic*

11 May 1895, xxvi, 349

Arthur Waugh (1866–1943), English literary critic and editor, and chairman (1926–36) of the publishing house of Chapman & Hall. The notice is an extract from his 'London Letter'.

The 'parochial' spirit in fiction has extended to Borneo, a tract hitherto untouched by the novelist, but now annexed by Mr. Joseph Conrad, a new writer, who sets forth this week under the ægis of Mr. Fisher Unwin. I have read *Almayer's Folly*, the story in question, and can easily credit the publisher's note, which declares that 'the author is intimately acquainted with Borneo and its people.' The book has more than the qualifications of a volume of travel: it understands, not only the scenery, but the inhabitants. The tragedy of it lies in the revolt of the half-savage daughter of a European—himself the husband of a Malay—to the passions of her mother's people. The European has hoped to educate his daughter and make a reasonable creature of her: she is all he has to care for in the world, and she elopes with a Malay. There is certainly material for fiction in Borneo, and, although Mr. Conrad is far from being a master of his art, and tells his story with plentiful circumlocution, he has hit on a strong motive, and he knows something of human nature. The only hope is that the wily brotherhood of novelists, hunting about for new material, may not suddenly involve us in a torrent of Bornean fiction. If Mr. Conrad's book has the least success, that, in the light of experience, will be the logical sequence.

5. Unsigned review, *World*

15 May 1895, 31

Almayer's Folly, by Joseph Conrad, is a dreary record of the still more dreary existence of a solitary Dutchman doomed to vegetate in a small village in Borneo. The only European in the place, he pits his wits against those of the astute Arab dealers, much to the advantage of the latter. His is a life of bitter disappointment; the half-caste wife he marries turns out a bad bargain, his only daughter leaves him, not unwillingly, for a native lover, and he sinks into the depths of opium degradation. The life is monotonous and sordid, and the recital thereof is almost as wearisome, unrelieved by one touch of pathos or gleam of humour. Altogether the book is as dull as it well could be.

6. Unsigned review, *Athenaeum*

25 May 1895, 3526, 671

In this story of the loves and hates, the intrigues and counterplots of Dutch, Malay, and Arab traders on 'an Eastern river'—the Pantai in Borneo—Mr. Conrad (like Mr. Becke[1] among the Pacific islands) breaks new ground, and presents us with a series of unfamiliar pictures evidently drawn from life. The central figure of the book, the dreamy unpractical Dutchman Almayer, is a pitiable creature, whose sorrows are ultimately buried in gin and opium, and whose nerveless doings arouse but little interest. His Malay wife (the curse of his existence) and his attractive, but semi-savage daughter Nina—who, with an old servant, Ali, and sundry other retainers, compose the uncomfortable household—succeed better in arresting the reader's attention. The love of Nina for her wild Malay suitor Dain, and the revolt of her half-tamed nature from the restraints of civilization, are well depicted, though in a style which suffers from exuberance, so that at times one feels all but stifled by its convolutions. Mr. Conrad has, we imagine, studied Zola[2] to some purpose, as witness the following overloaded, but powerful description of a Bornean forest:—

[quotes ch. 5 'In a moment . . . from which they sprang']

Almayer's Folly is a genuine piece of work, and, in spite of several crudities and awkwardnesses, shows considerable promise. We shall await with interest Mr. Conrad's next appearance as a novelist. Why should he not give his readers, if he can, a sketch of the Straits Settlements,[3] whose petition for fairer treatment, in respect of their military contribution, at the hands of the Government at home has brought them into temporary prominence?

[1] Louis Becke (1855?-1913), Australian author of adventure stories—*By Reef and Palm, The Ebbing of the Tide, The Mutineer.*

[2] Emile Zola (1840-1902), French novelist. Between 1871 and 1893 he published *Les Rougon-Macquart,* 20 novels dealing with the 'natural and social history of a family under the second empire'.

[3] Straits Settlements—Malay Peninsula, comprising Penang, Malacca and Singapore—established 1867, dissolved 1946.

7. H. G. Wells, unsigned review, *Saturday Review*

15 June 1895, 797

Two other books were reviewed in the same article—*Windabyne* by George Ranken and *Sinners Twain* by John Mackie. In his auto-biography, Wells writes: '[Conrad] had been excited by a review I wrote of his *Almayer's Folly* in the *Saturday Review*' (*Experiment in Autobiography*, 1934, ii, 615). Wells is most probably recalling Conrad's response to his review of *An Outcast of the Islands* (see Introduction, p. 8).

All three of these books may be spoken of as 'local colour' stories. *Almayer's Folly* deals with Borneo, *Windabyne* with the vanishing Australia of the squatting days, and *Sinners Twain* with the North-West Territory. Only one of them is to be regarded seriously as a work of art. Mr. Ranken relies on his intimate knowledge of the early settlements, Mr. Mackie on his mounted police business and his reputation for blizzards. But *Almayer's Folly* is a very powerful story indeed, with effects that will certainly capture the imagination and haunt the memory of the reader. Almayer is a Dutchman who marries a Malay woman, and the central conception is the relapse of their daughter from the colonial version of civilization to a barbaric life. It is a gloomy tale, but its gloom is relieved by the rare beauty of the love-story between Nina and Dain, and by such flashes of humour as Babalatchi's grinding at the hand-organ when the Rajah, his master, could not sleep. It is indeed exceedingly well imagined and well written, and it will certainly secure Mr. Conrad a high place among contemporary story-tellers.

8. James Ashcroft Noble, review, *Academy*

15 June 1895, 1206, 52

The Asiatic Archipelago is an unfamiliar background for romance; but its very novelty gives it a certain attractiveness, and Mr. Joseph Conrad has the art of laying on just sufficient local colour to make his work attractive, without adding those final touches—often so tempting to an expert—which are apt to make an artistic work unintelligible to 'the general.' *Almayer's Folly* is not a book which it is easy to appraise with confidence, because it is so much more of a promise than of a performance, and it is difficult even to say what the promise amounts to. It certainly cannot be declared an unqualified success. Its faults are as thick as blackberries in autumn, but many of them are plainly faults of inexperience rather than of incapacity, and are, therefore, not worth emphasising. The only weakness which may really be significant is a certain indistinctness of portraiture. Almayer, the disappointed, broken-down European—alone among the wily, half-savage Malays—is certainly distinct enough, and is not wanting in sombre impressiveness; but some of the other characters are terribly deficient in outline. Still, the book somehow leaves an impression of grasp and power.

9. Unsigned review, *Speaker*

29 June 1895, 722–3

The *Speaker*, a weekly founded in 1890, amalgamating with the *Nation* in 1907 and becoming the *Nation and Athenaeum* in 1921. It was incorporated in the *New Statesman* in 1931.

Two other books were reviewed in the same article—*At the First Corner, and Other Stories* by H. B. Marriot Watson and *The Story of Ursula* by Mrs Hugh Bell.

The Press has already given utterance to very favourable criticisms on the new story by a new writer called *Almayer's Folly*, and it only remains for us to join in the expression of the hope that this may not be the last work from the same pen. It is true that *Almayer's Folly* is a somewhat sombre tale, and that it departs altogether from the conventional happy ending, as well as from many other conventions of the novelist's art. But it is distinctly powerful, and not less distinctly original. It is written with manifest knowledge of the life which it portrays—the life of a solitary European in one of the remoter possessions of the Dutch in the East. Nor is it less convincing as a work of art because the author has not over-coloured either his scenery or his character-drawing. He makes no direct appeal to our sympathies on behalf of Almayer, the white man who has gone through all the bitter experiences of a life-long exile among an inferior race, and who, amid all his struggles and reverses, has been buoyed up by the hope of returning some day to his far-off home in Holland with wealth sufficient to secure his ease and comfort. But though there are no sentimental appeals to us on Almayer's behalf, the deterioration of character consequent upon his life of semi-barbarism is faithfully and forcibly presented, it is impossible not to feel a deep pity for the man, and even a certain respect for his character. His marriage with a native woman may have degraded him, but it has never turned him into a brute, and even the savage to whom he has given his name knows that she

CONRAD

can mock him without fear of the one punishment that she dreads. He
may have become drunken and dishonest, according to the Western
standard of honesty, but his love for his beautiful half-caste daughter
will redeem him in the eyes of all, save the most uncharitable. It is
for the sake of this daughter that he has remained in an obscure and
ignominious exile. It is to secure riches for her that he has broken the
laws, and, alas, it is through her that the tragedy of his life overwhelms
him. The beautiful girl, educated as a Christian among white people, is
the child of her mother as well as of her father, and in the end it is the
savage strain in her nature that conquers, and leads her to abandon
the comparative civilisation of her father's house for the squalid
luxury of a Malayan harem. The whole story is told with a delightful
reticence and self-restraint that only serve to make the tragedy the
more impressive. It is impossible to forget the book, with its vivid
glimpses of Eastern life and of characters that the novelist seldom ven-
tures to meddle with, after it has been laid aside. If Mr. Conrad can
give us another story as striking and life-like as this, his place in our
literature ought to be an assured one.

10. Unsigned review, *Guardian*

3 July 1895, 1001

Seven other novels were reviewed alongside *Almayer's Folly*—
W. E. Norris, *Billy Bellew*; Thomas A. Selby, *The Chinaman in his
own Stories*; Mrs Stevenson, *Woodrup's Dinah*; Lilian Bell, *A
Little Sister to the Wilderness*; Anon., *Under God's Sky*; F. H.
Balfour, *Cherryfield Hall*; Harry Lindsay, *Rhoda Roberts*.

Almayer's Folly is one of the most charming romances that it has been
our fortune to read for many a long day. It is a romance in all senses of
the word; the scene laid in the strange, weird world lying within the
Malay Archipelago, and the actors, Dutch, Arab, Malay, and half-
caste, essentially romantic personalities. Joseph Conrad must have had
unusual opportunity for becoming intimate with his surroundings.
We cannot pretend to criticise him with any real knowledge; we can
only say that our author seems to touch with unerring finger the
characteristic points of his varying nationalities, and to bring them into
a prominence which takes convincing shape. We do not know Mr.
Conrad's name as a writer, but his is evidently not the hand of a novice,
and we can only hope that he will give us more of such pure ore from
the virgin mine which he has struck. The story takes its name from
Almayer, a Dutchman, the only European in that wild land.

[gives summary of the plot]

. . . We will not further trace the workings of the story. Its chief charm
cannot be epitomised. It lies in the freshness and loveliness of theme, of
expression, of grouping; it lies, perhaps, in the fascination of the land
which Mr. Conrad knows so well; it lies above all in the pen of Mr.
Conrad himself, and we cannot hope to transfer that gift to our own.

11. Unsigned review, *Bookman*

September 1895, 176

The *Bookman* (1891–1934) was a popular monthly dealing with literature and subtitled *A Journal for Bookreaders, Bookbuyers and Booksellers*.

Almayer's Folly stands far apart from the common run of novels. Why it does not take its place among those of first-rate power and excellence is difficult to say with any precision, for indeed it has great qualities, picturesqueness, poetry, deep human sympathy, restraint, and literary ability of a very marked kind. It is the story of a Dutchman, an Asiatic Dutchman, who spends his life among the Malays, the only white man on the coast.

[gives summary of the plot]

. . . A bald summary is the most unsuitable way of presenting any idea of the book, which is vague, and subtle, and mysterious, and whose story is rather told by suggestion than in asserted fact. Almayer, the weak and pathetic central character, Abdullah the crafty, Nina the silent, passionate, uncompromising girl, are all finely and unerringly portrayed, though human nature has not in Mr. Conrad so powerful a painter as have the wood, the river, the Eastern sky by night and day. Beautiful, delicate, and sympathetic is his work when it deals with the out-of-door world. What is wrong with *Almayer's Folly*? In bits it is excellent and earns instant admiration. As a whole it is a little wearisome. The author is intensely interested in his subject, pities profoundly the weak, luckless Almayer; but he gives you the idea of muttering the story to himself. It is indeed hard to follow, and the minor characters are very hard to distinguish till the story is well advanced. The action drags. He stops to describe in what should be breathless dramatic moments. The style has beauty, but it lacks swiftness. The slow, vague, mysterious East has cast its spell over Mr. Conrad, with results not conducive to the interest of volatile European readers. But he has written pages of singular fascination.

12. Unsigned review, *Literary News*

September 1895, xvi, 268–9

This review was reprinted from the *Bookman* (U.S.A.), 1895, ii, 39–41, where it was signed by James McArthur. A review in the *British Weekly*, 30 May 1895, p. 86, contains certain phrases which appear also in the *Bookman*, which suggests that McArthur was author of this review also.

Almayer's Folly is unmistakably a serious and valuable contribution to literature. The idea is not only original, but the subtle development of the central and ruling motive is splendidly conceived and carried out. The gradual sapping of Almayer's moral and mental powers, the unequal contest going on in his mind between the essential selfishness of a weak moral nature and the affection for his daughter Nina, born of a Malay wife whom he married for the dreams of avarice which she was expected to realize for him; the sudden gust of passionate uprising against fate—which shows the dignity there is even in the ruins of a man—ere his hopes sink in the night of absolute despair are only equalled by the same masterly portrayal of Nina—poor Nina!—in whose breast there slumbered, despite her education and early training among her father's people, the ineradicable instincts of the Malay mother, which, under favoring circumstances, asserted their racial strength and encompassed the overthrow of the white man. Civilization had not shown its good side to her, and was only the more despised and detested by contrast with the bravery and vigorous manhood of the Malay lover for whom Nina abandoned her loved and loving European father. She is a fine illustration of what may happen to the Malay in the transition which Mr. Swettenham[1] sees is imminent. The phase of character is a revelation to us, and in this whole story of an Eastern river we are impressed with the fact that a new vein has been struck in fiction. It is a work to make one long for more from the

[1] Mr (later Sir) Frank Swettenham (1850–1946), Governor of the Straits Settlements (1901–4), author of many books about the Malays.

same pen. In the novelty of its local color, in the daring originality of its dramatic force, in the fresh disclosure of new scenes and characters, in the noble and imaginative handling of life's greatness and littleness, *Almayer's Folly* has no place in the prevalent fiction of the hour, which, like a flooded stream, sweeps past us into oblivion. It leaps at once to a place of its own—a place which ought to rank its author high among novelists worthy of the name in its best sense. In the scenery and atmosphere of the story the hand of the artist reveals itself. The sombre and languid air of a semi-civilized life is most skilfully conveyed—the dreamy river, its islands and reed banks, the thunder-storms, the thirst for the gains of civilization, and the contempt for its restraints, are vividly impressed on the imagination. Mr. Conrad has not only achieved a great success in realizing for us the fundamental truths underlying existence in a land and among a people almost unknown to the Far West—he deserves it. His book is one to be read and reread.

13. Unsigned review, *Nation* (U.S.A)

17 October 1895, lxi, 278

A novel in which the only white man of importance is a Dutch Trader, while all the women are Malays or half castes, does not promise much entertainment. It is, well, therefore, to approach *Almayer's Folly* with no expectations. The figure of Almayer is pathetic, but almost lost in a mob of raging heathen engaged in battles for rum and wives on the banks of a river of Borneo. We have become inured to tiresome fiction supposed to be descriptive of outlandish places, but a feeling of resentment smoulders. *Almayer's Folly* offers a good opportunity for protest. Borneo is a fine field for the study of monkeys, not men. The only interesting native of Borneo got away and was long ago introduced to an astonished civilisation as 'The old man from Borneo/Who's just come to town.'

14. Unsigned review, *Spectator*

19 October 1895, 530

This is a decidedly powerful story of an uncommon type, and breaks fresh ground in fiction. Almayer, a Dutchman, tries his fortune in Macassar among Englishmen, who are mostly adventurers of a rather low type, and some of whom are little better than pirates. He marries a Malay, and otherwise his prosperity does not come up to his dreams as a young man. He tries, however, to save Nina from sinking back into Malaydom. How he fails, how Nina's blood asserts itself, and how she leaves him to live her own life with her native lover, this story tells. It is extremely powerful all through, though the plot is not so well compacted as it might have been. All the leading characters in the book—Almayer, his wife, his daughter, and Dain, the daughter's native lover—are well drawn, and the parting between father and daughter has a pathetic naturalness about it, unspoiled by straining after effect. There are, too, some admirably graphic passages in the book. The approach of a monsoon is most effectively described:—
'Round her all was as yet stillness and peace, but she could hear afar off the roar of the wind, the hiss of heavy rain, the wash of the waves on the tormented river. It came nearer and nearer, with loud thunderclaps and long flashes of vivid lightning, followed by short periods of appalling blackness. When the storm reached the low point dividing the river, the house shook in the wind, and the rain pattered loudly on the palm-leaf roof, the thunder spoke in one prolonged roll, and the incessant lightning disclosed a turmoil of leaping waters, driving logs, and the big trees bending before a brutal and merciless force.'
The name of Mr. Joseph Conrad is new to us, but it appears to us as if he might become the Kipling of the Malay Archipelago.

AN OUTCAST OF THE ISLANDS

4 March 1896

---

15. Conrad on the literary profession

10 March 1896

Letter to Karol Zagórski, *CPB*, p. 216. Zagórski was a distant cousin of Conrad with whom he corresponded for some years. The extract shows Conrad's wish still to go to sea and his view of the literary profession at this early stage.

. . . A few days ago I was offered the command of a sailing vessel—the idea had pleased my Jessie (who likes the sea) but the terms were so unsatisfactory that in the end I refused. The literary profession is therefore my sole means of support. You will understand, my dear Karol, that if I have ventured into this field it is with the determination to achieve a reputation—in that sense I do not doubt my success. I know what I can do. It is therefore only a question of earning money—'Qui est une chose tout à fait à part du mérite littéraire'. That I do not feel too certain about—but as I need very little I am prepared to wait for it.

16. Unsigned review, *Daily Chronicle*

16 March 1896, 3

Review entitled 'A Romance of the Far East'. This is the first occasion on which Conrad was compared favourably with Herman Melville and R. L. Stevenson. 'Dangerous food' for youth is from 'Ruth': 'The tumult of a tropic sky,/Might well be dangerous food for him, a Youth.'

Mr. Conrad has justified the expectations roused by *Almayer's Folly*. That was altogether as remarkable a first venture in fiction as we can remember. *An Outcast of the Islands* is a work of extraordinary force and charm. The tentative stage, we find, is overpast. We have gained the 'ampler ether and diviner day' of mature achievement. This, too, is a Malayan romance. Once more we breathe the languorous air of those mysterious islands set amid the far Eastern seas. Here is an old world indeed made new by the romancer's magic—a strange world of greedy traders, of adventurous seamen, of wild piratical rovers, of all manner of half-caste rogues. With an intense art does Mr. Conrad depict the present aspects of this little-known Archipelago, where an ancient Aryan civilisation has flourished and died out, leaving no traces but some vague legends and a few monuments which the incurious white settlers scarce wonder at and wholly disregard. Hither the Portuguese came, and have since decayed. Here are now the Dutch and the English, but they have failed to exhaust the mystery or the resources of the island-world. Mr. Conrad's romance suggests its vastness and vagueness with astonishing effect. Excepting in Melville, perhaps, we know nothing to match his scenic descriptions of tropical islands, and to say that they recall *Typee* and its fellow romance is to give the highest and justest meed of praise. But the characters—whites, Arabs, Malays—are presented with not less brilliant definition than the scenes of their ruined paradise. They affect us as with a haunting presence that cannot be evaded.

It was a favourite speculation of certain eighteenth-century philosophers whether the civilised white man tended to deterioration under the condition of life in tropical climates. Some have stoutly denied the truth of Wordsworth's assumption that the influences of tropical nature were 'dangerous food' for youth. Mr. Conrad does not expressly take a side on this question. He has, however, represented these influences as playing an important part in the tragic progress of the outcast's ruin, by exasperating his self-abasement and accentuating his despair.

[gives an outline of the plot]

Here in this opulent and mysterious land of forest and river—Lingard's river, where Lingard ruled unquestioned—Willems met his fate. The process of degradation is set forth, stage by stage, with a power and an insight that are truly Stevensonian. But un-Stevensonian is the conception of the exalted infatuation of Aïssa, the daughter of Omar el Badavi, for the outcast. Her love for him is worship. He is the biggest man she has ever seen—a white man, too—and for him she will abjure faith, family, everything. And he, who is eager for freedom and leadership, becomes hopelessly her slave:—

[quotes part i, ch. 7: 'Willems never remembered . . . in the water'; concludes outline of the plot]

We shall not risk marring the actuality of this climax by quotation. Mr. Conrad's romance does not allow of the ordinary illustration of its qualities by extracts.

Mr. Conrad has been justly commended for his skill in depicting a situation and its environment. He must be on his guard, however, against over-insistence in points of detail. We note a tendency here and there in the present volume towards superfluity. Some of the descriptive passages are a trifle over-wrought, touches are added to what is already complete, and the surplusage weakens the whole picture. In characterisation, as in his previous story, Mr. Conrad shows remarkable resources. Lingard, Willems, Aïssa, these are very finely drawn; strong, enduring, vital personalities. Excellent also, is Joanna, the little Portuguese half-breed wife of Willems, while the crafty Arab, Babalatchi, is a master-sketch.

17. Extracts from notices in two Scottish papers

March 1896

(a) Unsigned review, *Scotsman*, 16 March 1896:

The setting of Mr Conrad's story, *An Outcast of the Islands* is in itself sufficient to render it remarkable. The scene is laid on the banks of a river in the West Indies [sic]—a spot almost untrodden by the foot of white men . . .

The strange effect of the story is mainly due to the skill with which the life on this western [sic] river is described. The two white men, outcasts from civilisation, stand out strongly in their isolation against the background of tropical forest and the contrast between them and those among whom they dwell is drawn with a sure hand . . . It is a weird story of a life that is strange and unnatural, yet there is in it sufficient of human nature to make it real and convincing. Some, perhaps, may find that the atmosphere is too depressing, and that Mr Conrad is inclined to linger too much over his effects, yet none can fail to recognise in it the work of a writer of singular power, and with a strong vein of imagination and originality.

(b) Unsigned review, *Glasgow Herald*, 19 March 1896:

No one who read Mr Conrad's previous work, *Almayer's Folly*, is likely to have forgotten it. If anything, this new novel is still stronger and better work . . . There is distinction in [his] style. Mr Conrad's books might be read for it, apart from any story at all . . . *An Outcast of the Islands* is a book of singular and indefinable power; to be read carefully, some times even with labour, but always beautiful in its style, rich alike in passion and in pathos.

18. James Payn, review, *Illustrated London News*

4 April 1896, 418

James Payn (1830–98), popular novelist, also editor of *Chambers' Journal* (1859–74) and later editor of *Cornhill* (1882–96). Conrad wrote to Mrs Sanderson, mother of his friend Edward Lancelot Sanderson, two days after this review: 'I had a few reviews. Nothing remarkable. The *Illustrated London News* says I am a disciple of Victor Hugo, and is complimentary! Very! So are the Irish papers,—the *Whitehall Review* and the *World*' (*L & L*, i, 187). The *World*, 1 April 1896, was not too complimentary: '. . . we could wish Mr. Joseph Conrad—whose first novel we unfortunately have not seen—had been a little more geographical in his second . . . The Malay Archipelago, even supposing we have got it rightly, is so very vague! . . . The worst faults of the romance are its redundancy and the absence of greatness of any kind in the persons concerned.'

As a general rule, the British novel-reader likes the scenes of his story to be laid in British soil. He is insular in his tastes, not easily interested in places and people who are outside his experience. When a writer contrives to hold his attention with such topics it is a proof that he has handled them exceptionally well. The author of *Almayer's Folly* has already made us feel quite at home in the Indian Archipelago: before his time we knew little of Borneo and its neighbourhood, except that it was beginning to grow good tobacco; and now he revives our acquaintanceship with it, to our great advantage, in *An Outcast of the Islands*. The story is a little disjointed, always a drawback, but especially when it treats of alien subjects; but the characters and descriptions are admirable. Here is the arrival of evening in the islands of the Indian Sea—

A sigh under the flaming blue, a shiver of the sleeping sea, a cool breath as if a door had been swung upon the frozen spaces of the universe, and with a stir of leaves, with the nod of boughs, with the tremble of slender branches, the sea breeze struck the coast, rushed up the river, swept round the broad reaches, and travelled on in a soft ripple of darkening water, in the whisper of branches, in the rustle of leaves of the awakened forests.

Abdulla ben Selim, the great Mohammedan trader of the Straits, is a fine portrait, and new, so far as I know, to the gallery of fiction. For forty years he has walked in the way of his Lord, and been a very religious person after his kind, who do not, however, exclude the idea of poisoning a commercial rival—

[quotes part ii, ch. 3: 'Restless like all his people... splendid rewards.']

The story, such as it is, is found on the rivalry between this man and Captain Lingard, the great white trader, a noble character, with only such little drawbacks (as, for example, in the way of shooting at sight) as are inseparable from his profession, and, to judge by the work under consideration, the only good man (plain or coloured) that has ever existed in the whole Malay Archipelago. As for the outcast himself, never did so mean a skunk figure as the hero of a novel. Yet on or about him the finest thoughts of our author are shed; they are often very striking, now sublime, and now grotesque, reminding us of the utterances of a writer who has had, to my knowledge, no other disciple, Victor Hugo. The keynote of *An Outcast of the Islands* is 'the tremendous fact of our isolation, of the indestructible loneliness that clothes every human soul from the cradle to the grave and perhaps beyond.' So skilfully is this dwelt upon that the sense of it, as he lays down the book, is communicated to the reader.

19. Unsigned review, *Daily News*

4 April 1896, 6

This review provides a paraphrase of the plot and I have omitted much of this. I include the review as it points to the fact that Conrad tended to go beyond permitted limits in his characterization.

Mr Conrad's second book, *An Outcast of the Islands*, bears out the extraordinary promise given by his first romance, *Almayer's Folly*. It is a story of the Malayan Archipelago, and it tells how in these summer islands was enacted the tragedy of the downward course of Willems, until, in his moral degradation, he touches depths of infamy.

[Willems, losing his job as confidential clerk to Hudig & Co, is taken by Captain Lingard to his secret river and established alongside Almayer. Willems falls in love with Aissa.]

... The author treats very frankly the influence of passion upon this nature hitherto poised in absolute egoism. First, the man's struggle against the something inarticulate and masterful that has suddenly possessed him, then his complete and abject surrender. It is an impressive and repulsive picture of one drunk with the poison of passion. The girl's infatuation for the superior white man is drawn with imaginative insight. She is ambitious for him. She would see him ruler of Sambir, and she listens readily to the honied promises of the leader of the malcontents, tired of the rule of Lingard, and who see in Willems the tool by which they may upset their benefactor's authority. This story of cold-blooded treachery is told swiftly and with ruthless directness. When the great betrayal is achieved, then Willems discovers that he will profit nothing by his crime, and his passion for Aissa turns to loathing. The scene between the traitor and Lingard is presented with a gruesome realism of detail. Some of the touches are over-violent, and pass the restraint of true tragedy. The last act of the drama is as unforeseen as it is convincing; it is one of many scenes that haunt the memory of the reader. This well-told story of an ignoble life is at once captivating and repellent.

20. Unsigned review, *National Observer*

18 April 1896, 680

National Observer, originally named *Scots Observer*, but W. E. Henley changed its name when he brought this weekly journal to London. Henley (1849–1903), poet, playwright, critic and editor. After leaving the *National Observer* started the *New Review*. He admired Kipling very much and published *Barrack-Room Ballads* (1892) in his journal. He was a friend of and collaborator with R. L. Stevenson. The identity of the 'enthusiastic critic' is not known, but his review appeared in the *Spectator* (No. 14). The reviewer's reference to Conrad's being 'diffuse' is a notion put forward in the *National Observer*'s notice of *Almayer's Folly*: '... its artistic possibilities are constantly thrown aside and sacrificed to a laboured and muddle-headed involution' (14 September 1895, p. 513).

When Mr. Conrad's former book, *Almayer's Folly*, appeared an enthusiastic critic seems to have declared that he might become 'the Kipling of the Malay Archipelago.' Judging by *An Outcast of the Islands* we fear that this prophecy has not been fulfilled. Mr. Kipling is a master of rapid delineation of character, of vivid directness of style. He excels in the short story because he can put into a small compass an amount of incident which, with lesser men, suffices for a whole volume. Mr. Conrad, on the contrary, is diffuse. He spreads his story over a wilderness of chapters and pages. Instead of the few vivid touches with which Mr. Kipling paints a scene, his narrative wanders aimlessly through seas of trivial detail. It is a pity, for Mr. Conrad is evidently equipped with a very thorough knowledge of the scenes which he describes and at times, when he resists his besetting sin of wordiness, he can be extremely effective. The opening scenes of this book for example, in which the early career of Willems is summarised, are good. But later on he seems to lose grip of his subject. The story melts away among a desert of words, and the desert alas is dry. Unhappily, his characters, on

CONRAD

whom he has evidently expended considerable pains, are not in themselves particularly effective. Lingard is not impressive and even Willems is not a very interesting scoundrel. As for Babalatchi, Lakamba, Patalolo and the rest, they are, it must be confessed, a bore. Mr. Conrad does not possess Mr. Kipling's extraordinary faculty of making his natives interesting. We are sorry not to be able to write more appreciatively of what is evidently a careful and conscientious piece of work, but as it stands, *An Outcast of the Islands* is undeniably dull. It is like one of Mr. Stevenson's South Sea stories, grown miraculously long and miraculously tedious. There is no crispness about it and the action is not quick enough, a serious charge to make against a book of adventure. Even schoolboys will probably have some difficulty in getting through it and we fear adults will find it impossible.

21. Unsigned review, *Sketch*

6 May 1896, 62

Those intent 'watchers of the sky,' the critics, who are ever sweeping it to distinguish fireworks, meteors, planets, and fixed stars from each other, will probably pronounce Mr. Conrad a nebula. This astronomical illustration, by the way, is Schopenhauer's,[1] who classifies writers as either meteors, that make a startling but momentary effect; planets, that outshine the fixed stars, only because they are nearer us, with an influence confined to their own orbit—to their contemporaries; and fixed stars, which, unlike meteors, are eternal, and, unlike planets, are original, shining by their own light; and, unlike both meteors and planets, belong not to one system, one nation only, but to the universe. Mr. Conrad, however, cannot be ranged and ranked under any of these three classes, since he is but a star in the making. His light is all his own, and is unquestionably brilliant, but it is nebulously diffused. A lack of

[1] Schopenhauer (1788–1860), German philosopher; his chief work was *The World as Will and Idea* (1819).

70

proportion and of concentration, in fact, is the chief fault, almost the sole fault, which the most exacting critic is likely to find with *An Outcast of the Islands*. Every mood and movement of the mind of each of his personages, and every mood and movement of nature in the Malay Archipelago, are described with a vividness and power that surprise you; but the descriptions submerge the story—

[gives an outline of the plot and quotes part v, ch. 4: 'Who is she? . . . Night already?']

Here end Willems and the story. Aïssa goes mad; the only other character that is not abjectly base, Lingard, disappears like that cloud to which Mark Antony[1] compares himself, no one knows when, where or how. Mr. Conrad has Stevenson's power of interesting us even sympathetically in the fortunes of unredeemed scoundrels; but he lacks, though he will not lack it long, the master's reserve and reticence. 'By what he omits,' says Schiller,[2] 'show me the master of style'; and Mr. Conrad occasionally becomes ineffective through overstraining after effect. To paint a field he must needs paint every blade of grass with pre-Raphaelite minuteness, while he observes through a microscope every thought that floats, however casually, through the minds of his personages. That the painting is done either exquisitely or powerfully is unquestionable, but its over-elaboration defeats itself. However, over-luxuriance, if it is the fault of youth, is also its promise, and the very elaboration which embarrasses and impedes the singular power shown in *An Outcast of the Islands* assures you almost as much as that power itself that Mr. Conrad has a future before him.

[1] Shakespeare's *Antony and Cleopatra*.
[2] Johann Christoph Friedrich Schiller (1759–1805), German dramatist and poet.

22. Unsigned article, *Bookman*

May 1896, 41

Article entitled 'New Writers—Mr. Joseph Conrad'. This is the first account, apart from reviews, that I have found of Conrad. It looks suspiciously like a publisher's handout, but it clearly served to satisfy the curiosity of a public who knew nothing about this strange new author. Conrad married Jessie George on 24 March 1896 and left for Brittany. He did not, as this article suggests, continue to live on the Continent, but returned to England in September.

It will not surprise readers of *Almayer's Folly*, that remarkable novel where wild nature and strange humanity were so powerfully portrayed, to learn that its author has led an adventurous life. Material for such books can only be brought to the writing table by the track of personal experience. It is as unmistakeably the book of a wanderer who has lived far from the ways and the atmosphere of European capitals as are Loti's[1] exotic romances. An unfamiliar something in its tone, too, which now expressed itself as poetry, and now was too vaguely illusive for readers here in London to grasp very easily, roused a curiosity as to its origin. Perhaps the unfamiliarity is explained by the fact that Mr. Conrad, for all his skilful adoption of our language, is not an Englishman. He is a Pole by birth, and his early years were spent in Poland. From at least two generations he inherited a keen interest in literature; his father, or his grandfather, was a translator of Shakespeare. But they were men of action, too. The grandfather had belonged to Napoleon's Grande Armée. His father attached himself to the revolutionary movement in Poland, and suffered imprisonment for his opinions. Indeed, we believe young Conrad and his mother shared the confinement. After his father's release and his mother's death, he accompanied his

[1] Pierre Loti, pseudonym of Louis Marie Julien Viaud (1850-1923), French novelist. His *Rarahu* (1880), published in 1882 as *Le Mariage de Loti*, describes the love of an Englishman for a Tahiti girl.

father to Warsaw, where the latter also died. At the age of thirteen he found his way to Paris, drifted to Marseilles, to a merchant house, and afterwards to a seafaring life. As a merchant seaman he has gone through all the grades, and is now full captain in the English marines. He has served in most quarters of the globe, but chiefly in the Pacific and on the Borneo coast, and has commanded a steamer on the Congo. During all his active, wandering life, literature has always had a fascination for him, though he has let the world see none of the experiments that perhaps prepared the way for *Almayer's Folly* and *An Outcast of the Islands.*

Mr. Conrad recently married an English lady, and is now living quietly in France with a view to further literary work. If he meets with the success which he deserves, his seafaring days are probably over.

23. H. G. Wells, unsigned review, *Saturday Review*

16 May 1896, 509–10

Conrad wrote to the reviewer in this instance and discovered that it was Wells (see Introduction, p. 8).

Last year there was published an East Indian romance, *Almayer's Folly*, which was praised, it is to be feared, rather more than it was read. Reviewer after reviewer hailed the new writer more or less pithily, promised him a brilliant future, and thought no more of the matter. 'Mr. Conrad,' said the *Daily Chronicle*, thumbs up, so to speak. 'Mr. Conrad may go on.' 'We have been struck by the book.' 'He will find his public, and he deserves his place.' And Mr. Conrad has availed himself of this generous permission, and has gone on—to a remarkably fine romance indeed. One fault it has, and a glaring fault; and that one may deal with first, and put aside to proceed to the more grateful enterprise of praise. Mr. Conrad is wordy; his story is not so much told as seen intermittently through a haze of sentences. His style is like river-mist; for a space things are seen clearly, and then comes a great grey bank of printed matter, page on page, creeping round the reader, swallowing him up. You stumble, you protest, you blunder on, for the drama you saw so cursorily has hold of you; you cannot escape until you have seen it out. You read fast, you run and jump, only to bring yourself to the knees in such mud as will presently be quoted. Then suddenly things loom up again, and in a moment become real, intense, swift.

Here, to get this painful part over, is Mr. Conrad at his worst. In Chapter iii. of Part V. he wishes to show us the intolerable boredom of Willems, the outcast, left alone, satiated, in Lakamba's deserted settlement, with the woman he loved so passionately. He has to give us a glimpse of the savage woman's aching perplexity at this changed demeanour, and of her gleam of happiness when for a moment he tried to relieve his tedium by blowing at the whitened ashes of his passion. Indisputably, Mr. Conrad has imagined it all; for if you feel about in this chapter, however hastily and eager, grasping the tangible facts, and letting the haze drive by you, you will, after an interval, see quite distinctly the pathetic beauty of the episode he has conceived. And this is how he begins: 'On Lingard's departure solitude and silence closed round Willems.' This apparently misses the effect sought, because of the turn of the phrase—'closed' cripples the idea of being derelict almost as much as if one spoke of a man being thickly swathed in isolation. Silence and solitude do not close round any one; they sit down afar off and watch. So much Mr. Conrad seems to have felt, and to modify it he adds, 'The cruel silence of one abandoned by men,' and still dissatisfied proceeds, 'the reproachful silence which surrounds an outcast rejected by his kind.' But there is something unsatisfactory about that silence, and the only remedy within Mr. Conrad's reach seems to be more words; so 'the silence unbroken by the slightest whisper of hope,' and then, getting angry, 'an immense, an impenetrable silence, that swallows up without echo the murmur of regret and the cry of revolt.' And having given the battered silence its unsatisfactory quietus with this, Mr. Conrad leaves it. The curious thing is that this trampling army corps of dependent clauses, this silence correcting silence, leaves no impression of silence at all. For ten pages altogether does Mr. Conrad toil away, multiplying words. Here is a sample chosen haphazard, which, indeed, might almost serve as a criticism of him in itself:—'His wandering feet stumbled against the blackened brands of extinct fires, kicking up a light black dust of cold ashes that flew in drifting clouds and settled to leeward' (naturally enough) 'on the fresh grass sprouting from the hard ground, between the shade trees. He moved on, and on; ceaseless, unresting, in widening circles, in zigzagging paths that led to no issue; and the marks of his footsteps, pressed deep into the soft mud of the bank, were filled slowly behind him' (not in front, mind you) 'by the percolating water of the rising river, caught the light, and shone in a chain of small reflected suns along the broad expanse of black slime, of the dull and quivering mire where he struggled on, objectless, unappeased; struggled on wearily with a set, distressed face behind which, in his tired brain, seethed his thoughts: restless, sombre, tangled, chilling, horrible and venomous, like a nestful of snakes.'

Notice here how the one finely expressive symbol of the shining footsteps is lost in this dust-heap of irrelevant words, and in particular how the last eleven words, with that needless inappropriate image of snakes, rob the whole of its last vestige of effect. It never seems to occur to Mr. Conrad to put forth his effect and leave it there stark and beautiful; he must needs set it and explain it and refer to it, and thumb and maul it to extinction; and it never seems to dawn upon him that, if a sentence fails to carry the full weight and implication it was meant to do, the remedy is not to add a qualifying clause, but to reject it and try another. His sentences are not unities, they are multitudinous tandems, and he has still to learn the great half of his art, the art of leaving things unwritten.

Now all this is set down without any desire of detraction. It is the least any one must say who is setting out to give Mr. Conrad his meed of praise as a romancer. After all this has been said, one can still apply superlatives to the work with a conscience void of offence. Subject to the qualifications thus disposed of, *An Outcast of the Islands* is, perhaps, the finest piece of fiction that has been published this year, as *Almayer's Folly* was one of the finest that was published in 1895. It is hard to understand how the respectable young gentlemen from the Universities who are engaged in cutting out cheaper imitations of the work of Mr. Stanley Weyman[1] and Mr. Anthony Hope[2] can read a book like

1 Stanley Weyman (1855–1928), a popular historical novelist, known in particular for *A Gentleman of France* (1893) and *Under the Red Robe* (1894).
2 Anthony Hope, pseudonym of Sir Anthony Hope Hawkins (1863–1933), famous at this time for *The Prisoner of Zenda* (1894).

this and continue in that industry. Think of the respectable young gentleman from the University, arrayed in his sister's hat, fichu, rationals, and cycling gauntlets, flourishing her hat-pin, and pretending in deference to the supposed requirements of Mr. Mudie's public, to be the deuce and all of a taverning mediæval blade, and compare him with Willems the Outcast, late confidential clerk to Hudig & Co. Here you have (a little pruned of words) the picture of Willems in his glory:—

[quotes part i, ch. 1: 'In the afternoon . . . Night already!']

Then compare Mr. Conrad's wonderful Aïssa with the various combinations of Mr. Hope's 'Duchess' and Mr. Weyman's fitful lady that do duty in contemporary romance. How she lives and breathes through all this jungle of tawdry pretentious verbiage!

[quotes part i, ch. 6: 'At the end . . . one's old self.']

Surely this is the real romance—the romance that is real! Space forbids anything but the merest recapitulation of the other living realities of Mr. Conrad's invention—of Lingard, of the inimitable Almayer, the one-eyed Babalatchi, the Naturalist, of the pious Abdulla—all novel, all authentic. Enough has been written to show Mr. Conrad's quality. He imagines his scenes and their sequence like a master, he knows his individualities to their hearts, he has a new and wonderful field in this East Indian novel of his—and he writes despicably. He writes so as to mask and dishonour the greatness that is in him. Greatness is deliberately written; the present writer has read and reread his two books, and, after putting this review aside for some days to consider the discretion of it, the word still stands. Only greatness could make books of which the detailed workmanship was so copiously bad, so well worth reading, so convincing, and so stimulating.

24. Unsigned review, *Manchester Guardian*

19 May 1896, 5

An Outcast of the Islands is an astonishingly clever book, and ought to make a mark. If it does not, it will probably be due to a certain turgidity and affectation of style which may prevent people from appreciating its genuine imaginative power and subtle, strong character-drawing. There is an extraordinary vitality and virility about the book, too. It is as masculine as Kipling, but without that parade of masculinity which Kipling loves. The account of the final meeting between Captain Lingard and Willems, the man who owes everything to him and who yet betrays and robs him, is one of the most curiously intense bits of writing we ever remember to have read. The account, too, of Willems's infatuation for Aissa, the half-caste girl, simply palpitates with life, and the meeting between her and his wife at the end of the book, and his death at Aissa's hands, are episodes which send one's heart into one's mouth as one reads. The scene is laid in the Malay Archipelago, and the bitter struggle that goes on endlessly between the white race and the yellow [sic] is described with force and insight. The only real fault to be found with the book is a certain tendency towards affectation and mannerism in the writing. This Mr. Conrad must beware of, for if he lets it grow upon him it will mar what is in other ways really first-rate work. This said, we have nothing but admiration for *An Outcast of the Islands*. It is, in our opinion, a genuinely remarkable book, and we shall be surprised if Mr. Conrad does not make a name for himself in the near future.

25. Unsigned review, *Spectator*

30 May 1896, 778

In this review, for the third time, Conrad is called a 'genius', the first time being in the *Weekly Sun* (see Introduction, p. 6).

We do not often come across a novel of so much power as Mr. Conrad's *An Outcast of the Islands*. The action takes place on an island of the Malay Archipelago, and the descriptions of tropical scenery glow with life and colour. There is not less power in the descriptions of character. But unfortunately the situation yields a richer crop of evil passions than of noble ones, and the book on the whole suggests the view of the well-known hymn that in the tropics it is as much a matter of course for man to be vile as for Nature to be beautiful. There is however, one grand character in the book—that of the old seaman, Tom Lingard. This personage, who is conceived on the colossal scale of primitive romance, looms through the lurid atmosphere of crime and sensuality like a legendary type of rugged, incorruptible manhood. The man who plays the largest and most detestable part in the story is a *protégé* of Lingard,—one, Peter Willems, whom he has taken compassion on as a runaway boy and put in the way of making a fortune. Willems is as incapable of loyalty or even honesty as Lingard is incapable of the opposite faults. Willems cheats his employer, and is turned out of a good berth, and flung disgraced upon a prospect of ruin. But Lingard gives him another chance, and he plays false again. This time he falls in love with a native woman, who is a magnificent embodiment of savage passion, and by his treachery causes a disastrous revolution in Lingard's island. The description of this revolution is extraordinarily graphic, and it abounds in horrors which are, however, partly condoned by the beauty and poetry of the style. The redeeming human point is the magnanimity of Lingard towards Willems. There is an exquisite poignancy of pathos in the words with which the hardy old sailor finally takes leave of the man he has benefited, and by whom he has been betrayed:—'You are not a human being that may be

78

destroyed or forgiven. You are a bitter thought, a something without a body, and that must be hidden. . . . . You are my shame.' Much is forgiven to genius, and there is genius in this novel. But even genius will not win forgiveness for the repulsive cynicism of the dialogue between Almayer and the Professor in the last chapter.

26. Unsigned review, *Athenaeum*

18 July 1896, 3586, 91

The remarkable promise displayed by Mr. Conrad in *Almayer's Folly* is fully maintained in *An Outcast of the Islands*, which is unquestionably one of the strongest and most original novels of the year. There are many people whose residence in outlandish quarters of the globe has furnished them with the raw material of fresh and interesting works of fiction; but it is only one in ten millions who can turn such opportunities to literary account, and transmute these raw materials into a work of art. This is what Mr. Conrad has achieved, and his achievement is all the more remarkable from the entire absence of all artifice or affectation in his method. From beginning to end of this vivid story of the Malay Archipelago there is not a single literary allusion, not a single evidence of his indebtedness to any other author. It is a perfectly genuine piece of work, the outcome of extensive experience and close observation allied to a subtle power of analysis and an intense and poetic appreciation of the beauties of the tropical landscape. Mr. Conrad's characters are almost without exception entirely fresh and unfamiliar, but instinct with vitality. The moral atmosphere of the book is one which can best be described as magnificently sordid. Apart from the old captain, who has a certain grandeur of purpose and nobility of temper, the *dramatis personæ* do not reflect much credit on humanity. But there is nothing gratuitous about the book, which marches on to its close with the inevitableness of a Greek tragedy, unless we except the somewhat cynical epilogue, which might, perhaps, have been spared. Mr. Conrad's style is at times rough hewn and occasionally obscure; but his book has fascination, and in face of that rare quality it would be ungracious to dwell further on the shortcomings of this brilliant novel.

27. Unsigned review, *Nation* (U.S.A.)

15 April 1897, 287

Belief in the benefits of foreign travel have long been a cherished superstition, and might survive eternally if travellers would keep their impressions to themselves, guarding them as jealously as the spoils picked up and paid for by the way. It is when the foreign air goes to their heads, persuading them that it is a specific for the creation of brilliant novelists, that the faith of the untravelled begins to waver and complete disillusion threatens.

The novels written by Mr. Joseph Conrad illustrate this effect of foreign travel which one cannot help regarding as rather curious than beneficial. There is no reason to suppose that he is by nature irrational or vain, or that he would have mistaken his vocation had he clung to centres of civilization. But the accident of residence in Borneo, Celebes, and circumambient isles has tempted him to write novels, and has therefore made him appear a person of little discernment and poor judgment. The climate and the vegetation of the East Indies instigated a book; and the society, black and white, of a sort which no reputable person would meet at home, commanded a novel. In the first novel, entitled *Almayer's Folly*, the most prominent member of that society is an immoral and bad-tempered trader, named Almayer. He appears in the second, entitled *An Outcast of the Islands*, almost virtuous and pleasing in comparison with Willems, a Dutchman, who adds hypocrisy and ingratitude to a variety of cruder vices. Rightly to understand the intrigues carried on by Arab adventurers and negro potentates, one would need the unlimited leisure of Borneo and a positive aversion for edification. The moral of the books seems to be that white Christians can be much worse than black pagans, and generally are, along the Straits of Macassar.

The point to be made is, not that a competent novelist would be beaten in a struggle with the Spice Islands, but that just having been there is not enough to make a good or even passable novelist.

28. Arnold Bennett on Conrad and Kipling

8 December 1897

Extract from a dated letter to H. G. Wells (*LAB*, ii, 94). Conrad had already been compared, both favourably (No. 24) and unfavourably (No. 20), with Kipling. Such comparisons had a long history.

I owe you a good turn for pointing out Conrad to me. I remember I got his first book, *Almayer's Folly*, to review with a batch of others from Unwin, & feeling at the time rather bored (*you* know the feeling —I get through 50 or 60 novels a month for two papers) I simply didn't read it at all—wrote a vague & discreet par. & left it.

I have just read his new book *The Nigger of the 'Narcissus'*, which has moved me to enthusiasm. Where did the man pick up that style, & that *synthetic* way of gathering up a general impression & flinging it at you? Not only his style, but his attitude, affected me deeply. He is so consciously an artist. Now Kipling isn't an artist a bit. Kipling doesn't know what art is—I mean the art of words; *il ne se préoccupe que de la chose racontée*. He is a great writer but not an artist.

29. Unsigned notice, *Daily Mail*

7 December 1897, 3

In a letter dated 6(?)December 1897 to R. B. Cunninghame Graham, Conrad quickly responded to the *Daily Mail* critic: 'There are twenty years of life, six months of scribbling in that book—and not a shadow of a story. As the critic in to-day's Dly Mail puts it tersely: "the tale is no tale at all". The man complains of lack of heroism! and is, I fancy, shocked at the bad language. I confess reluctantly there is a swear here and there. I grovel in the waste-paper basket, I beat my breast' (*LCG*, p. 49).

The conspicuous ability which Mr. Joseph Conrad displayed in his East Indian novel, *Almayer's Folly* and in his novel of the Malay Archipelago, *An Outcast of the Islands*, led one to open with confident hope his new tale of the sea *The Nigger of the 'Narcissus'*. Possibly our expectation was too high; anyhow we must admit that in many respects this present work is a disappointment. Mr. Conrad, indeed, is in this instance in the position of the needy knifegrinder—'Story! Lord bless you, sir, I've none to tell.' The tale is no tale, but merely an account of the uneventful voyage of the *Narcissus* from Bombay to the Thames. One of the ship's crew is an intelligent negro named James Wait. He lies in his bunk most of the voyage, and at last he dies and is buried at sea. This is positively all the story in the book. There is no plot, no villainy, no heroism, and, apart from a storm and the death and burial, no incident. The only female in the book is the ship herself, which Mr. Conrad describes lovingly and with an intimate knowledge of seamanship unrivalled even by Dana[1] or Clark Russell.[2]

The one surpassingly good quality of this masculine narrative is the distinctness of Mr. Conrad's characterisation of old Singleton . . . and

[1] Richard Henry Dana (1815–82), author and lawyer. He shipped as a common sailor and described the voyage in *Two Years before the Mast* (1840).

[2] In 1874 William Clark Russell (1844–1911) began publishing a long succession of sea stories. The *Glasgow Herald* (see No. 31) and the *Standard* (24 December 1897, 6) compare Conrad with Clark Russell to Conrad's advantage.

the rest of them. Their talk and their swearing, especially the latter, is absolutely natural. One only regrets that they never do anything else than their mere commonplace duties, and that they are not connected with a story.

30. W. L. Courtney, review, *Daily Telegraph*

8 December 1897, 4

W. L. Courtney (1850–1928) was for many years a reviewer for the *Daily Telegraph*. Garnett described him as 'that donnish British critic who ruled the literary roost in the *Daily Telegraph* for many years'.

Stephen Crane (1870–1900), American war correspondent and famous for his novel, *The Red Badge of Courage* (1895). Courtney's speculation on the influence of this on Conrad is shrewd, for Conrad himself wrote, many years later: 'Crane dealt in his book (*The Red Badge of Courage*) with the psychology of the mass—the army; while I—in mine (*The Nigger of the "Narcissus"*) had been dealing with the same subject on a much smaller scale and in more specialized conditions—the crew of a merchant ship' (introduction to Thomas Beer's *Life of Stephen Crane*, p. 3). Pierre Loti (see note on No. 22): some years later, Henry James compared *The Nigger of the 'Narcissus'* with Loti, probably recalling Courtney's original reference (letter to Gosse, 26 June 1902). Courtney's criticism of the title as 'the ugliest conceivable' clearly concerned Conrad's publisher. Jean-Aubry recalls that Conrad suggested to his publisher 'thirteen different titles' for the novel (*L&L*, i, 322) and the novel was published as *The Children of the Sea* in America.

Mr. Joseph Conrad does not shrink from the conditions involved in his literary art. He is an unflinching realist and, therefore, has no hesitation in giving to his singularly vivid and powerful tale of the sea the ugliest conceivable title. No one would say that *The Nigger of the 'Narcissus'* was a pretty or attractive inscription to stand at the head of an exceedingly careful and minute study; but we know that aesthetic considerations are held to be of no value by those who are determined to paint with exact and merciless severity facts as they know them. I believe that some excellent persons have objected to Captain Marryat's[1]

[1] Captain Frederick Marryat (1792–1848), popular writer of sea stories, his best known being *Mr. Midshipman Easy* (1834) for which he received £1,200.

stories of the sea, because his heroes and his heroines use somewhat rough and explicit language, and swear a good deal. Captain Marryat's realism, however, is not a patch upon Mr. Joseph Conrad's for various reasons, and principally for this, that the latter-day 'naturalist', as we now understand him, had not in his time burst upon an astonished world. Captain Marryat was sometimes inclined to invest a spade with the literary distinction of being an agricultural implement. Mr. Joseph Conrad, inspired by different ideals, remorselessly refers to it as a shovel, with a singularly effective and sanguinary adjective attached. Hence it comes that the seamen of the *Narcissus*—very real, picturesque, and living personages—are heard talking as undoubtedly they ought to talk, and would have talked, without any squeamishness on the part of the author in deference to our sensitive and refined nerves.

There is no doubt an advantage in this form of literal veracity; there is also a disadvantage. A man who is going to delineate an incident, a scene, or the cruise of a merchantship as it actually occurs, will not care for his story so much as for his technique. He is keen to give us the right atmosphere; he will surround his characters with elaborate descriptions of sky and sea, storm and calm; he will spend pages and pages prodigal in careful touches, and deliberate word-painting, so that at the end we may be under the illusion that we have listened to a tale, instead of being invited to a man's studio to see how he works. Mr. Conrad works like an artist—of that we are quite certain when we have finished his book; but we are left with only the vaguest idea of what the story has been all about.

[gives an outline of the plot]

It is not a story at all, but an episode, which Mr. Conrad has chosen to extend to 250 pages, and to adorn with all the resources of his knowledge, of his artistic skill, and of his unflinching realism.

Everyone will remember what a singular effect Mr. Stephen Crane produced some little time ago by his *Red Badge of Courage*. Mr. Joseph Conrad has chosen Mr. Stephen Crane for his example, and has determined to do for the sea and the sailor what his predecessor had done for war and warriors. The style, though a good deal better than Mr. Crane's, has the same jerky and spasmodic quality; while a spirit of faithful and minute description—even to the verge of the wearisome—is common to both. If we open any page of *The Nigger of the 'Narcissus'* we are told with infinite detail what each one was doing, what the ship was doing, and what sky and sea were doing. If Mr.

Conrad has to present to us a scene of hesitation, the angry interval of doubt and self-criticism, which often precedes a mutiny, he does it in the following fashion:

[quotes ch. 4: 'What did they want . . . A murmur died out.']

This is undeniably effective as a picture of indecision and vagueness, but Mr. Conrad luxuriates in such effects. He builds up his scenes piece by piece, never by one large and comprehensive sentence, but through a mass of commas, semi-colons, and full-stops, especially when it is his business to depict character or narrate incidents. It is in these that the example of Mr. Crane is most obvious and potent upon him. But observe how different the style becomes as soon as the author turns from man to nature, and gives some scope to that pictorial instinct of the artist when he is dealing with a large canvas and big brushes. Here is a passage which Pierre Loti might have written—and not very frequently even such an artist as he:

[quotes ch. 4: 'It looked as if it would be a long passage . . . in a voice mournful, immense, and faint.']

There are many scenes of this kind which only a man could paint who knew the sea and was aware of all its changing aspects and beautiful metamorphoses. It is for these, and such as these, perhaps, that some readers will delight in *The Nigger of the 'Narcissus'*; and, indeed, even as a moving panorama of the phases of ocean the book is admirable. But it has a value apart from its picturesque setting. There are few characters among the crew of the *Narcissus* which do not stand out with vivid and lifelike presentment; we know them all as though we, too, had partaken in the lengthy cruise, and had laughed and grumbled at all their idiosyncrasies and failings. Old Singleton, the Nestor of this company, with his immense knowledge and his impressive taciturnity; blue-eyed Archie, with his red whiskers; Belfast, with his touching fidelity to the nigger; Mr. Baker, the chief mate, with his grunts and his sovereign common-sense; little Captain Allistoun, as hard as nails, and with a will tempered like the finest steel; Donkin, the wastrel and outcast of metropolitan life, shifty, indolent, and sly; and the nigger, James Wait himself, with his mysterious authority and his racking cough—one and all are our familiar friends before the voyage is over. They are not a pleasant lot altogether, yet they are very human—big children in their petulant moods, and heroes in times of crisis. It is Mr.

Conrad's merit that we part with them with regret, for, as he says himself, they were a good crowd—'as good a crowd as ever fisted with wild cries the beating canvas of a heavy foresail; or tossing aloft, invisible in the night, gave back yell for yell to a westerly gale.'

31. Unsigned review, *Glasgow Herald*

9 December 1897, 10

On 14 December 1897, Conrad wrote to R. B. Cunninghame Graham that 'it was a friendly thought to send me the *Glasgow Herald*'s cutting. It came in the nick of time and send [sic] me to bed at peace with my fellow men' (*LCG*, pp. 52–3).

A new novel by the author of *Almayer's Folly* and *An Outcast of the Islands* may well be welcomed by critics, for there is no novelist of the day who is more original in his methods than Mr Conrad. He has chosen this time to turn from the steamy heat of the Far East to describe simply a voyage from Bombay to England. But how well he does it! Accustomed as we are to the admirable word pictures of Mr Clark Russell,[1] new marine story-tellers subject themselves to no mean comparisons, but Mr Conrad's book bears the test triumphantly. Nor does he seek any adventitious aid by the introduction in mid-ocean of beautiful but athletic young ladies who have been yachting with their papa, and have suffered some extraordinary ill-fortune at the whim of Father Neptune. There is not a petticoat in all Mr Conrad's pages. Nor is a burning ship descried on the horizon, nor do the crew land on an uninhabited island. Mr Conrad is all for plain, unvarnished realism, but realism which only the hand of a master could make attractive. He looks at the crew of the *Narcissus* as if he had lived with them (which we cannot but believe he actually did), and he makes us

[1] See note to No. 29.

know them, and if not exactly love them, at least respect them as only a shipmate could. The unfortunate Nigger is to the *Narcissus* even as was the man who shot the albatross to the companions of the Ancient Mariner. He is a hindrance, a curse, a reproach. Yet he fascinates them, and an almost insane devotion to him, a hypnotic unaccountable pathos overcomes them when they try to deal with his harassing ways. On the voyage a storm is encountered. It takes very many pages to describe, but the reader follows the description breathlessly, and feels as if a storm had never been described before. We have nothing but the highest praise for this distinguished contribution to modern literature, except on one point; Mr Conrad, like Mr Blackmore,[1] betrays an occasional fondness for the use of most unusual words. Is this a result of the wide circulation of Dr Murray's Oxford Dictionary? One example will suffice from p. 99—'French nails polished and slim. They lay in a solid mass more *inabordable* than a hedgehog.'

32. Unsigned review, *Daily Chronicle*

22 December 1897, 3

On 23 December 1897, Conrad wrote to Edward Garnett: 'The *Daily Chronicle* gives special article with a leaded heading—but you must have seen it as that is your household idol—isn't it?' (*LEG*, p. 123). The review was headed 'The Old Sea Salt'.

There may be better tales of the sea than this, but we have never read anything in the least like it. There is no pirate in it, no wreck, no desert island, no treasure trove. The story is simply an account of an ordinary voyage made by an ordinary sailing ship from Bombay round the Cape to the Thames. Nothing particular happens. There is a big storm, some dissatisfaction among the crew, which never ripens into

[1] Richard Doddridge Blackmore (1825–1900), author of *Lorna Doone* (1869).

anything like mutiny, and the least admirable of the men dies and is shot into the water. That is all. Yet there is in that story which sounds so simple a freshness, reality, and peculiar interest which raise the book far above the ordinary level of tales of the sea, and appear to us to leave it in a distinct place by itself. For it is written by a man who knows every phase of the sea, and has sailed as a seaman with varied crews. And (what we may be allowed to think at least as rare a qualification in an author) it is written by a man who can write.

It is true that his power of phrase and a most laudable desire to be brief and full-packed in style sometimes drive the author into the faults of strength. Sometimes too, we recognise the Meredithian[1] oddities which seem so infectious, but are none the less irritating in the master, and unendurable in every imitator. To say of a man that he 'rolled bloodshot eyes' or stood 'hanging a peaked nose' is natural and inevitable in Meredith, yet even from him we take it with regret. But from others we simply reject it. Again, we can forgive a seaman when he writes, 'he would lay blinded and invisible in the midst of an intense darkness.' It is not English, but it is seaman's language. But it is neither one nor the other to write of 'a slimy soft heap of something that smelt like does at dead low water a muddy foreshore.' And we hope that in his next book Mr. Conrad will forget to tell us quite so often that his men were 'breathing hard.' These are but small points, and in speaking of an ordinary book we should not think of taking the trouble to mention them. But Mr. Conrad has so fine and distinctive a style of his own that it is worth while for him to be on his guard about things apparently so insignificant. For, indeed, he has irony, humor, a sense of words, a power of choice, and also a steady sympathy with old mankind—all of them qualities that go to make up a rare and powerful writer.

[gives outline of plot]

That is all the plot, and it does not matter about betraying it; for the value of the book lies in the telling, and not in the events of the tale. It is the character of the men, the strangeness of the sea, the irony and pathos of it all that hold our attention fast. In a book almost overloaded with knowledge and telling phrase, the choice of quotation is difficult. But we may take these extracts from a passage on the old salt

[1] George Meredith (1828-1909), English novelist who achieved popularity with *Diana of the Crossways* (1885).

seamen, older even than those who are continually threatening 'to chuck going to sea for ever and go in a steamer':—

[quotes ch. 1: 'Singleton stood at the door . . . or loved the men.']

Or let us take this from the description of the captain, a silent king of men:—

[quotes ch. 2: 'He had commanded . . . out of sight of the sea.']

Or here, again, is a passage which goes to the heart of the tragedy which underlies all the stern humor of the book. James Wait, or Jimmy, is the malingering nigger himself:—

[quotes ch. 2: 'One day at dinner . . . wiping perspiration off his chin.']

The main event, if it may be called so, is that tremendous storm off the Cape. The description of it is long, but we doubt whether the state of a sailing ship during a storm at sea has ever been described with greater truth and power. We may take one short extract near the crisis. The ship had nearly capsized, and the men had rushed to cut down the masts, but had been stopped by the captain's word:—

All became still. They waited for the ship to turn over altogether, and shake them out into the sea; and upon the terrific noise of wind and sea not a murmur of remonstrance came out from those men, who each would have given ever so many years of life to see 'them damned sticks go overboard!' They all believed it their only chance; but a little hard-faced man shook his grey head and shouted, 'No!' without giving them as much as a glance. They were silent and gasped. They gripped rails, they had wound ropes'-ends under their arms; they clutched ring-bolts, they crawled in heaps where there was foothold; they held on with both arms, hooked themselves to anything to windward with elbows, with chins, almost with their teeth; and some, unable to crawl away from where they had been flung, felt the sea leap up, striking against their backs as they struggled upwards. Singleton had stuck to the wheel. His hair flew out in the wind; the gale seemed to take its life-long adversary by the beard, and shake his old head. He wouldn't let go, and, with his knees forced between the spokes, flew up and down like a man on a bough.

The burial of Jimmy, the return to England, the passage up the Thames, and entrance into the docks—all are admirable. And in the mothers and one or two other women waiting on the quay we get the one touch of womanhood in the tale; for otherwise the book is entirely free of that eternal feminine.

33. Unsigned review, *Spectator*

25 December 1897, 940

This review must have been a pleasant Christmas bonus for Conrad
—for the second time the *Spectator* refers to him as a genius (see
No. 25).

Mr. Joseph Conrad, whose intimate knowledge of the Malay Archipelago was impressively illustrated in those two powerful but sombre
novels, *Almayer's Folly* and *An Outcast of the Islands*, has given us in
The Nigger of the 'Narcissus' an extraordinarily vivid picture of life on
board of a sailing-vessel in the merchant marine. The incidents described all take place during a single cruise from Bombay to London;
there is no heroine in the plot—for the excellent reason that there is no
woman in the ship's company—no love interest, and practically no
hero. The central figure is a negro, who ships as a new hand at Bombay,
is soon invalided, but rather than admit the truth—for he is dying of
consumption—accuses himself of malingering, and when the captain
refuses to let him work, appeals so successfully to the feelings of his
shipmates as nearly to stir up a mutiny. Eventually he dies in sight of
land, having been robbed while in his death-agony by a villainous
guttersnipe named Donkin; and at the very moment his body plunges
into the sea the long spell of calm ends and a favouring breeze springs
up. 'Jimmy Wait,' alternately the mascot and the Jonah of the *Narcissus*,
is a type of West Indian negro—he comes from St. Kitt's—that we
confess ourselves wholly unacquainted with, in or out of books, but
Mr. Conrad's portraiture in every other instance is so convincing that
we are content to admit its accuracy here also. As a picture of rough
seafaring life, frank yet never offensively realistic, and illustrating with
singular force the collective instincts of a ship's crew, as well as the
strange and unlikely alliances that spring up on shipboard, this book is
of extraordinary merit. What is more, Mr. Conrad has an abiding sense
of the mystery of the immortal sea, and the happy gift of painting her
changing moods in words that glow with true poetic fire. Lest this

should seem exaggerated praise, let us quote the passage describing the view from the *Narcissus* as she entered the Channel:—

[quotes ch. 5: 'Below its steady glow . . . in the open sea.']

Mr. Conrad is a writer of genius; but his choice of themes, and the uncompromising nature of his methods, debar him from attaining a wide popularity. Illumined though it is by such shining moments as the passage just quoted, we own to having found *The Nigger of the 'Narcissus'* at times almost unbearably depressing.

34. I. Zangwill, Unsigned review, *Academy*

1 January 1898, 1-2

In a letter of 7 January 1898 to Garnett, Conrad wrote: 'I had 23 reviews. One indifferent (*The Standard*) and *one bad* (*The Academy*) . . . The rest unexpectedly appreciative' (*LEG*, pp. 125–6). This review was headed 'A Reviewer's Puzzle' and is a serious attempt at criticism.[1] Twelve days later, the *Glasgow Evening News* (13 January 1898) referred to the *Academy* review as 'depreciatory fudge, written obviously by some one incapable of recognising a good thing when he sees it'. It is possible that this review led Conrad to introduce in *Lord Jim* and 'Heart of Darkness' Captain Marlow as a narrator whose language is appropriate to his position as a sailor: '. . . abundant passages show that he [the narrator] was one of the common sailors. But the tense, exaggerated, highly poetic diction is not suitable to such a character.'

It is in dealing with such a book as this that a reviewer is apt to come to grief. At the risk of stepping outside the usual convention the present critic will endeavour as candidly as possible to explain why. He fully recognises that the author has vividly imagined his scenes, that he has originality and energy, and that he can write well. The human nature is presented with insight and sympathy, and the sea-pictures are beyond praise. Take the following as an example:

The passage had begun; and the ship, a fragment detached from the earth, went on, lonely and swift like a small planet. Round her the abysses of sea and sky met in an unattainable frontier. A great circular solitude moved with her, ever changing and ever the same, always monotonous and always imposing. Now and then another wandering white speck, burdened with life, appeared far off and disappeared; intent on its own destiny. The sun looked upon her all day, and every morning rose with a burning round stare of undying curiosity.

In vision this is poetry. The writer's observation is presented in the same strong, clean-cut way. Here is his description of a storm abating:

[1] A Conrad letter (22 Feb. 1898), a copy of which was sent to me by Dr Mario Curreli, suggests that this review was by I. Zangwill.

94

The sky was clearing and bright sunshine gleamed over the ship. After every burst of battering seas vivid and fleeting rainbows arched over the drifting hull in the flick of sprays. The gale was ending in a clear blow which gleamed and cut like a knife.

We select these passages not as representing the author at his best, but because in each a complete thought is briefly expressed, and they are typical of his style. There is so much good writing that one is reluctant to be absolutely frank and say that the book as a whole is not liked. Yet that is the truth, though possibly we may be misjudging genius, possibly the very cleverness and novelty may stand in the way, and the author may improve on a longer acquaintance. We shall, as far as we can, analyse the reasons for this bad impression, and leave the reader to judge how far they are reasonable and to what extent they might be removed.

In the first place, then, it seems to us that there is a small allowance of material for the length of the book. The story is simply that of a voyage from Bombay to London in a sailing-ship, and the incident consists only of a storm and the death of a nigger. The tale has no plot and no petticoats; its interest is thrown on the play of character in a crew of sailors, and the descriptions by the way. Up to a certain point it is refreshing to dispense with the love of women and the love of money, those hackneyed themes of the common novelist. But the writer who sets them aside assumes the responsibility of finding adequate substitutes, and this Mr. Conrad has not succeeded in doing. His material is barely enough for half the number of pages, and he has not invented any *motif* that will lead the reader on from page to page.

Again, he has not realised the seeming paradox that a long story differs from a short one in more than the number of words used. What we mean by a short story is a single incident or a series of incidents illustrating one phase of character. Nearly all recent romances, whatever their bulk, are but short stories 'writ large'. A long story must be organic, it demands atmosphere, it exhibits character under many lights. Now of these essentials, Mr. Conrad only gives us one—atmosphere. From embarkation to landing he keeps us consistently at sea and compels us to look at life as it appears to the ordinary mariner. In that the book is a pronounced and brilliant success. But he has not built up his little world well. He has given far too much detail for a short story, too little for a long one; the book should have been half or twice its present length.

The very style shows that he has not apprehended this necessity of artistic treatment. The tale is told in the first person, and though the narrator does not appear by name, abundant passages show that he was one of the common sailors. But the tense, exaggerated, highly poetic diction is not suitable to such a character. Jack Tar does not speak of 'incomparable repose', he is by no means so fond of the word 'incomparable' as our author is. He commands no such stilted language as this:

The men turned in wet and turned out stiff to face the redeeming and ruthless exactions of their glorious and obscure fate.

Nor of his ship would he say that:

She was born in the thundering peal of hammers beating upon iron, in black eddies of smoke, under a grey sky on the banks of the Clyde.

No language can be really fine unless it is appropriate; and there is scarcely a sentence in the narrative that could have proceeded naturally from the mouth of a sailor. Besides, if Mr. Conrad had not made a tar his spokesman, it still would have been a mistake to be always pressing the emphasis. His only weapons are Gatling guns, and he brings them to bear on the trivial and insignificant in the same way as on what is important. In consequence the gradations of light and shade are lost, the many excellent passages are not shown up by artistic contrast. Style which should allure the reader here repels him. Our first impulse on glancing at the book was to select a few passages to show that what Martin Scriblerus[1] called the 'art of sinking in poetry' was not lost. And these expressions would have been classified in Division 5 of the famous satire: 'Lastly I shall place the Cumbrous, which moves heavily under a Load of Metaphors and draws after it a long Train of Words. And the Buskin or stately frequently, and with great felicity, mixed with the former. For as the first is the proper Engine to depress what is High, so is the second to raise what is Base and Low to a ridiculous visibility.'

We have written all this with a considerable amount of dissatisfaction. Work so able and conscientious, scenes so vividly imagined and clearly described, rarely come in the reviewer's way; it is a cause of unfeigned regret that the presentation lacks tact and discrimination, so that merits which should have been open and attractive are to be discovered only by conquering a sense of repulsion. We are grateful for the author's cleverness, yet venture to remind him that the first duty of a writer is to interest.

[1] *Martinus Scriblerus peri Bathous*; or *the Art of Sinking in Poetry*, by Alexander Pope, appeared in *Miscellanies*, the last volume (1728).

35. Arthur Symons on Kipling and Conrad, *Saturday Review*

29 January 1898, 145–6

This reference to Kipling and Conrad appeared in Symons's review of a translation of Gabriele d'Annunzio's *Trionfo della Morte*. It disturbed Conrad. He wrote to R. B. Cunninghame Graham on 31 January: 'Symons reviewing *Trionfo della Morte* (trans:) in the last *Sat. Rev.* went out of his way to damn Kipling and me with the same generous praise. He says that *Captains Courageous* and the *Nigger* have no idea behind them. I don't know. Do you think the remark is just? Now straight!' (*LCG*, p. 71); and two days later he wrote to Garnett: 'Symons criticising trans: of Annunzio mentions Kipling and myself as you can see. Frankly—is the remark true?' (*LEG*, 131).

... Had it been translated quite adequately and in full, it could scarcely have failed to be, in various ways, a revelation. D'Annunzio is a man of wide culture, and this book is not without traces of English as well as of German influence; the influence of Shelley and of Pater, as well as the influence of Nietzsche and of Wagner. But it is the sort of book in which the English literature of the present day is very lacking, and which it is very good for Englishmen to be put in the way of reading. We have a surprising number of popular story-writers, some of them very entertaining, some of them with great ability of the narrative kind. Look only at the last year, and take only two books: Mr. Kipling's *Captains Courageous* and Mr. Conrad's *Nigger of the 'Narcissus'*. In one of these what an admirable mastery of a single bit of objective reality of the adventure of a trade, of what is external in the figures who are active about it! In the other there is an almost endless description of the whole movement, noise, order, and distraction of a ship and a ship's company during a storm, which brings to one's memory a sense of every discomfort one has ever endured upon the sea. But what more is there? Where is the idea of which such things as these should be but servants? Ah, there has been an oversight; everything else is there, but that, these brilliant writers have forgotten to put in. Now d'Annunzio, whether you like his idea or not, never forgets to put it in. . . .

36. Harold Frederic, unsigned review, *Saturday Review*

12 February 1898, 211

Harold Frederic (1856–98), American novelist and journalist and good friend of Stephen Crane, himself a friend of Conrad. His best novel is *The Damnation of Theron Ware* (1896). In a postscriptum to his letter to R. B. Cunninghame Graham, 5 March 1898, Conrad wrote: 'It was Harold Frederic who wrote the criticism of the *Nigger* in the Satur: R.' (*LCG*, p. 79). Frederic's criticism that Conrad had not realized the importance of 'human interest' was answered by the *Academy* in an unsigned review of *Tales of Unrest*, 16 April 1898: 'Like the great landscape artists, he brings equal facility to a sunset or to a man working in a field, and the man is real, part of the harmony, not a lay figure dumped down as a sop to those who clamour for "human interest".'

Mr. Joseph Conrad is visibly improving. His second book, *An Outcast of the Islands*, was much better than *Almayer's Folly*, the work which introduced him to the public. What in point of publication, at least, may be called his third production—'An Outpost of Progress,' recently published in *Cosmopolis*—was distinctly superior to that earlier couple, both in style and in grasp of the principles of construction. It may be as well to speak briefly of the qualities these three works have in common, before passing to a consideration of *The Nigger of the 'Narcissus'*.

In this trio of tales there is a single theme—the degeneracy of the white man under the influences of the South Sea islands. The term is geographically inexact, no doubt, for Mr. Conrad's chosen scene is in the Malayan Archipelago, where Dutch gunboats and a Mohammedan hierarchy affect at least the surface conditions of native life. In essentials, however, one does not detect many variations from the type studied by Robert Louis Stevenson in Samoa. There is always the Caucasian enslaved by the forces that he came to conquer, the non-militant, alluring, poisonous forces which insidiously sap the courage and conscience and manhood of the superior alien. Whether the natives are Malays or Papuans seems not to matter. The white man, confronted in his idleness by the great solitudes, tempted by the seductions of drink and gluttony, cannot maintain a sufficient hold upon himself to preserve his individuality. His environment softens and disintegrates him. Through delirium tremens, or simple madness or some other of the abhorrent rear gates which it is civilisation's task to keep closed, he degenerates. He is scarcely a profitable subject for study in himself—is indeed the emptiest and least significant of humanity's failures. But his background can be made so strikingly picturesque, and the sensuous aspects of his undoing can be painted with such safe breadth of handling that the popular vogue he has enjoyed in the fiction of the past half-dozen years is quite easily to be understood. It is enough to say that Mr. Conrad's books of this sort, along with their defects, have merits which put them, and especially the latest of them, among the best of their kind.

In *The Nigger of the 'Narcissus'*, however, the author turns his back abruptly upon what one had begun to fear was his 'speciality.' Nothing in his earlier works, moreover, had hinted at the possibility of this *volte face*. In them the sea was felt rather than discussed. There was always the suggestion of the illimitable ocean wastes, but at most the reader saw them through the eyes of the lonely trader, strained to catch the longed-for smudge of steamer-smoke on the pitiless horizon. Nowhere can we recall a passage in which the sea becomes less impersonal than is the desert of the *Talisman*.

But now Mr. Conrad, wisely leaving the degenerate sots of the islands to their unlamented fate, takes ship, and gives us the sea as no other story-teller of our generation has been able to render it. This is high praise, but it is precisely the praise which the description of the 'Narcissus' in the storm compels. We know nothing else so vivid and so convincing in contemporary fiction as the way in which the reader is forced, along with the crew, to hang on for dear life to the perilously slanting deck. The rest of the book, however, makes no such potential demand upon our enthusiasm. Its best features continue to be those which have to do with the ships and the deep. A vast deal of excellent observation and much hard work have obviously been lavished upon the crew, but considering the space they occupy, the interest they arouse is surprisingly slight. The cook is rather well done, and the second officer, Creighton, though seen only in glimpses, produces a distinct impression of reality. Other figures, like Old Singleton and the Captain, though delineated with almost an excess of detail, somehow do not come out of the canvas. The cockney loafer and ruffian, Donkin, although given by far the largest 'speaking part' of the lot, remains shadowy. We are far from assuming plagiarism, unconscious or otherwise, and if *The Ebb Tide* had never been written, it is conceivable that Donkin might have established himself as the type instead. As it is, he only reminds one of somebody else. It cannot be said that the 'Nigger' himself attains even that limited success. He wearies the reader from the outset, as one feels he bored and fatigued the writer.

In a word, Mr. Conrad has not realised, as yet, the importance of what is called the 'human interest.' There is, however, such substantial promise in Mr. Conrad's steady progress up to the present, and there is so much really fine work in this latest book, that we look with some confidence to see him strengthen himself in this weak point.

TALES OF UNREST

4 April 1898

37. Unsigned review, *Daily Telegraph*

9 April 1898, 8

Literature, 30 April 1898, criticized Conrad on other grounds than that of gloom: 'We could pardon his cheerless themes were it not for the imperturbable solemnity with which he piles the unnecessary on the commonplace.'

Mr. Joseph Conrad has chosen an appropriate title for the five stories which form his new volume. Tales of unrest—the unrest that is born, not of adventurous spirit, but of a constant struggle against a gloomy and burdensome fate—they undoubtedly are, and they leave the reader oppressed by the spirit that animates them. Incomparably the finest is the opening one, entitled 'Karain, a Memory,' a story of a magnificent savage, a Malay chieftain, who is haunted by the ghost of his friend whom he had shot down deliberately when he was about to take the life of his sister and the Dutchman with whom she had fled from her own people. Karain was in love with the girl, and, in the company of her brother, had tracked down the fugitives after a long and weary search, while the brother thought that his friend was animated by the same longing for revenge as himself. Mr. Conrad is known as a writer of Malay sketches, and he brings vividly before us the wild picturesque life of the curious, untamable race that inhabits the Archipelago. His figures are real flesh and blood, drawn to the life, and the scene in the cabin of the little schooner, which has been trafficking with the Malays in powder and guns, when Karain tells the story of his life, with his gleaming kriss on the table in front of him, and madness in his eyes and voice, is perfectly described. How he was pacified and sent away happy with a Jubilee sixpence, sewn up in a girl's white kid glove and suspended from his neck with a blue ribbon, as a charm to rid him of the haunting face of the dead man, Mr. Conrad relates with exquisite humour and striking skill. The concluding story also deals with Malay life, and is excellent, but in the other three he breaks new ground. For sheer morbid horror the story entitled 'The Idiots' would be bad to beat in the whole range of fiction. It may be founded on fact, but such subjects hardly lie within the proper province of the novelist, and not even the power with which the story is told reconciles us to the morbid, loathsome picture that it presents. Gloomy again, and morbid to a fantastic degree, is the tale, called 'An Outpost of Progress,' of the two incompetent Belgian officials left in charge of an up-river station in Africa, presumably on the Congo. They are left there for six months, and they loaf the time away doing nothing, the end of it being that their provisions run short, they quarrel, and one shoots the other in a panic of terror and then hangs himself, and is found thus by the managing director, who comes upon the scene as the tragedy is ended. This is how the tale concludes: 'His toes were only a couple of inches above the ground, his arms hung stiffly down; he seemed to be standing rigidly at attention, but with one purple cheek playfully posed on the shoulder; and irreverently he was putting out a swollen tongue at his managing director.' This is vivid, but assuredly it is ghastly. Mr. Conrad, we may hope, will in his next volume choose more pleasant themes.

38. Unsigned review, *Daily Mail*

12 April 1898, 3

This review is somewhat unusual in accusing Conrad of 'lack of literary training', but it was not alone in commenting upon his incorrect grammar—numerous reviewers made the same criticism: '. . . why will he make us shiver in the middle of a fine piece of writing by using "like" for "as"?' (*Black and White*, 23 April 1898); 'his grammar, by the way, is apt to stumble; he has an unaccountable habit of using the adverb "like" as if it were a conjunction' (*Manchester Guardian*, 26 April 1898).

Like all Mr. Joseph Conrad's previous work the stories grouped in *Tales of Unrest* show great breadth of view, much power, and a conspicuous lack of literary training. It is sufficient testimony to Mr. Conrad's power that we accept and enjoy him as we do, considering the continual weakness of his grammar and the frequent slipshodness of his general method. In this book, for instance, a story of quite ordinary London people, moving in quite ordinary London life 'The Return' grips and holds us by sheer force of the author's psychological insight and his unusual ability to see common things in an uncommon way. It is because of this ability that we reconcile ourselves to tolerate laxities of style which would be unpardonable were they less richly redeemed. We are bound to say that we like Mr. Conrad in London [the setting for 'The Return'] as well as on the *Narcissus*, and better than in the somewhat monotonous—fictionally—Malayan archipelago.

39. Edward Garnett, unsigned article, *Academy*

15 October 1898, 82–3

This was the first general article on Conrad to appear. Conrad wrote teasingly to Garnett: 'I am very anxious to see the horrors of the *Academy*. You are a dear old generalizer. I fancy you've generalized me into a region of such glory that no mortal henceforth will succeed in finding me in my work' (*LEG*, p. 145). Three months later, Conrad's *Tales of Unrest* shared the *Academy* award with two other writers (see Introduction, p. 14). The aim of this award was 'to encourage, to seek for promise, sincerity, and thoroughness in literary art rather than to acknowledge fulfilment' (*Academy*, 14 January 1899).

The sun rises and sets through all the wonderful ages on a prosaic and a commonplace spectacle: the every-day world. To men busied in their little crowd's concerns, struggling to best others, the daily life is seen in the morning light as a succession of hard facts to be squared, suffered, or ameliorated, a life of well-known surfaces and confused depths, with odd varieties of sensation stringing it, and the necessity for action always hurrying the crowd past self-realisation and deep perception. And in the midst of this light-of-day, solid world of matter-of-fact appearances and startling confusions occasionally comes a glimpse of a mysterious world behind the apparent, a shattering of the human surfaces that death or love perchance brings us; but the revelation passes, and the tide of events, people, circumstances, rolls on again mechanically, and as shockingly natural as faces crowd upon us in the streets of our inevitable and ridiculous civilisation.

And so with life everywhere. A generation passes away, to the last man; and to the immense new concourse of people that throngs the old streets, the old fields, the daily trivial round appears to have always been cast for them, to be always going to be theirs. But each generation, because it lives on surfaces and is so dull in its imagination, so harassed by work, so desperate or so contented in its environment, has always a baffled feeling that if it could but get a connected view of itself life would be illumined. And always the generation looks round for the men who are articulate, and passing by the orators, preachers, politicians, recognises that in so far as the past generations have been illumined it is through the work of the artists.

Whenever the artists are absent—in enormous tracts of life, that is—human nature appears to the imagination absolutely uncanny and ghost-like. But wherever the artist has been there the life of man appears suddenly natural and comprehensible. When we think of Romanised Britain our imagination becomes as a blank wall with a few historical facts staring at us from it. But in Rome under the Cæsars human life is as fresh and actual to us as in London to-day; we see and hear the people going down the street, the world of Horace, Juvenal, Catullus. The appearance of the artist makes an astonishing difference. Was it not yesterday that one of them appeared, and Anglo-Indian life started up coherent out of the huge mass of historical facts, statistics, and home letters that had stood for India in the British imagination? Individual life in general is an *ego* asserting itself in a chaos of experiences, and the man of the world who (touching spectacle!) fails to grasp the nature of his wife and misunderstands his own children, is seen holding fast by his Thackeray and his Dickens, creators who have resolved his world and made it less uncanny to him. To mention these two names is forthwith to see two lamps shining in the strange darkness of the unexplored oceans of humanity. The darkness of human nature is really everywhere, the commonplace darkness, and the lights are very few; and so the least unintelligent of us cluster round the artists' lamps.

In the unillumined tracts of swarming life the artist suddenly appears, unexpected, and never to be foreseen. They come, the artists, and they are always welcome (the impostors are always welcomed by humanity, but they can never stay); they come to us, and each brings along with him new worlds, spiritual, powerful, or complex, brutal or subtle, the worlds that have come to them through contact with the old prosaic spectacle of the everyday world. They come, and at the first word from them we know that that strange new world lives and dies with that individual artist. And always we realise how unillumined that particular tract of life, stretching before us, was before we heard coming from it the artist's voice.

So with the work of all true artists, and so with the work of Joseph Conrad. The unexpected has happened, and the artist has appeared where he was least looked for. From the far away, material, jumbled world of seamen, from the strange places of the earth where the emphatic, hardfisted, cautious men of action 'civilise' and subjugate alien races, from the forecastle and the Eastern ports and the high seas, suddenly springs this artist's living world of men and shadows, of passions, shapes, and colours, swiftly arranging itself in meaningful outline. The artist has spoken: a new world finds a voice; and we understand. The blank solid wall of the familiar, the strange world of new and old that fronts the puzzled sensations of those people far away, has melted away before this artist, and he has seen in everything *the significant fact*, he has seen and shown us the *way* that that man spoke or this wave curled before breaking. It is always what the artist *sees* that defines his quality; and whether he can connect this tangible world with the vast unseen ocean of life around him, that determines whether he is a poet. Mr. Conrad has seen the life that has been given to few poets to behold, and to no other artist to recreate. Of necessity, the civilisations that rear and nurture the artist keep him bound close to them, and rarely send him into the great world waiting outside; but Mr. Conrad's fortune it has been early to leave his country and his civilisation, and to sail in English ships to the ends of the earth. There are illimitable worlds, all the inarticulate oceans of life, waiting for the poet, but the poet rarely comes. Mr. Conrad has lived intimately, familiarly the sailor's life he describes, and he brings us from its monotony, its routine, its hardships, and its vast strangeness, a world of beauty intensely real, intensely delicate. He has seen.

What is the quality of his art? The quality of Mr. Conrad's art is seen in his faculty of making us perceive men's lives in their natural relation to the seen universe around them; his men are a part of the great world of Nature, and the sea, land and sky around them are not drawn as a mere background, or as something inferior and secondary to the human will, as we have in most artists' work. This faculty of seeing man's life in relation to the seen and unseen forces of Nature it is that gives Mr. Conrad's art its extreme delicacy and its great breadth of vision. It is pre-eminently the poet's gift, and is very rarely conjoined with insight into human nature and a power of conceiving character. When the two gifts come together we have the poetic realism of the great Russian novels. Mr. Conrad's art is truly realism of that high order. *The Nigger of the 'Narcissus'* is a masterpiece—not merely because the whole illusion of the sailor's life is reproduced before our eyes, with the crew's individual and collective attitude towards one another and their officers, with the daily round of hardship, peril, love for their ship; but because the ship is seen as a separate thing of life, with a past and a destiny, floating in the midst of the immense mysterious universe around it; and the whole shifting atmosphere of the sea, the horizon, the heavens, is felt by the senses as mysteriously near us, yet mysteriously aloof from the human life battling against it. To reproduce life naturally, in its close fidelity to breathing nature, yet to interpret its significance, and to make us see the great universe around —art cannot go beyond this, except to introduce the illusion of inevitability.

We find life's daily necessity in Mr. Conrad's art, we find actuality, charm, magic; and to demand inevitability from it is perhaps like asking for inevitability from Chopin's music. For Mr. Conrad's art, in its essence, reminds us much of his compatriot's—it is a very delicate, not a powerful instrument. There is a story, 'The Lagoon' in the *Tales of Unrest*, which flows out of itself in subtle cadence, in rise and flow and fall of emotion, just as you may hear Ernst's delicate music rise and sweep and flow from the violin. For occasionally the author's intense fidelity to the life he has observed seems to melt and fade away in a lyrical impulse, the hard things of actual life die and are lost in a song of beauty, just as the night comes to overwhelm the hard edges of the day.

So much goes to make up the world of the *Outcast of the Islands*, the *Tales of Unrest*, and *The Nigger of the 'Narcissus'*, that we have no time for dwelling on the author's gifts of irony, as shown in *An Outpost of Progress*; characterisation, as in 'Babalatchi' and 'Madame Levaille'; humour, as in the crew of the *Narcissus*; feminine insight, as in 'Aissa' and 'The Return'; and his particular gift of flashing a scene or episode upon us in a dozen lines. His power of making us *see* a constant succession of changing pictures is what dominates the reader and leaves him no possible way of escaping from the author's subtle and vivid world. He throws a mirage magically before you; he enmeshes your senses, you are in his universe, you accept it all.

Some talents in their character seem to come to us from the North, others are of the South; but Mr. Conrad's art seems to be on the line that divides East and West, to spring naturally from the country that mingles some Eastern blood in the Slav's veins—the Ukraine. His technique is modern in the sense that Flaubert and Turgenev are modern, but he develops at times a luxuriance, and to English people an extravagance, of phrase which leads us towards the East. He has seen! The artist *pur sang* always reveals himself by his incorrigible love of beauty, and this is the secret of humanity's love for the artist it secretly distrusts; he always shatters the hard prosaic surface of life, he always throws the light of beauty into the commonplace spectacle of the matter-of-fact world.

They are incorrigible, these artists; they juggle with reality till they make life yield up all its beauty to them; they are impostors, humanity angrily feels, for why should they have deep in them these organic worlds of beauty while the daily life stares stonily, prosaically, at you and me? Yes, they are impostors, these artists, even as old Nature, the only thing they love in their hearts, is the greatest artist and impostor of them all. For she, as they, deals in perpetual illusions, perpetual appearances, dreams and shifting phantasies, the hope and vision of beauty; she, as they, creates dissolving worlds, fading mirages out of the stuff men call reality, out of the earth which mothers everything —the good and the bad. Mr. Conrad is an artist of artists, his love is for Nature, his sure instinct is for beauty. He has brought the seen universe before us, he has interpreted it through the vast unseen ocean of life flowing around us. And that is the gift of only those who are born to sing to mankind—it is the gift of only the true poets.

40. Unsigned article, *Academy*

14 January 1899, 65–7

The title of the article was 'Our Awards for 1898—The "Crowned" Books', and the sub-title 'Mr. Joseph Conrad and "Tales of Unrest" '.

Mr. Conrad, in the five years or so that he has spent on land, setting down for our beguilement some of the stories that had come to him during his life at sea, has produced only four books; but they have been, in the fullest sense of the word, written. It might be said that the work of no novelist now working gives so much evidence of patient elaboration of style, without, however, leaving any sense of elaborateness. Mr. Conrad's art conceals art. With the nicest precision of epithet (a precision the more remarkable when we recollect that he lived so long at sea) Mr. Conrad tells his tales of strong men fighting the elements, of emotional crises, of settlers in foreign lands among alien people, by the conflict of the East and the West, of savagery and civilisation. This contrast between his own calm and the turbulence of his subject-matter lends his work a peculiarly impressive character. If his work reminds us of anyone it is Turgenev. His aloofness is Turgenev's. But his poetry, his outlook on life, his artistic conscience—these are his own.

Another of Mr. Conrad's distinguishing qualities is that he keeps man in his place. He has an eye ever vigilant both for the transitory persons of his drama and for the permanent forces at their back. He blends human beings and nature. The puppet never fills the universe, as with certain other novelists. Everything is related and harmonised. This comprehensiveness of vision, this amplitude of outlook, makes Mr. Conrad more than just a story teller. He seems to us to have some of the attributes of the Greek tragic dramatists. He has their irony. He sees so much at once, and is so conscious of the infinitesimal place a man can fill. Hence his work belongs never to cheerful literature; it is sombre, melancholy, searching. Yet Mr. Conrad is poet too. At the same time that he is aware of man's shortcomings he is profoundly in love with his capacities for grandeur, with his potential nobility. He recognises that an emotion may be as beautiful as a night of stars, a passion as tremendous as a typhoon.

It is Mr. Conrad's achievement to have brought the East to our very doors, not only its people—others have done that conspicuously well —but its feeling, its glamour, its beauty and wonder. He is one of the notable literary colonists. He has annexed the Malay Peninsula for us. With him it is not merely an array of names and ethnological facts, it is the real transference to paper of something of the very heart of the country, the nation, described. Here, from 'Karain,' in *Tales of Unrest*, is a passage from a picture of a Malayan paradise. The writer is observing the land from the sea—looking upon it for the first time:

[quotation begins 'A torrent wound about' and ends 'colours and stillness.']

This description opens a new world to the untravelled reader. It is the East. And Mr. Conrad's works have many such passages, quietly written, deliberate and reserved, yet full of atmosphere and the savour of the land. He makes us see it and, what is more, feel it; and, having done so, we are—thus familiarised with the conditions—in tune for the story, or the incident that is to follow.

During the year just closed Mr. Conrad has given us not only *Tales of Unrest*, the volume which we crown, but also a short story—*Youth: a Narrative*—which appeared in *Blackwood* in the summer. Both contributions strengthen our opinion that much is to be expected from him. *Youth* is merely the record of an ill-starred voyage, yet there is magic in it. In a way it is Mr. Conrad's most humanly touching work. We wish to associate *Youth* with *Tales of Unrest* in this award.

LORD JIM

9 October 1900

41. Unsigned review, *Manchester Guardian*

29 October 1900, 6

On 26 October 1900 D. S. Meldrum (literary adviser to Black-wood) wrote to Blackwood: '. . . I am glad to see excellent notices of *Lord Jim* in D. *Chronicle* and in *Manchester Guardian*: the latter especially is quite unusually enthusiastic. I have sent both notices to Conrad, who lives in need of these encouragements . . .' (*LWB*, 113). Five days later, on 3 November 1900, the *New York Daily Tribune* used similar terms to those used in this review to describe the novel: '. . . a book of great originality, and it exerts a spell such as is rarely encountered in modern fiction.'

Mr. Joseph Conrad's work has long been known to novel readers who search for their literature, and to them the publication of *Lord Jim* may rank as a memorable event. It is not to be accepted easily, it cannot be read in a half dose, and by the great public which multiplies editions it may remain neglected or unknown. Yet it is of such remarkable originality and merit that one may look for an emphasis of critical opinion which, as in the case of Mr. Meredith, can force a great reputation in the face of popular apathy or distaste.

The mechanism of the story is curious, and it includes a convention which may be attacked. The hero is introduced to us as a 'water clerk' —a kind of commercial traveller whose duty it is to board arriving ships,—employed successively at various Eastern ports. He is able, efficient, popular, but from time to time, at the breath of a sinister rumour, he resigns his position and dives into a temporary obscurity. The reason is presently explained. As first mate of the *Patna* he had been concerned in an incident that had roused the amazement and indignation of all reputable seamen. The ship, with eight hundred pilgrims bound for Mecca, had been deserted by the white men of its crew in a sinking condition, and it had not sunk. It had been taken in tow, had safely reached port, and the scandal of its desertion preceded the explanation of the captain, whose plausible concoction was annihilated by the damning facts. The narrative is taken up by a ship's captain who happened to be present at the inquiry. Some years afterwards he tells the strange story to an after-dinner party of men, and Mr. Conrad throws himself open to the obvious objection that the night must have been artificially prolonged to contain it. Later, again, the conclusion is conveyed to a privileged auditor. It may be that there is something distracting in a convention physically impossible. The essential construction—not a matter of shapeliness but a means to an end—is nevertheless fine and right. Without any formalities of art, it is the full expression of a natural concentration, and even the parentheses, which are numerous, are never irrelevant. Here we must quote a passage from the meeting of Captain Marlow with Jim, the hero of his own romances, an egoist but a noble one, here confronted with the incredible possibilities of his own nature, condemned to a perpetual regard of his own incredible act:—

[quotes ch. 5: 'I watched the youngster there' to 'the solicitation of ideas.']

Marlow is more than interested. He is grasped by the very desperation of curiosity, a pity that is almost a terror. His is the purity of friendship, independent of time or habit, absolutely without sentimentalism. It is impossible here to give any conception of the force and subtlety of Jim's confession, so human, intimate; its dreadful humour, its austere pathos; the close, minute investigation into a mind infinitely mysterious, an investigation broadening beyond our grasp.

[quotes ch. 16: 'It is when we try to grapple with another man's intimate need' to 'I would never forgive myself.']

This tremendous experiment in explanation, possible to the stranger, hopeless to the people at home from whom he is for ever exiled, opens to him the possibilities of life, an opportunity for rehabilitation in his own eyes. He tastes the sweets of love and power, of adventure and of devotion. He regains a 'belief in himself snatched from the fire,' he gratifies his own 'exalted egoism.' The Malay girl who shares this final period of his life, in the purity of her emotions, her natural nobility, her impregnable simplicity, may be a convention, but, if so, it is a convention that we cannot spare. 'She had seen nothing, she had known nothing, she had no conception of anything ... by nothing but his mere presence he had mastered her heart, had filled all her thoughts, and had possessed himself of all her affections.' Sharing the life, aspiring to share the burdens of this impenetrable lover, she is 'a brave person groping in the dark.' Her colloquy with Marlow is one of the finest passages in the story:—'It had the power to drive me out of my conception of existence, out of that shelter each of us makes for himself to creep under in moments of danger, as a tortoise withdraws into its shell.' The development need not be detailed. We pursue it with excitement, with trepidation, with a sympathy that projects itself into the unknown. The final catastrophe comes in part as the work of chance. He has conquered himself, he has worked out his expiation; it seems to be in vain when the bolt falls. The epilogue concludes with the strange irony of his romantic success curiously qualified by the moral victory: 'He goes away from a living woman to celebrate his pitiless wedding with a shadowy ideal of conduct,' while the woman remains, ignorant, unforgiving, incapable of understanding.

Mr. Conrad has done well before, but *Lord Jim* gives us the delighted surprise that is never the attribute of second-rate work. It is a book to make the world wider and deeper, a piece of life not over vivid but full of colour, moral because morality is at the root of humanity, touched with romance and profoundly true. The book is long, and even remarkably long, for it is written almost without a pause and with a concentration of purpose, a grasp of material, a deep energy which make it a great performance. In the more intense passages Mr. Conrad has the pregnant brevity of a master of form. His great effects are the simple revelations of his own insight; we recall the indication of tragedy in Jim's unfinished letter, the few words of dialogue between Jim and the girl before he leaves her. There is a whole gallery of sketches and portraits, duly subordinated, hardly less than perfect of their kinds. Such are the skipper of the *Patna*—a small masterpiece of grim humour —the trader Stein, the treacherous Cornelius, the Malay steersmen who give evidence at the inquiry, the amazing Brierly. All of these have their uses; they are strictly relevant, and they form part of a whole greatly conceived and finely executed.

42. W. L. Courtney, review, *Daily Telegraph*

7 November 1900, 11

In his review of *The Nigger of the 'Narcissus'* (No. 30), Courtney had emphasized Conrad's 'unflinching' realism. Here he concentrates upon criticizing his 'methods of story telling'. He finds an answer, perhaps, in the *Daily Chronicle* review of *Lord Jim*: 'The construction of the story is peculiar, and one would say that it sinned against all the rules except that it achieves a success, and the construction therefore is right' (29 October 1900). With *Lord Jim* Courtney was reviewing A. T. Quiller-Couch's collection of short stories, *Old Fires and Profitable Ghosts*.

There are many points of resemblance, curious similarities lying below the surface, in these widely differing stories. Mr. Quiller-Couch has the touch of the artist, the academic self-restraint so admirable in literature. John Emmett's life history is unfolded with a conciseness which is particularly refreshing in contrast with Mr. Conrad's flood of words. It is only a short story, but the effect produced is quite as powerful as that of the long novel. Mr. Conrad suffers from an exuberance of ideas. In striking antithesis to many writers of to-day he gives us too many episodes, too many side issues in his book. We are constantly longing to quote Rudyard Kipling, and say, 'But that's another story,' or to urge a study of Stevenson's maxim that the most important factor in the art of writing is a knowledge of what to omit. We have to wade, positively wade, through some eighty or ninety pages before we arrive at any conception of the author's design. Mr. Conrad has such unusual strength and power that his faults of method are specially regrettable. There are moments, as in Jim's story of his escape from the injured ship, his horror and his remorse, his pitiful desire that his version of the story shall be believed by his confidant, when the very faults of style which mar the book as a whole give an additional sense of power, thoughts and words flow unrestrained, the minutest details are described, and the forceful effect is enhanced. But, on the whole, the method of story telling adopted in *Lord Jim*, the constant wandering from the point, the recurrent introductions of incidents which do not affect the main issue, are distinctly weakening to the general end and aim of the book. The author gives us many charming character sketches, many fantastic, many tender situations, but the appetite is wearied with an excess of good fare.

43. Unsigned review, *Academy*

10 November 1900, 443

The author of this review could well be Edward Garnett. Conrad defended himself against the reviewer's criticism of the length of this 'after-dinner story' in his Author's Note to *Lord Jim* of 1917.

Lord Jim is a searching study—prosecuted with patience and understanding—of the cowardice of a man who was not a coward. A moment of great trial came to Jim when he was mate of a steamer. He failed. For years he lived dully, never forgetting this failure; and then came an opportunity to retrieve (before God), and he took it. That is the story, in barest outline, which Mr. Conrad has lavished his energy upon, omitting not the minutest tittle of evidence in Jim's favour (and, through Jim, in favour of us all—for Jim's trial and subsequent penance typify the trials and penances of all men); omitting nothing in Jim's disfavour; reproducing every shaft of light that played upon Jim from all sides; and giving us, too, the wonderful bizarre setting of the drama: the mysterious tropical sea, the odd parti-coloured life of the Eastern port, with its natives, its captains, and its traders; and, later, the inner life of the tiny State in the Malay Peninsula where Jim worked out his salvation—all done with a poetical, romantic, half-wistful air for which we go in vain to any other English writer. That the book is of the sea and the East is in a certain way an accident: its application to life, to all of us, is in no way diminished by this chance. For Jim, as we have said, stands for the universal; he has something in common with us all.

We may, perhaps, return to the subject again, more particularly to Mr. Conrad's revelation of the East. But now we may just refer to the vividness of the glimpses which the story gives us, here and there, of some of the men who are engaged in relating the East to the West; those strange links with the two civilisations, voluntary exiles from this country, denationalising themselves that the British flag shall find trade wherever it penetrates. The romance of the merchant service is not a whit less enthralling, and is many times more curious, than that of the Navy, and Mr. Conrad knows it all. There is in this book, *Lord Jim*, a wonderful figure of a latter-day buccaneer; and the old trader Stein, with his butterflies and his resignation and his memories and his power, is a figure that fills the eye. They are embodied forth, these odd so-journers in their wrong hemisphere, so subtly, so almost magically, in this poignant narrative; they come silently and suddenly, and stay. And the strange thing is that the story all the time is of Jim and his poor boyish conscience, and his lost opportunity, and his far-reaching egoism (reaching even to the most confident of Mr. Conrad's readers); and yet, though Jim is the subject, and the beginning and the end, there is the crowded, mysterious East too, and there are these notable men—Brown and Stein, Brierley and Brierley's mate, the German captain and the Swedish chandler, Cornelius and Doramin, Jewel and Tamb 'Itam and, more than all, Marlow. And yet, though so fully drawn, they have a place in the book only and solely by virtue of their relation to Jim. How Mr. Conrad can tell so much so incidentally we cannot explain. But the secret gives him a double claim; for not only does he command attention for his story, but also for his art. He is at once a reader's and a novelist's novelist.

The blemishes are very slight. We are a little doubtful if the picture of Jim given in the opening pages is the right one: we do not quite follow Mr. Conrad's scheme in choosing to place him before the reader as a water-clerk at the outset. His water-clerking was not the most important phase of his life. Indeed, we do not quite see why this adult presentation was called for just there at all: why not have begun with page 3, at the words, 'Originally he came from a parsonage'? Again, there is a slight jerkiness in the passages immediately following that might have been smoothed away. Lastly, there is the mechanical con-vention of the story itself, which decrees that Mr. Conrad shall retire at page 34 and hand over the rest of the narrative to a story-teller in an arm-chair on an evening after dinner. There is good precedent for this mannerism. One of the finest short stories ever written—Turgenev's 'Lear of the Steppes'—is modelled on precisely the same lines; yet we own to a prejudice against it. In the case of *Lord Jim*, the objection is twofold, for it is not credible. This after-dinner story, told without a break, consists of about 99,000 words. Now it is unreasonable to suppose that the narrator, who chose his words with care, spoke at a greater rate than 150 words a minute, which means that he was telling that after-dinner story to his companions for eleven solid hours. Mr. Conrad, we fancy, in his zeal, lost sight of this amusing prolixity. He has also occasionally made his spokesman employ phrases such as no oral story-teller would be likely to compass. As an example, take this interlude on the moon:

There is something haunting in the light of the moon; it has all the dispassionateness of a disembodied soul, and something of its inconceivable mystery. It is to our sunshine, which—say what you like—is all we have to live by, what the echo is to the sound: misleading and confusing whether the note be mocking or sad. It robs all forms of matter—which, after all, is our domain— of their substance, and gives a sinister reality to shadows alone.

That is all right; but we have some difficulty in believing it just there. It is not thus that men speak.

One other point: the suicide of Brierley. We are not persuaded that that is proved.

But these, after all, are nothings. We mention them more in the hope that (for our own pleasure) Mr. Conrad may, perhaps, come to revise his preference for story by story-teller above story by himself than because they really matter. *Lord Jim* is too fine for such spots to injure its beauty.

44. Unsigned notice, *Sketch*

14 November 1900, 142

This notice carried the initials O.O.—perhaps Oliver Onions, the pseudonym of George Oliver, English novelist (1873–1961). One of the notice's themes was taken up and expressed more strongly in *Public Opinion*: 'This would make an excellent short story; in its present form it covers 451 pages' and 'pages are devoted to conversations between [Jim] and Marlowe, in which his past career and chances for the future are threshed out. Words cannot describe the weary effect of all this . . . [Conrad] cannot check his love of . . . morbid dissection of character, and the result is that the story is choked' (23 November 1900). In his Author's Note to the novel, Conrad commented that there was nothing 'morbid in the acute consciousness of lost honour'.

I doubt if the year will produce a more remarkable book than Mr. Joseph Conrad's new novel, *Lord Jim*. More readable novels, better novels in every way, have already been published by the score, but none more strange, none more genuinely extraordinary. *Lord Jim* is an impossible book—impossible in scheme, impossible in style. It is a short character-sketch, written and re-written to infinity, dissected into shreds, masticated into tastelessness. The story—the little story it contains—is told by an outsider, a tiresome, garrulous, philosophising bore. And yet it is undeniably the work of a man of genius, of one who, wrongly I think, despises every popular and accepted method. Mr. Conrad will do great things when he consents to follow advice.

45. Unsigned review, *Spectator*

24 November 1900, 753

It may be that amongst the hundred and twenty-five novels still awaiting notice on our shelves some work of uncommon talent may reveal itself to gladden the heart of the reviewer; in the meantime, we have no hesitation in pronouncing Mr. Conrad's *Lord Jim* to be the most original, remarkable, and engrossing novel of a season by no means unfruitful of excellent fiction. That it may not strike all readers in this light we readily concede. Mr. Conrad's matter is too detached from 'actuality' to please the great and influential section of readers who like their fiction to be spiced with topical allusions, political personalities, or the mundanities of Mayfair,—just now the swing of the pendulum is entirely away from the slums, and almost altogether in the direction of sumptuous interiors. Mr. Conrad, in a word, takes no heed of the vagaries of fashion or of pseudo-culture—he only once mentions an author and only once makes a quotation—he eschews epigrams, avoids politics, and keeps aloof from great cities. His scenes are laid in unfamiliar regions, amid outlandish surroundings. But if you once succumb to the sombre fascination of his narrative—as the present writer did years ago on reading *An Outcast of the Islands*—your thraldom is complete. Several writers have derived literary inspiration from their sojourn in the Malay Archipelago; but Mr. Conrad, beyond all others, has identified himself with the standpoint of the natives, has interpreted their aspirations, illumined their motives, and translated into glowing words the strange glamour of their landscape. Such an achievement, though remarkable in itself, seems to indicate a de-nationalisation that might inspire a certain amount of distrust. But in the volume before us, though the 'noble savage' is once more prominent, the story is half finished before we reach Malaya, and the central figure who rivets our interest throughout, though intensely romantic by temperament, is the son of an English country parson, and throughout all his long exile never loses touch with the sentiment, the ideals, the essential *ethos*, of his race.

[gives a summary of the plot]

We despair within the limited space at our disposal of conveying any adequate notion of the poignant interest of this strange narrative, the restrained yet fervid eloquence of the style, the vividness of the portraiture, the subtlety of psychological analysis, which are united in Mr. Conrad's latest and greatest work. The wizardry of the Orient is over it all. We can only congratulate him on an achievement at once superlatively artistic in treatment and entirely original in its subject.

46. Unsigned review, *Speaker*

24 November 1900, 215–16

The review was signed L.R.F.O. To Meldrum Conrad wrote on 27 November 1900: 'Many thanks for the *Spectator* ... The review is good is it not. The *Speaker* too reviewed me the same week—Whig and Tory. That was also a good review. Upon the whole the "Press" is good' (*LWB*, 115).

Many prophecies, extravagant we thought at the time, were made with regard to the author of *The Nigger of the Narcissus*. Those prophecies, have been more than fulfilled in *Lord Jim*, which is a very remarkable and interesting book. Mr. Conrad has found a problem of universal interest, is never in doubt as to what he has to say about it, and expresses himself with consummate art, reinforced by a wide and peculiar store of information. In its way *Lord Jim* is a psychological study as profound, if not as illuminating, as any of Meredith's. It brings Mr. Conrad at once into the front rank of living novelists.

The general theme considered in *Lord Jim*, is suggested by the following quotation from Novalis[1]:—'It is certain my conviction gains infinitely, the moment another soul will believe in it.' The

[1] Novalis, pseudonym of Friedrich von Hardenberg (1772–1801), German romantic poet who was called the 'Prophet of Romanticism'.

particular problem with its refinements and side issues is not easily summarised—it takes Mr. Conrad over two hundred pages to enunciate it. Briefly, however, we may say that it is concerned with the discovery by a romantic young sailor, 'one of us' Captain Marlow calls him, that is, an Englishman and a gentleman—that he is not the brave man he thought himself. He has not the habit of courage, and on an occasion when the eye of others was not upon him and the example of others was in favour of cowardice, he neglects his clear duty and shows himself a coward, thereby losing his honour, which is to the Frenchman who diagnoses his case the important point. Unable to get any encouragement in his attempt to believe that he was not really a coward, he searches for an opportunity to disprove it. Before he finds it, however, the conviction of a wife and a savage tribe of which he has become the providence almost gives him complete confidence. Accident removes this conviction from the savages, and Jim takes the opportunity which this accident also provides. 'He goes away from a living woman to celebrate his pitiless wedding with a shadowy ideal of conduct. Is he satisfied quite now, I wonder?'

There is an apparent artlessness about the arrangement of the book which seems to arise from a determination that the reader shall not be led away by the interest of the mere external events of the tale. Events are almost contemptuously forestalled, in order that the how and the why of them alone shall get the best attention of the reader. The story doubles back on itself continuously when a theory of conduct wants illustrating and elucidating. The scheme of arrangement allows, too, for the easy introduction of different points of view. Jim's story is chiefly told by the man who comes to his help in his great time of need, an extremely good device. But opinions on Jim's case are sought from men of all classes and all nationalities, from the Frenchman who undertook the actual act of bravery in which Jim failed and who believes that all men are born cowards, from the German who knows the power of a romantic imagination, from the captain who had himself some secret shame that led him soon after to suicide, from Gentleman Brown, robber on the high seas, who wants to take his revenge upon the world, and from many others. The arrangement of the book is original and effective; it seems to have solved one of the great difficulties of the philosophical romance.

Mr. Conrad's style still seems to suffer something from lack of simplicity. He has some of the tricks of those who try to express more than they mean. 'He had Ability in the abstract, which is good for no other work but that of a water-clerk' is an example of this. On the whole, however, Mr. Conrad's command of language in this book is remarkable, and he is generally so sure of what he means that he is able to express the most subtle ideas with quite unusual clearness. Occasionally there are passages of real beauty—for example, that most tragic interview between Marlow and the poor girl who loves Jim, but believes that some unknown force will take him from her.

[quotes ch. 33: ' "What is it?" . . . and then arise and go.']

47. Unsigned review, *Pall Mall Gazette*

5 December 1900, 4

The review was entitled 'The Phantasmagoria of the East'. This was the first occasion on which *Lord Jim* was criticized for being a 'broken-backed' narrative. There is a suggestion that Garnett had already made a similar comment. In his letter to Garnett of 12 November 1900, Conrad writes: 'Yes! you've put your finger on the plague spot. The division of the book into two parts' (*LEG*, p. 171).

It is, perhaps, not Mr. Conrad's fault that on reading his last contribution to the atmosphere of the East, ghosts are inclined to rise upon us. When Jim, the burly German Captain, and his two engineers come up from the sea, as Marlow describes it, we are faintly conscious of some old familiar acquaintants. Is it out of *The Wrecker* that these people have strayed; or is it, perhaps, *The Ebb Tide* that has been brought to our recollection by their faces and characters and destinies?[1] It may, indeed, be that derelicts from any land and in any part of the world carry with them an air which may be described as generic. Again, it is

[1] R. L. Stevenson brought out *The Wrecker* in 1892 and *The Ebb-Tide* in 1894.

probably not Mr. Conrad's fault that his methods and his style remind one irresistibly of a strange commingling of Mr. Henry James and the late Mr. Stephen Crane. To each is his individuality, which must be accepted as it stands.

Yet it may be safely affirmed of Mr. Conrad that he belongs to a certain school which is represented by some distinguished writers, and which finds its expression best in very intense and subtle analysis. Mr. Crane was bent on building up, brick by brick and tone by tone, a huge effort, which should be so elaborate, even so laborious, and so detailed, as to give one the picture required from every point of view. He abandoned that theory of *plein air*, in which R. L. Stevenson matured to perfection, and which consisted of broad brushes, of elimination, of simplicity of arrangement, of abstention, of sudden and long-calculated audacity. It is a monstrous procession of facts, signs, and colours which the new school uses, and, to do it justice, it flings its imagination about most riotously and generously.

But the result, as we take it, makes for a definite formlessness, an unwieldiness sometimes, and always, we are inclined to say, for a disproportion, for the overwhelming of main facts in a sea of minor verities. The proportion of Mr. Conrad's tale is—well, it can hardly be said to be in proportion. Paragraphs in various papers have informed us (whether correctly or incorrectly we know not) that *Lord Jim* was begun as a comparatively short sketch, and developed subsequently into its present length of (we should guess) 120,000 words. We should judge that the story is true, for *Lord Jim* is a very broken-backed narrative. The first 150 pages or so are devoted to the episode of the *Patna*, told, for some reason, partly in the third person and partly (by Captain Marlow) in the first. But the remaining 300 pages seem to be an afterthought, the extension of which rumour speaks. The formlessness which haunts such work as we have endeavoured to describe is vastly augmented by this plan. Indeed, for all the qualities which Mr. Conrad undoubtedly possesses, and which are manifest in many places in this book, *Lord Jim* is tedious, over-elaborated, and more than a little difficult to read. The first episode might have stood by itself, and the concluding narrative, again, might well have been worked up into a separate tale. But, although there is a kind of weak-backed unity in the tale, the various fragments of narrative do not hold the interest, or, rather, pass it on from point to point. We have spoken of a unity, and there is undoubtedly one. It is the character of Jim—the blind spot in his character comes in once, and we have the *Patna* episode; it comes in again, after many weary years, and we have—the end. It is tragedy, of course, and a tragedy which would have been greatly effective if another method had been adopted. But Mr. Conrad has his own style, and we must bow to the inevitable. As it is, the main impression left upon the reader's mind will be, we think, a phantasmagoria, a changing scene of life in Eastern seas, and chiefly in that Malaysia which has found of recent years so many exponents. As such it is graphic, vigorous, conscientious, and full of knowledge and penetration.

48. Unsigned review, *Daily News*

14 December 1900, 6

Lord Jim's own account of his 'jump' from the *Patna* is omitted.

Mr. Joseph Conrad's new book *Lord Jim*, which has recently run through many pages of *Blackwood's Magazine*, is really more of an epic than of a story. It is grandiose, it is poetic, it is thoughtful; in a word, it is masterly, yet it is hardly the sort of thing that will tend much to the enjoyment of the butterflies of fiction. The obstructions set in the way of the reader are many, and, moreover, are mainly owing to Mr. Conrad's idiosyncrasies. His manner of telling his story is involved; it wanders, moreover, back and forth, up and down, with regard to the main story, in a fashion that can hardly be described as lucid. He apparently altogether abjures paragraphs, and, to make the puzzle more complete, Lord Jim's history is, almost throughout, told of him by a third person, and in inverted commas. Thus, to begin with, and before the story has taken hold of the reader, he feels as though wandering in a morass of wonderful language and incomprehensible events. But, apart from these faults, which are, after all, merely defects of style, the story is powerfully enthralling. Its central idea, and the book is all built round this central idea, is splendidly conceived and ably carried out; while for background there is the ever-shifting panorama of the great Pacific, varied by the picturesque islands of the Indian Sea. No one talks, unless it be to discuss Lord Jim; there is no conversation; the book has all the effect of an impassioned monologue, delivered 'en plein air,' amid the eternal and kindly-neutral forces of sky and sea. 'Lord' Jim, whose prefix, it may be stated, is a nickname, a translation from the Malay 'Tuan' Jim, is a sailor and a visionary, originally a mate in the merchant service; in youth he 'goes under a cloud' and loses his credentials, his offence being that in a moment either of mental paralysis, compulsion, or merely sudden, unreasoning terror, he, with three others, had deserted a sinking and crowded ship. . . .

In that terrible moment Jim's life goes under. Yet he is no coward, as after-events prove. During his subsequent career he shows even an absolute recklessness of his own life, which, nevertheless, appears a charmed one. The long mental agony of self-reproach and unavailing self-introspection, acting on a naturally conscientious and sensitive spirit, is realistically told. His old sin ever tracking him, he throws up one employment after the other, finding at last a perilous refuge from his own kind as trader's agent at Patusan, a primitive island village in the Malay Archipelago. Stein, the trader and entomologist, whom Lord Jim serves, is a wonderful creation. The reader should not miss the pathos of his early life-story—hidden, as are so many other good things, in the crowded pages of this tremendous and paragraph-less volume. The Malay island, where 'Tuan Jim' successfully establishes himself as counsellor, guide, and warrior, offers fine opportunities for local colour and adventure. Here love also comes into Lord Jim's life —a love, however, that 'never finds its earthly close,' but leads rather to self-sacrifice and death, the hero 'going away from a living woman to celebrate his pitiless wedding with a shadowy ideal of conduct.' Mr. Conrad's descriptions are vivid and wonderfully true. His knowledge of the sea, of sailors—indeed, of all he writes—is amazing; but, apart from all this, he has given us in *Lord Jim* the dramatic history of an uncomprehended and tortured soul—the soul of a dreamer, rising, under affliction, to ever higher flights of altruism and self-sacrifice. All will not be able to read the book, but those who do will pronounce it to be an artistic success.

49. Unsigned review, *Bookman*

February 1901, 161

This was reprinted unchanged in the U.S.A. *Bookman*, April 1901.

If Mr. Henry James had a consummate knowledge of life at sea and in the Pacific Coast towns and settlements, he would write a novel very like *Lord Jim*. Is this praise or blame? Granting the supreme talent of Mr. James, would it be rightly or wrongly devoted to analysing the soul behind the rough-and-tumble life of a sailor and a ship-chandler's water clerk? Is it well for us to be reminded that such persons may be as infinitely complicated, as civilisedly degenerate as any dweller in refined and sophisticated circles? We do not know. Mr. Conrad may have written an unwise—he certainly has written an interesting book. Let not the tired reader, the reader only in want of amusement or distraction, approach *Lord Jim*; for it is more than usually serious, more than usually depressing, and to such as are not psychological students it must seem very tedious. There is no bad work in it, but there is far too much good—which amounts to the same thing: half of it should have been mercilessly sacrificed, and no essential of the pathetic and attractive and hopeless Jim would have suffered. The book is all Jim—there is nothing else in it that counts. He is a romanticist, a sentimentalist, a sailor made of fine stuff, who had all his young life 'been elaborating dangers and defences, expecting the worst, rehearsing his best.' But the worst came in an unexpected way; and, speaking brutally, he proved himself a coward; speaking charitably, he lost his opportunity. He never will face that part of him that made 'the mistake,' but he knows he has to expiate it. The 'mistake' dogs him. In the end he goes out of his way to seek a bullet, so that with his last consciousness he may feel he is no coward. And his biographer, who loves him, yet must comment thus on the fact: 'He goes away from a living woman to celebrate his pitiless wedding with a shadowy ideal of conduct.' Judged as a story, *Lord Jim* may find various criticism. Judged as a document, it must be acknowledged a masterpiece.

126

50. Unsigned review, *Critic* (U.S.A.)

May 1901, 437–8

This review carried the initials J.B.P.

Imagine a fat, furry spider with green head and shining points for eyes, busily at work, some dewy morning, on a marvellous web,—and you have the plot of *Lord Jim*. It spins itself away, out of nothing, with side tracks leading, apparently, nowhere, and cross tracks that start back and begin anew and end once more—sometimes on the verge of nowhere, and sometimes in the centre of the plot itself;—and all with an air of irresponsible intentness and a businesslike run at the end that sets the structure trembling on gossamer threads.

The completed web is a marvel of workmanship, built with a foresight and a careless ease that suggests instinct rather than art. But the real plot interest is too subtle for the instinct theory to cover. The psychologic study of a romantic youth who meets fear and is conquered offers problems that are not solved by instinctive skill in plot.

For the primal ape—and his kind—the fear of fear has no existence. He knows fear only as a commonplace,—something to be depended upon in time of danger to point the warning finger at which he takes, —in hordes,—to the woods. For Lord Jim, the guileless youth, and for the rest of us, fear is something to be reckoned with, but something to be ashamed of, forever at our shoulder. It should have been dropped, long since, with the caudal appendage, when usefulness was done. If we may no longer take to the woods at its warning voice, why should we be haunted by it night and day,—always at hand to whisper horror? It whispered in the ear of Lord Jim and he took the fatal jump that landed him with cowards. Let the man who is without fear cast the first stone. For such a man, if he exist, the story of Lord Jim will have, perchance, neither fascination nor moral lesson. It will be simply the involved and somewhat tedious history of a young man who yielded to an impulse of fear and who gave his life to living down the consequences,—inside and out. Add to the situation a romantic temperament and an inability to grasp the fact that he has shown himself a shadowy scoundrel at heart—and you have the very pretty problem.

Mr. Conrad works it out—as has been intimated—in his own peculiar fashion. If he keeps on writing the same sort, he may arrive at the unique distinction of having few readers in his own generation, and a fair chance of several in the next.

13 November 1902

51. Conrad on 'Heart of Darkness'

1898-9

'Heart of Darkness', which dealt with Conrad's experiences in the
Congo, was the second story in the *Youth* volume and appeared
first in *Blackwood's Magazine*, 1899, in issues of February, March,
and April. William Blackwood at this time had been editor for
twenty years.

R. B. Cunninghame Graham (1852–1936) was one of the great
personalities of his age, socialist and Scottish laird, traveller and
writer. His friendship with Conrad began when he wrote to Conrad in 1897 praising 'An Outpost of Progress', which appeared
in *Cosmopolis* in June and July that year. Their friendship lasted
until Conrad's death in 1924.

(a) Conrad to William Blackwood, 31 December 1898 (*LWB*, p. 37):

The title I am thinking of is 'The Heart of Darkness' but the narrative
is not gloomy. The criminality of inefficiency and pure selfishness when
tackling the civilizing work in Africa is a justifiable idea. The subject is
of our time distinctly—though not topically treated. It is a story as
much as my *Outpost of Progress* was but, so to speak 'takes in' more—is
a little wider—is less concentrated upon individuals.

(b) Conrad to R. B. Cunninghame Graham, 8 February 1899 (*LCG*,
p. 116):

I am simply in the seventh heaven, to find you like the *H of D* so far.
You bless me indeed. Mind you don't curse me by and bye for the

very same thing. There are two more instalments in which the idea is so wrapped up in secondary notions that You—even You! may miss it. And also you must remember that I don't start with an abstract notion. I start with definite images and as their rendering is true some little effect is produced. So far the note struck chimes in with your convictions—mais après? There is an après.

52. Edward Garnett, unsigned review, *Academy and Literature*

6 December 1902, 606

Earlier reviews of this volume of stories tended to concentrate on 'Youth'. The *Sketch*, 3 December 1902, referred only to 'Youth'; the *Daily Telegraph*, 26 November 1902, was rapturous over 'Youth', and gave 'Heart of Darkness' and 'The End of the Tether' less than their due. The *Daily Mail*, 25 November 1902, spoke of 'The Haunt of Darkness' [sic]—'application of the methods of Mr. Henry James to Central Africa'. This review by Garnett was the most intelligent appreciation of 'Heart of Darkness', and responding to it on 22 December 1902, Conrad wrote: 'My dearest fellow you quite overcome me. And your brave attempt to grapple with the foggishness of H. of D., to explain what I myself tried to shape blindfold, as it were, touched me profoundly' (*LEG*, p. 184). It is the 'foggishness' which Conrad mentions here which was taken up much later by E. M. Forster in his criticism of Conrad: '. . . he is misty in the middle as well as at the edges . . . the secret casket of his genius contains a vapour rather than a jewel' (*Abinger Harvest*, 1936, p. 135).

The publication in volume form of Mr. Conrad's three stories, 'Youth,' 'Heart of Darkness,' 'The End of the Tether,' is one of the events of the literary year. These stories are an achievement in art which will materially advance his growing reputation. Of the stories, 'Youth' may be styled a modern English epic of the Sea; 'The End of the Tether' is a study of an old sea captain who, at the end of forty years' trade exploration of the Southern seas, finding himself dispossessed by the perfected routine of the British empire overseas he has helped to build, falls on evil times, and faces ruin calmly, fighting to the last. These two will be more popular than the third, 'Heart of Darkness,' a study of 'the white man in Africa' which is most amazing, a consummate piece of artistic *diablerie*. On reading 'Heart of Darkness' on its appearance in *Blackwood's Magazine* our first impression was that Mr. Conrad had, here and there, lost his way. Now that the story can be read, not in parts, but from the first page to the last at a sitting, we retract this opinion and hold 'Heart of Darkness' to be the high-water mark of the author's talent. It may be well to analyse this story a little so that the intelligent reader, reading it very deliberately, may see better for himself why Mr. Conrad's book enriches English literature.

'Heart of Darkness,' to present its theme bluntly, is an impression, taken from life, of the conquest by the European whites of a certain portion of Africa, an impression in particular of the civilising methods of a certain great European Trading Company face to face with the 'nigger.' We say this much because the English reader likes to know where he is going before he takes art seriously, and we add that he will find the human life, black and white, in 'Heart of Darkness' an uncommonly and uncannily serious affair. If the ordinary reader, however, insists on taking the subject of a tale very seriously, the artist takes his method of presentation more seriously still, and rightly so. For the art of 'Heart of Darkness'—as in every psychological masterpiece—lies in the relation of the things of the spirit to the things of the flesh, of the invisible life to the visible, of the sub-conscious life within us, our obscure motives and instincts, to our conscious actions, feelings and outlook. Just as landscape art implies the artist catching the exact relation of a tree to the earth from which it springs, and of the earth to the sky, so the art of 'Heart of Darkness' implies the catching of infinite shades of the white man's uneasy, disconcerted, and fantastic relations with the exploited barbarism of Africa; it implies the acutest analysis of the deterioration of the white man's *morale*, when he is let loose from European restraint, and planted down in the tropics as an 'emissary of light' armed to the teeth, to make trade profits out of the 'subject races.' The weirdness, the brilliance, the psychological truth of this masterly analysis of two Continents in conflict, of the abysmal gulf between the white man's system and the black man's comprehension of its results, is conveyed in a rapidly rushing narrative which calls for close attention on the reader's part. But the attention once surrendered, the pages of the narrative are as enthralling as the pages of Dostoevsky's *Crime and Punishment*. The stillness of the sombre African forests, the glare of sunshine, the feeling of dawn, of noon, of night on the tropical rivers, the isolation of the unnerved, degenerating whites staring all day and every day at the Heart of Darkness which is alike meaningless and threatening to their own creed and conceptions of life, the helpless bewilderment of the unhappy savages in the grasp of their flabby and rapacious conquerors—all this is a page torn from the life of the Dark Continent—a page which has been hitherto carefully blurred and kept away from European eyes. There is no 'intention' in the story, no *parti pris*, no prejudice one way or the other; it is simply a piece of art, fascinating and remorseless, and the artist is but intent on presenting his sensations in that sequence and arrangement whereby the meaning or the meaninglessness of the white man in uncivilised Africa can be felt in its really significant aspects. If the story is too strong meat for the ordinary reader, let him turn to 'Youth,' wherein the song of every man's youth is indeed sung.

The third story, 'The End of the Tether,' is not, we think, so remarkable an artistic conception as are the other two; but in the close study of the old English captain, a seaman of the old school, Mr. Conrad has given us the best piece of character painting he has yet achieved.

[gives an outline of the plot]

As a picture of sea life the story is absolutely convincing; it is only in the total effect on the reader's nerves that 'The End of the Tether' strikes us as being less subtle in arrangement, less inevitable in its climax than is 'Heart of Darkness.' If we are to judge the story, however, as a series of continuous and interdependent pictures of life, cunning mirages of actual scenes, exquisitely balanced and proportioned, delicate mirages evoked as by an enchanter's wand, then indeed Mr. Conrad is easily among the first writers of to-day. His special individual gift, as an artist, is of so placing a whole scene before the reader that the air, the landscape, the moving people, the houses on the quays, the ships in the harbour, the sounds, the scents, the voices in the air, all fuse in the perfect and dream-like illusion of an unforgettable reality. 'The End of the Tether' is a triumph of the writer's art of description, but we must repeat that 'Heart of Darkness' in the subtlety of its criticism of life is the high-water mark of the author's talent.

53. Unsigned review, *Manchester Guardian*

10 December 1902, 3

The review was entitled 'Mr. Conrad's New Book'.

Mr. Joseph Conrad's latest volume, *Youth*, contains three stories, of which the one that gives the title is the shortest. This and the second one may be regarded as a kind of sequence. The third and longest, 'The End of the Tether,' is admirable, but in comparison with the others the tension is relaxed. It is in a manner more deliberate, less closely packed; this is Conrad, but not Conrad in his fine frenzy; it gives an engaging picture of a noble old man, pathetic, imaginative, deserving a whole array of eulogistic adjectives, but it is not of the amazing quality of Mr. Conrad at his best. The other two, though not of such scope and design, are of the quality of *Lord Jim*—that is to say, they touch the high-water mark of English fiction and continue a great expression of adventure and romance. Both stories follow Mr. Conrad's particular convention; they are the outpourings of Marlow's experiences. It would be useless to pretend that they can be very widely read. Even to those who are most impressed an excitement so sustained and prolonged, in which we are braced to encounter so much that menaces and appals, must be something of a strain. 'Youth,' in this conception of Mr. Conrad's, is not the time of freedom and delight, but 'the test, the trial of life.' No labour is too great, no danger is too close for this great adventure of the spirit.

[quotes from 'Youth', pp. 11–12: 'There was for us not sky . . . and had the eyes of idiots.']

And through this come the precious moment, the exultation of endeavour, the joy in a strength to be broken on the wheel, the splendours of agony, a sense of the awfulness of life. The story is told with a surprising humour, and its details are perfectly devised. Closely relevant are the old captain, pathetically anxious to save his first command, dogged against all unhappy chances, and the indomitable crew, upborne in their enormous labours by 'something solid like a principle and masterful like an instinct—a disclosure of something secret, of that hidden something, that gift of good or evil that makes racial difference, that shapes the fate of nations.' The narrative does something to enlarge our conceptions of heroism; the seafaring man is justified, he has found a friend in high places.

'Heart of Darkness' is, again, the adventure of youth, an adventure more significant than the mere knockabout of the world. It is youth in the toils, a struggle with phantoms worse than the elements, 'a weary pilgrimage amongst hints for nightmares,' a destructive experience.

[gives an outline of the plot with quotations]

It must not be supposed that Mr. Conrad makes attack upon colonisation, expansion, even upon Imperialism. In no one is the essence of the adventurous spirit more instinctive. But cheap ideals, platitudes of civilisation are shrivelled up in the heat of such experiences. The end of this story brings us back to the familiar, reassuring region of common emotions, to the grief and constancy of the woman who had loved Kurtz and idealises his memory. It shows us how far we have travelled.

Those who can read these two stories in sympathy with Mr. Conrad's temperament will find in them a great expression of the world's mystery and romance. They show the impact upon an undaunted spirit of what is terrible and obscure; they are adventure in terms of experience; they represent the sapping of life that cannot be lived on easy terms. Mr. Conrad's style is his own—concentrated, tenacious, thoughtful, crammed with imaginative detail, breathless, yet missing nothing. Its grim earnestness bends to excursions of irony, to a casual humour, dry, subdued to its surroundings. Phrases strike the mind like lines of verse; we weary under a tension that is never slackened. He is one of the greatest of sea-writers and the most subjective of them. His storms are not the picturesque descriptions of gigantic phenomena, we see them in the 'weary, serious faces,' in the dreadful concentration of the actors. Mr. Conrad is intensely human and, we may add with some pride of fellowship, intensely modern. By those who seek for the finest expositions of the modern spirit 'Youth' and 'Heart of Darkness' cannot be neglected.

54. Unsigned review,
The Times Literary Supplement

12 December 1902, 372

The Times Literary Supplement's suggestion that 'The End of the Tether' should have been put 'in the forefront of the book' receives, by implication, an answer from Conrad when he wrote to F. N. Doubleday during the last year of his life on 7 February 1924: '. . . take the volume of *Youth*, which in its component parts presents the three ages of man (for that is what it really is, and I knew very well what I was doing when I wrote "The End of the Tether" to be the last of that trio)' (*L & L*, ii, 338).

Telling tales, just spinning yarns, has gone out of fashion since the novel has become an epitome of everything a man has to say about anything. The three stories in *Youth* by Joseph Conrad are in this reference a return to an earlier taste. The yarns are of the sea, told with an astonishing zest; and given with vivid accumulation of detail and iterative persistency of emphasis on the quality of character and scenery. The method is exactly the opposite of Mr. Kipling's. It is a little precious; one notes a tasting of the quality of phrases and an occasional indulgence in poetic rhetoric. But the effect is not unlike Mr. Kipling's. In the first story, 'Youth,' the colour, the atmosphere of the East is brought out as in a picture. The concluding scene of the 'Heart of Darkness' is crisp and brief enough for Flaubert, but the effect—a woman's ecstatic belief in a villain's heroism—is reached by an indulgence in the picturesque horror of the villain, his work and his surroundings, which is pitiless in its insistence, and quite extravagant according to the canons of art. But the power, the success in conveying the impression vividly, without loss of energy is undoubted and is refreshing. 'The End of the Tether,' the last of the three, is the longest and best. Captain Whalley is racy of the sea, and an embodiment of its finest traditions; and the pathos of his long-drawn wrestle with the anger of circumstance is poignant to the end. Mr. Conrad should have put him in the forefront of the book. There are many readers who would not get beyond the barren and not very pretty philosophy of 'Youth'; more who might feel they had had enough horror at the end of 'The Heart of Darkness.' But they would miss a great deal if they did not reach 'The End of the Tether.' It has this further advantage over the other two tales, that it is much less clever, much less precious.

55. Unsigned review, *Athenaeum*

20 December 1902, 3921, 824

The art of Mr. Conrad is exquisite and very subtle. He uses the tools of his craft with the fine, thoughtful delicacy of a mediæval clock-maker. With regard to his mastery of the *conte* opinions are divided, and many critics will probably continue to hold that his short stories are not short stories at all, but rather concentrated novels. And the contention is not unreasonable. In more ways than one Mr. Conrad is something of a law unto himself, and creates his own forms, as he certainly has created his own methods. Putting aside all considerations of mere taste, one may say at once that Mr. Conrad's methods command and deserve the highest respect, if only by reason of their scholarly thoroughness. One feels that nothing is too minute, no process too laborious for this author. He considers not material rewards, but the dignity of his work, of all work. He does not count the hours of labour or the weight of weariness involved in the production of a flawless page or an adequately presented conception; but he has the true worker's eye, the true artist's pitilessness, in the detection and elimination of the redundant word, the idle thought, the insincere idiom, or even for the mark of punctuation misplaced. The busy, boastful times we live in are not rich in such sterling literary merits as these; and for that reason we may be the more thankful to an author like Mr. Conrad for the loyalty which prevents his sending a scamped page to press.

A critical writer has said that all fiction may roughly be divided into two classes: that dealing with movement and adventure, and the other dealing with characterization, the analysis of the human mind. In the present, as in every one of his previous books, Mr. Conrad has stepped outside these boundaries, and made his own class of work as he has made his own methods. All his stories have movement and incident, most of them have adventure, and the motive in all has apparently been the careful analysis, the philosophic presentation, of phases of human character. His studious and minute drawing of the action of men's minds, passions, and principles forms fascinating reading. But he has another gift of which he himself may be less conscious, by means of which his other more incisive and purely intellectual message is translated for the proper understanding of simpler minds and plainer men. That gift is the power of conveying atmosphere, and in the exercise of this talent Mr. Conrad has few equals among our living writers of fiction. He presents the atmosphere in which his characters move and act with singular fidelity, by means of watchful and careful building in which the craftsman's methods are never obtrusive, and after turning the last page of one of his books we rise saturated by the very air they breathed. This is a great power, but, more or less, it is possessed by other talented writers of fiction. The rarity of it in Mr. Conrad lies in this, that he can surround both his characters and his readers with the distinctive atmosphere of a particular story within the limits of a few pages. This is an exceptional gift, and the more to be prized in Mr. Conrad for the reason that he shows some signs of growing over-subtle in his analysis of moods, temperaments, and mental idiosyncrasies. It is an extreme into which all artists whose methods are delicate, minute, and searching are apt to be led. We have at least one other analyst of temperament and mood in fiction whose minute subtlety, scrupulous restraint, and allusive economy of words resemble Mr. Conrad's. And, becoming an obsession, these characteristics tend to weary the most appreciative reader. With Mr. Conrad, however, these rather dangerous intellectual refinements are illumined always by a vivid wealth of atmosphere, and translated simply by action, incident, strong light and shade, and distinctive colouring. The title of the present volume is perhaps a little misleading, but its sub-title explains: *Youth: a Narrative, and Two other Stories.* The story which gives its name to the book is emphatically a narrative, and of a very stirring sort. It fills some forty-seven pages, and deals, in the author's own manner, with the voyage of a little coal-laden barque from England to Bangkok. Then comes 'The Heart of Darkness,' consisting of a hundred and thirty odd pages, and lastly 'The End of the Tether,' a story of nearly two hundred pages. All three appeared in *Blackwood's Magazine*, and all three are better suited for publication and perusal in book form. 'Youth' is a wonderful narrative, an epic in little of the life of those who use the sea. It might very well have been called by any other name, since the mental attitude of its hero, of youthful zest and youthful appreciation of the dramatic and adventurous in life, is incidental to the story, and the most carefully drawn character is that of an old man, the skipper. There is not a wasted word in it, and it forms a valuable record, as well as a beautiful and vivid picture. 'The Heart of Darkness' is a big and thoughtful conception, the most important part of the book, as 'The End of the Tether' is the most fascinating. The first deals with life on the Congo and the Belgian ivory-hunt; the second is the story of a fine old merchant-service captain who finds himself rapidly becoming blind, and who, for the sake of the daughter who relies upon him for support, retains command of a coasting steamer among the Malays (where keen eyesight is perhaps a skipper's most essential qualification) long after he has ceased to be capable. A more deeply moving story it would be hard to find, vivid, full of movement, even of stirring inci-dent, yet piercingly analytic, and here and there almost too subtle in its descriptive *minutiæ*, as where the steamer-owner's cabin is described as showing 'no traces of pipe-ash even, which, in a heavy smoker, was morally revolting, like a manifestation of extreme hypocrisy.' Here, we think, intensity verges upon the kind of exaggeration which may become ridiculous. But the story is masterly.

The reviewer deliberately abstains both from quotation and from any attempt at analysis of a story like 'The Heart of Darkness.' Any such attempt in a limited space would be a painful injustice where work of this character is concerned. Further, the reader is warned that this book cannot be read understandingly—as evening newspapers and railway novels are perused—with one mental eye closed and the other roving. Mr. Conrad himself spares no pains, and from his readers he demands thoughtful attention. He demands so much, and, where the intelligent are concerned, we think he will command it.

56. George Gissing on Conrad

24 December 1902

Letter to Miss Collet (*Letters of George Gissing to members of his family*, ed. A. & E. Gissing, 1927, p. 391).

... Read Conrad's new book. He is the strongest writer—in every sense of the word—at present publishing in English. Marvellous writing! The other men are mere scribblers in comparison. That a foreigner should write like this, is one of the miracles of literature.

57. John Masefield, review, *Speaker*

31 January 1903, 442

John Masefield (1878–1967), English poet and novelist, served his apprenticeship on a windjammer and thus acquired a real knowledge of the sea. His earliest poetical work, *Salt Water Ballads*, appeared in 1902. He became Poet Laureate in 1930. Masefield was to write some very complimentary, though unsigned, reviews of Conrad's later work in the *Manchester Guardian*. William Rothenstein's comment on Conrad's attitude to Masefield is therefore intriguing: 'Masefield himself had a passionate admiration for Conrad. When later I got to know Conrad, I took him Masefield's *Salt Water Ballads*, and some of his stories; but Conrad had conceived one of his odd prejudices against Masefield, and indulged in a violent outburst against him.' Since Rothenstein had drawn Conrad's portrait by 1903, we can assume that he took Masefield's book to Conrad only a few months after this hostile review by Masefield. By this time, Conrad must have been tired of being compared to his detriment with Kipling and Stevenson (see letter to Pinker, *L&L*, ii, 250: 'Professional critics ... live on comparisons, because that is the easiest method of appreciation. Whereas I hate them, even if made in my favour').

Mr. Conrad's stories, excellent though they are, leave always a feeling of disappointment, almost of regret. His is a rare temperament, an exotic, a poetic temperament, and its artistic expression, though tense, nervous, trembling with beauty, is always a little elusive, a little alien, of the quality of fine gum from Persia, or of a precious silk from Ghilan.

In this volume Mr. Conrad gives us three stories, and in each shows a notable advance upon the technique and matter of his former work. His manner, indeed, shows a tendency towards the 'precious,' towards the making of fine phrases and polishing of perfect lines. He has filled his missal-marge with flowerets; he has planted his forest full of trees;

till both prayer and forest are in some danger of being hid. In the story called 'Youth,' and still more in the story called 'Heart of Darkness' (both of them stories written as told by one Marlow to a company of friends), he has set down page after page of stately and brilliant prose, which is fine writing, good literature, and so forth, but most unconvincing narrative. His narrative is not vigorous, direct, effective, like that of Mr. Kipling. It is not clear and fresh like that of Stevenson, nor simple, delicate, and beautiful like that of Mr. Yeats. It reminds one rather of a cobweb abounding in gold threads. It gives one a curious impression of remoteness and aloofness from its subject. Often it smells very palpably of the lamp, losing all spontaneity and becoming somewhat rhetorical. An instance of Mr. Conrad at his very best is to be found on page 39:

[quotes from 'Youth', pp. 34–5: 'Between the darkness . . . mass of coal within.']

That is finely said, with a keen feeling for rhythm, and with a subtle appreciation of the musical value of vowel sounds, but it is hardly the sort of thing a raconteur would say across the walnuts. Oil and the file went to the making of it, not the after-dinner glow, the wine-cup, and the circle of attentive friends.

The story from which we quote ('Youth') is the best of the three tales the book contains, and is, indeed, a valuable addition to our sea-literature. In 'Heart of Darkness' the author is too much cobweb, and fails, as we think, to create his central character. The third story, 'The End of the Tether,' is a more precise piece of creation, though a trifle tedious and diffuse. Prose and scenery cling round the central character like so much ivy, though the picturesqueness of the result is undeniable.

'Youth' is, without doubt, the best thing Mr. Conrad has done. Tales of just that quality are rare, and the book should establish Mr. Conrad in the high position he already holds, even if it should fail to add to his laurels.

TYPHOON, AND OTHER STORIES

22 April 1903

58. Unsigned review, *Morning Post*

22 April 1903, 3

Mr. Conrad is admittedly one of the most powerful writers of short stories, and there are many nowadays who write excellent short stories. Few, however, are as good as his. Mr. Kipling is the only one who can be compared with him. They have much in common. In the matter of style they are much on a level. Mr. Conrad's is perhaps less forced. Both again have written stories of the sea, but if we allow Mr. Kipling to be supreme on land, Mr. Conrad has no equal on the seas. His story of 'Typhoon' contains the most amazing description of the utter madness of the sea when tormented by a force almost as great as itself that we have ever read. And yet there is no apparent straining after effect. Of course, there is intention to give you the effect of something superhuman or infinitely inhuman. But there are different ways of achieving such an effect. Mr. Conrad does it in the most simple manner. It is the height of the storm, and you are to imagine yourself in the engine-room. Comes the sudden command to stop the engines.

[quotes 'Typhoon', part v: 'Nobody—not even . . . with her bows.']

It has only been possible to give hints, but is it not just right? You can feel the horror of it all and the terrible appalling beauty of that wonderful sea. But it is not only description of the elements at war with each other that you get in 'Typhoon.' There is slowly developed a magnificent picture of a man—not a magnificent man except when he fought the typhoon, and all for love of the ship, and because he was a man and a captain. Mr. MacWhirr has had his portrait done once for all, and there are many just like him who sail the seas, and no one is any the wiser for the splendid things they do in the darkness and with death at their elbows.

Another story which might almost be compared with 'Typhoon,' because of its portraiture of another extraordinary man, is that called 'Falk.' There is a strong dash of horror in it, but it in no way distresses you. Mr. Conrad has the courage of the artist who accepts all things as more or less explicable on reasonable lines. Falk was a huge man, a sort of savage if you like, yet intelligent and kindhearted. The description of him is curiously interesting. He had only one movement. He pulled his hands over his face and shuddered slightly. But the face remained unchanged. All the passion was in the hands. It is impossible to give an idea of the subtlety shown in drawing this portrait of an elemental creature like Falk. As the story progresses all resentment against him fades away, though when you know him and his story neither is attractive. Mr. Conrad, it must be stated, rather affects what is unaccustomed and even terrible in nature and in human nature. He does not altogether shine as a humourist. He affects those terrible imaginings which give us some glimpses of the pain and terror which have been and must be. The story of 'Amy Foster' is an illustration of this. Here you have a wretched Austrian, shipwrecked on an English coast, shunned by the natives, incapable of holding converse with them. One woman is attracted by him, marries him, and bears him a son. Then she becomes frightened of him—of the strange words that he speaks to his little son. He dies beseeching her to give him some water. She flies from him in blind terror. Then there is the last story of the volume, 'To-morrow.' Perfectly written, curiously imagined, it is a little master-piece. But there, again, you have a touch of the grotesque—the old man is waiting for his son, and growing quite mad in the process. He comes to expect him 'to-morrow.' The son does suddenly appear; but to the father 'to-day' does not exist—everything can only be explained in terms of 'to-morrow.' It is very good, but it is almost cruel. But what would you have? With such an imagination Mr. Conrad must do as he chooses, and we can only admire him. These four stories are sufficient in themselves to place the author in the first rank of living writers. There is a lack of that genial humour which makes what is terrible and full of pain less to be feared, but he wants nothing else. We are not even sure that he does want it. There is an ease and a quietness about his manner that suggests even greater breadth than appears. One can only wonder that Mr. Conrad is not more universally accepted as the fine master he is. Certainly no one has grasped so wondrously as he, and no one has expressed so finely, the mystery and terror of the sea and its effect on those who live on it.

59. Unsigned review, *Daily Mail*

22 April 1903, 4

This review was entitled 'The Sea between Covers: Mr. Joseph Conrad's New Book'. Conrad clearly had it in mind when he wrote his Author's Note to *Typhoon* in 1919: 'At its first appearance *Typhoon*, the story, was classed by some critics as a deliberately intended storm-piece'.

It is an accusation often brought against our literature that it produces few great writers inspired directly by the sea, although we are an island race, and owe our place among the nations to a conquest, both military and pacific, of the sea itself. It may be that England is only geographically, strategically, an island; it may be that our interests as a race are so wide and so complex that the sea has lost its meaning for us as an insulating, protecting element, and has come to be merely a belt or zone in our communications with the world. If this is so, it accounts for the fact that even those among our authors of distinction who write about the sea seldom give themselves wholly to its influence, or permit themselves to be wholly immersed in its mysterious, tragic melancholy.

Of those living writers of secured reputation who have been inspired by the sea, Mr. Kipling is still pre-eminent, for the simple reason that he is artist first and lover of the sea second. If, however, his best work, as some of us believe, has been that in which he has been most closely in touch with the great salt element, it still remains only a part of his work, and a small part at that. Mr. Clark Russell and Mr. Frank Bullen[1] come into a different class; they are specialists, with a limited range of subjects within which they are magnificent, but outside of which they make no special appeal to a sense of art or literature. But Mr. Joseph Conrad—who in this last book writes of the sea and the sea only, its moods and influences, the people who live upon it and by it—is more nearly than any existing author a real and intimate interpreter of the sea in literature.

[1] Frank Thomas Bullen (1857–1915), a sailor until 1883 and then a writer on the sea, is best known for the *Cruise of the Cachalot* (1898).

In this book he conveys exactly the right impression—that he does
not care about anything else but the sea; that he has no ear for any but
its voices; that he has no eye but for its furrowed expanse, its panoramic
scenery of storm and calm. His characters appear, as it is proper they
should, vaguely and in a half-light; it is only as the sea acts upon them
that Mr. Conrad sees and reveals them to us. The result of this treatment, conveyed through the medium of a vivid, elastic, and yet
dynamic style, simple where simplicity is needed, complex where
complexity is the note, is that we have a little epic of the sea and sea
life not far from perfect in its intimacy, its truth, its mastery.

Of the four stories contained in this volume, the first and longest,
'Typhoon,' is the most elaborate storm piece that one can recall in
English literature. It is nothing but an account of a cargo steamer in a
typhoon in the China Sea, with a subordinate study of her master,
Captain MacWhirr, and of his behaviour in new and staggering
circumstances. It comes near to deserving a description similar to that
which Stevenson applied to one of his own stories; it is a sonata of ships
and storms and breaking waves. One may give some idea of its
elaboration by quoting a passage in which the engine-room and its
occupants are under observation in the height of the storm:—

[quotes 'Typhoon', pp. 68–9: 'Gleams, like pale long flames . . . as a
sharp cry captures attention.']

Of the other three stories, 'Amy Foster' is the story of a village girl
who married a foreign, elemental creature who was shipwrecked at
her doors, and the developments of character consequent on their
marriage and parentage are brilliantly conveyed. But here, again, it is
not so much the characters in the story who live and move as the great
neighbouring sea that lives and moves within them, working out its
mysterious will, influencing them even beyond the margins of its
tides.

The third story, 'Falk,' is again a sea study, the characters a morose
pilot of a China river fairway and a German skipper and his family.
The river pilot, a strong, silent giant of a man, had once, in extremity,
eaten the flesh of men; and it weighed upon his conscience, shaming
him in the company of his fellows, combating the pride of sexual love
in him with a monstrous, Titanic struggle. The description of Hermann,
the German captain, has all the merit of obscure truth.

[quotes 'Falk', p. 148: 'With his shaven chin . . . act of tilting a water-
ing-pot.']

Perhaps one of the most remarkable of Mr. Conrad's qualities, and one that stamps him as a master, is his treatment of the passion of love. It is not the love of men and women in cities or in country places, nor is it the crude passion of the brute. It is a big and simple thing, primitive if you like, but primitive as ideal romance should be, knowing no civilised complications, comprehending no social interference. It sweeps through the lives of these sea people as a wind sweeps across and troubles the waters.

For those who know and love the element in which he rejoices, this book of Mr. Conrad's will come as a rare and valuable gift. Between its covers is caught and preserved some essence of the fragrance, the cleanness, the cruelty, the coldness, the hoary age, the salt youth of the sea. Nor need the reader fear monotony. Mr. Conrad is a consummate artist, and there is in these pages the variety of the sea. We are not always out of soundings; often we pass from the splendid and bursting clamour of the shore to some quiet garden where behind the sheltering wall ivy clings and small fragrant flowers unfold themselves in the silence.

60. Unsigned review, *Glasgow Evening News*

30 April 1903, 2

In a letter to Henry S. Canby, 7 April 1924 (*L & L*, ii, 342), Conrad wrote with reference to *The Nigger of the 'Narcissus'* that 'the problem that faces them is not a problem of the sea, it is merely a problem that has arisen on board a ship where the conditions of complete isolation from all land entanglements make it stand out with a particular force and colouring'. This review, antedating by some twenty years Conrad's remarks, puts forward a similar notion. The review was entitled 'Mr. Conrad's Philosophy'.

It is very probable that a good many readers, seduced by hearsay praise into taking up one of Mr. Conrad's books, have laid it down with the disappointed remark that 'there is no love in it.' As it happens, such a criticism, however banal and illiterate it may sound, is one which will occur with a good deal of force to readers considerably more discerning than the average young lady who is the mainstay of the novel-writer. In fact, it embodies the perception of a certain very notable characteristic of the author. It is true that in *Almayer's Folly* and again in *Lord Jim* we had subsidiary sketches of savage womanhood. But in his other tales Mr. Conrad has either ignored women, or at best made use of them as figures to fill a space in the background of his painting.

It is easy, of course, to frame more or less cheap and obvious explanations of this singular characteristic. Somebody said the other day that Mr. Conrad seems intent on giving us fiction without sex in it, as Stevenson wanted to do, and one might hazard the guess that we had here a hint of the conscientious artist trying to keep himself clear of the debasing influence of the love-story market. Mr. Conrad, however, knows as well as anyone that the more profoundly a writer deals with the relations of the sexes, the less likely he is to sink to the level of the love-story.

Another and much more plausible suggestion would be that Mr. Conrad has simply determined to write of the life he knows—the life of the sea and its strange Eastern shores—in which women have comparatively little part. This, too, might be held to account for another striking feature of his work, namely that he so persistently avoids the busy throngs, the common haunts of everyday life, expending all his strenuous skill on one or two isolated figures on some lonely ship, some desolate coast, or by-way of the world.

Somehow, the solution, plausible as it appears, is rather less than convincing. A writer of art so masterly, of understanding so sympathetically profound, is not to be held as limited in his outlook on life to a few odd bits of abnormal experience gathered in out-of-the-way corners. And it seems, to the present writer at least, that one must look for the explanation to something deeper in Mr. Conrad's philosophy of life. That something which seems to lie at the bottom of all his writing is his intensely individualistic regard. He has felt—possibly felt more than perceived—the essential loneliness of the human soul, face to face with the universe.

In all his writing one feels that his problem has been the revelation of the soul wrestling with or sinking beneath its own weakness, the elemental forces of Nature, or the mysterious force of circumstances —struggling, yielding, suffering, but always solitary, individual, isolated. It is not, indeed, that he bungles the relationship of his figures to each other—he is too sure in his grip of character for that. It is that character is for him an essentially individual creation, separate from, comparatively untouched by ordinary human relationship.

For this reason it is, surely, that he avoids so constantly alike the sexual factor and that social aspect of man which has so deeply modified the thought of the past century. While Zola, for example, always tended to make his characters mere social types, representative of great streams of tendency, Mr. Conrad, following rather the old mystics, pushes towards the other extreme of regarding his types as self-pivoted units, though, it is true, always with an aim less directly ethical and more artistic than that of Zola.

It is here, one conjectures, that one is able to detect the underlying tendency which directs his choice of subject to those simple sailor-folk, those crude and primitive souls who are by circumstance and nature cut off from all the complex inter-action of organised society, and therefore nearer the purely individual problems of existence. Unhampered by the superficial intricacy of social life, or the disturbing and fluctuating influences of sexual relations, he plunges into the inmost hearts of these beings, whose springs of action are so few and simple.

And he places them for us with art consummate in its powerful security against a background sometimes vague, sometimes luridly vast, but always serving to throw the human figures in the foreground into sharper relief.

Of the four stories which make up this volume, there is little of importance to be said, apart from the general artistic problem we have been discussing. While the title-story may be fairly set on an equal footing with that which gave its name to Mr. Conrad's last volume, *Youth*, the story of the cannibal sailor, Falk, hardly touches the level of the earlier 'Heart of Darkness' in its subtlety. The other two sketches, admirable as they are, lack importance mainly by reason of their themes. One returns inevitably to the question whether a writer, however masterly within his limits, can rank with the great masters of literature while he ignores some of the fundamental factors of human life. The answer must be that no artist can be classed with the Olympians without visibly possessing a philosophy of life rounded and adequate within the limitations of his age. Mr. Conrad's philosophy is not that yet. But one may perhaps look to the future with hope.

61. Unsigned notice, *Academy*

25 April 1903

The *Academy*'s comment on the praise Conrad received in the *New York American* is perhaps justified, but the *New York American* account does indicate something of the way in which Conrad's popularity was growing at this time.

The *New York American* has discovered that Mr. Joseph Conrad is the 'New Great Figure in Literature.' We read:—

In the early criticisms of his work Conrad was compared to Kipling and to Bret Harte. He is a greater than either. He equals their intimacy with their scenes and characters and presents them as vividly, but with this skill he combines a largeness of literary purpose and a universality beyond them.

Unlike Kipling, the mechanism of his composition is noiseless and all hidden. He leads you into brilliant passages and you are only dazzled, when you turn back the pages to re-read the lines that have moved you so deeply.

As for the people of his books, they are the actual beings of the life he describes. The second mate of a trading ship is a good enough hero for him. He can make a fascinating chapter of a ship sailing without incident over a glassy sea, and a whole book of a single storm—and make you regret there is not more of it.

When a man writes like this it does not matter what he writes about or whether he lays his scene in the Eastern seas or on Broadway. He chooses the background for his drama instead of fabricating a story to fit a background.

Every book he has written bears the unmistakable mark of genius. The stories he tells brim with life and strength and interest; the manner of their telling is as good as the matter.

There is a buoyant certainty about all this, but it is not criticism.

62. Unsigned review, *Academy*

9 May 1903, 463-4

Review entitled 'Mr. Conrad's Way'. Charles John Cutcliffe Wright Hyne (1865–1944) is especially remembered for *Captain Kettle*, the other book dealt with in this article.

Of the many orders of romance perhaps the romance of the sea is the most constant in its appeal, and this, primarily, because it touches so nearly the uncertainty of human life and brings men face to face with a force mysterious, alluring, and unconquerable. It represents the unknown, and demands a humble affection and something of a shuddering worship. In our time the cult of the sea has changed the tone of its interpreters; the old rollicking sea-story has still its representatives, but writers have arisen who have brought to the old subject a different outlook and a different method. They have seen with a more subjective eye and realised the inner meanings of power in relation to individual temperament. The first of the new school, perhaps, was Herman Melville, who is still, in his particular way, unapproached; but he did not bring to his subject the creative imagination which we find, say, in the work of Mr. Kipling and Mr. Conrad.

Two books largely concerned with the sea lie before us: Mr. Conrad's *Typhoon* and Mr. Cutcliffe Hyne's *Captain Kettle, K.C.B.* Mr. Hyne treats the sea jovially, objectively, in a way vividly; he understands the handling of a ship and he gives us characters reasonably in keeping with their environment. Captain Kettle is something of a creation; he has stood the strain of several volumes, and in this latest volume we are glad to meet him again. But Captain Kettle is, after all, a convention; he occupies a stage and appeals to the suffrages of a popular audience. He is presented from the outside; we never approach to any intimacy with the soul of the man. This does not detract from the excellence of Mr. Hyne's work; it merely marks its limitations; limitations, no doubt, deliberately accepted by the author as necessary to a popular scheme. Mr. Conrad, on the other hand, has no idea of popular appeal; he is a writer who is so possessed with the terror and wonder and beauty of the sea that he brings to his work a sense, as it were, of profound responsibility, a consciousness of vastness and of wide and sinister horizons. And against this background move his characters—characters most faithfully observed, alive, full of nerve, or smitten down by the fear of sudden and awful death. We never question the truth of Mr. Conrad's characters. We may sometimes dislike his method, we may find fault with his construction, but the essential human element of his dramas stands beyond cavil. In a word, his psychology has the accuracy of brilliant diagnosis.

Many critics have complained of Mr. Conrad's indirectness; he leaves his main theme to go off on a side issue, to introduce the point of view of a minor character into his narrative, to pick up a thread apparently dropped with something of the carelessness of a child. There is reason in the complaint; though, for ourselves, we are willing to accept Mr. Conrad's work just as it stands. For this indirectness, this returning upon himself, this effect, often disconcerting, of an abruptly introduced outside comment, are inherent parts of the extraordinary subjectivity of Mr. Conrad's method. When Jukes, in the 'Typhoon,' is writing to his friend in the Western Ocean trade we feel that Mr. Conrad is endeavouring to correct his own conception of Captain MacWhirr by the commonplace conception of the first mate; the result is to heighten the effect of MacWhirr's simplicity, stolidity, and sublimely unimaginative pluck. The course of the terrific storm is followed with a cumulative and crashing power; it is, indeed, the typhoon itself which is the vital personality of the story; it is against that implacable monster that the battle is waged in turmoil and darkness. Mr. Conrad has the rare faculty of investing with a kind of savage personality the forces which are themselves subject to the unknown and invisible force which is at the heart of the world. His winds move upon the clamourous waters like driven and helpless deities. We must quote a passage from 'Typhoon.' The storm has not yet reached its climax, but the boats are going. Jukes sees 'two pairs of davits leaping black and empty out of the solid blackness':—

[quotes 'Typhoon', ch. 3: 'He poked his head forward . . . stands to reason.']

The main incident of 'Typhoon' is the fight amongst the battened-down Chinamen when their boxes break loose and the hoarded dollars get adrift; it is an admirably told incident, but just in that place we hardly need it, it is not one of Mr. Conrad's characteristic digressions. It strikes us, indeed, as an interpolation, a concession to those who insist on incident. Mr. Conrad, in our view, should make no concessions.

The remaining stories in the volume deal less directly with the sea, though through all of them runs the note of it, and over all of them broods the spirit of it. 'Falk' is a most remarkable study; it illustrates Mr. Conrad's way in Mr. Conrad's most elaborate manner. It is as certain that no other living author could have written it as that no other living author would have attempted it. In its way, the thing is architectural, or rather, like a mosaic, built up out of infinite fragments. The heart or secret of it is almost unimportant; we should have been content to let Falk's misfortune remain undiscovered. We are almost inclined to resent anything in the nature of a plot in Mr. Conrad's work; he has no need of adventitious aids. He is an interpreter not of incidents mechanically contrived, but of moods and the human spirit. At times we seem to hear a cry of revolt, the first breathings of a passionate protest against the pain and mystery of the world; again, we are carried away by the splendid energy of action and the insurgence of immortal youth. Mr. Conrad is one of the few writers who think intently and express lucidly; the apparent diffuseness of his method indicates the eager searching of a masterful mind.

The story in this volume called 'Amy Foster' is a piece of true tragedy—the tragedy of attraction and misunderstanding. But the misunderstanding is not of that sort which is the current coin of fiction, it is rather an absolute lack of understanding which reaches to the deeps of essential and inevitable tragedy. The simplicity of it leaves no room for side issues; from first to last we are engrossed by the narrative as by a dream made actual. Here is bare life, handled with extraordinary skill—life free from any kind of sentimentality, bare to the nerve. The concluding story is more commonplace both in idea and treatment, yet one of the characters raises it far above the level of ordinary fiction. Mr. Conrad can give us in a few strong touches the history of a quiet, half-developed and baffled soul.

There is no secret about Mr. Conrad's power: he who runs may read and understand. It lies in an intense reality of observation, a profound sense of the mystery of all creation, a deep pity for the human tragedy, and an unshakable belief in the joyous possibilities of life. This, of course, should be the full equipment of every writer who essays to interpret life; we know how seldom any writer has a real grip of even one of these necessary qualities. Mr. Conrad, of course, has faults; it would be easy to criticise certain points in any one of these stories. But before such distinct achievement criticism may well lay down its arms. To recall in quietness the massed impressions which this volume leaves with us is to be convinced that in Mr. Conrad we have a writer whose work is worthy of a time which, though great in a hundred ways, is still not great in literary expression. Mr. Conrad is great in literary expression; but he is greater in a breadth of outlook which takes into account the actual forces which move and console the world.

63. A. T. Quiller-Couch, review, *Bookman*

June 1903, 108-9

This review was entitled 'Four Tales by Mr. Conrad'. It is dis-appointing and shows up Q's limitations as a critic when he places 'To-morrow' as 'the finest essentially' in the collection.

Of men writing fiction just now many are wonderful to me; but the two most wonderful, being almost admirable, are Mr. Henry James and Mr. Joseph Conrad. I am not thinking just now of that particular wonder which is excited by a touch of genius—in a tale, say, by Mr. Barrie or by Mr. Kipling. Genius in itself is always wonderful; but anyone decently acquainted with literature ought to be familiar enough with the shock produced by it. You know the method; you follow it with joy and delight; you come upon the stroke which you know to be masterly, and say, 'Here—just here—is the thing which only one man in ten thousand can do.' It astonishes; nevertheless you may be said in a fashion to understand it. But Mr. James and Mr. Conrad move in an atmosphere in which I feel myself inexpert, and follow as an amateur, fairly active on another level, stumbles after a Swiss guide. I know that here is good literature; I guess that it is literature touched with genius; I am pleased and even proud to find myself enjoying it whole-heartedly, instead of falling foul of it as certain minds fall foul of Maeterlinck,[1] for instance, because he happens to talk strangely. Still, as an experimenter, over many years, in more objective methods of story-telling (and as a convinced believer, let me say, that the synthetical, objective method of presenting your characters is so much the better than the analytical, as it is the briefer), I begin to stare helplessly when Mr. James and Mr. Conrad tuck up their sleeves and begin to weave a situation round with emotions, scruples, doubts, hesitancies, misunderstandings, understandings, half-understandings; cutting the web sometimes with the fiercest of strokes; anon patiently spinning it again for another slice; and always moving with the calmness of men entirely sure of their methods, and confident that the end of the tale will justify them—as it always does.

Of the four tales in this new volume of Mr. Conrad's I should (from my own inveterate point of view) call the last, entitled 'To-morrow,' the finest essentially. It tells of an old man with a missing son, who is always to return 'to-morrow'; and of a girl forced to listen to his unending tale, until this prospectively returning prodigal becomes a real figure to her; and of the son actually turning up at last—half in jest—only to be beaten from the door by his crazy father, and to wound the heart of the girl—how subtly yet poignantly, you must go to the story to discover. It is brilliantly told, yet not more brilliantly than the first tale 'Typhoon'—a small masterpiece in the style of *The Nigger of the 'Narcissus'* built around a delightfully humourous character. I don't know when downright matter-of-factness (call it not Scotch!) has been more happily hit off than in Captain MacWhirr of the ss. *Nan-Shan*; witness his argument with the chief mate, Mr. Jukes, whose feelings were hurt by the steamer's transference from the British to the Siamese flag:

[quotes ch. 1: 'The first morning . . . Union Jack in the flag.']

Of the other two stories, 'Amy Foster' seems to me not quite worthy of the author of 'Youth,' and 'Falk' is spoilt for me by a natural repugnance, which perhaps has nothing to do with criticism. But the book as a whole proves amply that Mr. Conrad is not, as some feared, a worker on a vein of ore which may run thin and disappear; that

---

[1] Maurice Maeterlinck (1862–1949) poet and dramatist. His play *Pélleas et Mélisande* was used by Debussy for his opera. Maeterlinck was awarded the Nobel prize for literature in 1911.

romance with him is rather a spring running fresh and strong, and able to fill as many buckets as time may allow to be brought to it. He has too fine a conscience to permit the buckets to be brought too fast.

64. Unsigned review, *Speaker*

6 June 1903, 238–9

While we are waiting for Mr. Conrad to eclipse *Lord Jim* with another really important novel, we welcome such interesting exercises in his art as he gives us in the four stories which make up the volume before us. They are characteristic stories, all directly or indirectly concerned with the sea, Mr. Conrad's source of inspiration, and all written with more or less of that intensity which characterised *Lord Jim* and the earlier short stories, and which seems to suggest that the stories had to get themselves written, whether Mr. Conrad wanted to write them or not.

It is difficult to say which holds the imagination most, the story of the terrible storm through which the *Nan Shan* and her commonplace, unimaginative captain, MacWhirr, passed, with a cargo of coolies battened down under hatches; or the story of Falk, the monopolist pilot of some Eastern river, who had proved himself the best man even at the expense of cannibalism, which, in his days of solitude, hung round him as a curse, though not a remorse, till he found companionship in marriage; or the story of the great misery of isolation which tells of a Suabian peasant wrecked on the South Coast of England, meeting with a reception which one would merely call unfriendly were it not for the piteous effect it had on the mind of the beautiful stranger. Perhaps the last is the most astonishing example of Mr. Conrad's power of building up an effect. It is one of the most perfect short stories we have ever read. It opens with a description of a peaceful south country village on the seashore—everything, martello tower, church spire, and farmyard, combining to make a picture of one of the most familiar of home scenes that suggest quietness and uneventful lives. Yet here come mystery and fear, the most horrible. They come, too, in a beautiful form, for the Suabian peasant who is washed ashore when the emigrant ship is sunken in the bay is like a young Greek god.

[gives an outline of the plot]

The fourth story has not the same intensity as the other three. It tells of an old man who lives for the return of his only son who has run away to sea as a boy. He believes that he will be back 'to-morrow,' and saves for him and plans out his life in that belief. The son, who has suffered as a boy from the arbitrariness of the father, comes back at last, but the father refuses to admit him because it is not 'to-morrow.' The story is saved from the mere cleverness of the good magazine tale by the fine interview between the girl whom Captain Hagberd has destined for his son and the young roving sailor himself, and the whole story is enlightened by the last sentence. The son has gone, and the father rejoices at having 'got rid at last of "something wrong." ' This is how it appears to the distracted Bessie: 'It was as if all the hopeful madness of the world had broken out to bring terror upon her heart, with the voice of that old man shouting his trust in an everlasting to-morrow.'

Mr. Conrad is in the line of our great writers of the romance of the sea, Smollett, Michael Scott[1] and Marryat, and he has also introduced something new into our fiction. By no other author have we had the psychology of action so subtly and yet so vividly presented. There are times in reading his work when we think that Stevenson with new experiences has taken up his work when it broke off in his noble fragment *Weir of Hermiston*, and there are others when we think we are reading a translation of a work by Tolstoi or Maxim Görki. But always we realise that Mr. Conrad writes from the fullness of his own experience—passing through a mind that with great and almost painful efforts snatches from it some secret of life and reveals it in the glow of a brilliant imagination.

---

[1] Michael Scott (1789–1835), Scottish author, went to the West Indies but returned and settled in Glasgow. He wrote stories such as *Tom Cringle's Log* (1829–33) and *The Cruise of the Midge* (1834–5).

65. Conrad on writing *Nostromo*

1903–17

(a) Extract from a letter to R. B. Cunninghame Graham, 8 July 1903 (*LCG*, p. 145):

I am dying over that cursed *Nostromo* thing. All my memories of Central America seem to slip away. I just had a glimpse 25 years ago—a short glance. That is not enough pour bâtir un roman dessus. And yet one must live.

(b) Extract from a letter to John Galsworthy, 22 August 1903 (*L&L*, i. 317):

The book is, this moment, half done and I feel half dead and wholly imbecile . . . I feel myself strangely growing into a sort of outcast. A mental and moral outcast. I hear nothing—think of nothing—I reflect upon nothing—I cut myself off—and with all that I can just only keep going . . .

(c) Extract from a letter to J. B. Pinker, 22 August 1903 (*L&L*, i. 315–16):

This is half of the book, about 42,000 or so. . . . I have never worked so hard before—with so much anxiety. But the result is good. You know I take no credit to myself for what I do—and so I may judge my own performance. There is no mistake about this. You may take up a strong position when you offer it here. It is a very genuine Conrad. At the same time it is more of a Novel pure and simple, than anything I've done since *Almayer's Folly*.

(d) Extract from *A Personal Record* (pp. 98–9), Conrad's account of being interrupted while writing *Nostromo*:

All I know, is that, for twenty months, neglecting the common joys of life that fall to the lot of the humblest on this earth, I had, like the prophet of old, 'wrestled with the Lord' for my creation, for the headlands of the coast, for the darkness of the Placid Gulf, the light on the snows, the clouds on the sky, and for the breath of life that had to be blown into the shapes of men and women, of Latin and Saxon, of Jew and Gentile. These are, perhaps, strong words, but it is difficult to characterise otherwise the intimacy and the strain of a creative effort in which mind and will and conscience are engaged to the full, hour after hour, day after day, away from the world, and to the exclusion of all that makes life really lovable and gentle . . .

'How do you do?'

It was the greeting of the General's daughter. . . . I jumped up from my chair stunned and dazed, every nerve quivering with the pain of being uprooted out of one world and flung down into another—perfectly civil.

(e) Extract from a letter to Edward Garnett, 3 September 1904 (*LEG*, p. 190):

I drop you these lines just to say that *Nostromo* is finished; a fact upon which my friends may congratulate me as upon a recovery from a dangerous illness.

(f) Extract from Author's Note to *Nostromo* (p. xviii):

It took the best part of the years 1903–4 to do; with many intervals of renewed hesitation, lest I should lose myself in the ever-enlarging vistas opening before me as I progressed deeper in my knowledge of the country. Often, also, when I had thought myself to a standstill over the tangled-up affairs of the Republic, I would, figuratively speaking, pack my bag, rush away from Sulaco for a change of air and write a few pages of the 'Mirror of the Sea.' But generally, as I've said before, my sojourn on the Continent of Latin America, famed for its hospitality, lasted for about two years. On my return I found (speaking somewhat in the style of Captain Gulliver) my family all well, my wife heartily glad to learn that the fuss was all over, and our small boy considerably grown during my absence.

66. Arnold Bennett on *Nostromo*

22 November 1912

Arnold Bennett to Joseph Conrad (*LAB*, ii, 321–2). Higuerota, the mountain in *Nostromo*—'The dawn breaks high behind the towering and serrated wall of the Cordillera, a clear-cut vision of dark peaks . . . Amongst them the white head of Higuerota rises majestically upon the blue' (*Nostromo*, pp. 5–6). In reply to Bennett's letter Conrad wrote: 'The joy your praise of that novel has given me is immense. With the public it was the blackest possible frost', letter of 25 November 1912 (*L&L*, ii, 143).

I read *Higuerota* again not long since. I always think of that book as *Higuerota*, the said mountain being the principal personage in the story. When I first read it I thought it the finest novel of this generation (bar none), and I am still thinking so. It is 'majestic and orbicular' and just peerless, and there's no more to be said. It's the Higuerota among novels.

67. Conrad as a personality in modern literature

Academy, 20 February 1904

This account, whilst jejune, does indicate that Conrad had 'arrived'.

Since Mr. Joseph Conrad wrote *The Nigger of the 'Narcissus'* there has been no question of his being a personality in modern literature, and personalities in modern literature are not too numerous. His point of view, his knowledge, his mode of expression are emphatically his own.

I have a theory that it is almost impossible to entirely understand a man's work without knowing something of the man. The personality of the artist is often the explanatory note of his art. This is, of course, the apology of the journalist who is responsible for interviews and personal sketches, and there is much to be said for it.

Unfortunately, perhaps, the man whose work is most worth understanding is generally most loth to supply this personal annotation. Genius is often shy, and to this rule Mr. Joseph Conrad is not an exception.

I once 'interviewed' Mr. Conrad and I vividly remember the terror with which he regarded me when he met me at the station. Happily I was soon able to convince him I had no curiosity for trivial impertinences, and it was my fortune, while chatting to him in an old-world farmhouse garden through a long summer afternoon, to catch something of his unique individuality.

Joseph Conrad is a Pole and a sailor—in itself a strange combination. Born far inland, he caught the sea fascination in some mystic way in his youth and was never contented till he lived upon it. Essentially a stylist in English, it is only to him a borrowed language, though his love for it may perhaps be not a little due to the fact that he learnt it from East Coast fishermen with whom he worked for a while.

I can think of no other instance of a foreigner learning to write English as Mr. Conrad writes it, while certainly few native writers

have anything approaching his veneration for its beauties and its possibilities. He takes infinite pains to express thoughts and ideas in what
to him is the most perfect manner. In a real sense he is an artist in
words.

Here then are the facts of the personality that surely illustrate the
work—a Pole, one of the strange unconquerable race that Seton
Merriman[1] called the 'Frenchmen of the North,' a sailor with a poet's
insight and imagination, and a foreigner with a knowledge of more
than one other language, deliberately choosing English for the expression of his imaginings.

In appearance Mr. Conrad suggests the seaman. His figure is stalwart and short, his dark beard well trimmed, and his walk nautical.
Meet him near the docks and one would write him down 'ship's
captain' without hesitation.

But his eyes, curiously distinctive and striking, mark him out from
his kind. Ship captain he may be, but his eyes proclaim him an artist.

It is some time since my talk with Mr. Conrad, but he is not a man
to be easily forgotten, for, apart from his personal charm, he has all
the qualities to include him within Schopenhauer's famous definition
of genius: 'The mind of genius is among other minds what the car-
buncle is among precious stones, it sends forth light of its own, while
the others reflect only that which they have received.'

One remark of Mr. Conrad's is worth quoting as illustrating his
attitude to criticism:—

'Praise and blame to my mind are of singularly small import, yet
one cares for the recognition of a certain ampleness of purpose.'

[1] Henry Seton Merriman, pseudonym of Hugh Stowell Scott (1862–1903), a novelist
in the tradition of Dumas—*The Sowers* (1896) and *The Velvet Glove* (1901).

68. Unsigned review,
The Times Literary Supplement

21 October 1904, 320.

We have heard it urged by fairly intelligent judges against *Lord Jim*, which we consider Mr. Conrad's finest novel, that its unwinding is intolerable. For ourselves it is more than tolerable, such is the fascination of Mr. Conrad's conscientious method when applied to such a problem as Jim presented. But what we shall reply when the same critics impugn the unwinding of his new book, *Nostromo*, we dare not think; for its defence, even among Mr. Conrad's most stalwart upholders, will not be easy. The fact is that in *Nostromo* Mr. Conrad has definitely succumbed to a danger which must often have beset him—he has made a novel of a short story. When he began *Lord Jim*, we understand, he intended it to run through a number or so of *Blackwood* and come out the length of his 'Typhoon' or thereabouts; and behold it grew under his hands, became worthier and yet more worthy of the expenditure of his genius, until it stands now secure in its place as one of the finest (and longest) of our later novels. In *Nostromo* the very reverse has happened; Mr. Conrad has written and written his five hundred pages, only to discover that it was in essence a short story after all. In the result the book is rather like one of those modern scenic plays where the drama is overwhelmed by machinery. We do not object to an author's finding his way by first losing it, or at any rate by first trying many others—probably it is the safest means—but we do object to being taken with him on the search. In other words, we think that the publication of this book as it stands is an artistic mistake. Let Mr. Conrad write his way in as he will, but let us be called upon to join him only when he has found it. The first third of *Nostromo* should have been compressed into a few pages. The story—another of Mr. Conrad's studies in self-respect—tells us how a Genoese sailor, a slave to the good opinion of others, in a South American port sinks to theft and his own contempt. The actual relation of Nostromo's tragedy, which occupies less than half of the book, is always strong and moving; Mr. Conrad's hand there is sure, his sympathy lively. There is a scene, in his best manner, of three men at night on a lighter, in imminent peril of being run down by a steamer; a scene, in his best manner—a manner quite unique—of two men fencing intellectually by the dead body of a third; and in each of these scenes it is, we feel, the presence of Nostromo that nerves the author to do greatly. The book has other passages that are fine, but for the most part the narrative is allegation rather than proof—a long and not too absorbing history of revolutions and revolutionary motives, of plot and counter-plot. The drama of Nostromo, and his friends the Violas, is apart, although it is in reality the only matter. What we maintain is that a writer of Mr. Conrad's genius, in order to introduce Nostromo's case, should not have to ask us to accompany him, backwards and forwards, through such a labyrinth of South American politics and into the careers of so many persons. Mr. Conrad's retrospective habit has always been a little difficult to follow; but in *Nostromo* there are moments when it is impossible to feel sure whether the past or the present is being described. All this, which is at its worst in the first two hundred pages of the book, before the narrative really becomes single, ought, we think, to have been ruthlessly cut. Many readers will never survive it. Yet Mr. Conrad is Mr. Conrad, his mind is his own, and always curiously interesting. Hence *Nostromo*, although a shapeless work, is yet a shapeless work by a man of genius, satisfying only occasionally, but never undistinguished. Shapelessness is its only fault. The writing is always good, the character drawing is always subtle, and now and then the author gives us an unforgettable figure—the old Garibaldino, Nostromo himself, the dispirited and disillusioned Dr. Monygham, and Martin Decoud of the Parisian boulevards, who would overthrow a State for the fun of it. But as a whole *Nostromo* is disappointing. It is not on a level with Mr. Conrad's best work.

69. Unsigned notice, *Review of Reviews*

1 November 1904, 539

Then there is Mr. Conrad's *Nostromo*, though it is hardly up to the level of his previous work.

70. Unsigned notice, *Black and White*

5 November 1904, 668

The reviewer had already reviewed *There and Back* by Frank Richardson, *The Affair at the Inn* by Kate Douglas Wiggin, and *Park Lane* by Percy White, before coming to *Nostromo*.

Oddly enough, the humour of the books I have mentioned seems to me to be far more in tune with reality than are most of the so-called serious volumes that have recently been published. I do not understand, for example, what truth of life Mr. Joseph Conrad intended to represent when he decided to write *Nostromo*. There are South American silver mines here, and stolen treasure, and love, and fighting, and civil uprisings in abundance. Here is the stuff either of romance or of fierce realism, according as the artist chooses. Mr. Conrad, however, has hidden what grain of romance or of realism was in him under a multitude of words and lowering paragraphs. Only here and there does he now catch anything of the terrible mystery of the sea. Only here and there does he come in touch with the still more terrible mysteries of the human heart. In *The Nigger of the 'Narcissus'* he set afloat a cockleshell of plot on a sea of marvellous descriptive passages. But in *Nostromo*, unfortunately, the descriptive passages themselves are not marvellous.

71. Unsigned review, *Daily Telegraph*

9 November 1904, 4

Mr. Joseph Conrad's work is stamped with an abounding personality. There is something tempestuous in the manner in which he flings himself upon his work. He has many of the qualities which go to the making of a great novelist; ideas, characters, situations throng so thickly round him that he is unable to cope with them. He has extraordinary vigour of conception, his canvas is immense, and yet it is overcrowded. He sees clearly, he describes vividly. He has almost a touch of genius, yet not enough of that divine spark to atone for the lack of artistic instinct which always mars his work as a whole. Not for the first time do we regret the inability to see the wood for the trees. True, each tree stands distinct and strong, well grown, clearly defined, brilliant or subdued in colouring, but the beauty of the scene as a whole is lost, the sense of proportion is absent. While parts of *Nostromo* have an absorbing interest, the impression is not preserved when the book is viewed in its entirety. It has longueurs of a wearisome nature; vital situations hang fire while the author indulges in characteristic digressions; detail absorbs the position of outline, which becomes impossibly blurred; the story which held us by its vigour, its wide human interest, becomes narrowed to some small personal issue; the spell is broken.

Had Mr. Conrad the selective gift which has been denied him, his book might well have proved a master-piece. The initial conception of Charles Gould, slowly dominated by the idea which had been his father's undoing, steering it to success when to his father it had meant ruin, is fine. The Gould concession, the San Tomé silver mine of

Sulaco, had been forced upon Gould, senior, by the intrigues of a venal South American Republic. It had haunted him, preyed upon him, killed him. To his son, kept apart from this vampire of the family fortune in his youth, it had revealed itself under another guise; it was at once his revenge, his triumph, and his divinity. To the woman who in their mutual youth had shared his love, his aspirations, his ambitions, it became the cruellest of rivals; it broke her heart, though she said no word. The San Tomé mine became an important asset in the politics of Costaguana, and in these politics we find ourselves immersed. Gradually the attraction with which the Goulds had inspired us fades; they fall into the background, and are absorbed in the crowd. Other issues supervene, the original interest disappears. Yet, in some strange way, this original conception of the man dominated by the spirit of a treasure hidden in the earth which, becoming his evil genius, withers all that is fine and generous—even human—in his nature, endures though the person of the protagonist changes, and Nostromo steps into the foreground—Nostromo, the factotum of the Oceanic Steam Navigation Company, indeed, of all the European population of Sulaco. We see dimly the effect at which the author is aiming; many of the means which he uses to arrive at it are admirable; but the faculty of construction being absent, he fails to achieve it in the end.

Mr. Conrad shows an extraordinary power in dealing with his minor characters. Don José Avellanos, Don Pépé, Martin Decoud, Dr. Monygham, Giorgio Viola are drawn with wonderful insight and with an elaboration which makes each figure a careful study, a human document. The author is not content with giving us each man as he is, he goes far back into the past, showing us the hidden springs which have gone to the moulding and making of the man of to-day. This method, while it gives a remarkable individuality to each person, hampers materially the progress of the book. But it is characteristic of the writer. We must accept him as he is. Curiously enough in his handling of the most conspicuous figures he has been less successful. An admirable portrait of Nostromo in the early stages of his career is presented to us, but the strange, unexpected change in the man, his deterioration under the influence of the hidden treasure, is scamped. We are told of the facts, but are hardly allowed to watch the subtle working of the spell. And a similar criticism may be applied to Charles Gould whose youthful years, hopes, and ideals are so carefully chronicled, but whose personality is allowed to evaporate as the book progresses. But perhaps our greatest regret lies in the failure of interest in Mrs. Gould after the first half of the book. Mr. Conrad's inability, or, shall we say, disinclination to concern himself with the delineation of feminine nature, has often been commented upon. It seemed as if on this occasion he would transcend his limitations. And, indeed, in Mrs. Gould, as we first meet her, he gives us a very beautiful, lovable picture. But it is only a sketch. It is never permitted to develop, it remains in statu quo.

72. C. D. O. Barrie, review, *British Weekly*

10 November 1904, 129

Nostromo sounds the call to meet adventure: Mr. Conrad, however, does not summon us to melodrama. He offers, instead, a serious study of human characters, working, indeed, in an atmosphere volcanic with action and passion, but all fitly causing tragedy.

When at the opening of the novel we are asked to know Captain Mitchell, 'a thick, elderly man, wearing high, pointed collars and short side-whiskers, partial to white waistcoats, and really very communicative under his air of pompous reserve,' we are entering a society where every fresh introduction proves Mr. Conrad possessed of that first quality of a novelist, the power of making his men and women not only recognisable as real and in a real world, but inevitably the subject of curiosity. Nor are we hopelessly in his secret and their confidence from the first.

So far, in fact, is interest excited that we take refuge in criticisms, are angry with Nostromo's reticence, and complain that we too seldom have his company. For Mr. Conrad is master of the ceremonies, and will not have his chief figure always seen. Nostromo, with his 'peculiar talent when anything striking to the imagination has to be done,' is a Mediterranean sailor. He has deserted into Sulaco, the seaport of Costaguana, a convulsive South American republic, and there, with the position and pay of Capataz de Cargadores or foreman of the wharf, is engaged in playing hero to the populace and practical providence to the Europeans. So this magnificent Nostromo, too garish never to be extravagant, and too useful never to be incredible, is by intention only heard of until his peculiar talent can be shown.

With such easy power of writing of character it is natural that the most insistent merit of the book is its life. There is a sense of movement through every chapter. A reader feels he must reckon personally with the emotions of the men and the deliberations of the women, the very white mules beat their hoofs audibly in the dusty road. Then there is the country of romance whither we have sailed before the wind of Mr. Conrad's imagination—to meet his people. Scenery, to be given the glamour of bright, loose robes or glances from dark eyes, is built slowly above our horizon or springs into view at the turning of a page. Thus 'There is the Great Isabel; the Little Isabel which is round; and Hermosa which is the smallest.' It is not much, but we have seen the three Isabels, come upon them lying there in the bay of Sulaco.

Judged as an ordinary story, however, *Nostromo* is not well told. The plot is confused; the tale does not run smoothly from incident to incident; it is often difficult to say when or where we are. But the object of a good novel is the display of character, and this is no bold-tongued narrative of an adventurer. Mr. Conrad has not a cunning plot to unravel. He would have us acquainted with a number of men and women and scenes among which figured his Nostromo, 'a man for whom the value of life seems to consist in personal prestige,' and he takes the world's way to achieve his end. So we also must have imagination wherewith to understand hints and broaden glimpses. Real life has few confessionals.

Thus there is a breadth and vigour and freshness about Mr. Conrad's method as well as boldness in his character conception and vividness of description. It is as though he had chosen a new way to impart reality. The story reaches us by all manner of accidental natural ways—hearsay, narrative, conversation, letter. Lists of facts worked out in sequence do not come to give pause for humdrum satisfaction. Instead, we capture information and are fascinated; we appease curiosity. The method of thus directly holding up the mirror is so well managed as to leave an effect of extraordinary vividness. We have no feeling that an actual life would require touching up to be thus logical. *Nostromo* is so excellent a novel that it demands judgment of the highest standard, originality.

73. Unsigned review, *Manchester Guardian*

2 November 1904, 5

Mr. Conrad's collaboration with Mr. Ford Madox Hueffer in *Romance* seemed to mark a relaxation from the strenuous period of *Lord Jim* and *Heart of Darkness*. This latest story does not follow with a single mind the spiritual history of an individual, and so it lacks, perhaps, something of the intensity and concentration that we associate with some of its predecessors; but it is a very serious and absorbing piece of work, and it contains several remarkable characters and many striking and picturesque ones. Mr. Conrad has imagined again a vast and solemn world full of passion and mystery, and he has risen indomitably to cope with this tremendous nature of his imagination. There is again that blend of character and adventure that gives to his books such an extraordinary quality, and he is once more the story-teller who cares immensely about the means, and, unhastening, dwelling on the intense life of the moment or pursuing the episode to its vital issues, seems sometimes to lose sight of the end or to obscure the design. While he is content to hint at things that seem of prime importance, he enlarges along unexpected lines, and we are compelled to follow, until at last, it may be, we perceive something of a design that is independent of formal construction and follows the bent of a peremptory instinct. We may have some lingering regret that our great novelists to-day do not happen to take any of the ways of popularity, and Mr. Conrad with this story can hardly hope for any wide extension of that patience and sympathy that must with some readers precede the amazed absorption in his narratives. But though his exposition is not easily grasped and the interests are so active and insistent that the scope seems at first to widen beyond our control, the art of the narrative does at last bring the strange array of characters and figures into significant relation. Most of us have from time to time read idly of some crisis or revolution in a South American republic, and perhaps dismissed idly the 'farcical' episodes in the life of a community which seems to change its government with the weather. It is to one of these episodes—the separation of the 'Occidental Republic' from 'Costaguana'—that Mr.

Conrad has addressed himself. It need hardly be said that he does not lack the humorous perception of the events that he records, and in a corner of the world that is hardly worthy of our perfunctory and impatient regard he finds a richness and variety of life that cannot be matched in our careful civilisations.

A prime mover in the great liberal revolution of Costaguana is General Montero, and here is his finely graduated description:—

[quotes from part i, ch. 8, p. 122: 'On one side, General Montero . . . the homage of worshippers.']

And this barbaric ruffian has had as a predecessor in usurped power the atrocious Guzman, of whom it is said that 'the power of supreme government had become in his dull mind an object of strange worship, as if it were some sort of cruel deity.' Against such forces are ranged respectable patriots, vaporous Parliamentarians, a general who had received a command out of consideration for his creditors. Prominent, too, among the institutions which make for stability and order is the San Tomé Mine, the great silver concession, worked by Gould, an Englishman of Costaguanan birth. The rapacity of the various un-scrupulous adventurers is centred in this mine, which plays a great part in the story. From a welter of revolutionary, rapacious, or con-servative parties, into the details of which it would be vain to enter, a remarkable character emerges in Martin Decoud, a Spanish creole of Parisian traditions,

[quotes Nostromo, part ii, ch. 3: '. . . an idle boulevardier. . . . intellectual superiority.']

To such a man 'any government anywhere is a thing of exquisite comicality' and Costaguanan politics are a burlesque. But, contemptu-ous as is Mr. Conrad's description, it is no dismissal, and it is a significant stroke of irony that the creation of a new republic is primarily the work of Decoud, who promotes a revolution as a detail in the pursuit of his amour—an amour, it must be said, of a quality that redeems him from the stagnation of a mere idler. To Decoud, Gould, with his intense preoccupation in his work, is one of 'the people who will never do anything for the sake of their passionate desire unless it comes to them clothed in the fair robes of an idea,' for Decoud has a perfect intellec-tual perception of the qualities he despises. He sees in Gould's relations with his wife the subtle wrong, 'the sentimental unfaithfulness which surrenders her happiness, her life, to the seduction of an idea,' while he, in Mr. Conrad's fine antithesis, will sacrifice all to the service of his passion. In the growing interest and excitement of the narrative Mr. Conrad makes Decoud his mouthpiece. It is a remarkable stroke of imagination that makes him in the extremity of danger, provoked by circumstance into the expression of his highest capacity, turn, not to his love, but to his sister in Paris:—

[quotes *Nostromo*, part ii, ch. 7: 'It occurred to him. . . . to his sister.']

Of Nostromo himself, an Italian sailor with a mispronounced name, captain of the lightermen and caretaker of the jetty, Mr. Conrad has made a curious and perhaps not quite convincing study. He is an egotist with a passion for reputation, a man of heroic vanity, incorruptible yet finally corrupted by the silver which, representative once of stability and social regeneration, seems destined in a menacing forecast of the future of the new republic, purged of the grosser abominations, to become a vast industrial tyranny. Nostromo's adventures and his simple but curious organism are prominent in the latter part of the story, and the irony of a great political movement dependent for inception and execution upon such persons as Decoud and Nostromo is apparent, but Nostromo is not, to our sense, a natural dominant force in the story, and his prominence is part of what seems an arbitrary and baffling design. But the whole presentation of this new and strange world, crowded with characters and incidents to which we cannot even refer, is very powerful and very fascinating, with a rapid humour of phrase, a steady vision, and noble qualities of imagination.

74. Edward Garnett, review, *Speaker*

12 November 1904, 138–9

This is Garnett's first signed review of Conrad. As usual with his reviews, it is highly intelligent and sensitive. It carried the title 'Mr. Conrad's Art'.

In *Nostromo*, a tale of the seaboard of Central America, Mr. Conrad has achieved something which it is not in the power of any English contemporary novelist to touch. His genius, that rose to the consummate art of 'The Heart of Darkness' and the beauty of 'Youth', has in *Nostromo* descended a step or two to a lower plane to weave the more orthodox, structured novels, with a plot and *dénouement*. For we cannot disguise that the worst thing about the modern novel is the conventionalised plan of its structure. Happily, however, Mr. Conrad's gifts have triumphed over the regular form prescribed for the public's consumption: *Nostromo* is not particularly orthodox in its structure, and the larger canvas Mr. Conrad has chosen on this occasion gives him more elbow room to show the working unity and harmonious balance of his fascinating gifts.

We draw attention to the harmonious balance of the author's vision in *Nostromo*, for to speak frankly we did not expect that the creator of *Lord Jim* would have threaded the mazes of the situation exposed in *Nostromo* with such unerring and easy steps, or would have so clearly shaped the minor clues that lead us to the broad main issue. If we put aside the somewhat lengthy handling of the early history of the San Tomé silver mine and the abrupt and hurried final chapters that describe Nostromo's death, which are artistically too violent, there is scarcely a line in the book that is not essential to the development of this dramatic pageant of life in a South American State. For the book's theme is not, indeed, the life and death of the hero Nostromo, El Capitan de Cargadores, as Mr. Conrad no doubt originally conceived it, neither is it the story of the vicissitudes of the great San Tomé silver mine and of the Europeans who develop it in Sulaco, as in Part I. it

174

threatens to become. Mr. Conrad's artistic instinct has perhaps unconsciously led him to clear the reefs of these subsidiary issues, and
has brought him and his readers safe into the open sea, whence they
can look back at the sharp outline of the Costaguanan coast, the
placid waters of the Golfo Placido, and realise that his subject is the
great mirage he has conjured up of the life and nature of the Costaguanan territory lying under the shadow of the mighty Cordilleras.
The foreground of *Nostromo* is, indeed, the dramatic narrative of the
political and revolutionary vicissitudes of the town of Sulaco.

[gives an outline of the plot]

—all this is told us through the medium of various characters, as Captain Mitchell, the pompous old resident officer of the O.S.N. Co.,
Nostromo himself, Martin Decoud, Spanish creole, Parisian boulevardier and Rivierist journalist, Dr. Monygham, a broken and gloomy
army doctor, who has seen too much of Costaguana and its revolutions
to have any illusions left; and indirectly through the medium of Mrs.
Gould, the wife of the mine-owner, Giorgio Viola, an old Garibaldian
soldier, and Colonel Sotillo, military bravo and torturer of the miserable
Hirsch, the German Jew. Mr. Conrad has never before attempted to
group together such a variety of characters, to exhibit so many conflicting issues, and to make pass before us such a dramatic pageant as in
this wonderful mirage of S. American life. How has he been able to do it,
and what is the nature of the artistic method by which scene after scene
flows clearly, freely, in natural and convincing sequence, leaving the
impression on the reader of having seen and assisted at a whole national
drama?

The critic, pressed for an explanation of Mr. Conrad's special power
by which he accomplishes artistic feats beyond his rivals, may boldly
declare that he has a special poetic sense for *the psychology of scene*, by
which the human drama brought before us is seen in its just relation
to the whole enveloping drama of Nature around, forming both the
immediate environment and the distant background. In Mr. Conrad's
vision we may image Nature as a ceaselessly-flowing infinite river of
life, out of which the tiny atom of each man's individual life emerges
into sight, stands out in the surrounding atmosphere, and is lost again
in the infinite succession of the fresh waves of life into which it dis-
solves. The author's pre-eminence does not lie specifically in his
psychological analysis of character, but in the delicate relation of his
characters to the whole environment—to the whole mirage of life in

which their figures are seen to move. Thus, the character drawings *per se* of Mrs. Gould and Dr. Monygham, Captain Mitchell and Old Viola, though admirable studies, cannot be called deeply original creations, but their human significance is very great if we consider them as figures which serve as arresting points by which we can focus the character of the national drama around them and so penetrate to the larger drama of Nature. Thus, while the psychology of certain characters, as Charles Gould, Decoud, and Nostromo himself, is indeed not always clear and convincing, when we take the figure of Mrs. Gould and analyse the effect made on us by the vision of her exquisite and gracious nature, moving 'with her candid eyes very wide open, her lips composed into a smile,' amid the electric and sullen atmosphere of this South American town, weighed down by the ever-hanging menace of her husband's danger, ministering to all the world in turn seeking her ear, while conscious in secret that her husband, in his fanatical devotion to the interests of the San Tomé mine, has surrendered, merged, and lost sight of his love for her—if we consider the spirit of this woman we shall recognise how exquisitely just is the author's sense of perspective which has led him to place her so that, like a figure in a landscape, she serves as the gleam of light against the sombre and threatening horizon. And so against the devotion to duty of Giorgio Viola, the old Garibaldian hero, the Spanish-American revolutionary rabble of Sulaco shows up 'sullen, thievish, vindictive, and bloodthirsty.' And thus against the wooden-headed unimaginativeness of the Britisher, Captain Mitchell, the hard-headed idealism of Charles Gould, and the gloomy disillusionment of Dr. Monygham, the whole racial genius of this captivating and gracious South American land, semi-barbarous, with its old-world, Spanish traditions and its 'note of passion and sorrow,' stands forth triumphantly; and its atmosphere, which is, indeed, an artistic quintessence from both Central American and South American States, penetrates home to our European consciousness. And if this is so—and if in Mr. Conrad's art the whole mirage of Nature be everything, and the series of flowing scenes in which are reflected the subtly shifting tides of human emotion and human passion—we shall see why it is that the artistic imperfections of some of his figures seem of curiously little importance. It is because with most writers the whole illusion of the scene is centred in their characters, but with Mr. Conrad the central illusion is the whole mirage of Nature, in which the figures are, strictly speaking, the human accessories. Thus in the 'Heart of Darkness', that sinister presentment of the imbecility, the cruelty and rapacity of the white man in the Dark Continent, the effect is got by the tropical atmosphere of a savage environment dominating the white man's *morale*, and sapping him, body, mind, and soul: thus in *Lord Jim*, Jim's actions and words and thoughts are not nearly so convincing in themselves as is the poetic conception of his figure placed by fate, and by the force of his one great *défaillance*, in the environment of the wanderer of the Eastern seas. It is not, indeed, essential to the author's spell over us that they should be. This great gift of Mr. Conrad's, his special sense for the *psychology of scene*, that he shares with many of the great poets and the great artists who have developed it each on his own chosen lines, it is that marks him out for pre-eminence among the novelists. His method of poetic realism is, indeed, intimately akin to that of the great Russian novelists but Mr. Conrad, inferior in the psychology of character, has outstripped them in his magical power of creating the whole mirage of Nature. It is for this reason that we regret that the last two chapters describing Nostromo's death are included in the novel. Their touch of melodrama does violence to the evening stillness of the close. The narrative should have ended with the monologue of Captain Mitchell and the ironic commentary of Dr. Monygham on the fresh disillusion-ment in store for the *régime* of 'Civilisation' planted by European hands on the bloodstained soil of the Republic of Costaguana.

75. John Buchan, unsigned review, *Spectator*

19 November 1904, 800–1

Mr. Conrad's new book shows in the highest relief the characteristic merits and defects of his work. He has a greater range of knowledge—subtle idiomatic knowledge—of the strange ways of the world than any contemporary writer. He has an imaginative force which at times can only be paralleled among the greatest; he has a profound sense of drama, and the logic of events which lesser people call fate; and he has a style which is often careless, involved, and harsh, but, like all true style, has moments of superb inspiration. On the other hand, he is burdened with the wealth of his equipment. A slender talent finds it easy to be lucid and orderly; but Mr. Conrad, seeing his people before him with such tremendous clearness, and entering into their loves and hates with such gusto, does not know where to begin or to end their tale. His characters crowd upon him, demanding that each have his story told with the same patient realism, till the great motive is so overlaid with minor dramas that it loses much of its appeal. His books, in consequence, tend to be a series of brilliant episodes connected by a trickle of narrative, rather than romance with the stream of story running strongly to the close. And the misfortune is that the drama which is pushed into the background is nearly always of exceptional power, capable, were the rest only duly subordinated to it, of raising the work to the highest level of art. In the book before us the story, which gives the title to the whole, is of one Nostromo, an Italian sailor, who becomes Capataz de Cargadores in the service of a steamboat company at a port in a South American Republic. He is the masterly egotist, the leader among his own class, trusted and used by his masters, happy in his second-rate greatness. But there come events which show, or seem to show, that he is a tool rather than a principal. His pride takes fire, he is all but in revolt, but his egotism comforts itself, and he does heroic work for his masters. And then somehow the story ebbs away. We see Nostromo an embryo revolutionary, spending himself in amours and a hurry to get rich, and killed at last by an accident. And the reason is that another and stronger drama comes athwart his. An Englishman and his wife have taken upon themselves the regeneration of the Republic of Costaguana by means of the silver industry which they control. The story of the regeneration, the revolution, and the creation of the Occidental Republic is the compelling interest of the book, and Nostromo comes in only as a handy *deus ex machinâ* in the greater story. The true story ends with the reminiscences of old Captain Mitchell, and the bitter reflection of Dr. Monygham that some day it would have to be done all over again,—the justification of the moral on the title-page: 'So foul a sky clears not without a storm.' The last two chapters belong to Nostromo's story alone, and are therefore irrelevant to the main drama, and a narrative which at times is profoundly moving and inspired with a kind of cosmic dignity ends bewilderingly with a mishap to a minor character. Either the politics of Sulaco should have been a mere background to Nostromo's tragedy, or his career should have been merely an episode in the story of the Republic. The separate interests are too potent to harmonise within one romance.

But though the construction of the book is topsy-turvy, beginning in the middle and finishing at the start, the story, considered even as narrative, is of surpassing interest. Mr. Conrad has flung around his work the mystery of a cloud-covered sea and high remote mountains. All his characters, in spite of the close realism of his method, are invested with the glamour of romance. No one is perfunctorily treated; each is a living man or woman, adequately understood, drawn with firm, clean strokes. He has gone for many to the backways of life, but, strange as some are, the human blood of each is unmistakable. The most elaborate study is Nostromo, who misses being a masterpiece because of his habit of suddenly becoming a puppet in the development of another tale. But in the scene where he is adrift alone with Decoud and the treasure, in the fog, listening to the beat of the enemy's screws, there comes one of those intense moments of natural self-revelation which are the triumph of the psychologist. Mrs. Gould is an exquisite figure, the good angel of a troubled time; and if any one desires proofs of Mr. Conrad's genius, let him turn to those wonderful scenes during the Revolution when she sees for the first time the defects of her husband's regenerating policy, and shuts her lips to accept the second-best. But the greatest achievements are in the minor personages, —Decoud, the cynical and belated nationalist; Antonia; Hernandez, the brigand; the old Garibaldist Viola and his daughter; and the amazing crowd of schemers and swaggerers who play at politics in those Republics. We have said that every character is an adequate portrait. But Mr. Conrad's achievement is still greater, for he has managed to make clear the strife of ideals in a sordid warfare, and to show the core of seriousness in mock-heroics. It is not a book which the casual reader will appreciate. The sequence of events has to be sought painfully through the mazes of irrelevancy with which the author tries to mislead us. But it is a book which will well repay those who give it the close attention which it deserves. It shows signs of haste both in style and construction, and we trust that this may be the explanation of the main defects. It would be a thousand pities if an author who has few equals in talent should habitually spoil his work by an inability to do the pruning and selecting which his art demands.

76. Unsigned notice, *Illustrated London News*

26 November 1904, 774

To say that *Nostromo* is the great achievement in fiction of the year is to state altogether imperfectly our appreciation of Mr. Conrad's latest novel. There are few years in which it would not be the notable achievement. The criticism certain to be levelled against it—that it is formless—is in reality a criticism of its extreme length. It is longer even than it appears, because, to a degree unparalleled in any other novelist we can think of, every word goes to the development of the story and the enlightenment of the appreciative reader. It is not exaggeration to say that an imperfect understanding of the author's intention may result from a moment's slackness of attention and the failure to read between two (no more) particular lines. Now, of course, too great a demand upon our concentration—upon our enthusiasm even—is open to legitimate criticism. It is for the novelist to take account of the angle of human vision, so to say, and to set limits accordingly to the width of his scheme. We think it possible that Mr. Conrad would have admitted some failure on his part to do so when he realised that Nostromo's ride to Cayta must be compressed into half-a-dozen pages of description put into the mouth of Captain Mitchell. So much may be conceded to the objectors. But while *Nostromo* is not Mr. Conrad's most perfect piece of work, it is incomparably the work which most clearly shows his extraordinary powers. There is no falling off in the variety, beauty and charm of the parts; there is, on the other hand, a greater sweep and breadth in the general design; and if the result is less faultless than sometimes hitherto, the ease and confidence of the author with his means of attaining it are more manifest. *Nostromo* will set the seal upon Mr. Conrad's title to rank in the forefront of living novelists.

THE SECRET AGENT

10 September 1907

77. A. N. Monkhouse, review, *Manchester Guardian*

12 September 1907

Review signed A.N.M. Monkhouse's son, Paddy, for many years with the *Guardian*, identified the review as his father's. Alan Noble Monkhouse was literary editor of the *Guardian* (1926–9). For the first time, in this review Conrad's 'sordid' tale was considered comic, a view later put forward by Douglas Hewitt, *Joseph Conrad: A Reassessment* (1952), pp. 85–8. Monkhouse was also one of the few critics of the day who recognized that *The Secret Agent* 'breaks fresh ground'. In a letter to R. B. Cunninghame Graham, 7 October 1907, Conrad stressed that the novel 'had some importance for me as a new departure in *genre* and as a sustained effort in ironical treatment of a melodramatic subject' (*LCG*, 169). W. H. Chesson, the day after this review, in his notice of the novel in the *Daily Chronicle*, 13 September 1907, also stressed that Conrad's 'characteristic humour is happily in evidence'. The *Morning Post*, 19 September 1907, called it a 'comedy of the Inferno'. Oblique reference is made to the Greenwich 'bomb outrage' of 15 February 1894, Conrad's original source for the bomb explosion in the novel.

Fiction can give us nothing more stimulating than a story by Mr. Joseph Conrad, and *The Secret Agent* which is dedicated to Mr. Wells, has been heralded by the curious announcement that it is 'based on the inside knowledge of a certain event in the history of active anarchism.' Mr. Conrad excites our curiosity and he does not satisfy it, but perhaps surmises as to the limits of history and invention would be relevant only to the hidden technics of his work. Of course this work is extremely interesting, and it breaks fresh ground. *Nostromo* brought a change of continents, but it was still concerned with romantic adventurers; it would be an ingenious definition of romance that should include the Secret Agent and his companions. We associate Mr. Conrad with memorable experiences of thrilling adventure, of heroical tension, of the glowing East; we seem to be losing something very precious when he compels us to the grim comedy of anarchism. *The Secret Agent* absorbs, but it does not exalt, as did the tragedy of *Lord Jim* or the revelation of 'Youth'; there is nothing that warms our heart like Captain MacWhirr or startles our imagination like the defiance of the dying Jew in *Nostromo*. It is close and fine, but it does not often flash upon us, and it seems that interests are somehow less associated with sympathies than they were. Some very solid, ugly things are described, and if Mr. Conrad's people must always be human, his revolutionaries and their opponents are not engaging. The amiabilities of the anarchists are generally effaced, and they have no very deep enthusiasms. They are strangely wanting in ideals, and, half-desperate as they are, they remain the prey of vanity. Mr. Conrad approaches them with a nimble and even whimsical humour.

Mr. Adolf Verloc is a protector of society in the pay of a great foreign embassy, to which he betrays his comrades when it becomes necessary to do something for his wages. He has come to this frightful vocation through a love of ease and dislike of the fixed occupation. His patron was the eminent Baron Stott-Wartemheim, a ponderous diplomatist, who is said to have exclaimed on his death-bed and in the presence of his august master: 'Unhappy Europe! Thou shalt perish by the moral insanity of thy children!' The loss of this great man brings unhappy days to Verloc, who is told that he must do something more than compile voluminous reports, and the brilliant young secretary of the embassy makes a remarkable proposal, and develops it with an ignorance of the aims and methods of revolution that fills Mr. Verloc with dismay. The Great Power wishes Great Britain to come into line with Europe in her treatment of militant anarchists, and this can only be accomplished by outrages, inexplicable and illogical, to be performed on her own soil. Attacks on crowned heads and even malignant attacks on the crowd are intelligible, if not calculable, and it is madness alone that really terrifies a community.

[quotes ch. 2: 'The attack must have. . . . . a go at astronomy?']

Thus the ingenious secretary, who is a confident, scornful personage, quite ready to take on the management of the world. Poor Verloc merely desires a life of quiet treachery and domestic happiness, but he realises that 'there is no occupation that fails a man more completely than that of a secret agent of police.' Something must be done, and there is an agent ready to his hand in his brother-in-law, one of the few characters in the story that can hardly be comprehended in a comic scheme. It is Mr. Conrad's ironical conception that what is noble and pitiful in these attempts to regenerate society concentrates in this poor idiot, a very moving and finely devised figure. With his accident in Greenwich Park we come to the surface of common knowledge, for most of us can recall that curious, alarming incident. So this great intrigue fizzles out, and Mr. Conrad pursues briefly the private fortunes of some of the individuals concerned. He is always interested in the psychological relation of persons roughly disturbed from a conventional setting, and the selection for imaginative analysis first of Verloc and his wife, and then, after another tragedy, of Mrs. Verloc and a peculiarly base specimen of the anarchist, seems instinctive rather than arbitrary.

If it be straining the conception of comedy to find it in the idea of madness and despair attempting the renovation of the world, the story that enforces this idea is rich in comic types and details. The Verloc household is a great and original accomplishment, and it does justice to the insatiable curiosity of the artist. Among those queer people, whose comparatively innocent and ostensible means of living is a trade banned by all decent folk, Mr. Conrad moves with senses quite unperturbed. His moral sense is not blunted, but, like the surgeon in another field, he has ceased to be squeamish. His investigation is coloured with humour and imagination; the obscure and terrible is revealed as comic, but it is not merely comic. Verloc, the mysterious agent, mentioned in important despatches by a symbol, with his husky, confidential voice, changing inopportunely into the booming, oratorical one that has done duty at open-air meetings, turns out to be rather stupid and almost pitiful. The 'Professor', an ascetic old man profoundly ignorant of worldly conditions, walks the streets meditating on his power, and grasping always an india-rubber ball, the squeezing of which would annihilate him and any captor. Even he, however, has his fits of discouragement, 'moments of dreadful and sane mistrust of mankind. What if nothing could move them? Such moments come to all men whose ambition aims at a direct grasp upon humanity—to artists, politicians, thinkers, reformers, or saints. A despicable emotional state this, against which solitude fortifies a superior character.'

There is, too, the anarchist patronised by a fine lady because 'she liked to watch what the world was coming to'—a man who had thought things out in his fifteen years of imprisonment, and was painfully disconcerted if his monologues, so long uninterrupted, were broken in upon by a voice; there is the police inspector, with his incredulous attitude towards these incomprehensible anarchists and his revulsion in favour of thieving, which at least is not a sheer absurdity; there are certain official personages, very well done; there is the casual and memorable introduction of a cabman and his horse. We are shown the seamy side of a preposterous world, a festering society that is commonly left to the pathologist or philanthropist. It is all vital and surprising in Mr. Conrad's narrative.

78. Unsigned review,
The Times Literary Supplement

20 September 1907, 285

Mr. Joseph Conrad, by a stroke of fine humour, has appended to his new book, *The Secret Agent*, a history of anarchists and spies, the sub-title 'A Simple Tale'; and in thinking it over we have suddenly realized that a part at least of this great novelist's mission is to remind his readers how simple men really are, even when they are the destroyers of society or their pursuers. To show how narrow a gulf is fixed between the maker of bombs and the ordinary contented citizen has never before struck a novelist as worth while, the subterranean world in which the terrorists live having up to the present time been considered by him merely as a background for lurid scenes and hair-raising thrills. And then comes Mr. Conrad with his steady, discerning gaze, his passion for humanity, his friendly irony, and above all his delicate and perfectly tactful art, to make them human and incidentally to demonstrate how monotonous a life can theirs also be. Stevenson just dipped into this nether world, bringing away only what was needed for his more or less sensational purpose; it was left for Mr. Conrad once again to hold the lantern that was to light every cranny; just as it was left for him fully to illumine the darkest places of the forecastle, the swamps of the Congo, and the mysteries of the heart of the revolutionary, the Ishmael, the derelict, and the coward. Englishmen cannot be too grateful that this alien of genius, casting about for a medium in which to express his sympathy and his knowledge, hit upon our own tongue. *The Secret Agent* is more of a portrait gallery than a story, although it is a story too, and a really exciting one. It is notable we think, chiefly for the portrait of the Professor the maker of bombs, Mr. Verloc the spy, and Chief Inspector Heat, of Scotland-yard, hunter of men; but there is no one scamped in it; all are made vivid, and their interaction is marvellously managed. The logic of the story is of iron. We do not consider *The Secret Agent* Mr. Conrad's masterpiece; it lacks the free movement of 'Youth' and the terrible minuteness of *Lord Jim*, while it offers no scope for the employment of the tender and warm fancy that made 'Karain' so memorable; but it is, we think, an advance upon *Nostromo*, its immediate predecessor. That canvas was a little overcrowded, while in *The Secret Agent* one's way is clear throughout. But the Professor is its triumph. It is the Professor who principally increases Mr. Conrad's reputation, already of the highest.

79. Unsigned review, *Country Life*

21 September 1907, 403–5

The review was signed with the initial Z. It is a very ignorant attack on Conrad's novel, its strengths taken as weaknesses, its humour misconstrued. That the source of Sir Ethelred should have been recognized so early is interesting. Conrad's description of Verloc's murder, attacked here on dubious grounds, is praised by the *Star* (No. 85).

Until *The Secret Agent* came into my hands my ideas of Mr. Joseph Conrad were of the vaguest. Some years ago I looked into a book, a novel of sea life, written by him, and formed a high opinion of his potentialities. Since then rumour has been busy with his name, and he is now almost invariably spoken of in respectful terms as a writer of very great ability, who has a magnificent future before him. Possibly this may be quite true, but the augury is not borne out by the latest of his publications. *The Secret Agent*, subjected to any test that can be imagined, will not entitle the author to a place beside Scott and Thackeray. One would begin by saying something about his selection of characters, although it may be said that the first, second, third and last essential is that they should be interesting. Unless the creations of an author's brain seize the attention and exercise the mind of his readers they are not worth considering at all; but a less amusing set of people never filled the imaginary world of a novelist than have been chosen for the pages of *The Secret Agent*. There used to be an old song of which the refrain, if we remember rightly, was: 'It's naughty, but it's nice.' Now, Mr. Conrad, in this book, is naughty, without being at all nice. His chief male character is a Mr. Verloc, a sort of spy and informer in the service of revolutionists. In portraying him the author appears to have taken M. Zola as model, for he introduces him with a certain kind of respectability, making him decent in his indecency, and honest in his dishonesty. The thing strikes us at once as a paradox. The sort of shop kept by Mr. Verloc is one where shady photographs, obscene

186

literature and other articles of a similar kind are sold. The people who keep such places are, generally speaking, the most unmitigated black-guards who hold on to the edges of civilisation. The man, however, as depicted by Mr. Conrad might have been an honest plasterer or stone-mason, who has even gone on the path of respectability so far as to get married, instead of forming one of the slight and fleeting attach-ments which are more common in the order to which he belongs. His wife—and thereby hangs a tale—is the daughter of a woman who has kept a boarding-house and is the widow of a low type of licensed victualler or publican. The man is a very dull dog who, apparently, has a gift for spouting in parks and places where Socialists assemble, but shows very little trace indeed of eloquence in the conversations he holds with the various people during the course of this story. Indeed, it would appear as if Mr. Conrad had set himself the impossible task of trying to make dulness interesting, for he lets Verloc only use a hoarse whisper in private, instead of a voice that was said to carry over the greater extent of Hyde Park; and he is distinguished, more than in any other way, by an utter lack of wit and *esprit*. He is called upon by an ambassador to destroy one of the great scientific institutions in Great Britain.

I would never dream of directing you to organise a mere butchery, even if I expected the best results from it. But I wouldn't expect from a butchery the result I want. Murder is always with us. It is almost an institution. The demon-stration must be against learning—science. But not every science will do. The attack must have all the shocking senselessness of gratuitous blasphemy. Since bombs are your means of expression, it would be really telling if one could throw a bomb into pure mathematics. But that is impossible.

This reminds us curiously of one of Mr. Gilbert's phantasies, only it is a Gilbertian idea clothed in very bad prose. The respectable vendor of photographs is, to use a colloquialism, 'knocked silly' by this demand upon his energies, and yet he has to set about carrying out the command laid upon him with diligence, lest those of his own brotherhood should fall upon and slay him. The brotherhood consists of a number of very stagey revolutionists. One of them is a little man, who goes about armed with a new detonator, with which he is prepared to blow him-self into eternity when any attempt is made to arrest him. He, too, might have figured quite appropriately in Gilbert and Sullivan's opera; but all this is not germane to Mr. Conrad's intention, which is obviously to develop the latent capacity for murder in Mrs. Verloc. She has married this agent without any question of love coming in the way, but merely because she had two people to provide for—her mother and a half-witted brother. Jilted by a butcher boy, in the days when she was serving-maid at the boarding house, all that she has of love and passion has flowed out to this half-witted brother. Him Mr. Verloc chooses as the agent to carry out his plan of destroying the Hall of Science. The youth fails to do it, and is blown into so many pieces that —as our author tells us with a realism that seems to have tickled his palate—they have to be collected in two shovels. About half-a-dozen times these implements and their grim contents are referred to in the story. This catastrophe enrages Mrs. Verloc, who stabs her husband and afterwards commits suicide. That is the sum and substance of the story. If Mrs. Verloc had been interesting, the tale would have been so as well; but, if possible, she is still duller than her husband. This fact is emphasised by the very bad style in which Mr. Conrad tells his story. You can tell a great writer at once, because his analysis is all done, as it were, behind the curtain. He makes his people speak and act, and leaves the reader to judge what is passing in their minds. The course followed by Mr. Conrad is exactly the opposite of this. In page after page he discourses fluently about the ideas that were coursing through the brain of a woman who never spoke at all. The sort of writing we refer to may be shown by a specimen:

[quotes *The Secret Agent*, ch. 11: 'Every nook and cranny. . . . covered the voice.']

But when we tell the reader that this sort of thing goes on for seventy-five pages—to be exact, from page 301 to 376—he will see what we mean. Of course, the art that perpetrates this sort of thing is very bad indeed. Nothing can be called art except that which is convincing, and the reader knows absolutely that Mr. Conrad is guessing and guessing very badly, at the intricate movements of a woman's mind. There is no way by means of which he could get within it. Indeed, we had thought that the style of writing here exemplified belonged to an earlier and less enlightened stage in our literary history. It places Mr. Conrad not in the van, where he ought to be but in the rear of the movement. Again, we have no hesitation in saying that the whole thing is indecent. Of course, we do not apply the term in the vulgar meaning; what we call indecent is that the whole inception, process and accomplishment of a murder should have been planned as it were, on the stage and in the sight of the spectators. Killing, undoubtedly, is a necessity but it is as indecent to exhibit a murder done in this slow and tedious manner as it would be to have the shambles of a butcher in the public streets. Many chapters before it takes place we know perfectly well what is coming. The art that conceals art is not Mr. Conrad's: but this is not the fault we have to find with *The Secret Agent*. Critics generally have agreed that even very great authors, such as Fielding, made a mistake in keeping to the example of Cervantes, and introducing short stories into the middle of their novels. Mr. Conrad is not guilty of that mistake, but of one equally inartistic, and that is the fault of bringing in minor and unessential characters and making far too much of them. It is best to give specific examples, so that any reader can, if he wishes, turn up the book and see for himself, or herself, how far these strictures are justified. Let us take Chapter VIII as an example. It tells us how Mrs. Verloc's mother went about to get admitted to an almshouse. The incident in itself is well enough, and might be helpful in developing the character of Mrs. Verloc; but considering that the woman never comes into the story again, the enormously-drawn-out tale of her departure must be considered as an excrescence, was not wanted in the slightest. Again, the characters of the Assistant Commissioner, the Inspector of Police, and the Minister, whose portrait seems to be intended as a burlesque of the late Sir William Harcourt, are all unnecessary to the picture, and might have been left out, or their parts curtailed, to very great advantage. In fact, if Mr. Conrad was aiming at art and immortality instead of at filling up a definite number of pages, he could have reduced his story to a tenth part of its present dimensions, and still rather added to than taken away from its merits. The book might fairly be described as a study of murder, by a writer with a personality as egotistical as that of Mr. Bernard Shaw, only lacking in the wit and humour which goes some way to justify the existence of the latter.

80. Arnold Bennett on *The Secret Agent*

25 September 1907

Extract from Bennett's Journal (*JAB*, i, 256–7). Some years later in a letter to Conrad of 22 November 1912, Bennett was much kinder to *The Secret Agent*: '. . . I wish I could acquaint you with my state of mind—intense satisfaction in seeing a thing truly *done*, mixed with anger because I know I can never do it as well myself —when I recall the quiet domestic scenes behind the shop in *The Secret Agent*, here is rather the sort of thing I reckon to handle myself—but I respectfully retire from the comparison.'

A certain amount of reading has been done lately. Conrad's *The Secret Agent*. A sort of sensationalism sternly treated on the plane of realistic psychology. A short story written out to the length of a novel. Nothing but a single episode told to the last drop. The Embassy scenes did not appear to me to be quite genuine, but rather a sincere effort to imagine events for which the author had nothing but psychological data of a general order. But the domestic existence of the spy, and the character of his wife—the 'feel' of their relations, very masterly indeed, also the invention of the idiot brother-in-law for the doing of the crime. On the other hand, the contrivance of the mother-in-law's departure, though the departure in itself was excellent, seemed clumsy; and the final scenes between the wife and the anarchist after her husband's death rather missed fire in their wildness; they fail, not in the conception but in execution. On the whole, coming after *Nostromo*, the book gives a disappointing effect of slightness.

81. Edward Garnett, unsigned review, *Nation*

28 September 1907

It is good for us English to have Mr. Conrad in our midst visualising for us aspects of life we are constitutionally unable to perceive, for by his astonishing mastery of our tongue he makes clear to his English audience those secrets of Slav thought and feeling which seem so strange and inaccessible in their native language. They are not inaccessible, those secrets, not in the least; through the gates of literary translations we can all enter into the alien spirit of those distant peoples; but so poor is the imagination of most of us that we linger outside, puzzled and repelled by their strange atmosphere and environment, even when mirrored clearly by art. Mr. Conrad, however, is to us as a willing hostage we have taken from the Slav lands, in exchange for whom no ransom could outweigh the value of his insight and his artistic revelation of the world at our gates, by us so imperfectly apprehended. By *The Secret Agent* he has added to the score of our indebtedness, and he has brought clearly into our ken the subterranean world of that foreign London which, since the death of Count Fosco,[1] has served in fiction only the crude purpose of our sensational writers.

[gives an outline of the plot]

In tracing the outline of this appallingly futile tragedy the reviewer may remark that Mr. Conrad's possession of a philosophy, impartial in its scrutiny of the forces of human nature, is the secret of his power— we had almost added, of his superiority to contemporary English novelists. The laws that govern human nature are often as disconcerting to our self-esteem as they are chastening to our spiritual egoism. And our English novelists, unlike the Slav, are apt to work too assiduously on the side of the angels, and hold, avowedly or in secret, an ethical brief. But the advantage of keeping the earthly horizon on a low plane is that there is more space around and beyond, in the picture, for the background of those eternal elements which both govern and

---

[1] Count Fosco, the villain of Wilkie Collins's *The Woman in White* (1860), was a secret agent for a foreign government.

dwarf man's petty endeavour. Mr. Conrad's achievement in his novels and tales of seamen's life in the Eastern seas, was, in fact, a poet's achievement; he showed us the struggle of man's passionate and wilful endeavour, cast against the background of nature's infinity and passionless purpose. And in *The Secret Agent* Mr. Conrad's ironical insight into the natural facts of life, into those permanent animal instincts which underlie our spiritual necessities and aspirations, serves him admirably in place of the mysterious backgrounds of tropical seas and skies to which he has accustomed us. He goes down into the dim recesses of human motive, but though his background is only the murky gloom of old London's foggy streets and squares, the effect is none the less arresting. His character sketches of Michaelis, the ticket-of-leave apostle of anarchism, of Karl Yundt, the famous terrorist, the moribund veteran of dynamite wars, 'who has been a great actor in his time, on platforms, in secret assemblies, in private interviews,' but who has never, strange to say, put his theories into practice; of Comrade Ossipon, who lives by exploiting the servant-girls whom his handsome face has seduced; and of the Professor, the dingy little man whose ferocious hatred of social injustice inspires him with a moral force that makes both his posturing comrades and the police shudder, acutely conscious, as they are, that he has both the will and the means to shatter a streetful of people to bits—these character sketches supply us with a working analysis of anarchism that is profoundly true, though the philosophical anarchism of certain creative minds is, of course, out of the range of the author's survey. And not less well done is the scrutiny of the official *morale* and personal incentives that govern the conduct of those guardians of social order, Chief Inspector Heat and the Assistant-Commissioner of Police. The two men, who have different ends in view, typify the daily conflict between Justice as a means and Justice as an end, which two are indeed rarely in harmony.

But Mr. Conrad's superiority over nearly all contemporary English novelists is shown in his discriminating impartiality which, facing imperturbably all the conflicting impulses of human nature, refuses to be biassed in favour of one species of man rather than another. Chief Inspector Heat, the thief-taker and the guardian of social order, is no better a man than the inflexible avenger of social injustice, the Professor. The Deputy Commissioner of Police, though a fearless and fine individual, moves our admiration no more than does the childlike idealist, Michaelis, who has been kept in prison for fifteen years for a disinterested act of courage. Whether the spy, Mr. Verloc, is more contemptible than the suave and rosy-gilled favourite of London drawing-rooms, M. Vladimir, is as difficult a point to decide as whether the latter is less despicable than the robust seducer of women, the cowardly Comrade Ossipon. And, by a refined stroke of irony, the innocent victim of anarchist propaganda and bureaucratic counter-mining is the unfortunate and weak-witted lad, Stevie, whose morbid dread of pain is exploited by the bewildered *agent provocateur*, Mr. Verloc, in his effort to serve the designs of his Embassy, and preserve both his situation and his own skin. Finally, as an illustration of our author's serene impartiality, we may mention that the real heroine of the story is concealed in the trivial figure of Mr. Verloc's mother-in-law, whose effacement of self for the sake of her son, Stevie, is the cause contributory to his own and her daughter's ruin. For Mr. Verloc, growing desperate, sends the half-witted lad with an infernal machine to blow up Greenwich Observatory, and, Stevie perishing, Mr. Verloc is attacked by his wife in a fit of frenzy and killed.

While the psychological analysis of the characters' motives is as full of acumen as is the author's philosophical penetration into life, it is right to add that Mr. Verloc and his wife are less convincing in their actions than in their meditations. There is a hidden weakness in the springs of impulse of both these figures, and at certain moments they become automata. But such defects are few. Mr. Conrad's art of suggesting the essence of an atmosphere and of a character in two or three pages has never been more strikingly illustrated than in *The Secret Agent*. It has the profound and ruthless sincerity of the great Slav writers mingled with the haunting charm that reminds us so often of his compatriot Chopin.

82. Unsigned notice, *Truth*

2 October 1907, 817

Mr. Conrad's latest work, *The Secret Agent* would be notable if only for the reason that the author has managed to shake himself free from those intricacies of style which are the despair of all but devotees of the Henry James school of fiction. His story gains immeasurably from its simplicity. The plain intelligence may comprehend Mr. Conrad's 'simple tale,' and enjoy his subtle analysis of character. There is much to enjoy, even though Mr. Conrad has chosen to illuminate some very sordid and ugly things with the light of his wit, for he brings the same fine gift of critical insight to deal with the crawling reptiles of anarchism which he has devoted in the past to romantic adventure on the confines of civilisation. He shows us the seamy side of unfortunately too possibly real a world, but he does so with humour and imagination— one may almost say genius. *The Secret Agent* is a book to read.

83. Unsigned review, *Glasgow News*

3 October 1907, 5

The review was entitled 'A Great Book'. It follows Garnett's review in the *Nation* (No. 81) quite closely and is perhaps the source of Conrad's complaints (see Introduction, pp. 25–6), 'I've been so cried up of late as . . . an amazing bloody foreigner writing in English'.

It is not an irrelevant reflection upon *The Secret Agent* that its author, Joseph Conrad, is of Polish birth. Nor is that reflection forced upon one by the fact that the book deals with the underworld of revolutionary intrigue with an authority of first-hand, almost instinctive knowledge, which is something entirely different from the crudely sensational and improbable imaginings of the average English novelist who writes of underground Russian politics. There is much more in the author's origin than that. For the fact is that he has imported into English literature a quality, a mood, a temperament which has never appeared in it before—something perhaps entirely alien to our national genius, at any rate something which we can only parallel in the great Russian writers. That something, not easily defined, may be suggested as a spirit of complete and impassive sincerity, a dry north light in which nothing escapes, nothing is forced or exaggerated or obscured, in which everything appears exactly as it is in its own shape and place. The author never takes a side, never betrays any of the personal feeling, the sentiment or humour or geniality or cynicism or contempt or bitterness that British writers either parade or visibly attempt to suppress—nothing but tranquil comprehension and passionless statement. At the utmost there is a grave irony, or a faint tinge of melancholy, as of one brooding without resentment over the futility and pettiness of human efforts and desires. But this is a new note in our literature—Hardy's sombre tragedy is something quite different—so new that one does not feel it British at all; it is Slavonic. And surely it is a strange accident that has thrown this great writer, imbued with the genus of a race so different from our own, into using our language as his medium of expression, and using it with the power and grace of a born master.

Here in this book he takes a sordid story of underground intrigue and crime among some of the foreigners who make London their refuge. It is such a story as in the hands of nine British novelists would have been a mere hash of old improbable plots, sensational incidents, and crude character-drawing. In his hands it becomes not only a masterly revelation of some unfamiliar aspects of London—the foreign anarchists, the average capable but limited police official, the high Russian bureaucrat, the great politician 'behind the scenes,' the respectable London woman engaged in a shady trade, and so on—but a revelation of all human life itself, its impossible mixture of triviality and dignity, of striving and frustration, of beauty and vulgarity, of meanness and terror and unheroic tragedy. This is not one of those books which can be spoiled for the reader by fore-knowledge of the 'plot,' and we may, therefore, briefly sketch its outline. Verloc, a spy in the pay of the Russian Embassy, who has dodged along comfortably for years without doing much, is suddenly sent for on a change at the Embassy, and told by his new masters that he must do something for his money, and it is suggested that he should instigate some crime which will rouse British opinion and the London police. In terror of losing his job, he finally procures an infernal machine, and incites a half-witted lad, his wife's brother, to blow up Greenwich Observatory. The lad stumbles, and blows himself to pieces, and the whole story by a trifling accident comes into the possession of the authorities. Before they can do anything, however, Verloc's wife discovers what has happened, murders him in a fit of frenzy, and then, flying from justice, is robbed and deserted by a scoundrel to whom she had turned for help and throws herself from a cross-Channel steamer.

That is all, so far as 'plot' goes, and in the outline it looks like anything that might have been written by more than one contemporary whom it will be kinder not to name. But no outline can convey the impression of absolute truth, of profound and comprehensive knowledge of human nature that the reader gets from the book. To take only two instances, no one who has any knowledge of even the outer side of anarchism can fail to be delighted with this portrayal of some typical anarchists as they are to be met in life, and not as they are wildly imagined by writers of popular fiction; no one who has had anything to do with policemen can fail to recognise the searching truth with which the character of that admirable type, Chief-Inspector Heat is described. And the other characters are etched with the same calm, unwavering, unemotional precision. *The Secret Agent* is the work of a great writer, and more than ever may we be grateful for the fortunate chance or chances which threw that writer on our literary shores. He remains, it is true, somewhat aloof; he may always be somewhat remote from popular comprehension, not to say affection. But we shall, for our own sake, do well to pay him honour.

84. Conrad's reply to the Garnet review

1 October 1907

Extract from letter to Edward Garnett (*LEG*, p. 204). Jack is John Galsworthy.

I only heard from Jack yesterday of your review in the Nation. I sent to the Railway Station today for the No.

It makes a fine reading for an author and no mistake. I am no end proud to see you've spotted my poor old woman. You've got a fiendishly penetrating eye for one's most secret intentions. She *is* the heroine. And you are appallingly quick in jumping upon a fellow. Yes O! yes my dear Edward—that's what's the matter with the estimable Verloc and his wife: 'the hidden weakness in the springs of impulse'. I was so convinced that something was wrong there that to read your definition has been an immense relief—great enough to be akin to joy. The defect is so profoundly temperamental that to this moment I can't tell *how* I went wrong. Of going wrong I was aware even at the time of writing—all the time. You may imagine what a horrible grind it was to keep on going with this suspicion at the back of the head.

85. Unsigned notice, *Star*

5 October 1907, 1

Another book that emerges from the inky torrent is *The Secret Agent* by Mr. Joseph Conrad. Its imaginative force is terrible. It is the first book in which Mr. Conrad has put London into his magic crucible. The soul of London is not easily transmuted into literature, and few of our novelists have managed to achieve the alchemy of vision. The realists have all failed. Since Dickens no novelist has caught the obscure haunting grotesquerie of London. Now Mr. Conrad has caught it, and caught it as wonderfully as he caught the magic of the Malay forest and the magic of the sea. He stirs and mixes London into his characters, although they are nearly all alien anarchists. You feel its fat, foul, heavy, mysterious presence behind these strange dim folk who move like fish in a dingy aquarium. Verloc, the foreign spy, and his wife, and the idiot boy, and the sensual Ossipon, and the horrible old Professor, are all alive. The murder of Verloc is one of the most intensely dramatic murders in fiction. Its imaginative realism is amazing. Mr. Conrad's pictorial gift is diabolical. He makes you see the whole scene. The moment of the crime is intolerably visible. You see Verloc seeing the shadow of the arm with the clenched hand holding the carving-knife. You think out the plan of defence which he thinks out. You feel that there was not time for him to move, although there was time for him to think. You hear the ticking which is not the ticking of the clock, for the clock has stopped, and you shudder when you realise with Mrs. Verloc that it is the sound of the drops of blood falling on the floor-cloth, with a sound of trickling growing fast and furious like the pulse of an insane clock. But the most ghastly piece of pictorial imagination is Mr. Verloc's round hat on the floor which rocks slightly on its crown in the wind of her flight. That is a stroke of genius. It is the fine art of murder in fiction.

86. Stewart Edward White, review, *Bookman* (U.S.A.)

January 1908, pp. 531–2

An undistinguished review, it nevertheless makes certain points as to Conrad's personal bias which have been taken up by critics in recent years, especially by Irving Howe: 'Where Conrad presumes to render the London anarchists in their characteristic haunts and accents, he drops to a coarse-spirited burlesque' (*Politics and the Novel*, 1961, p. 97).

Mr. Joseph Conrad renders difficult the task of reviewing *The Secret Agent* by already having written *Lord Jim, Youth* and the rest of his splendid list of titles. By them we know what he can do. Therefore we cannot dismiss *The Secret Agent* with a few well-chosen words to the effect that it is a readable story, with flashes of humour and passages of gripping realism.

The book has to do with anarchists, diplomats, policemen and stodgy middle-class English people. Of the lot, all but the Professor with his nth power explosive are either opéra bouffe or treated as such. In that we touch the chief fault of the book. Mr. Conrad sketches for us a half-dozen characters from the standpoint of delicately satiric contempt, the sort of contempt that refuses to take seriously either the motives, temperaments or actions of the specimens at which it laughs. Mr. Hichens[1] in *The Londoners* and *The Prophet of Berkeley Square* offers a good example of what I mean. The Secret Agent himself pays 'visitations' which 'set in with great severity.' He is 'steady like a rock—a soft kind of rock.' The diplomat has 'the air of a preternaturally thriving baby that will not stand nonsense from anybody.' The three anarchists gathered in the little back shop are cowardly, fat, decrepit, futile. Probably they were so, and Mr. Conrad intends to show just these

---

[1] Robert Smythe Hichens (1864–1950), best known for his novel *The Green Carnation* (1894).

qualities in apposition to the swift terror of the dynamite outrage. But he overdoes it. One feels that after the fall of the curtain they will go forth to the consumption of beer—real beer, not the property beer they drink in the book.

And then, without any real reason for it, we are offered mangled flesh scooped up with a shovel, and gentlemen with carving knives in their bosoms, and abandoned crazed ladies leaping from channel steamers.

The only excuse for a book with a 'disagreeable ending,' so-called, is an exact realism that makes the tragedy inevitable from the first. Witness 'The Heart of Darkness.' When an author's personal bias is permitted in any way to intrude, it weakens by just so much the convincing quality of his work.

In several other ways *The Secret Agent* seems to have been written from the blind spot of Mr. Conrad's literary vision. The long and rambling description of the old mother on her way to the poorhouse —excellent enough in itself—has absolutely 'nothing to do with the case.' Comrade Ossipon's intrusion into the big tragedies at the end seems to me a trifle irrelevant, not to say impertinent. Mr. Verloc, after having the book named for him, holds with difficulty the title rôle, and is finally knifed and left on the sofa while the story, with unexpected tenacity of life and fickleness of affection, fastens on the heretofore unimportant Mrs. Verloc and follows her through fifty-odd pages, only to abandon her with equal unexpectedness in favour of the Professor. And heretofore the Professor's sole mission in life seemed to have been that of picturesqueness and the invention of an explosive.

With it all is Mr. Conrad's marvellous faculty of fixing a scene in suspension as by a flash of lightning, his power of bringing out a character by a multiplicity of little touches, the insight that has made his work a delight. The imaginative reader can see readily enough what he is after. Only he has not done it.

87. Unsigned article, *Edinburgh Review*

April 1908

Extract from an article entitled 'On Ugliness in Fiction'. The following novelists and novels were condemned as well as *The Secret Agent*: Margaret L. Woods, *The Village Tragedy* (1892), Thomas Hardy, 'An Imaginative Woman' (1894), *Tess of the D'Urbervilles* (1891), Horace Vachell, *Brothers* (1904), Maxwell Grey, *The Silence of Dean Maitland* (1902), W. H. Maxwell, *The Guarded Flame* (1906), John Galsworthy, *The Man of Property* (1906), J. C. Snaith, *Henry Northcote* (1906), May Sinclair, *The Helpmate* (1907), S. R. Lysaght, *Her Majesty's Rebels* (1907), Hon. Mrs Grosvenor, *The Thornton Device* (1907). Arnold Bennett, under his pseudonym Jacob Tonson, attacked this article in *New Age*, 9 May 1908:

> The Reviewer has the strange effrontery to select Mr. Joseph Conrad's *Secret Agent* as an example of modern ugliness in fiction: a novel that is simply steeped in the finest beauty from end to end. I do not suppose that the *Edinburgh Review* has any moulding influence upon the evolution of the art of fiction in this country. But such clotted nonsense may, after all, do harm by confusing the minds of people who really are anxious to encourage what is best, strongest, and most sane. The Reviewer in this instance, for example, classes, as serious, Thomas Hardy, Joseph Conrad, and John Galsworthy, who are genuine creative forces, with mere dignified unimportant sentimentalisers like Mr. W. H. Maxwell and Miss May Sinclair.

The Secret Agent is another variant of the type. This personage has long been in the employ of a foreign embassy. He has given satisfaction to his former chiefs, but to the present ambassador he seems inactive, lethargic, unprofitable. He is given to understand that England must be startled into more cordial co-operation in the suppression of the revolutionaries whose refuge is London. He must therefore turn himself into an *agent provocateur*, and provide some telling outrage. He accordingly plans that abortive, but historic, explosion in Greenwich Park, which was intended to work the destruction of our world-famed observatory. He is surrounded by a small group who are drawn with much skill, but upon whose repulsiveness no redeeming lights are attempted to be thrown. One of their number supplies him with the necessary bomb. He chooses for his companion a half-witted brother of his wife. The latter, though not unfaithful hitherto to her uninteresting husband, expends all the love of which her nature is capable upon the boy. Following the lines of the actual incident, the boy is sent forward to lay the bomb at the gate of the observatory. He stumbles in the darkness over the root of a tree, the bomb explodes, and he is literally blown to pieces. The husband makes full confession to his wife, and gives into her custody a large sum of money which he has provided for their flight. Having done this, he eats his supper, and lies down peacefully to sleep upon a sofa in their sitting-room. The woman goes upstairs, and returns dressed for departure. After a brief self-colloquy, in her wrath and hate she takes up a carving-knife and stabs the man in his sleep. Smitten, not by remorse, but by fear of the gallows, she leaves the house, intending to commit suicide by leaping from one of the bridges. On her way she meets with the 'lady-killer' of the anarchical group, and, straightway changing her mind, throws herself into his arms. The most interesting point to him in her narrative is her possession of 500l. He takes this in charge, and procures two tickets in the night-train for the Southampton and St. Malo service; the tickets he gives to his companion, and tucks her up quietly in a first-class carriage, out of which he leaps himself just as the train is leaving the station. The woman travels on, and, still haunted by her terror of the hangman, goes on board the steamer. In despair she leaps overboard in mid-Channel, and we are left in doubt as to what the conspirator does with the money. If any embellishment of art, or service to society, is done by the concoction of such a story, clever as it may be, we confess that we fail to detect either.

88. John Galsworthy on Conrad

1 April 1908

This remarkable tribute to his friend entitled 'Joseph Conrad: A Disquisition' appeared in the *Fortnightly Review* (April 1908) 89, 627–33. Conrad had clearly read it in typescript for he refers to it in a letter to Galsworthy, 29 October 1907 (*L&L*, ii, 63):

The reading of your article soothed my spirit of profound discontent. The thing is magnificently all right in its general considerations. As to their application to my personality, it is not for me to say. A too protesting modesty would be uncivil to you. To show all my gratification would be perhaps indecent. But since your friendship is too sincere to deal in anything but truth, I will tell you that I am glad the truth is *this* and no other. There are sentences I would bind about my brow like a laurel wreath and rest content.

In the composition of a certain plant, chemists have found a liquid volatile alkaloid, known by the name of nicotine. Found nowhere else, this essence makes the plant tobacco.

And so it is with writers—at least, with great ones. To the composition of them many qualities and powers contribute, but at the back of all there is secreted something that differentiates the species.

Now in the writer Joseph Conrad there is present behind his art, and the conscious qualities ranged in service to express it, a certain cosmic spirit, a power of taking the reader down below the surface to the earth's heart, to watch the process that, in its slow, inexorable courses, has formed a crust, to which are clinging all our little different living shapes. He has the power of making his reader feel the inevitable oneness of all things that be, of breathing into him a sense of solace that he himself is part of a great unknown Unity.

The irony of things is a nightmare weighing on man's life, because he has so little of this cosmic spirit; the little that he has he frequently distrusts, for it seems to him destructive of the temples that he builds, the gardens he lays out, the coins he circulates from hand to hand. He goes in fear of death and of the universe in which he lives, nor can he bear to think that he is bound up with a Scheme that seems to him so careless of his own important life.

The Universe is always saying: The little part called man is smaller than the whole!

Man cannot grasp that statement. He ducks his head resentfully beneath his wing, and hides from contemplation of this truth. It is he who thus creates the irony of things.

Joseph Conrad's writings have the power of persuading man to peep out now and then and see that whole of which he is so small a part. There is no other living English novelist that so reveals the comfort and the beauty of the mystery in which we live, no other that can make us feel how small and stupid, how unsafe and momentary, solution is. If, at the bottom of our hearts, below our network of defences, we did not feel uncertainty, we should expire—suffocated in the swaddling bands of safety—we could not breathe the stagnant air with which we try to fill our houses. It is the essence of this writer to let in the wind with its wild, mysterious savour.

To understand nothing is to love everything. The moment that we really understand, we are no longer curious; but to be curious is to be in love. The man who has the cosmic spirit knows that he will never understand; he spends his life, inquiringly, in love. Nothing is too squalid, too small, too unconventional or remote for him to gaze on and long to know. Joseph Conrad was born in love with knowledge, but he was also born in love with mystery; in a word, he is a lover of the Universe. And so it is that on his canvases the figures he has loved pass and repass across a background that he has loved as much or even more; they step forth and sink back into the great Scheme from which all came and into which we all return. They stand before a backcloth that has not only the dimensions of height and breadth, but that of thickness, a backcloth into which is woven the whole cosmic plan; they live and breathe without detachment, phenomena of the process which has brought them forth. Epic, often, in their tragedy and comedy, what makes them epic is the feeling they inspire, that, for all their firm reality and detailed, everyday existence, they are shapes embodying the evolution and the devolution of the spheres. Neither exalted to the abasement of the Scheme that brought them forth, nor abased to the exaltation of their author—they have their just position on the plan of life.

In the novels of Balzac and Charles Dickens there is the feeling of environment, of the growth of men from men. In the novels of Turgenev the characters are bathed in light; Nature with her many moods is all around; but man is first. In the novels of Joseph Conrad, Nature is first, man second. The certainty of this is not obtruded on the reader, it reaches him in subtle ways; it does not seem conveyed by conscious effort, but through a sort of temperamental distillation. And it is this feeling for, and prepossession with, the manifestations of mysterious forces that gives this writer his unique position among novelists. The cosmic spirit is not in many men, but in all that have it there is something of the unethical morality of Nature. Things, for them, have no beginning and no end. Such men stand and watch the plants spring up; watch those plants growing by the same process that brought them into life; watch them in the end returning to the mould from which they came. The virtues of this cosmic spirit are a daring curiosity and courageous resignation; its value to the world is in correspondence with its rarity.

If men were not disharmonic, there would be no irony of things. We jut out everywhere, and fail to see how we are jutting out. We seek solutions, raise our flags, work our arms and legs loyally in the isolated fields that come within our vision, but having no feeling for the whole, the work we do is departmental. The work of the departments is the game we understand; we spend our lives keeping up the ball and taking down the score. The race of men is a race of partisans feeding their pigeon-holes with contradictory reports of life, and when a fellow comes and lays a summary on the desk, they look at him askance; but the future pays attention, for the impartial is all that it has time for.

Art inspired by cosmic spirit is, in fact, the only document that can be trusted, the only evidence that Time does not destroy. Artists are the eyes of that human figure which symbolises human life, and if this figure is to see its way at all, its eyes must pierce and be unflinching. Myopia, a cast or squint, a habit of looking on the ground or at the sky—these sight-defects are dangerous to the whole body; the things such eyes perceive are not the things that are; and in the voyage of long discovery that man is set on, all shoals not definitely marked, all rocks not accurately seen, all winds not strictly registered, together with the ungauged fluctuations of the man himself, his tides of temper, his caprices, and his dreads—these are set-backs to the fortune of the voyage.

The just envisagement of things is the first demand we make of art;

it is art's spirit; then comes the manner of expression, for the quality of art is obviously the quality of its technical expression. No man can change the spirit born in him, but daily, hourly, he does change the manner of its setting forth. All that he sees and hears, reads, writes, and thinks of, even what he dreams, mould and modify the form of his production. The fuller the traditions and life that flood an author's consciousness, the finer, so long as he keeps his powers, will be the texture of his output.

This writer, Joseph Conrad, born of families of Polish gentry who suffered in the rebellion of 1863, sharing as a child his parents' exile, spending his early manhood as a sailor, has laid up a strange store of thought, tradition, life, and language, and on his manner of production this has stamped itself. As in a fine carpet, with lapse of time, the colours grow more subtle, more austere, so in the carpet of this writer's weaving the bewildering richness of his earlier books is sobered to the clearer, cooler colours of the later. *Almayer's Folly*, *An Outcast of the Islands*, *Tales of Unrest*—his first three books—were in a sense surcharged; they gleamed, they were luxuriant, like the tropics where their scenes were laid; they had a certain animal delight in their abundance; they rioted. With *The Nigger of the 'Narcissus'*—that real epic of the sea—the carpet begins to tone; through *Youth* and *Lord Jim* this process of toning is at work, till in 'Typhoon' and, above all, in 'Falk' a perfect mellowness is reached. *Nostromo*, in some respects his most amazing work, reveals the carpet, as after a visit to the cleaner's, harsher again in colour, somewhat patchy, but *The Mirror of the Sea*, which followed on *Nostromo*, displays it in an evening light, worn to a soberer beauty. As to *The Secret Agent*, our latest glimpse of Joseph Conrad's carpet, the colours are clear and quiet, though we are shown them in a hard, unsparing light.

The writing of these ten books is probably the only writing of the last twelve years that will enrich the English language to any great extent. Other writers will better clarify and mould; this writer, by the native wealth of his imagery, by a more daring and a subtler use of words, brings something new to the fund of English letters. The faults of style are obvious, the merit is the merit of unconscious, and unforced, and, in a sense, of accidental novelty. Style is inseparable from that which it expresses, and all that we should fling aside, and rightly, as exotic, if it expressed a futile spirit in new words and images, we instinctively accept with all its flaws when it clothes true insight into life. A language is avid of fresh blood, of all that ministers to health and stamina; like a human being, it assimilates the cake and rejects the country rock. All that is country rock in Joseph Conrad's writings falls away; all that is not has passed into the English tongue.

Writers of any courage sometimes descend on to the little earth of creatures they have created, and ask: 'Are these persons really living—is it blood, or is it sawdust, in these veins? I'll try them with a pin!' And with a pin they go, searching for soft spots, but they never run it in; they are not looking for another's vulnerable spots—any blood or sawdust that came out would, unfortunately, be their own. Precious to themselves, they must preserve the little creatures they have made. So that, though when they return to heaven they say: 'This or that one's very woodeny!' in their hearts they do not feel them so, for it was they who made them.

But the reader of any courage need not, nor to do him justice does he often, spare the bodkin.

On the earth of Joseph Conrad the population teems; and, having tried them with a bodkin, we find very few with sawdust in their veins. Some, it is true, such as the hero in *Lord Jim*, or the husband in the story 'The Return', have been so violently attracted by the man who made them that, like true worshippers, they refuse to stand upon their legs. Intended for stupid men with the brains and nerves of such, they will not, out of longing to resemble their creator, admit that they are stupid. They pray so to be like him, that their prayer has sometimes been a little heard; they voice too much the thoughts of their creator. But they are few. Oftener—like Captain MacWhirr and Mr. Jukes in 'Typhoon', and Mr. Baker of *The Nigger*; like the girl in 'Falk'; the elderly French lieutenant in *Lord Jim*: 'a quiet, massive chap in a creased uniform, sitting drowsily over a tumbler half-full of some dark liquid'; like the ragged Russian in the 'Heart of Darkness': like Karain the Malay, and Stein the naturalist; like Nostromo's Doctor Monygham; Stevie, Inspector Heat, the Perfect Anarchist, and Mrs. Verloc in *The Secret Agent*—they stand up very straight and undismayed, not in the limelight needful to the figures of more fashionable children of the brain; not in the high, dry light of Fielding, Thackeray, or Henry James; not in Turgenev's limpid, sorrowing sunlight; but in a shadowy glamour of their own. Breathing and palpable, clothed firmly in their suitable flesh, they are yet elusive, as though jealous of displaying those dynamic powers which they concrete. They have something of the quality and something of the colouring seen in a Leonardo picture; they quiver with the strength of their vitality; they move amongst black shadows. For Joseph Conrad is an artist who paints in orange, Vandyke-brown, blue, silver, and lamp-black, whose poetry is science, and whose science poetry. And always round these figures, above them, and below are felt those restless forces, too potent in their restlessness for man, too little potent for the unchanging rhythm that keeps their restlessness controlled.

There is a natural tendency in departmental man, and perhaps especially in Englishmen, to demand of authors that they shall make for our enjoyment so-called 'interesting' characters—not common sailors, anarchists, or outcasts of the islands—but persons of a certain rank and fashion; persons living not in 'sordid squalor,' but in gilt-edged certainty; persons not endued with the heroism and the failings of poor human nature, but with gentility; in a word, persons really 'interesting.' This is the great defect of Joseph Conrad's writings. Lamentably lacking in the power of envisaging the world as the private property of a single class, lamentably curious, lamentably sympathetic with all kinds of men, he has failed dismally to produce a single book dealing solely with the upper classes. All sorts of common people come upon his stage, and in such a careless way; not that we may laugh at them, or note the eccentric habits of their kind, but that we may see them breathing-in their oxygen, loving and dying, more alive and kicking than the veriest *bourgeois* of us all. It is a grievous fault! That one who paints a gentleman as well as Joseph Conrad can, should choose to paint Verloc, and give us insight, such as few have given, into a fellow-creature so remarkably deficient in gentility—this is indeed a waste of force! For, departmental as we are, we feel we only want to know the things that help us to be departmental. Before the departmental man there shines a climbing star. The stars that he who has the cosmic spirit sees are stars that never climb; fixed as fate, they throw their rays.

But there is one faculty of Joseph Conrad's writings for which even departmental Britons may be grateful. It is his kindly diagnosis of the departmental Briton. Prisoners in the cells of our own nationality, we never see ourselves; it is reserved for one outside looking through the tell-tale peep-hole to get a proper view of us. So much the better when the eye that peeps is loving! In the whole range of his discovery there is no man that better pleases Joseph Conrad than this same departmental Briton, man of action, man of simple faith, man un-visited by hesitation—in sum, the man of enterprise, with all his qualities and limitations. He has painted this type a dozen times—Captains

Lingard, Allison, MacWhirr, Mr. Baker, Mr. Jukes, Mr. Creighton, Inspector Heat, and many more.

Detached by temperament and blood, this writer sees that sort of Briton with a tender irony that brings out all his foibles, but also an essential sturdiness of soul which makes him one to have beside you on a dark and windy night. Seeing him objectively and without confusion, knowing him personally in all those hours that test the temper of the heart, and having felt his value at first hand, Joseph Conrad has hung on our too-little grateful walls the most seizing portraits of the man of action that our literature can show. For evidence as poignant of this type we have to go to Speke's[1] delicious, naïve presentment of himself in his journal of the Nile's discovery. We learn, subjectively, from that what Speke had no desire to tell, no interest in telling, no power of seeing when the tale was told; we learn, reading between the lines, with our tongues pressed against our cheeks, what a force is 'no imagination'; we learn, too, with our tongues restored, the meaning of the word 'indomitable.' But to learn from Speke's unconscious revelation we must have our wits about us and construct his figure for ourselves; to learn from Joseph Conrad's object-pictures we need only eyes.

Side by side with these impervious spirits he has been through all the peril of the sea, watching to see how they would take it, and he has found they took it very well. So there has grown up in his heart a laughing admiration, a sense of safety and reliance on a kind of man who really would be frightened if he could; and with that laughing admiration he has set him down, not once, but many times.

In the features of those truthful portraits one seems to read the kindly artist's verdict: 'On a lee shore, sirs, there are worse things than "no imagination"!'

There hang the pictures if we had eyes!

Eyes; it seems a little thing! But to 'see' is the greatest gift of all. The surface of the world is open enough to everybody's gaze; that which lies behind the surface is what lies in the gazer's soul, the beauty which everyday phenomena evoke out of the seer's consciousness. Everything is beautiful to those who have the humour to perceive. Birth and decay, virtue and vice, youth and old age, even the real and touching value of the departmental Briton—all these the seer Joseph Conrad sees, and has put in terms of a profound philosophy.

[1] John Hanning Speke (1827–64), explorer who discovered Victoria Nyanza. Galsworthy is referring to Speke's *Journal of the Discovery of the Source of the Nile* (1863).

A SET OF SIX

6 August 1908

---

89. Robert Lynd, review, *Daily News*

10 August 1908, 3

Robert Lynd (1879–1949), Irish essayist and for many years literary editor of the *News Chronicle*. A different version, modified but in essentials the same, appeared in *Black and White*, 29 August 1908. This review irritated Conrad enormously, particularly Lynd's extraordinary reference to Constance Garnett. To Galsworthy he wrote:

The above *D[ai]ly News* genius exclaims that my novels would have been much better if translated by Mrs. Garnett. That's an idea. Shall I send her the clean type of *Razumov*? But why complicate life to that extent? She ought to write them; and then the harmless reviewer could begin something like this: 'Mr. Joseph Conrad's latest novel written by Mrs. Garnett is a real acquisition for our literature, not like the others previously published, which, on the whole, were rather noxious, if amazing, phenomena, etc., etc.' [letter wrongly dated July 1908, *L&L*, ii, 71].

Mr. Conrad, as everybody knows, is a Pole, who writes English by choice, as it were, rather than by nature. According to most people this choice is a good thing, especially for English literature. To some of us, on the other hand, it seems a very regrettable thing, even from the point of view of English literature. A writer who ceases to see the world coloured by his own language—for language gives colour to thoughts and things in a way that few people understand—is apt to lose the concentration and intensity of vision without which the greatest literature cannot be made. It was a sort of nationalism of language and outlook that kept wanderers like Turgénieff and Browning from ever becoming cosmopolitan and second rate. Mr. Kipling, who has never had a native country, but only a native Empire, is a writer who has not been entirely saved from the cosmopolitan danger, despite the fact that he is fortunate enough to write in a language to which he was born.

Mr. Conrad, without either country or language, may be thought to have found a new patriotism for himself in the sea. His vision of men, however, is the vision of a cosmopolitan, of a homeless person. Had he but written in Polish his stories would assuredly have been translated into English and into the other languages of Europe; and the works of Joseph Conrad translated from the Polish would, I am certain, have been a more precious possession on English shelves than the works of Joseph Conrad in the original English, desirable as these are. What greater contribution has been made to literature in English during the past twenty years than Mrs. Constance Garnett's translations of the novels of Turgénieff? But suppose Turgénieff had tried to write them in English!

Perhaps it was one of Mrs. Garnett's dedications that first set me making comparisons between Turgénieff and Mr. Conrad. I doubt, however, if any lover of Turgénieff could read 'Gaspar Ruiz,' the first story in Mr. Conrad's new volume, without noticing a curious similarity in the methods of the two writers. 'Gaspar Ruiz,' one feels, could only have been written by one who knew the author of 'A Lear of the Steppes' inside and out, backwards and forwards. It is one of those rare stories which, in the enthusiasm of reading, one is inclined to put among the greatest short stories in the English language. Gaspar Ruiz, like the Lear of the Steppes, is a magnificent giant—gigantic in his muscles, in his simplicity, in his single-minded devotion.

[a summary of the plot is given here]

Mr. Conrad, however, is a creator of impressions, not a teller of anecdotes, and one learns little of his stories from a bare account of their plots. In regard to the incidents of 'Gaspar Ruiz' it is enough to say that, not since Turgénieff's Lear tore down the walls of his house with the fury of his hands, has there been in fiction so terrible a vision of the mad output of strength as when Gaspar makes a gun carriage of his body in order that the gates of the enemy may be burst open and the woman of his devotion brought out alive. Compared with Turgénieff's story Mr. Conrad's has this weakness: that Gaspar's end is pathetic rather than tragically magnificent. There was no need to allow him to die happy with his wife speaking her first words of love to him. The last few pages read too much like a story-teller's smoothing out of things.

This possibly brings us near the secret of a peculiar quality in Mr. Conrad's stories. Mr. Conrad is not, when all is said, a tragic writer. His characters are not, in Pater's phrase, 'aristocrats of passion.' We might call them rather 'aristocrats of fascination.' One remembers 'Youth,' for instance, that story of a fascination almost as wonderful as passion—the fascination of youth and command amid all dangers and the sea. Gaspar, too, is a creature not so much of passion as of fascination, and in 'An Anarchist'—a whimsical story of a Frenchman who is convicted in the most absurd way of being an Anarchist, and who escapes from a penal settlement in South America to a cattle-breeding island—we have another case of a man who always acts as though under a spell. In 'The Informer' we have a story about real Anarchists, and here again the man who gives his name to the story is a spell-bound sort of person. In his case, however, the spells—one the hatred of Anarchism, one the love of woman—conflict; but as he is only a very ordinary piece of imagination this story does not count for much.

'The Brute' is a wonderful impression of a spell-bound ship, a ship that seems to have as living a personality of its own as a vicious horse, and delights in the death of its victims like a heathen god. Only one other living writer, perhaps, could have told this story so well. Splendidly told, too, is 'The Duel', the fantastic story of two soldiers who began fighting a duel for a scarcely-known reason as lieutenants of Napoleon's, and met at intervals and tried to kill each other till they were Generals, and Napoleon had been shipped off to St. Helena. This is an excellent example of Mr. Conrad's whimsical, half humorous, decorative method. The picture of General Feraud and General D'Hubert tracking and dodging each other through the wood in the hope of bringing the epic duel to a mortal close is a masterpiece of story-telling. Still, the first story, to my mind, is worth all the rest of the book. 'Gaspar Ruiz' alone would make *A Set of Six* memorable among the books of the year—perhaps among the books of many years. Mr. Conrad, as we have said, has here written a story to compare with 'A Lear of the Steppes.' Had he remained a Polish writer, he might—who knows?— have given us novels to compare with *On the Eve* and *Virgin Soil*.

90. W. L. Courtney, review, *Daily Telegraph*

12 August 1908, 4

See No. 92 for Conrad's comments on Courtney's review. Courtney also wrote in his letter book, 12 August 1908:

And what is the general impression that Joseph Conrad in all his works leaves on our minds? It is a little difficult to describe. In general outlines his philosophy seems to resolve itself into an inculcation of the littleness and insignificance of humanity. We make a great fuss about ourselves, but we are in reality only playthings, puppets, dolls in the hands of the overmastering forces outside us—Nature and circumstance. But what I am more especially concerned with is the impression which Conrad gives us of his own personality. He possesses a singular neutrality and detachment. He stands apart from all his creations. Sometimes he does not appear very much interested in them himself; often he seems to suggest that we need not be interested either. After all, if humanity is such a little thing, there is no special reason why we should show excitement in the matter. But then, what sort of artist can he be who is not interested in humanity? Take away the human drama, and the occupation of the literary artist is gone. Or is it that Joseph Conrad also is a prophet of violence, in that he desires to show his contempt of the infinitely touching hopes and despairs, loves and hatreds of men and women, and, painting with a full brush, wishes to portray us all as dupes or slaves? [*Rosemary's Letter Book*, The Wayfarer's Library, 1908, 88–9.]

In this essay, Courtney was concerned with the literary fashion of the time, which he saw as 'a certain crude and harsh violence, a desperate desire to produce an effect, and to produce it in such a masterful fashion that the nerves tingle with the strain' (p. 82). Those writers he condemned were W. E. Henley in poetry and Conrad, Arthur Morrison (1863–1945: *Tales of Mean Streets*) and Rudyard Kipling in prose.

Among the most successful of the short story-tellers must assuredly be included the name of Joseph Conrad. He has just produced a collection of six stories, two, or, perhaps, three, of which are masterpieces, while all of them stand at an exceedingly high level of workmanship and literary value. Mr. Conrad arranges them in classes, a 'romantic tale,' an 'ironic' tale, an 'indignant' tale, and so forth, as though he were aware that some apology were needed for stringing diverse stories together, which are not obviously connected in spirit or method. But these appellations of his we can disregard. They tell us nothing, and, indeed, serve only to confuse our judgment. There is nothing very 'indignant' or very 'desperate' about the stories to which he chooses to affix these titles, though there may be about the feelings of the readers. The first deals with the malicious waywardness of a merchant vessel, the second about the absurd as well as desperate straits to which a supposed Anarchist was reduced in the attempt to gain his living.

Mr. Joseph Conrad appears, as we have said, to considerable advantage in these brief studies of his, based on his large experience of the world and of men, or else springing from his own inexhaustible imagination. A short time ago a brother novelist, Mr. John Galsworthy, published, in one of the current reviews, a disquisition on Joseph Conrad[1]—a generous estimate of an author's capacities, from one who knew the difficulties of the art of story-telling and the rarity of striking success. The encomium was a little extravagant, it may be, but it hit one characteristic which every reader of Joseph Conrad will appreciate. He has a certain quality about him which makes him a thing apart, almost elemental. He sees the world as a whole, and is under no misapprehension as to the insignificant part played therein by humanity. This is not a customary attitude for a novelist to take, for obvious reasons. By virtue of his office he is concerned with humanity and its doings, his business is to portray the drama of man's existence, and whether it turns to tragedy or comedy, it is the human figures which engross his attention, their faults, their failings, their efforts, their successes, their affections, and their animosities. Thackeray and Fielding would find their occupation gone if they did not put men and women in the very forefront of their romances as the main material and the proper objects of solicitude.

But when we come to a writer like Conrad, we are conscious that though he is interested in his puppets, they are not half so interesting to him as the vast forces of nature, the obscure dominion of fate, and the unyielding tyranny of circumstance, which crush the feverish

[1] See No. 88.

activity of men as their plaything. Many of Conrad's novels deal with the ocean, and one need only read the *Nigger of the 'Narcissus'* to comprehend how absolutely insignificant is man in the grip of such eternal and archetypal elements as the sea. Something of the same feeling is produced also by *Lord Jim*, by that amazing story entitled *Nostromo*, and a few others. In each case the reader is aware that all the pomp and circumstance of man's estate, so infinitely important to himself, become ridiculous when we look at the matter from the universal standpoint. The effect on Mr. Conrad himself is no less remarkable. There is a certain detachment in his way of regarding things; he is perfectly neutral, almost unconcerned. These or those things happen—tragic errors, humourous mistakes, wholesale catastrophes, conflagrations, revolutions. If men get mixed up with them, so much the worse for the men, and after all it does not much matter. The tragi-comedy of existence goes on all the same; only the dramatic characters are different. The best and wisest man is he who does the work immediately before his eyes, with the greatest amount of calm efficiency. And perhaps if our author has any preferences, he admires most the type of British official, a man of action, a man of simple faith, unvisited by hesitation, untroubled by imagination, men like Captain Lingard, Mr. Baker, Inspector Heat, MacWhirr, and Allison.

In the present book, the same attitude is revealed, almost unconsciously, for our author has probably no theories about his art, and writes in obedience to the obscure promptings of his genius. Now and again, when he has a subject which suits him, he writes a little masterpiece.

[a summary of the plot of 'Gaspar Ruiz' is given here]

. . . Mr. Conrad tells his story not as though he were particularly enlisted on the side of his hero, not even wishing us to be very interested but merely as one who draws up the veil of an unknown corner of life, and bids us watch the blind happenings of destiny. Man is but a toy. Things are what they are, and they will be what they will be. We, the spectators, should take the lesson home to ourselves, not in any spirit of cynicism or revolt, but as philosophers who know and who must needs be contented, acquiescing with sombre silence in what cannot be helped.

The same thing is revealed in another of these stories, entitled 'An Anarchist.' A young Frenchman, a mechanician, leading a tolerably harmless life, working hard to earn his daily bread, drinks one night too much in a café, gets mixed up with some Anarchists, and in his drunken ardour shouts out their watchwords, as though he himself were an acknowledged rebel. What is the result? He can never shake off the cloud of suspicion which from this moment broods over his existence. He is thrown into prison, swept off to a penal settlement, blunders into the middle of a riot, commits murder in order to escape, gets away at last from his pursuers, only to find himself in the hands of a very hard-headed Yankee manager, who keeps him in durance vile as the engineer of a little sea launch—condemning him to all sorts of servile employment, merely on the ground that he suspects the shadiness of his past. Here is the coil of circumstance and fate, a deadly chain ensnaring a man really innocent, and dooming him to a life of torture. To be the captain of one's soul, as Mr. W. E. Henley adjures us to be, is indeed a difficult business. For the most part human beings are slaves not because they like it, but because accident is too strong for them. If they resist, their sufferings are the more, but they are dragged along all the same. In circumstances like these, the only available temper is gloomy resignation, stoicism of the most austere type, the wide-eyed acknowledgement that though we are slaves we are not therefore dupes.

It is a dreary philosophy at best, but it is what Mr. Conrad's tales suggest. He, too, belongs to that modern school of violence which, whether in the form of Imperial violence, like that of Mr. Rudyard Kipling, or psychological violence, like that of our author, appears to be the most popular mode or pose among our writers of today. All the light, all the colours are crude and harsh. There is no softness in the landscape, no healing balm in the atmosphere. The world is an unfriendly place, and most of us, if we begin to think at all, are prisoners. It was not so with an earlier school, who envisaged their outlook on life with a tenderer grace; but they are now regarded as sentimental optimists, who refused to face stern facts. There is not much sentimentalism in a modern author like Mr. Conrad. There is abundance of strength, picturesque vigour, masterly handling of his materials; but no pity, no sorrow. Humour he certainly possesses, the grim humour of a man who declines to be deceived. As a story-teller he has few rivals; each tale of his arrests our attention from the very outset, and does not let us go till the very end. His so-called 'ironic' tale in this volume is, comparatively speaking, a failure, for we do not quite understand from the last few sentences what he is driving at. Another of his tales, entitled 'The Duel', becomes tedious through its unnecessary length. But 'Gaspar Ruiz', 'The Brute', and 'An Anarchist' are fine achievements—the work of a man who has conquered the difficulties of his task, and deals with his topics as a veritable artist, a recognised master of his craft.

91. Unsigned review, *Country Life*

15 August 1908, 234–5

Conrad correctly assumed that this review was by Anderson Graham (see No. 92).

On first looking at Mr. Joseph Conrad's new book, *A Set of Six*, we thought the author had been making some new studies in style, for on the cover of the work the six stories are described as 'A Romantic Tale, An Ironic Tale, An Indignant Tale, A Desperate Tale, A Military Tale, A Pathetic Tale.' What a miracle it would have been if the author had at one and the same time proved himself to be a master of romance, irony and pathos, to say nothing of the other three headings. But a little consideration led us to think that the compilation of this list was no more than an essay in the art of literary window-dressing. The book is no book in any real sense of the term. At any rate, it looks to the present writer as though Mr. Conrad had contributed his six stories to a magazine, or the magazines, and had invented the descriptive titles when he came to put them together between the same covers. Such descriptive titles do not greatly commend themselves. When Mr. Conrad or anybody else writes a story called 'The Duel', the reader might surely be trusted to find out upon perusal that it was 'A Military Tale,' and in the story called 'The Informer,' the sub-title, 'An Ironic Tale,' appears to be still more superfluous. . . . It is a pity, because Mr. Conrad possesses many of the attributes of the artist, and nothing could be more disappointing than his misuse, for example, of the term ironic. Mrs. Slip-Slop's 'irony' would have been more to the purpose. . . .

It is not here ['The Informer'], but in 'The Duel,' that Mr. Conrad shows his best command of the ironic spirit. If he had possessed the style that goes with it, this story would indeed have been a masterpiece. But irony is the most difficult to employ of all the literary man's weapons. At perfection it must be as delicate as the lines of a snowflake, yet as keen as the edge of a hollow-ground razor, and, more than that, it must be absolutely well bred. Irony at once becomes heavy and vulgar when used with a lack of breeding. The master of it in English undoubtedly is Fielding. Swift brought too much savage indignation for such a light weapon to carry. He was like a man trying to shave with a reaping-hook; but Fielding, with his all-round interest and sympathy, his detachment of mind and his broad toleration, could sit in his easy-chair and paint the world around him with this, the most delicate and still the most effective of brushes. Mr. Conrad conceives his story in an ironic spirit, but fails to write it in the ironic style. The little tale, nevertheless, is as fine as anything he has done recently. It concerns two soldiers of Napoleonic times, who might have been friends and comrades. Perversity and misunderstanding cause them to fight a series of the most truculent duels and to continue a life-long enmity. The author seems to have rejoiced in making fate play with the lives of men. Even so, he scarcely carries out the original intention, but winds up with a happy and sentimental ending. If anyone can sit down and imagine the manner in which Fielding would have told this story, he will be able to appreciate the force of the criticism that Mr. Conrad is too heavy of hand to use irony with the skill of that great master. It is difficult to believe that in the other stories he thought any more about what he was writing when he made his list than he did about the use of the word irony. The story he calls 'The Brute,' described as 'An Indignant Tale,' is one of those in which a ship is endowed with a kind of personality. The conceit is good enough for a paragraph, but it is beaten out very thin in this story, and to call 'Il Conde' 'A Pathetic Tale' is a gross misuse of the word. Pathos is as delicate an instrument as irony, and a much more beautiful one; but it is when the two are used in conjunction that the perfection of narrative style is reached. Probably Mr. Conrad himself would prefer to be judged by the first of his tales, 'Gaspar Ruiz.' He calls it romantic, perhaps because it is the history of a great passion. It might still more accurately have been named a study in brutality. If we were asked what is the strongest characteristic of Mr. Conrad, the unhesitating answer would be, the power of brutal realism. . . . The final scene of the drama is incredible. Gaspar Ruiz makes himself into a gun-carriage in order that his sweetheart may be relieved:

He lay there before me on his breast under the darkly glittering bronze of his monstrous burden, such as no love or strength of man had ever had to bear in the lamentable history of the world. His arms were spread out, and he resembled a prostrate penitent on the moonlit ground.

Not a detail of the breaking of the man is missed by the author, and indeed it is obvious that he depends for his effects in a large measure upon the power of producing horror. This, surely, is not very great art; it is not much greater than that of the sensational reporter who gathers together thousands of readers for the rag that will print his account of the last dying struggles of some wretched criminal hanged for murder.

92. Conrad's response to the reviews

21 August 1908

Letter to Garnett (*LEG*, 211–13). Conrad comments upon reviews in *The Times* (13 August 1908), *Daily News* (No. 89), *Daily Telegraph* (No. 90) and *Country Life* (No. 91).

. . . W. L. Courtney in a long article[1] calls the *Duel* tedious and 'Gaspar Ruiz' a masterpiece; and myself a heartless wretch with a pose of brutality like the rest of the moderns. Still, always according to W.L.C., there are two masterpieces and a half in the vol.—'G. Ruiz' being one of them, 'An Anarch': the other and the 'Brute' the doubtful one.

[1] See No. 90.

Your acceptance of the 'Duel' is balm to my soul. My first intention was to call that story 'The Masters of Europe' but I rejected it as pretentious. Anyway I did conscientiously try to put in as much of Napoleonic feeling as the subject could hold. This has been missed by all the reviewers, every single one being made blind by the mere tale. . . .

The *Times* review seemed to me insignificant. But there is a fellow in the *Dly News* who calls me—God only knows on what provocation— a man without country and language. It is like abusing a tongue-tied man, for what can one say. The statement is simple and brutal; and any answer would involve too many feelings of one's inner life, stir too much secret bitterness and complex loyalty to be even attempted with any hope of being understood. I thought that a man who has written the *Nigger, Typhoon*, 'The End of the Tether', 'Youth', was safe from that sort of thing. But apparently not. If I had made money by dealing in diamond shares like my neighbour here Sir Julius Wernher, of Hamburg, I would be a baronet of the U.K. and provided both with a language and a country. Still I suppose the man is simply an ass; and even the tribute he pays to your wife's unforgettable achievement fails to mollify me, for this once. For he goes on shoving me with incredible folly on to Turgeniev à propos of 'G. Ruiz', comparing it with *Lear of the Steppes* do you understand? *The Lear!!!* that infernal magazine fake with the *Lear of the Steppes*!!!! It is enough to make one wonder whether the man understands the words he writes—whether he has sense and judgement enough to come in when it rains? Has ever the Shade of a great artist been more amazingly, more gratuitously insulted? Who's the fellow? . . . Couldn't someone speak to him quietly and suggest he should go behind a counter and weigh out margarine by the six-pennyworth? I can understand Anderson Graham to whom I am such an offensive fraud that he can't even see me scratch the side of my nose without exasperation at the indecency of the thing. That's a genuine temperamental expression, frank and honourable enough in its way tho' certainly a little funny. He jumps on me with both feet in the *Country Life* 'book of the week'. But the *Dly News* article is beyond everything the gloomiest pessimism as to the good feeling and common decency of daily criticism could imagine.

93. Edward Garnett, unsigned review, *Nation*

22 August 1908, 746, 748

The review was entitled 'The Genius of Mr. Conrad'. Garnett here takes up points made in the *Times Literary Supplement* review of 13 August 1908, and by Robert Lynd ('another English critic', see No. 89). Garnett's ironic reference to our 'cosmopolitan and friendless' author's talent is a taking up (incorrectly) of Lynd's foolish remark, 'the vision of a cosmopolitan, of a homeless person'. Garnett's return to categorizing Conrad as a Slav (see No. 81) tried Conrad's friendship (see No. 94).

While a *Times* critic has patriotically declared that Mr. Conrad's stories are 'characteristically English by virtue of the humour that plays all about them and through them,' another English critic has hazarded the suggestion that had 'Mr. Conrad remained a Polish writer he might—who knows?—have given us novels to compare with *On the Eve* and *Virgin Soil*,' and has deplored that the author should have become denationalised and have written his books in English instead of in Polish. Both these criticisms, though complimentary to Mr. Conrad's powers, go wide of the main point—that it is impossible for a writer of genius to denationalise his spirit. Mr. Conrad's rare gifts may, indeed, have been fertilised by his cosmopolitan life, and have fructified through their transplantation into English soil, but anything less English than his ironic, tender, and sombre vision of life it would be hard to find. In fact, the 'humour that plays about his stories' is essentially Slav in its ironic acceptance of the pathetic futility of human nature, and quite un-English in its refinement of tender, critical malice. No doubt Poland lost much when this writer, who has literature in his blood, cast in his lot with our merchantmen and sailed to the ends of the earth in English ships; but what is of especial interest to the critic is that he has been a liberating force to our English insularity. The horizon of his human valuations is not bounded by the special illusions our English society cherishes, and yet none of our writers have paid so impartial, so fair a tribute to the integrity of the Englishman on active service, and the straightness of our English rule overseas. Mr. Conrad, indeed, has a special affection for the Englishman's bluff code, practical creed, and simplicity of outlook; but let us not presume on this, or conclude on such slender evidence that his stories are 'characteristically English', for they are nothing of the kind. They are Continental in their literary affinities, Slav in their psychological insight, and Polish in their haunting and melancholy cadence, and in their preference for dwelling on the minor.

[quotes 'An Anarchist', pp. 146–8: 'On his twenty-fifth birthday . . . folded his arms.']

The passage above cited is taken from 'The Anarchist,' a little story which is a gem of Mr. Conrad's art, and, indeed, an admirable illustration of our 'cosmopolitan and friendless' author's talent for finding himself at home wherever his human material gives him scope for his ironical, picturesque observation of men. Give Mr. Conrad an aged cabman and a bony, disillusioned horse, and he will invest this prosaic subject (as he has done in *The Secret Agent*) with a depth of human significance as arresting as Rembrandt's treatment of a group of beggars. Give him an advertisement of the B.O.S. Meat Extract Manufacturing Co., Limited, and his cosmopolitan vision transports us straightway to the Marañon cattle estancia in a South American estuary, where Mr. Harry Gee, the Americanised manager, collides with our unfortunate *soidisant* Anarchist, the victim of a Parisian law court, who had managed to escape, by favoring fortune, from the convict settlement at Cayenne. The end of the story has that poetic cadence on the minor strings which, as we have noted, is part and parcel of our author's birthright. It is simple and ironically profound, is this poor Anarchist's refusal to return to Europe and to '*them*,' which means the 'victims of society' who were ready to 'stick their comrade like a pig.'

Four of the stories in *A Set of Six* are not studies on which the artist probably sets any high value, though all of them, if published anonymously, would betray themselves to the connoisseur's eye as indubitable Conrads. The least successful is 'The Informer,' another study of an Anarchist *milieu*, and we attribute its failure to the three chief characters —X, the great publicist conspirator and active inspirer of secret societies; Comrade Sevrin, 'the most persistent, dangerous, craftiest, and systematic of informers'; and the girl Anarchist, with whom he is in love, not acting true to type, but being plausibly brought together for the purpose of the story. Much better is 'The Brute', a tale of a mad ship, 'the most evil-minded, underhand, savage brute that ever went afloat,' who invariably kills somebody every voyage she makes. The narrator, a seaman, justifies his charge of insanity against the 'Apse Family' by the terror she inspired among her crew whenever she broke loose, till finally she 'overreaches herself in her last little game,' and goes ashore off the Cape. The first story, 'Gaspar Ruiz,' a study of a heroic figure, 'a strong man who perished through his strength' in one of the South American wars of liberation, though admirable in its character sketches, is lacking in subtlety of atmosphere; but this criticism does not apply to 'The Duel,' which is a masterpiece of style—a story which, in the unerring delicacy of its artistic strokes, is worthy of Turgenev. Mr. Conrad's serene impartiality, his mordant humour, his special faculty of depicting the change and movement of life, flowing on even while it arrests us with some sharply stamped aspect, then gliding away to form anew some strangely significant episode—all his rare qualities unite happily in 'The Duel' to produce a perfect whole. The description of the first duel in Lieut. Feraud's garden (pp. 192, 193), the scene of Fouché's reception, in his Ministerial Cabinet, of General Baron D'Hubert (p. 240), and of the final duel in the pine wood between the exasperated adversaries, show the precision of a master's hand. So faultless is this story that indeed it creates the tests by which the companion stories reveal the nature of their achievement.

94. Conrad on Garnett's review in *Nation*

28 August 1908

Letter to Garnett (*LEG*, 213–14). The charges against him listed here by Conrad—'pose of brutality', 'lack of all heart, delicacy, sympathy—sentiment—idealism'—seem to derive from Courtney's review in the *Daily Telegraph* (No. 90) and Graham's review in *Country Life* (No. 91). The extraordinary accusation that Conrad gloated 'over scenes of cruelty' was made by Symons in an unpublished study of Conrad which Symons sent to him. Conrad replied (August 1908): 'I did not know I had "a heart of darkness" and an "unlawful" soul. Mr. Kurtz had . . . I did not know that I delighted in cruelty and that the shedding of blood was my obsession' (*L&L*, ii, 73).

I have the *Nation* and I must thank you for the article. No doubt to put one's tongue into both cheeks at once is an immoral trick and I suspect that it is on the ground that you and W. L. Courtney (bow) meet in the condemnation of the 'Informer.'

I don't defend him—it. But let me ask, is my earnestness of no account? Is that a Slavonic trait? And I am earnest, terribly earnest. Carlyle bending over the history of Frederick called the Great was a mere trifle, a volatile butterfly, in comparison. For that good man had only to translate himself out of bad German into the English we know, whereas I had to work like a coal miner in his pit quarrying all my English sentences out of a black night.

For that reason, I suppose, I read in a study (still unpublished) of Conrad, that I gloat over scenes of cruelty and am obsessed by visions of spilt blood.

At any rate I think I have always written with dignity, with more dignity than the above-alluded-to butterfly ever could command. And that not certainly from lack of conviction, which often takes that outward form. The fact is that I have approached things human in a spirit of piety foreign to those lovers of humanity who would like to make

224

of life a sort of Cook's Personally Conducted Tour—from the cradle to the grave. I have never debased that quasi-religious sentiment by tears and groans and sighs. I have neither grinned nor gnashed my teeth. In a word, I have behaved myself decently—which, except in the gross conventional sense, is not so easy as it looks. Therefore there are those who reproach me with the pose of brutality, with the lack of all heart, delicacy, sympathy—sentiment—idealism. There is even one abandoned creature who says I am a neo-platonist. What on earth is that?

95. Edward Thomas, review, *Bookman*

October 1908, 39

Edward Eastaway Philip Thomas (1878–1917), English poet. He was killed in the First World War and left behind him lyrical verse of great beauty.

Mr. Conrad's six new stories are labelled, rather whimsically, a romantic tale, an ironic, an indignant, a desperate, a military, and a pathetic tale. But they are all perfect tales, fascinating arrangements of character and event so as continually to delight and surprise. At a first reading we are inclined to think that here is an entertainment, of the oldest kind, that has just reached its hardest, clearest, least wasteful form—an entertainment and perhaps nothing more, except that it is unique in quality. Not, of course, that this would be a small or a common achievement. To excel in the telling of a story is to excel where all men are competitors. And the invention and external form of three of these six tales are in themselves so good that every one would be very much charmed if the colouring, the words, the filling in of the prescribed outlines had been done by less than a master hand. The other three tales, of a mad ship, of an anarchist, and of a quiet old gentleman and a *Camorra*, are not imaginable in any other man's hands. We are, however, much more than charmed. Some very good stories are 'writ in water'; they sting us for one short moment only and vanish away. These are not. The substance of them is of precious material, no less than the English of a master who seems to be practically incapable— except, where it is inevitable, in dialogue—of using words without that magic of labour and of character by which the whole, the sentence or the paragraph, becomes incomparably greater than the mere sum of its parts. Nor is Mr. Conrad only a lord of language. These stories, without any irrelevancy, bear a heavy weight of experience, of observa- tion and of reflection. With all their speed, therefore with all their ease and spirit, they produce a richness of effect which compels you to read them again in order to understand it. And then you notice the colour, both physical and spiritual, that is in the words—the cadence you must have noticed before, for such movement is not of every day. 'Tis the colour, first of all, of a man who is vowed to beauty. This is an admir- able sentence: 'In the colourless and pellucid dawn the wood of pines detached its columns of trunks and its dark green canopy very clearly against the rocks of the grey hillside.' But then he sacrifices nothing to produce such sentences. His are all equally good, though there is no harm in admitting that it is when they are used to depict the visible, the faces and forms of men and nature, that they have the most relish. And not only parts of things, and things still and waiting to be painted; but things moving, as in the description of the retreat from Moscow:

[quotes 'The Duel', pp. 211–12: 'Often from daybreak' to 'Immensity of the snows.']

But it is also the colour of a great character and a great courage, of one who has pathos, irony, wit, understanding, and always grace and an admirable air; above all, one who has the spirit of comedy.

96. Unsigned review, *Pall Mall Gazette*

11 October 1911, 5

Review entitled 'Betrayal'.

Keen and merciless in exposure and meticulously searching in analysis, *Under Western Eyes* is a psychologic study of remarkable penetration, and, as a novel, is entitled to rank with the best work that Mr. Joseph Conrad has given us. We are revolted by Razumoff's betrayal of his fellow-student (though Haldin's crime merited the swift and degrading execution that was its punishment), for Haldin had sought refuge in Razumoff's rooms and had confessed to his crime under the conviction that his host was, like himself, a Nihilist. But by subtle strokes of art our sympathy—that is, at least, 'a sympathy of comprehension,' to use De Quincey's striking phrase as applied to *Macbeth*—and perhaps something more, is enlisted with the betrayer. Except that by a quite arbitrary, and, it must be added, inartistic skipping of certain stages of his spiritual development and an equally arbitrary return to them, the narrative does not follow the sequence of events, we trace the various phases of his soul's disturbance from mere rage at being suspected by the police, through a tardy but ever-growing remorse, till, purified by love, he repents, and with high courage makes full confession to an inner circle of conspirators, to suffer at their cruel hands a punishment, horrible, brutal, and infinitely worse than death.

The book startles one by its amazing truth and by the intimate knowledge of the human heart that it reveals in its varied and masterly characterisation. Although, too, he still confuses the preterite with the perfect and often uses the wrong sign of the future, Mr. Conrad's remarkable gifts as a writer of nervous and polished prose are as note-worthy here as always. Quite a masterpiece of writing, for instance, amid much that is excellent is the account of a convict's escape in Siberia. The muffled clanking of his chains, a sound he deadened with strips torn from his clothing lest it should betray his presence, is almost as unforgettable as the tapping of blind Pew's stick.

97. Richard Curle, review, *Manchester Guardian*

11 October 1911, 5

Richard Curle (1883–1969) was Conrad's greatest friend from 1912 until Conrad's death. Curle himself wrote in 1955: 'There have, beyond doubt, been abler critics of Conrad's work than myself, but I do not believe it has ever had a better friend' (introduction to *Nostromo*, Dent Collected Edition, p. xiii). When this review appeared Curle had not yet come to Conrad's notice, and the review contains some adverse criticism.

A new work by Mr. Conrad is a literary event of the first importance. It is now three years since *A Set of Six*—that volume of stories which marked so distinct a change in his technique—was published, and one must not therefore be surprised to find that *Under Western Eyes* carries us still further on the fresh path. One need expect no longer, save in occasional sentences, the exuberant and monotonous vocabulary, that sea-like and sonorous ebb and flow. No; for that exotic style he has exchanged one very distinguished, it is true, very expressive, very artistic, but altogether less striking. It is the atmosphere which we miss (that impalpable thing which has no necessary relation to place), the atmosphere from which emerged people of an invincible reality, the atmosphere which gave us Jim, Mrs. Gould, and Winnie Verloc.

It was in his tropical books especially that it became so enthralling. The strange glow which hung over the tropics hung over his figures as well; the languor of Southern nights which stole into his words stole into the hearts of his people. Everything seemed surrounded by a mysterious and patient force, amidst which life, dimly conscious of it all, went on increasingly with an ironical intensity of joy and suffering. An immense power appeared to brood over the vanities and struggles of men, an impassive and relentless purpose to await them at every step. The fleetingness of individual life, the disenchantment of desire, the passing away of hope, were contrasted with the stillness of the forest, the might of the ocean, the teeming prodigality of the earth. Such is the kind of atmosphere of novels like *Lord Jim* and *Nostromo*, of stories like 'Heart of Darkness,' 'Youth,' 'An Outpost of Progress,' and 'The End of the Tether.' It was a romantic realism, colouring life with an extraordinary vividness. And such is not the atmosphere of *Under Western Eyes*. It is not simply that it is a novel of Europe instead of the tropics, for the typical Conrad atmosphere can be seen in European tales such as 'The Return,' 'To-morrow,' and *The Secret Agent*—it is something much more. *Under Western Eyes* is the work of a great writer for whom psychology is swallowing romance, of a great artist for whom form is becoming more and more impersonal, of a great creator whose creations are beginning to lack energy. The sentences are perfectly modulated, the whole style is exact and finished, but there is that something lacking which used not to be lacking. There are probably in this book a greater mastery of the detail of language, a nearer approach to complete avoidance of exaggeration, than in any of his books, but there is less of original genius. It is curiously as if he had been trying to model himself on Henry James, and in the effort had lost part of his own personality.

But *Under Western Eyes*, though not one of Mr. Conrad's typical achievements, is a remarkable book.

[the plot is briefly summarized]

Perhaps the finest part of the book is devoted to the midnight betrayal of Haldin, reposing trustfully in Razumov's bed. And the only result of it all is that Razumov is convinced that he is himself suspected by the Government. In a powerful scene between him and Councillor Mikulin, who has charge of the inquiry, a scene strangely reminiscent of those between Raskolnikov and the terrible Porphyrius in *Crime and Punishment*, he endeavours to probe their intention concerning him. Caught thus in the web of suspicion, he consents to go as a Government spy to Geneva, where there is a notorious colony of Russian conspirators. Here, as fate would have it, he meets with Haldin's mother and sister, who consider him a hero, as he is believed to have been Haldin's associate and helper. On all hands, indeed, he is greeted warmly, though as somewhat of an enigma. For he cannot hide the bitterness of his animosity nor the gnawing of the remorse which has been fully roused by contact with Miss Haldin. She is presented as a beautiful and strong nature whose trust in Razumov is unbounded. Slowly, under the awakening of his conscience, this life of lies grows impossible to him. It is not till all chances of his ever being discovered have disappeared, till he has felt that he is falling in love with Miss Haldin and that his love will be returned, that he resolves to confess. The end of the book is tragedy, not of an exalted but of a pitiful description. The novel is, as Mr. Conrad truly says, 'the sustained psychology of a mood,' and, as such, all other figures are subsidiary to the main one, and, in spite of their force, appear somehow insubstantial.

98. Unsigned review, *Morning Post*

12 October 1911, 3

Writing to Galsworthy, 15 October 1911, Conrad said:

Marwood [Arthur Marwood, friend of both Conrad and Ford Madox Hueffer] sent me the review out of the *Morning Post*. . . . It was all right: but there was a passage in it which is incomprehensible, unless meant as a hint that I, being a Jew, am especially fit to hold the balance between East and West! I believe that some time ago that preposterous C—— has been connecting me with Father Abraham, whether to hurt me or to serve me, or simply because he's an idiot,—I don't know . . . It's an absurd position to be in, for I trust I have no contemptible prejudices against any kind of human beings and yet it isn't pleasant to be taken out of one's own skin, as it were, by an irresponsible chatterer, [*L&L*, ii, 136.] The review was entitled 'The Riddle of Russia'.

Here is the book that admirers of Mr. Joseph Conrad's work have been waiting for for some time now, ever since, in fact, the publication of *Lord Jim*. *Under Western Eyes* is written with that intensity of vision, that complete absorption in and by the subject, and that astonishing mastery of the subtleties of language which have ever distinguished its author's best work. In addition it is constructed with greater ability than Mr. Conrad's longer stories usually are; it does not give one the idea that *Lord Jim* did, namely, that its author's mare had taken the bit between its teeth; here the man in the saddle is in complete mastery, and the result is a perfectly poised work of art.

The story of *Under Western Eyes* is told by an English professor, living at Geneva, and having some intimate knowledge of the Russian community which inhabits a quarter of that town. The significance of the title lies, of course, in the nationality of the imaginary narrator; the Russian character can only, at the best, be dimly comprehended by the Western mind. Acute and intelligent students of Russia, like Mr. Maurice Baring,[1] have frequently warned us of the complexity of the

---

[1] Maurice Baring (1874–1946), war correspondent, novelist and author of many books on Russia including *What I Saw in Russia* (1913) and *An Outline of Russian Literature* (1914).

problem which seems to Friends of Russian Freedom a mere matter of light and darkness. Mr. Conrad expresses the riddle in terms of personalities, and while he makes it extremely lucid he does not make it any easier to solve. The professor is made to disavow at the outset any intention of providing a key to the mystery. 'I confess,' he says, 'that I have no comprehension of the Russian character. The illogicality of their attitude, the arbitrariness of their conclusions, the frequency of the exceptional, should present no difficulty to a student of many grammars; but there must be something else in the way, some special human trait—one of those subtle differences that are beyond the ken of mere professors.' The most the professor can do for us, and that after all is a very great deal indeed, is to make it clear why he does not understand. Here is an example: 'You think it is a class conflict' (it is a Russian girl speaking of Russian unrest) 'or a conflict of interests, as social contests are with you in Europe. But it is not that at all. It is something quite different.' 'The propensity,' comments the professor, 'of lifting every problem from the plane of the understandable by means of some sort of mystic expression is very Russian. . . . I suppose one must be a Russian to understand Russian simplicity, a terrible corroding simplicity in which mystic phrases clothe a naïve and hopeless cynicism. I think sometimes that the psychological secret of the profound difference of that people consists in this, that they detest life, the irremediable life of the earth as it is, whereas we Westerners cherish it with perhaps an equal exaggeration of its sentimental value.' The professor, we cannot help fancying, must have been a Jew, holding the balance between the West and the East. However that may be, he does succeed in making us see a difference so large that it requires a large mind to appreciate its existence. Those of us who are but shallow observers of national distinctions are apt to strain at a gnat and swallow a camel.

It is not, however, the racial problem that is the only, or even the chief, interest of *Under Western Eyes*. Mr. Conrad is one of the few living novelists that are able to analyse character not only at rest but in motion. In this book we have a dynamic study of character comparable only in recent fiction to that which Mr. Conrad himself gave us in *Lord Jim*. In this case it is a study in remorse, mainly moving from within, but also affected by external forces of personality, according to the psychological theory propounded in the earlier work. . . .

[gives a summary of the plot]

. . . Mr. Conrad has given us an able and convincing study of a soul in the cruel, remorseless grip of fate. He has never done anything better.

99. Unsigned review, *Westminster Gazette*

14 October 1911, 12

Fatality enters your room while your landlady's back is turned; you come home and find it in possession bearing a man's name, clothed in flesh—wearing a brown cloth coat and long boots—lounging against the stove. It asks you 'Is the outer door closed?'—and you don't know enough to take it by the throat and fling it downstairs. You don't know. Mr. Conrad describes his book as 'the sustained psychology of a mood having its origin in a crime,' but we must go further back than the mood if we wish to understand the book as literature. We are not content, now, to accept the study of a fragment, however magnificently executed; we must see the fragment in some relation to the whole, and the whole is life, the urgent, significant life of an individual, a family, or a nation. We look to the masters of literature in fiction for some light on the larger problem; the psychology of a mood does not content us if it has no wider application. 'Fatality enters your room. . . .' That is, after all, the major premiss of Mr. Conrad's book. Fatality entered the room of Kirylo Razumov, a young Russian student without political bias. It entered in the person of Haldin, who had just 'removed' a Minister of State by the means of a well-aimed bomb. Haldin had not attracted notice, he had a chance to escape, he came to Razumov because his character begot trust. Razumov accepted his mission, endeavoured first to obtain the help he had been asked for, and then, suddenly resentful of the stigma that was cast upon him, changed his mind and betrayed Haldin to the authorities. It was quietly done and successfully. Thereafter Razumov found himself trusted implicitly by bureaucrat and Nihilist; and yet lived in a torture of suspicion. This is a starved description of the crime and the mood; in the novel itself both the reality and the spirit are brilliantly particularised; but while we may say that here is all the flesh of the story, we have as yet no indication of the soul. That soul is the soul of the Russian character. Mr. Conrad makes no such explicit statement, but we need have no hesitation. There is the title *Under Western Eyes*, with its suggestion that the Slav is not easily comprehensible to us, Teutons. More significant still are certain explanatory passages, of which we quote one of the most effective:

That propensity of lifting every problem from the plane of the understandable by means of some sort of mystic expression is very Russian. I knew her well enough to have discovered her scorn for all the practical forms of political liberty known to the Western World. I suppose one must be a Russian to understand Russian simplicity, a terrible corroding simplicity in which mystic phrases clothe a naive and hopeless cynicism. I think sometimes that the psychological secret of the profound difference of that people consists in this, that they detest life, the irremediable life of the earth as it is, whereas we Westerners cherish it with perhaps an equal exaggeration of its sentimental value.

That last sentence summarises the effect which Mr. Conrad has produced. It is not for us to say whether it is or is not a true reading of Russian character; but as we read we were conscious always that these Russian men and women were unconcerned with the detail of life as we know it, the detail which to so many English men and women constitutes the whole. We may take Razumov as typical in this, though we find some aspect of the same attitude in all the other widely differentiated characters depicted. And we may take as most representative Razumov's attitude towards the discovery of his secret. We see that he is never flattered by the confidence shown in him either by bureaucrat or revolutionist; he is at no pains to create an impression of himself on his hearers—save in this one regard of concealing his crime. He is not pleased by the high estimate of his abilities made by the leaders of the revolutionary party outside Russia and the high officials within. He has a strange detachment from all the minutiae of existence, a disregard for what we call comfort. He is wrapped in the contemplation of his own moral action, and this not because he has been placed by Fate in an extraordinary position, but because he is a Russian. *Under Western Eyes* becomes an explanation of the works of Russian novelists; it helps us to understand Turgeniev and Dostoievsky with greater clearness; it is a brilliantly successful effort to make the Russian comprehensible to the Westerner. That, in our opinion, is the essence of the book, and it is that which makes it acceptable as a piece of literature which should endure.

The machinery is admirably adapted to the exhibition of the theme, but it is very plainly machinery. As in the case of *Lord Jim*, so here we have a postulated narrator, but with this difference, that here he has the diary of Razumov—rarely quoted verbatim—from which to build his story. But never did a man know the detail of any life as this imagined teacher of languages knows that of Razumov. From construction we turn to characterisation, and in this particular we find some of the most vivid and convincing work that Mr. Conrad has ever given us. Peter Ivanovitch, the feminist, the escaped convict from Siberia, the patriot's hero, the 'inspired man,' is a brilliant portrait, so subtly are his vanities and weaknesses indicated. The little 'dame de compagnie,' his secretary, is no less perfectly sketched, and hers is a personality we may admire sympathetically. Peter's Egeria, 'painted, bedizened, dead-faced, glassy-eyed,' is a horror worthy of Poe; but as something sheerly abhorrent, even she is second to Nikita, nicknamed Necator, the killer of gendarmes and police agents, a great white fleshy creature with a high, squeaking voice. There are other characters no less brilliantly drawn, all of them with some touch to convince us that the man or woman is distinctly Russian. The whole is a work which must rank with the masterpieces of English fiction, as 'a Russian story for Western ears, which are not attuned to certain tones of cynicism and cruelty, of moral negation, and even of moral stress already silenced at our end of Europe.'

100. Conrad's defence of *Under Western Eyes*

20 October 1911

Letter to Garnett (*LEG*, 232–3). Conrad's letter is in reply to one from Garnett which has not survived, but there is clear evidence that Garnett had charged him with putting hatred into *Under Western Eyes*. Garnett was a known sympathizer with Russian revolutionaries and exiles, some of whom, in a disguised form, appear in the novel. For Garnett's retraction of the charge see Introduction, pp. 24–5.

There's just about as much or as little hatred in this book as in the *Outcast of the Islands* for instance. Subjects lay about for anybody to pick up. I have picked up this one. And that's all there is to it. I don't expect you will believe me. You are so russianised, my dear, that you don't know the truth when you see it—unless it smells of cabbage-soup when it at once secures your profoundest respect. I suppose one must make allowances for your position of Russian Embassador to the Republic of Letters. Official pronouncements ought to be taken with a grain of salt and that is how I shall take your article in the Nation which I hope to see tomorrow evening when the carrier comes back from Ashford. But it is hard after lavishing a 'wealth of tenderness' on Tekla and Sophia, to be charged with the rather low trick of putting one's hate into a novel. If you seriously think that I have done that then my dear fellow let me tell you that you don't know what the accent of hate is. Is it possible that you haven't seen that in this book I am concerned with nothing but ideas, to the exclusion of everything else, with no arrière pensée of any kind. Or are you like the Italians (and most women) incapable of conceiving that anybody ever should speak with perfect detachment, without some subtle hidden purpose for the sake of what is said, with no desire of gratifying some small personal spite—or vanity.

101. Edward Garnett, unsigned review, *Nation*

21 October 1911, 140–2

Garnett's admiration for Miss Haldin—'this exquisite type of Russian womanhood'—faded. A few weeks before his death, he wrote: 'Miss Haldin is the weakness of the book.'

The title of Mr. Conrad's novel is an artful one, presenting an apologia within a definition. 'I cannot pretend to any complete understanding of these people and their baffling actions,' the anonymous English chronicler, 'a teacher of languages,' seems to say to us. 'I can only narrate what happened, following Mr. Razumov's diary, and my experiences with the Russian exiles in Geneva.' Of course, this anonymous chronicler is merely a blank screen on which Mr. Conrad projects a series of psychological analyses of his people's deeds, moods, and temperaments. But the effect of his evasive, artistic method is artful in the extreme, reminding us of those ingenious puzzles which fall suddenly into place with a click. It is only when we look back that we recognise what a perfect whole has been framed of these imperfect parts. If to Western eyes his material seems to be eked out here and there with guess-work, to be fragmentary and puzzling, the artist has wrought it into meaning curves and a highly original pattern.

[gives a summary of the plot]

It is in these scenes of Razumov's life and moral struggles in Geneva that the irony of Mr. Conrad's method gathers weight and velocity like a wheel set rolling down-hill. In Parts I. and II. we see him skilfully arranging his chess board, in Part III. the drama of Razumov's 'moral revolt' coalesces with a corrosively bitter etching of types of the revolutionary party, such as the famous Feminist, Peter Ivanovitch, his companion, Madame de S——, Laspara, the philosophic anarchist, the sinister Nikita, slayer of gendarmes and spies, but himself another

Azev, and so on. This merciless picture, which is as formidable in its indictment of the revolutionists' claims as the figures of Prince K——, General T——, and Councillor Mikulin are destructive of the Autocracy's pretensions, would seem vindictive art, had not the author introduced into the group the admirable figure of Sophia Antonovna, a woman Nihilist of the old school, who recalls the heroines of the early 'eighties. Razumov, in his unwilling intercourse with these chiefs of the circle, is ravaged by a whirling anxiety of fear, contempt, hatred, malice, and self-loathing. It is a psychological study of cynical pride sustaining the hollowness of self-disillusionment, and throwing up volcanic, fresh defensive waves of lava, that is offered us in Razumov's portrait. The study is very special, and to the English reader, who knows nought of Dostoievsky, and is touchingly ignorant of his own soul's dark places, may seem a nightmare of hallucinations, but in fact, within its narrow lines, it is illuminating in its pathological truth. The artistic intensity of the novel lies, however, less in the remarkable drawing of characteristic Russian types than in the atmospheric effect of the dark national background. With almost uncanny adroitness, Mr. Conrad has both relieved and increased the blackness of his picture by the rare, precious figure of Natalia Haldin. How he has managed to concentrate in a few 'impressions,' conversations, and confidences the essence, profoundly spiritual, of this exquisite type of Russian womanhood, is worth the closest examination; but he has attained a degree of fineness that is extraordinary. The poignancy of the position of the bereaved mother watching for the arrival of her dead son is much heightened by the ironical fact that Haldin, in his last letter to his sister, has commended Razumov as 'a man of unstained, lofty, and solitary existence.' . . . In other passages the bitterness and irony of the artistic treatment seem to ignite in a flame to light up the obscurities of this drama of ignoble egotism and impure motives. It is, however, in the suggestiveness of the national background of the illusions of frustrated and blighted generations, stretching ominously like a gloomy curtain behind the figures in the drama, that the author's special triumph lies. Readers of 'The Heart of Darkness' will recall Mr. Conrad's special power of concentrating and blending the tragic essence of human stupidity and human futility with a poetic description of a place and an atmosphere. In *Under Western Eyes* he has concerned himself exclusively with flying aspects of Russia's mournful internal history, which many of her chief writers associate with deep-rooted vices in the national blood. And he has artfully underscored the stigma by skilfully placing his fanatical and impotent circle of 'reformers' against the bourgeois placidity and indifference of modern Switzerland. There is something almost vitriolic in Mr. Conrad's scathing rejection of the shibboleths of humanitarian lovers of their kind, and we confess to an enjoyment, positively indefensible, in such perfect little scenes as the one where we see the tortured Mr. Razumov seeking solitude on the little islet, 'a perfection of puerile neatness,' where stands the exiled effigy of Jean Jacques Rousseau![1]

There are pages, indeed not a few, where the talk between the characters seems a little strained, or obviously arranged for the particular purpose of the drama. But such flaws escape clean from the memory when we reach the last chapter of Razumov's confession of his crime to Miss Haldin, and, later, to the circle of exiles. The sinister force of the last twenty pages has the effect of a thunderbolt cleaving the brooding, sultry air. Here Mr. Conrad is at his best, and many of his pages may be placed by the side of notable passages in Turgenev and Dostoievsky, to both of which great masters Mr. Conrad bears affinities and owes a debt.

[1] Jean-Jacques Rousseau (1712–78), philosopher and educationalist and father of romanticism.

102. Ford Madox Hueffer, signed article, *English Review*

December 1911–March 1912, 69–83

When Hueffer (Ford) writes below 'I knew at one time very well a writer who collaborated with Conrad in one or two books' he is, rather childishly, referring to himself.

. . . I have thought very often that Conrad is an Elizabethan. That is possibly because he is a Pole—and the Poles have the virtues and the powers that served to make nations great in the sixteenth and seventeenth centuries. Roughly speaking, that was when Poland was a great Empire. They were Romantic, they were heroic, they were aristocrats—they were all the impracticable things. You could not expect their greatness to live on into the days of Mr. Carnegie or the cotton spindle. . . . But, though this could no longer be done, that is not to say that it is so long ago since Poland was the beloved of the world—of all the world that was not engaged in the breaking up of the prey. And if you cannot have a fortune in the two-and-three-quarter per cents. it is a very good thing to be beloved for showing a fine spirit. Thus for me Joseph Conrad is the finest of the Elizabethans.

His preoccupations are with death, destiny, an inscrutable and august force, with the cruel sea, the dark forests of strange worlds or the darker forests that are the hearts of our fellow men. It would not in the least surprise you to come upon a dance of madmen in one of his stories as in Webster's *Duchess of Malfi*; . . . For really there is hardly anything that was written by Marlowe or Massinger or Webster or Kyd or Heywood that would not fit into this author's works.

Of course I mean this in the sense of feeling—of what I should like to express by the word colour. For when we think of the works of the Elizabethans other than Shakespeare, we seem to see a darkness—a darkness of forests illuminated by torches, and when I think of the work of this author I always have the same image. And darkness has very curiously gone out of modern life and literature. We never see it—

not the real thick blackness that seems to invade the lungs, the heart, and the very circulation of the blood. Similarly, we never think of death, of ruin, of dishonour, of chivalry, of a careless pursuing of an ideal with nothing but a thin plank between us and the fathomless sea. We never think of them—or if we do it is only for a very short moment. We switch on the electric light and turn our attentions to the evening papers.

But these things—darkness, death, honour, and a careless chivalry are the constant preoccupations of Conrad. In the one particular of honour he differs from the Elizabethans, but they were preoccupied with all the other primitive things that we have forgotten, whilst we have grown kinder. Indeed it is very curious how little space kindness occupies in the work either of Conrad or of the Elizabethans. . . . Of course there is kindness rendered in *Lord Jim*—that book of all others that has a vivid moral for English readers. But even here it is the kindness of old wise and sad men like Marlow or like Stein for a boy who has failed upon the point of honour. That is what they can understand, for that they can feel. In all the rest there is a desperate sort of remorselessness.

If you consider the case of the sham escape of Razumov from the police you will see very plainly what I mean. Razumov is in league with—or let us say he is under the obsession of—the Russian secret police. He has to gain the confidence of the revolutionaries, so, to add a touch of verisimilitude, as it were, to advertise his escape, he goes to a madcap boy and announces his desire to borrow money in order to pay the expenses of his escape. The boy has no money; he must rob his father in order to find it. This he does. He comes to Razumov with the money:

Razumov nodded from the couch, and contemplated the hare-brained fellow's gravity with a feeling of malicious pleasure.

'I've made my little sacrifice,' sighed mad Kostia, 'and I've to thank you, Kirylo Sidorovitch for the opportunity.'

'It has cost you something?'

'Yes, it has. You see the dear old duffer really loves me. He'll be hurt.'

'And you believe, all they tell you of the new future, and the sacred will of the people?'

'Implicitly! I would give my life. . . . Only you see, I am like a pig at a trough. I am no good. It's my nature.'

Razumov, lost in thought, had forgotten his existence till the youth's voice, entreating him to fly without loss of time, roused him unpleasantly.

'All right. Well—good-bye.'

That is just all that Razumov had to say. He had forgotten the youth's existence, though he had made the boy rob his father in order to advertise his escape to the revolutionaries. . . .

When dawn broke, Razumov, very still in a hot, stuffy railway car . . . rose quietly, lowered the glass a few inches, and flung out on the great plain of snow a small brown paper parcel.

It was the stolen money. He was too disdainfully honourable a man to use stolen money. He could not have done it.

And this same unimaginative cruelty of a man blindly pursuing his lost honour dignifies Razumov to the end. It pursues him into the room and into the presence of the sister of the man he betrayed to death—the woman with the trusting eyes who loves him, and whom he loves. He just tells her with the fewest possible words.

'It ends here—on this very spot.' He pressed a denunciatory finger to his breast with force and became perfectly still.

You observe those are the fewest possible words in which he could tell her that he was the traitor. Razumov is so set upon regaining his lost honour that even for the sake of the woman with the trusting eyes he cannot take the trouble to prepare her for the revelation he has to make. Then he goes to the revolutionaries in council; denounces himself to them as a police spy, receives his terrible punishment, and his soul is at peace.

It is here that Conrad differentiates himself from the Elizabethans, for they could never have worked themselves up to the pitch of subtlety. They could, as it were, have conceived a Judas, and even the remorse of such an Iscariot. They had very certainly the conception of an avenging providence. But they could not prize honour quite so high. For here is the comment of the wise woman revolutionist on the case of Razumov.

'There are evil moments in every life. A false suggestion enters one's brain and then fear is born—fear of oneself, fear for oneself. Or else a false courage—who knows? Well, call it what you like; but tell me how many of them would deliver themselves up deliberately to perdition (as he himself says in that book) rather than go on living, secretly debased in his own eyes? How many? . . . And please mark this—he was safe when he did it. It was just when he believed himself safe and more—infinitely more—when the possibility of being loved by that admirable girl first dawned upon him, that he discovered that his bitterest railings, the devil work of his hate and pride, could never cover up the ignominy of the existence before him. There's character in such a discovery.'

Of course this labouring of, this preoccupation with the idea of the point of honour is very foreign—so foreign that it has obviously come to this author with his foreign blood. It is a thing wholly individualistic and wholly of the aristocrat. And that is what the Poles are—aristocrats and individualists; that is why their land is harried and held down in this age of limited companies and democracy.

For the honour that obsesses all the chief characters of this author is hardly ever a question of public polity—or it might be more just to say that their souls do not treat it as a question of public polity. Lord Jim commits of course a public mis-demeanour in deserting his ship be-cause it is full of Mohammedan pilgrims; but for the rest of his life he is haunted not by the thought of thousands of drowned brown men, but by his own honour: Captain Whalley falls from honour, but it is his private soul that is harrowed, so it is with Falk the cannibal—so it is with Razumov, and in an extraordinarily imaginative degree. For the problem of Razumov is hardly to be solved by anyone but the hardest of partisans, and hardly by them. . . . The problem of Razumov was much more terrifying.

. . . But at any rate that is the ceaseless moral of all this author's work—the being true to your own sense of personal honour. For my honour is not yours; you may with a good conscience commit crimes that would make me sick—you may split infinitives and praise bad books. Your honour is not mine—the other day I shot a fox, and I feel none the worse though truly the fox was among vineyards and in no English hen-roost. But there the moral of all Conrad's work just is—follow the lines of your private honour, and you will probably starve. But you will never have to confess to the woman you love that you have desecrated her ideals—you will never have to give the woman you love the pain of attending at your dishonoured deathbed, or you will never give the woman you love the infinitely greater pain of having to wait while you go to your death to satisfy the avenging providence that watches over personal honour.

Destiny! The woman you love! Deathbeds and death. How extra-ordinarily old-fashioned it all sounds! And for the matter of that how singular is Conrad's theory of the mysticism and awe of a man's private honour—for, as we see in the case of Razumov, that unfortunate's private honour was affected without so much as his will coming in question. He did his best to save the Revolutionist. . . . But to save Haldin was impossible—impossible! The man who was to have driven him away in a sledge was drunk. So that all that Razumov did was to bow to what appeared to him an august and inscrutable destiny. And then the august and inscrutable destiny pursued him to the journey's end, so that he presents the picture of a flying wretch in the night, to the light of sparse torches, hiding in his arms his face averted from the strokes of pursuing Furies!

I do not know that it is the moral of this author's whole work, but so it presents itself to me, and with an extraordinary vividness—that when our private and intimate honour is in conflict with the law, we must break the law. For the law is a conventional arrangement of the relations between man and man. But a man's heart knows! I think that that is what it comes to.

. . . I think that we have too much law; I think we think too much about law-making. There must come a time when the State can go no further, for the State is a clumsy and blind engine that can do no more than rough-square the material of human lives! We have our fingers too much on our moral pulse when it comes to enacting regulations for the relief of the Unfortunate in the mass: we have too little thought for what is called imagination—for our personal dealings with individuals whom destiny throws in our way.

. . . He is a deeply religious writer—for the figure of an avenging deity pursues a fearful course through all his pages. If you sin, he says, you must pay for it. Thus, illicit passions and theft, the breach of trust, are punished with death in the case of Nostromo. Thus a breach of the mercantile marine regulation that an officer must stick to his ship until all the passengers have left is punished with a life of penury and dishonour, with death at the end. (*Lord Jim.*) Falk the cannibal is punished as a cannibal should be punished, though the crew drop off his ship in Southern latitudes. Spying is punished with endless cares and a certain death (*The Secret Agent*). In the same work the Police Inspector, that symbol of rectitude and the law, is rewarded with the commendation of his superiors and a career of tranquil success. It is all as it should be—and it is all as it is in life. That is the wonderful thing about it. If there is any pitying of sinners it is not the author who writes the words, it is one of the characters who utters them. The writer, providing only the framework of the story, seems for ever to be enforcing the moral: 'Be sure your sin shall find you out.'

This is a sombre conviction, and it is all the more odd to find it in a writer of Conrad's class—for Conrad is one of the two or three English writers who uphold the despised standard of Art for Art's sake. And of course when I say odd I do not in the least mean that it is odd. For every work of true art must have a profound moral significance. And I will add, that nothing that is not a work of High Art can have any moral significance at all. A work of art is passionless, a work of art is a record, a work of art is above all a symbol and the highest expression of an individual's struggle for survival. Now all Law, all Morals are the symbol of the struggle for existence of a type. English Law and English Morals are designed to perpetuate the English type; Chinese morals are an attempt to mould a world such as shall be easy for the support of the typical Chinaman. And so it is all the world over. Morals are life; sin is death. The very household laws that a mother frames for her children are intended to lengthen their lives towards that immortality that every mother wishes for her child. And the artist looking upon life and rendering only the results of his considerations produces always for his own type the one lesson—morals stand for life, sin for death.

Of course the type changes; the Universe is very large, and in it there is room for an infinite number of moral cosmogonies. The legendary Chinaman murders his daughters and, in view of the terrible over-population of China he is right in so doing. Razumov—who was probably more a Pole than a Russian—was so fickle upon the point of honour that, although he gave the law its own, his conscience drove him to a death that was worse than a death. . . .

So that the artist drawing life, sombre more or less according to its latitude, is the true, is the only moralist. All the rest are only moralisers: they say what they like, not what is. . . .

But that is enough of morals; let us consider Conrad's methods. It has been said, and I think with truth, that this author is without an equal for getting an atmosphere; I will add that he is without an equal for describing action. Let us see how these results are arrived at. There is one technical maxim that jumps at the eye all through his work. It is this: *Never state: present.* And again: *Never state: present.* I am aware that these words will not be understood by the majority of my readers; I will try to make the meaning plain. The self-appointed work of an artist of Conrad's type is to make each of his stories an experience for his reader. That is his preoccupation; it is for that that an august and inscrutable providence has set him in the world; if he do anything else he offends against his personal honour.

Now in order to make a narration of events strike the hearer as an experience, the author must make the events narrated strike the senses as nearly as possible as they would be presented by nature herself. . . .

But the problem before Conrad when he wrote *Lord Jim* was to present to us a fair-haired capable son of an English parsonage, waiting in his white canvas tennis shoes upon a boat stage in the sun for the approach of the boat—and of inscrutable and august Destiny.

And never once, never once, during the whole book do we say—if we are unsophisticated readers—'*How clever Mr. Conrad is!*' We say, '*Oh, poor devil! Oh, poor devil!*' and we hope that God will be kinder to us poor Englishmen!

That is the great achievement of this type of art, . . .

. . . When it comes to *Lord Jim*—why, it is a part of me. Yes, it is a part of my soul, of my life. It has entered into me like the blood in my veins; it has given me my English outlook, though I am a foreigner and have every kind of intellectual contempt for the countrymen of Tuan Jim. But it has made me understand the English-English with such a perfect comprehension—and what one perfectly comprehends one loves!

Now that is a great achievement—for it is a great achievement to have overwhelmed any one soul, and there are few men's souls that can resist *Lord Jim* once they have found him out. . . .

We have seen that Conrad's method of treatment is to render. Now what about his powers of selection and what about the defects of his merits? He is, we know, concerned before everything else with getting an atmosphere. But is he? I knew at one time very well a writer who collaborated with Conrad in one or two books, and has very kindly presented me with the manuscript of these works. I transcribe two passages, underlining the words that are by Conrad:—

To yesterday and to-day I say my *polite* 'vaya usted con Dios.' What are these days to me? *But that far-off day of my romance when* from between the blue and white bales in Don Ramon's darkened store room, at Kingston, *I saw the door open before* the figure of an old man with the tired, long, white face, *that day I am not likely to forget.* I remember the chilly smell of the typical West Indian store, the indescribable smell of damp gloom, of locos, of pimento, of olive oil, of new sugar, of rum; the glassy double sheen of Ramon's great spectacles, the mahogany face, *while the tap, tap, of a cane on the flags went on behind the inner door; the click of the latch; the stream of light.* The door, *petulantly thrust inwards, struck against some barrels. I remember the rattling of the bolts on that door*, and the tall figure that appeared there, snuff-box in hand. In that land of white clothes, that precise, ancient Castilian in black was something to remember. The black cane that had made the tap, tap, tap dangled *by a silken cord*, from the hand whose delicate, blue-veined, wrinkled wrist ran back into a foam of lawn ruffles. *The other hand paused in the act of conveying a pinch of snuff to* the nostrils of the hooked nose that had, on the skin stretched tight over the bridge, the polish of old ivory; *the elbow pressing the* black cocked hat against the side; the legs, one bent, the other bowing a little back—this was the attitude of Seraphina's father.

Having imperiously thrust the door of the inner room open, he remained immovable, with no intention of entering, and called in a harsh, aged voice: '*Señor Ramon, Señor Ramon!' And then twice, 'Seraphina, Seraphina!' turning his head back* . . .

The second passage contains no description at all except the description of moods, but it is none the less instructive since it shows Conrad's desire for actualities, for hard and characteristic phrases set against his collaborator's more vague personality, so that it stands out in a strong relief:—

It takes long enough to realise that someone is dead at a distance. I had done that. But how long, how long, it needs to know that the life of your heart has come back from the dead. *For years afterwards I could not bear to have her out of my sight.*

Of our first meeting all I remember is a speechlessness that was like the awed hesitation of our overtried souls before the greatness of a change from the verge of despair to the consummation of a supreme joy. The whole world, the whole life, *had changed all round me:* it enveloped me so lightly as not to be felt, so suddenly as not to be believed in, so completely that that whole meeting was an embrace, so softly that at last it lapsed into a sense of rest *that was like the fall of a beneficent and welcome death.*

For suffering is the lot of man, *but not inevitable failure or worthless despair which is without end—suffering the mark of manhood, which bears within its pain a hope of felicity like a jewel set in iron.* . . .

Her first words were. 'You broke our compact. You went away whilst I was sleeping.' Only the deepness of her reproach revealed the depth of her love *and the suffering she too had endured* to reach a union that was to be without end— *and to forgive.*

And looking back we see Romance—that subtle thing that is mirage, that is life. It is the goodness of the years we have lived through, of the old time when we did this or that, when we dwelt here or there. Looking back it seems wonderful enough a thing that I who am this and she who is that, commencing so far away a life that, after such suffering borne together and apart, ended so tranquilly there in a world so stable—that she and I should have passed through so much, good chance and evil chance, sad hours and joyful, all lived down and swept away into the little heap of dust that is life. *That, too, is Romance.*

Now two main facts have occurred to me in studying these passages very carefully. One of them is that every word of description is by the other writer, and every word of action is by Conrad. This is a very curious fact, for it would be absurd to ascribe to the other writer greater powers of description, and certainly that apportionment of the task was never consciously made between the two.

And that is the great happiness, is the great good fortune of this author's temperament. We can most of us describe, some of us can get atmospheres—but it is only the very great writer who can so interpenetrate his characters with the seas and skies, or the houses, fabrics, and ornaments that surround them. For that is what Conrad seems to do. It is not what he actually does—actually he sends through all the seas and skies the very beings of the men that look upon them. For a descriptive writer—or rather for a writer noted for his descriptions—he describes very little. Consider this passage from 'Youth'—that most magical of all this author's pieces of work. The narrator, after having pulled nearly all night in the escape from a wreck, has been guided by a red light, in the depth of a great darkness, into an Eastern harbour. He has fallen asleep in the boat against an unknown quay:—

But when I opened my eyes again the silence was as complete as though it had never been broken. I was lying in a flood of light, and the sky had never seemed so far, so high before. I opened my eyes and lay without moving.

And then I saw the men of the East—they were looking at me. The whole length of the jetty was full of people. I saw brown, bronze, yellow faces, the black eyes, the glitter the colour of an Eastern crowd. And all these things stared without a murmur, without a sigh, without a movement. They stared down at the boats, at the sleeping men who at night had come to them from the sea. Nothing moved. The fronds of palms stood still against the sky. Not a branch stirred along the shore, and the brown roofs of hidden houses peeped through the green foliage, through the big leaves that hung, shining, and still like leaves forged of heavy metal. This was the East of the ancient navigators, so old, so mysterious, resplendent and sombre, living unchanged, full of danger and promise. And these were the men. I sat up suddenly. A wave of movement passed through the crowd from end to end, passed along the heads, swayed the bodies, ran along the jetty like a ripple on the water, like a breath of wind on a field—and all was still again. I see it now—the wide sweep of the bay, the glittering sands, the wealth of green, infinite, and varied, the sea blue like the sea of a dream, the crowd of attentive faces, the blaze of vivid colour—the water reflecting it all, the curve of the shore, the jetty, the high-sterned outlandish craft floating still, and the three boats with tired men from the West sleeping, unconscious of the land and the people and the violence of the sunshine. They slept thrown across the thwarts, curled on bottom boards, in the careless attitudes of death. The head of the old skipper, leaning back in the stern of the long boat, had fallen on his breast and he looked as though he would never wake. Farther out, old Mahon's face was upturned to the sky, with the long white beard spread out on his breast as though he had been shot where he sat at the tiller, and a man all in a heap in the bows of the boat slept with both arms embracing the stem-head and with his cheek laid on the gunwale. The East looked at them without a sound.

Now that passage renders the East as no writer has ever rendered it, and yet how little of real description there is in it. It is the men—the men whose destinies had brought them to that spot who really give the passage its tone—because something human is dearer to this writer than all the pictures of all the East.

And this great and desirable faculty is his not merely because of a technical self-consciousness. We most of us—those of us who have any technical knowledge at all—know that we must not introduce any descriptive writing just for the love of a description. Anybody knows enough to know that. But Conrad's eye is so formed that it does not notice anything save what carries the story forward. . . .

I am not by any means saying that there are no passages in the works of Conrad that are not simple pages of description. You will find, for instance, in 'The End of the Tether', whole long pages of descriptions of land-fretted seas. But the purposes of these are the purposes of the story. They make so plain to the reader the nature of the seas in which the *Sofala* carried the burden of the old Captain's tragedy that when the sinking of the ship comes there is no need to burden the narrative with topographical explanation. All the while one has been on the ship, one has seemed to be so conscious of the ledges of rock below one that when the knife-thrust has come it has seemed for long to be inevitable, and the whole conduct of the story need concern itself only with the feelings of the human beings.

And that is the great faculty of this author—that he can make an end seem inevitable, in every instance the only possible end. He does this by every means—by the explanations of heredity, of temperament, of the nature of sea and sky, by the sound of a song, by the straws in the street. His sense of Destiny differs in its means of expression from that of the Greeks, its intensity is always as great as theirs. Perhaps it is a part of a common Oriental temperament. The Greek Destiny was embodied, commented on, chorussed. It was an all-overwhelming cloud. The Destiny of Conrad's books is hymned by no Chorus of Captive Women, and by no Bacchantes. That is not the temper of his time or ours. When all sorts of things, all sorts of little coincidences, nowadays force us to a course of action we do not any longer say that Atropos compelled us—we say that it seemed as if every blessed thing conspired to make us do it. And what Conrad does for us is to express for us the Three Sisters in the terms of every blessed thing.

Now this is a very great achievement, a very great enlightenment for our age. I do not mean to say that Conrad is the only writer that does this for us. but I am certain that we have no other—nowhere in the Western World—so exclusively occupied with this consideration, which is, surely, one of the two most important considerations of the world and life. I have heard it said that his books are too long; that his elaboration is over great. But that is the case only for minds very hurried or temperamentally out of tune with this author. For myself I can only say that not one of his works has ever seemed tedious. I like one subject more than another, but the keen pleasure of observing the incidents, the certainty that every incident—that every word, however superfluous they may appear, will in the end show necessary and revelatory—this pleasure I am never without.

And when we consider the great obstacles of language with which this man has struggled, and the unswerving conscientiousness with which this writer has pursued his guiding lights—whether we like or dislike his books—we must be consoled. For if our age can have raised up such a conscience in any walk of life, and if our country can have attracted him to live amongst us, our age and our country must have in it something that is good—in its traditions and its teachings. Indeed, when I think that in a light-hearted way I have poked fun at the artistic conscience of this country I feel a little ashamed. For if Conrad has not earned any huge material success, he has secured a recognition, even from the more Academic, that few men of his greatness have ever secured in their age and their own day. And looking back it seems a wonderful enough thing that this writer, commencing so far away a life that after sufferings, perils, and vicissitudes borne under so many skies and upon so many seas, has its consummation here in a world so stable—that after the seas where he passed through so much, good chance and evil chance, upon this foreign shore he should receive the acknowledgement of his services from the State, and the applause alike of the Orthodox and of the Critical. That, too, is Romance.

103. Robert Lynd, review, *Daily News*

14 October 1912, 8

To Garnett Conrad wrote on 5 November 1912: 'I daresay *Freya* is pretty rotten. On the other hand the *Secret Sharer*, between you and me, is *it*. Eh? No damned tricks with girls there. Eh? Every word fits and there's not a single uncertain note. Luck my boy. Pure luck' (*LEG*, 243).

If anyone has any doubts of Mr. Conrad's genius he will do well to read 'The Secret Sharer,' the second story in this volume. I confess repentantly that I once had such doubts. But I had not read 'Typhoon' then. None of the three stories in *'Twixt Land and Sea* possesses the cosmic or rather the infernal, energy of 'Typhoon.' In reading 'Typhoon' one has constantly, as it were, to catch hold of something solid in order to keep oneself from being swept off one's feet by the fury of the author's sensitive and truthful genius. 'The Secret Sharer' is work of a quieter mood. It is as different from 'Typhoon' as still water is from a storm. But it is to an equal extent a mastering vision of a world which Mr. Conrad knows and nobody else knows—a world of artistically uncharted seas—a world the seas of which have at once the reality of the seas we know, and something of the still intenser reality of the phantom seas of 'The Ancient Mariner.'

Everyone who has read Mr. Conrad's stories knows how sensitively and how surely he can create a living atmosphere as he adds nervous sentence to nervous sentence. Every sentence has a nerve; that is one of the distinguishing features of his writing. It is not clever writing—at least, not deliberately so. If his genius fails him, he has none of those glittering reserves of cleverness to fall back upon, such as enable

Mr. Kipling always to achieve vividness even when he does not achieve life. But in what has been called the sense of life, Mr. Conrad is, within his limits, far richer than Mr. Kipling.

It is true that he expresses his sense of life rather through his winds and seas and ships than through his human beings. His human beings are, on the whole, small and eccentric creatures compared to those elements which spring upon them and lie in wait for them like the messengers of gods and devils. His characters, in other words, do not belong to that aristocracy of passion of which Pater[1] wrote. Even though they perform miracles of endurance in their warfare against wind and wave, it is the latter who are the mighty characters of his books. Compared with them, the captains and the sailors seem at times to be just a sort of odd playthings.

Thus his characters have frequently something of the quality of victims. One is very conscious of this as one reads 'Freya of the Seven Isles,' in the present book. This is a wonderful pitiless story of revenge in the Dutch East Indies. It tells how a Dutch naval lieutenant, an ugly, surly, thick-bodied man, was enabled to get his rival, a young English trading captain, into his clutches in a manner that cost a charming and generous young man his reason, and a charming and high-hearted girl her life. The especial pitilessness of the story arises from the fact that the Dutchman's bitterness would hardly have been able to plan the destruction of his rival unaided. It was fate that struck the young man down—struck him down, too, not through his vices, but his virtues. For a man to whom he had done a service stole, in a moment of drunken weakness, the firearms belonging to his ship, and sold them to the natives on one of the Dutch islands, with the result that the young trader was delivered into the lieutenant's power. No one but Mr. Conrad could have described with such intense imaginative excitement—excitement free from every trace of melodrama and rhetoric—that calculated devilish tragedy when the lieutenant man-œuvred Jasper Allen's beautiful white ship to its doom upon the reef where it would lie long afterwards, a grey ghost, haunting the insane eyes of its owner as he watched it, the ghost of a man, from the shore.

In his description of human beings subjected to some terrible fas-cination Mr. Conrad excels. 'Studies in fascination' would be a not inapt description of the three stories in this book. The first of the

---

[1] Walter Pater (1839–94), English critic and associated with the Pre-Raphaelites. He is particularly known for his *Studies in the History of the Renaissance* (1893) and *Marius the Epicurean* (1885). His style is highly polished.

three, 'A Smile of Fortune,' which also has its scene among tropical seas, is a study of the spell cast on the captain of a ship by a mysterious outcast, shy, untamed, animal of a woman. It is good, but not supremely good. 'The Secret Sharer,' on the other hand, which tells of the spell cast upon another captain by a mate charged with murder, who has taken refuge in his ship, is surely a masterpiece. Here Mr. Conrad himself casts a spell.

Ever from that midnight moment, when the captain, lonelily pacing the deck of his anchored ship in islanded eastern seas, looks over the side and beholds the apparently headless body of a man in the phosphorescent water at the foot of the ladder, the story grips one in its quiet, inevitable sentences. There is marvellous psychological insight shown in the way in which the captain, having clothed the man in his clothes and hidden him in his room and heard his strange story, like a secret, in intimate whispers, gradually comes to associate his own identity with the identity of the fugitive. It is the captain and not the fugitive who jumps at sudden sounds and at chances of discovery. The great elation of the story, however, does not arise from its study of the psychology of fascination or curious sense of identity or alarm. All this is necessary to produce it, but all this alone would not produce it. In his eagerness for the escape of his double, who insists upon dropping over the ship's side at night and swimming to one of the islands where he can live as one dead, a marooned and forgotten man, the captain compels his crew, almost still with horror, to bring the ship right up under the shadow of the land on a pretence of looking for land winds. That scene gives us one of the great thrills of modern literature.

Such a hush had fallen on the ship that she might have been a bark of the dead floating in slowly under the very gate of Erebus.

'My God! Where are we?'

It was the mate moaning at my elbow.

As the helmsman gives his answers to the captain's orders 'in a frightened, thin, childish voice' we, too, are still and tense like the horror-stricken crew. Then comes the fugitive's escape in the dark water. After that, the escape of that fine ship herself from the shadow, as it were, of the everlasting night—an escape that is one of the wonderful things of the literature of the sea. The elation that we get from this story is the elation which all great literature, even tragic literature, ought to give. Let all the bells of praise ring for so fine a piece of work.

104. John Masefield, review, *Manchester Guardian*

16 October 1912, 7

The review was signed 'J. M.' and, according to *Guardian* records, is by John Masefield.

'*Twixt Land and Sea*, by Joseph Conrad, contains three stories, written in the new and handy form (about a third the length of the ordinary novel) which will perhaps be the usual literary form in the decade after this. Mr. Conrad has always used this form with fine effect, and he uses it again here finely, with a complete mastery of his art and with his old colours of mystery, romance, and the strangeness of life. His three new stories illustrate the three kinds of creative writing for which he is best known. The first tale, 'A Smile of Fortune,' is another study in the manner of 'Heart of Darkness.' The suggestion of a strange and rather great character through a veil of mystery, which is plucked away, as it were, thread by thread, by a multitude of clever pickings, till the character behind it stands out, bigger perhaps than we had expected, but also stranger although revealed. The second story, 'The Secret Sharer,' is a new romance of the sea, a second 'Youth,' beautiful like that fine tale, with the suggestion that something done with difficulty and perhaps unavailingly has, after all, brought something into life, bigger than one thought, something to count as significant later on when the play is considered as a whole. The third story, 'Freya of the Seven Isles,' ends the symphony of the book with a study of blindness, mental this time, not physical, as in the tale at the end of 'Youth', but not less tragical, being the blindness of an old, kindly father to the depths of emotion in his tragically placed daughter.

Of the three tales the first two have most of that particular art and personal way of looking at life which give Mr. Conrad's books their new and fine flavour in the mind. All three are written in a firm and beautiful prose, at once precise and supple, good both in dialogue and in description. There is quality in the prose as in the subjects, difficult to define exactly, except as a personal quality of the kind sometimes got in loneliness by a strong and strange temperament who is more sensitive to impressions than his way of life gives warrant for. This quality in the choice of subjects and in the way of handling them is Mr. Conrad's own special quality. There is not and never has been anything in the least like it. Given an unusual temperament placed in a rough —and ready way of life which leads men into those unusual places unusual traits in character are called out, a quality of this kind is likely to develop; a quality of great mental sensitiveness, which is the real man, hidden behind the mask of the activity of the occupation. Having this special gift of sensitiveness, and having as a master mariner little occasion to use it in his daily work, it seems to have developed in Mr. Conrad a deep, never-sated curiosity about life, mostly about the life known to him, the life of sailors and of the men who deal with sailors, traders, charterers, consignees, consuls, and ship's chandlers, natives of various colours, and so on, and his main achievement is this—that he has brought these people into the imaginative kingdom in all the sincerity of their simplicity. His is not a vision of the world, like Shakespere's, nor of a society, like Chaucer's; but of unusual people outside the settled orders, and his vision is all the more intense from being focussed on individuals.

His power of focussing upon the out-of-the-way gives an uncanny flavour to the first of these three tales, told in the first person of a sea captain newly arrived at an island, where he is served by a profound and single being with a kind of elemental greatness in his singleness, who has an inexplicable daughter and a home like a private madhouse. Little by little one is made more intimate with the man and his home, one comes almost to dread him and it, then one changes to dislike him or despise him, and ends by thinking him rather great, rather sinister, but quite mysterious one way or the other, in the end (like life itself, sanely looked at). The second story is not less wonderful in its atmosphere; a captain newly come to a ship in a far-away Eastern road, with the masts of another ship (waiting to be towed up the river) just visible over an island, and night coming down, and a murderer, flying from the law, in the water alongside, having swum out on a last chance. This tale, made perhaps a little petty by some of its intrigue, gets a great lift of romantic beauty towards the end, and finishes with what musicians call a full close. The third tale, wonderful throughout for its colour, strikes one as having its movement rather clogged, and its

CONRAD

complications made a little slow, until the tragedy is at its height, when after a few swift moments, we are taken from direct contact with the characters.

105. Unsigned review, *Standard*

25 October 1912, 7

No volume that Mr. Conrad has ever published could offer more unmistakable proof of his genius than does this collection of three stories. In his greatest things—in 'Typhoon,' in 'Youth,' in *Lord Jim*, in *Nostromo*—he had big themes, motifs that lent themselves readily in his hands to great results. In two of the stories here presented to us there would seem to the ordinary writer scarcely any theme at all; never before have we realised so vividly the things that Mr. Conrad can do.

We may acclaim him perhaps as the first king of a new country—that country of story-tellers who will combine the sense of life proclaimed by the great mid-Victorians with the sense of form discovered here in England somewhere about 1890. He is as enthralled by the actual world that he beholds as were ever Dickens or Thackeray; his prose is as singing and haunting a melody as was ever Meredith's or Stevenson's. It is when he is concerned with the mean things of life, as, for instance, the little paper-shop in *The Secret Agent*, or Jim's fellow criminals on the pilgrim ship in *Lord Jim*, that this startling welding of vision and matter-of-fact is most plainly to be discerned. It is here again in the story entitled 'A Smile of Fortune,' when he describes for us the shabby, down-at-heels daughter of a scoundrelly trader, describes her as she is, but describes her also so that he places her in relation to all the most mysterious and beautiful things in nature. She stands—drab, dirty, neglected—in the heart of her scented garden like a picture by Leonardo.

Indeed this story is, from beginning to end, an invocation of beauty drawn from the most neglected things that the world can show. It

256

is simply the effect upon the most ordinary of seamen of a girl who might to the common-place eye reveal nothing but moral and physical degeneration. One may read the tale again and again, and still miss the secret of the pathos and power that Mr. Conrad extracts from it. There are, of course, passages of prose that are unforgettable in their beauty:

[quotes from 'A Smile of Fortune', p. 76. 'The evening closed upon me' to 'losing their glow one by one.']

But even here the secret is not to be obtained. Such prose might have been, and yet such poignancy and mystery as enclose this story might have escaped the reader. But if the secret of Mr. Conrad's genius is hidden in this first story, still more is it concealed in the second tale, 'The Secret Sharer.' We are inclined to name this as the most perfect of all Mr. Conrad's stories, although we have not forgotten 'Youth' nor 'The Duel,' nor 'Typhoon.' It tells of a captain of a ship walking his decks at night. He sees a swimmer approach him out of the darkness. He helps him on board, discovers that he is a murderer escaping from justice, hides him in his cabin until his vessel approaches the coast, when he assists him again to escape. That is all. You are presented with the effect on the captain's mind of the silent and secret presence of this other man. You are made to feel the rising of that secret presence through the very boards of the ship, so that the reader himself, as the ship moves and the tension grows, is almost impelled, as though he were himself a secret watcher there, to cry out, 'Take care! Take care!' to the other passengers on the boat. Mr. Conrad places these sensations in the mind of a quite ordinary matter-of-fact man, so that immediately the experience is brought into relation with us all—for all of us that moment may come when the prevailing menace of that Other Self, concealed as we think from the world, threatens us with instant disaster. The third story in the volume is less mysterious in its appeal, although equally magnificent in its workmanship. The pathos that is in it relies for its power on the blundering, ugly cruelty of the stupid and tyrannous. It has less of Mr. Conrad's unmistakable note in it, and it stands less obviously in relation to the mysteries of that visible and yet so secret world that is Mr. Conrad's kingdom. Nevertheless Freya is perhaps the most poignant of all his heroines. She takes her place with the girl who loved Lord Jim, with the woman in 'Falk,' with the daughter of the lighthouse keeper in *Nostromo*.

No work of English fiction since Mr. Conrad's own, *Under Western*

Eyes, has so beautifully interpreted the world. No work has left us with so haunting a conviction that in the heart of the darkest and dreariest things there is a great light shining.

106. Extract from *Spectator*

16 November 1912, 815

The reviewer is primarily concerned to assert that Conrad has thrown off the 'evil' influence of Henry James.

In one or two of the latest of Mr. Conrad's books some of his admirers have noticed with consternation signs of new and by no means happy developments both in his matter and style. This change first became evident in *The Secret Agent*, which, for all its brilliance and interest, lacked, except for a few pages the especial signs of its author's genius. Oddly enough, the most marked element in the new manner seemed to be the influence of a writer as far removed as possible in his inspiration from that of Mr. Conrad—the influence, we mean, of Mr. Henry James. Much might be written of the effects of Mr. Henry James upon contemporary English fiction. It may be questioned whether there is a single prominent novelist who has not at one time or another fallen under his sway. (Could even Mr. Kipling be confidently quoted as an exception?) At all events, *The Secret Agent* seemed often to echo Mr. Henry James, not merely in the characteristic formation of his sentences, but even in his equally characteristic method of character-painting. And, whatever may be the value of Mr. James's surreptitious permeations into English literature in general, upon Mr. Conrad the effect was entirely lamentable. It is with deep satisfaction therefore that we see that in his new book he has once more shaken himself free. He has returned with fresh vigour to his earlier course, and is as triumphantly successful in it as he has ever been in the past. . . .

CHANCE

15 January 1914

107. Conrad, letter to J. B. Pinker

2 June 1913 (L&L, ii, 146)

I can't tell you how relieved I am to be done with the book [*Chance*]. I have been very anxious—but I am so no longer. It's the biggest piece of work I've done since *Lord Jim*. As to what *it is* I am very confident. As to what will happen to it when launched—I am much less confident. And it's a pity. One doesn't do a trick like that twice—and I am not growing younger—alas! I will vanish in the ruck.

108. Conrad on selling his work in America

20 July 1913

Letter to Alfred A. Knopf (*L&L*, ii, 146–8). Knopf had recently been employed by Doubleday. The promotion of *Chance* was initiated by Knopf, and it must be to him that Conrad owed his ultimate success as a best-selling novelist. *Chance* was published by Doubleday, Page on 26 March 1914.

... I assure you that I am very sensible of the good opinion you have of my work (which dear Hudson also likes) and I congratulate myself on it—since if you had not 'happened along,' all these books would have remained on the back shelves of the firm where they have been reposing for the last ten years. I see in your letter that you suspect me of undue aloofness. It is not so. I am very much interested; I find it quite exciting to be rediscovered by my own publisher, after such a long time.

I have manifested as much interest in my publishers as my publishers have in me—nothing less; it would be unreasonable to expect more from a man—and I don't know that any angel has yet taken to literature. At any rate, I am not he.

Writing to you as to a good friend of my work, I must begin by saying that in business I am a partisan of frank speech as much as of frank dealing. I am glad to hear that Doubleday, Page & Co. has bought two of my vols. from Mr. Doran. It is a sign of interest. But the fact remains that Mr. Doubleday might have had all my books up to date in his hands if he had cared. Other people bought them and I haven't heard that they have been ruined by it; though I did not give away my work for ten cents a volume, I can assure you. I am not an amateur who plays at it. It's anything but play with me. Perhaps Mr. Doubleday does not know it, but it's a fact that ever since *Nostromo* (1904) every line of my writing has been serialized in the U.S.—with the exception of the *Mirror of the Sea*, of which however a good part appeared in *Harper's Weekly*. And the *Mirror* is not the sort of stuff to be read in the Elevated train or on the river-ferry while going home. Yet even here the *Pall Mall Mag*: (a popular sixpenny) published several papers out of it, *Blackwood* two or three, and a great penny daily the last two.

Why did these people do these things? Surely not from personal liking. I don't know a single magazine editor here, not even by sight. Of the men on your side, I have seen Col. Harvey once—years ago. Obviously there is something in what I do, some ground to go upon. It is also a fact that ever since *The Nigger* (published by Appleton 1898 under the absurdly sweet title, *Children of the Sea*) I have had in the U.S. a very good press—invariably. And you cannot deny that the majority of writers of notices in newspapers are men of average tastes. When it comes to popularity I stand much nearer the public mind than Stevenson, who was super-literary, a conscious virtuoso of style; whereas the average mind does not care much for virtuosity. My point of view, which is purely human, my subjects, which are not too specialized as to the class of people or kind of events, my style, which may be clumsy here and there, but is perfectly straightforward and tending towards the colloquial, cannot possibly stand in the way of a large public. As to what I have to say—you know it is never outrageous to mind or feeling. Is it interesting? Well, I have been translated into all the European languages, except Spanish and Italian. They would hardly do that for a bore.

There are two methods in the publishing business. The first is speculative. A book is a venture. Hit or miss. To a certain extent it must be so. But here and there a writer may be taken up as an investment. An investment must be attended to, it must be nursed—if one believes in it. I can't develop much feeling for a publisher who takes me on the 'hit or miss' basis. A gamble is not a connection. What position I have attained I owe to no publisher's efforts. Sixteen years of hard work begin to tell.

The question for me is: Has the Doubleday, Page Co. simply bought two books of mine or is it to be a connection? If it is the last, then you will find me responsive enough. I appreciate warmly the practical evidence of your good will towards my work. The writing of this long letter (which is not in my habits) is the best proof of it, for I should not have cared to open my mind like this to an indifferent stranger, I can assure you.

All I can do to help you form a stable connection between me and the firm I am ready to do—even to the sacrifice of my personal tastes.

To begin with I shall at once revise the notes on me and send them to you, I hope by the same ship with this letter. As to the portrait: I shall this week make arrangements with the Cadbys (a couple in great repute as photographers. Very artistic) to have more than one photograph taken in their best manner. The photos will be in your hands in good time before the publication of *Chance*. The Rothenstein portrait we like very much, but something more recent is needed, I think.

For the future: A young literary friend of mine, Mr. Richard Curle, was here some time ago and asked my permission to write a book on me, a critical monograph on my work. Don't think I mean a cheap puff: it would be an interesting attempt to describe my subjects and my methods. Say 50–60 thousand words. It would be exactly what's wanted to educate readers. He knows my work backwards. I may ask him to begin at once and the little book could be ready in some six months. But I can't very well ask him to drop everything and get on with that study unless I may tell him that you will, when the work is ready, consider it in a favourable spirit for publication in the U.S. Of course, I don't suggest you binding yourself in advance. What do you say?

And there is another thing. Last year I published with Harpers' a short volume entitled: *A Personal Record*. A bit of autobiography—and a bit of good writing as well. I let it go to them at a royalty of 10%, because Harpers' have in one way or another paid me a good lot of money in the last five years; thinking also that they would try to do something special with it. But apparently not. They sold a couple of thousand copies, I believe, on the strength of the name, and that's all. This book, rather intimate, quite readable, and for which I care in a special way—is just wasted. Now if you could buy it from Harpers' at once and put it before the public properly in a cheap edition (I am going to arrange for a 2/6 ed. here), say 50c., I believe it would do good. I would suggest extending the title, as thus: *A Personal Record*, by J. Conrad. *The Story of His First Book and of His First Contact with the Sea*. As a matter of fact it is just that. And if people really want that sort of thing they will be able to learn a lot about me from that little book.

Now if Doubleday, Page & Co. can and will do that and use it for the publicity (I don't mean sending men with loaded guns to force it on people, but everything short of that) then for my part I am ready to forego my royalties (under the agreement with Harpers') for three years—*except* in the case of that vol: coming out with others in a uniform edition before the three years expire.

I am ready to embody my proposal in an agreement as soon as

you have succeeded in extracting the thing from Harpers', which may not be difficult if attempted at once. I don't think I could do more to show my interest in the connection with your house, and my appreciation of your efforts on my behalf.

Believe me, my dear Sir with friendliest feelings.

P.S. I am very busy finishing my next novel—the one I told Mr. Doubleday all about. I hope he wasn't bored to death. Please give him my kind regards. I'll try to send you in time corrected galley slips to set up *Chance* from. I recommend to you that book very specially for, of its *kind*, it isn't a thing that one does twice in a lifetime!

109. Henry James's criticism

1914

From 'The New Novel' in *Notes on Novelists* (1931), pp. 271–80. Conrad said of this criticism that it was 'the *only time* a criticism affected me painfully' (letter to John Quinn, 24 May 1916, Baines, p. 383).

Let us profess all readiness to repeat that we may still have had, on the merest 'life' system, or that of the starkest crudity of the slice, all the entertainment that can come from watching a wayfarer engage with assurance in an alley that we know to have no issue—and from watching for the very sake of the face that he may show us on reappearing at its mouth. The recitals of Mr. Arnold Bennett, Mr. Gilbert Cannan,[1] Mr. D. H. Lawrence, fairly smell of the real, just as the 'Fortitude' and 'The Duchess' of Mr. Hugh Walpole smell of the romantic; we have sufficiently noted then that, once on the scent, we are capable of pushing ahead. How far it is at the same time from being all a matter

[1] Cannan (1884–1955) was for a short while dramatic critic of the *Star* (1909–10), also novelist and playwright.

of smell the terms in which we just above glanced at the weakness of the spell of the happy-go-lucky may here serve to indicate. There faces us all the while the fact that the act of consideration as an incident of the esthetic pleasure, consideration confidently knowing us to *have* sooner or later to arrive at it, may be again and again postponed, but can never hope not some time to fall due. Consideration is susceptible of many forms, some one or other of which no conscious esthetic effort fails to cry out for; and the simplest description of the cry of the novel when sincere—for have we not heard such compositions bluff us, as it were, with false cries?—is as an appeal to us when we have read it once to read it yet again. *That* is the act of consideration; no other process of considering approaches this for directness, so that anything short of it is virtually not to consider at all. The word has sometimes another sense, that of the appeal to us *not*, for the world, to go back— this being of course consideration of a sort; the sort clearly that the truly flushed production should be the last to invoke. The effect of consideration, we need scarce remark, is to light for us in a work of art the hundred questions of how and why and whither, and the effect of these questions, once lighted, is enormously to thicken and complicate, even if toward final clarifications, what we have called the amused state produced in us by the work. The more our amusement multiplies its terms the more fond and the more rewarded consideration becomes; the fewer it leaves them, on the other hand, the less to be resisted for us is the impression of 'bare ruined choirs where late the sweet birds sang.' Birds that have appeared to sing, or whose silence we have not heeded, on a first perusal, prove on a second to have no note to contribute, and whether or no a second is enough to admonish us of those we miss, we mostly expect much from it in the way of emphasis of those we find. Then it is that notes of intention become more present or more absent; then it is that we take the measure of what we have already called our effective provision. The bravest providers and designers show at this point something still in store which only the second rummage was appointed to draw forth. To the variety of these ways of not letting our fondness fast is there not practically no limit?— and of the arts, the devices, the graces, the subtle secrets applicable to such an end what presumptuous critic shall pretend to draw the list? Let him for the moment content himself with saying that many of the most effective are mysteries, precisely, of method, or that even when they are not most essentially and directly so it takes method, blest method, to extract their soul and to determine their action.

It is odd and delightful perhaps that at the very moment of our urging this truth we should happen to be regaled with a really supreme specimen of the part playable in a novel by the source of interest, the principle of provision attended to, for which we claim importance. Mr. Joseph Conrad's *Chance* is none the less a signal instance of provision the most earnest and the most copious for its leaving ever so much to be said about the particular provision effected. It is none the less an extraordinary exhibition of method by the fact that the method is, we venture to say, without a precedent in any like work. It places Mr. Conrad absolutely alone as a votary of the way to do a thing that shall make it undergo most doing. The way to do it that shall make it undergo least is the line on which we are mostly now used to see prizes carried off; so that the author of *Chance* gathers up on this showing all sorts of comparative distinction. He gathers up at least two sorts—that of bravery in absolutely reversing the process most accredited, and that, quite separate, we make out, of performing the manœuvre under salvos of recognition. It is not in these days often given to a refinement of design to be recognised, but Mr. Conrad has made his achieve that miracle—save in so far indeed as the miracle has been one thing and the success another. The miracle is of the rarest, confounding all calculation and suggesting more reflections than we can begin to make place for here; but the sources of surprise surrounding it might be, were this possible, even greater and yet leave the fact itself in all independence, the fact that the whole undertaking was committed by its very first step either to be 'art' exclusively or to be nothing. This is the prodigious rarity, since surely we have known for many a day no other such case of the whole clutch of eggs, and these withal of the freshest, in that one basket; to which it may be added that if we say for many a day this is not through our readiness positively to associate the sight with any very definite moment of the past. What concerns us is that the general effect of 'Chance' is arrived at by a pursuance of means to the end in view contrasted with which every other current form of the chase can only affect us as cheap and futile; the carriage of the burden or amount of service required on these lines exceeding surely all other such displayed degrees of energy put together. Nothing could well interest us more than to see the exemplary value of attention, attention given by the author and asked of the reader, attested in a case in which it has had almost unspeakable difficulties to struggle with—since so we are moved to qualify the particular difficulty Mr. Conrad has 'elected' to face; the claim for method in itself, method in this very sense of attention applied, would be some-how less lighted if the difficulties struck us as less consciously, or call it even less wantonly, invoked. What they consist of we should have to diverge here a little to say, and should even then probably but lose ourselves in the dim question of why so special, eccentric and desperate a course, so deliberate a plunge into threatened frustration, should alone have seemed open. It has been the course, so far as three words may here serve, of his so multiplying his creators or, as we are now fond of saying, producers, as to make them almost more numerous and quite emphatically more material than the creatures and the production itself in whom and which we by the general law of fiction expect such agents to lose themselves. We take for granted by the general law of fiction a primary author, take him so much for granted that we forget him in proportion as he works upon us, and that he works upon us most in fact by making us forget him.

Mr. Conrad's first care on the other hand is expressly to posit or set up a reciter, a definite responsible intervening first person singular, possessed of infinite sources of reference, who immediately proceeds to set up another, to the end that this other may conform again to the practice, and that even at that point the bridge over to the creature, or in other words to the situation or the subject, the thing 'produced,' shall, if the fancy takes it, once more and yet once more glory in a gap. It is easy to see how heroic the undertaking of an effective fusion becomes on these terms, fusion between what we are to know and that prodigy of our knowing which is ever half the very beauty of the atmosphere of authenticity; from the moment the reporters are thus multiplied from pitch to pitch the tone of each, especially as 'rendered' by his precursor in the series, becomes for the prime poet of all an immense question—these circumferential tones having not only to be such individually separate notes, but to keep so clear of the others, the central, the numerous and various voices of the agents proper, those expressive of the action itself and in whom the objectivity resides. We usually escape the worst of this difficulty of a tone *about* the tone of our characters, our projected performers, by keeping it single, keeping it 'down' and thereby comparatively impersonal or, as we may say, inscrutable; which is what a creative force, in its blest fatuity likes to be. But the omniscience, remaining indeed nameless, though constantly active, which sets Marlow's omniscience in motion from the very first page, insisting on a reciprocity with it throughout, this original omniscience invites consideration of itself only in a degree less than that in which Marlow's own invites it; and Marlow's own is a prolonged hovering flight of the subjective over the outstretched ground of the case exposed. We make out this ground but through the shadow cast by the flight, clarify it though the real author visibly reminds himself again and again that he must—all the more that, as if by some tremendous forecast of future applied science, the upper aeroplane causes another, as we have said, to depend from it and that one still another; these dropping shadow after shadow, to the no small menace of intrinsic colour and form and whatever, upon the passive expanse. What shall we most call Mr. Conrad's method accordingly but his attempt to clarify *quand même*—ridden as he has been, we perceive at the end of fifty pages of *Chance*, by such a danger of steeping his matter in perfect eventual obscuration as we recall no other artist's consenting to with an equal grace. This grace, which presently comes over us as the sign of the whole business, is Mr. Conrad's gallantry itself, and the shortest account of the rest of the connection for our present purpose is that his gallantry is thus his success. It literally strikes us that his volume sets in motion more than anything else a drama in which his own system and his combined eccentricities of recital represent the protagonist in face of powers leagued against it, and of which the dénouement gives us the system fighting in triumph, though with its back desperately to the wall, and laying the powers piled up at its feet. This frankly has been *our* spectacle, our suspense and our thrill; with the one flaw on the roundness of it all the fact that the predicament was not imposed rather than invoked, was not the effect of a challenge from without, but that of a mystic impulse from within.

Of an exquisite refinement at all events are the critical questions opened up in the attempt, the question in particular of by what it exactly is that the experiment is crowned. Pronouncing it crowned and the case saved by sheer gallantry, as we did above, is perhaps to fall just short of the conclusion we might reach were we to push further. *Chance is* an example of objectivity, most precious of aims, not only menaced but definitely compromised; whereby we are in presence of something really of the strangest, a general and diffused lapse of authenticity which an inordinate number of common readers—since it always takes this and these to account encouragingly for 'editions'—have not only condoned but have emphatically commended. They can have done this through the bribe of some authenticity other in kind, no doubt, and seeming to them equally great if not greater, which gives back by the left hand what the right has, with however dissimulated a grace, taken away. What Mr. Conrad's left hand gives back then is simply Mr. Conrad himself. We asked above what would become, by such a form of practice, of indispensable 'fusion' or, to call it by another name, of the fine process by which our impatient material, at a given moment, shakes off the humiliation of the handled, the fumbled state, puts his head in the air and, to its own beautiful illusory consciousness at least, simply runs its race. Such an amount of handling and fumbling and repointing has it, on the system of the multiplied 'putter into marble,' to shake off! And yet behold, the sense of discomfort, as the show here works out, *has* been conjured away. The fusion has taken place, or at any rate *a* fusion; only it has been transferred in wondrous fashion to an unexpected, and on the whole more limited plane of operation; it has succeeded in getting effected, so to speak, not on the ground but in the air, not between our writer's idea and his machinery, but between the different parts of his genius itself. His genius is what is left over from the other, the compromised and compromising quantities —the Marlows and their determinant inventors and interlocutors, the Powells, the Franklins, the Fynes, the tell-tale little dogs, the successive members of a cue from one to the other of which the sense and the interest of the subject have to be passed on together, in the manner of the buckets of water for the improvised extinction of a fire, before reaching our apprehension: all with whatever result, to this apprehension, of a quantity to be allowed for as spilt by the way. The residuum has accordingly the form not of such and such a number of images discharged and ordered, but that rather of a wandering, circling, yearning imaginative *faculty*, encountered in its habit as it lives and diffusing itself as a presence or a tide, a noble sociability of vision. So we have as the force that fills the cup just the high-water mark of a beautiful and generous mind at play in conditions comparatively thankless—thoroughly, unweariedly, yet at the same time ever so elegantly at play, and doing more for itself than it succeeds in getting done for it. Than which nothing could be of a greater reward to critical curiosity were it not still for the wonder of wonders, a new page in the record altogether—the fact that these things are apparently what the common reader has seen and understood. Great then would seem to be after all the common reader!

We must not fail of the point, however, that we have made these remarks not at all with an eye to the question of whether *Chance* has been well or ill inspired as to its particular choice of a way of really attending to itself among all the possible alternatives, but only on the ground of its having compared, selected and held on; since any alternative that might have been preferred and that should have been effectively adopted would point our moral as well—and this even if it is of profit none the less to note the most striking of Mr. Conrad's compositional consequences. There is one of these that has had most to do with making his pages differ in texture, and to our very first glance, from that struggle of ungoverned verbiage which leads us up and down those of his fellow fabulists in general on a vain hunt for some projected mass of truth, some solidity of substance, as to which the deluge of 'dialogue,' the flooding report of things said, or at least of words pretendedly spoken, shall have learned the art of being merely illustrational. What first springs from any form of real attention, no matter which, we on a comparison so made quickly perceive to be a practical challenge of the preposterous pretension of this most fatuous of the luxuries of looseness to acquit itself with authority of the structural and compositional office. Infinitely valid and vivid as illustration, it altogether depends for dignity and sense upon our state of possession of its historic preliminaries, its promoting conditions, its supporting ground; that is upon our waiting occupancy of the chamber it proposes to light and which, when no other source of effect is more indicated, it doubtless quite inimitably fills with life. Then its relation to what encloses and confines and, in its sovereign interest, finely compresses it, offering it constituted aspects, surfaces, presences, faces and figures of the matter we are either generally or acutely concerned with to play over and hang upon, then this relation gives it all its value: it has flowered from the soil prepared and sheds back its richness into the field of cultivation. It is interesting, in a word, only when nothing else is equally so, carrying the vessel of the interest with least of a stumble or a sacrifice; but it is of the essence that the sounds so set in motion (it being as sound above all that they undertake to convey sense,) should have something to proceed from, in their course, to address themselves to and be affected by, with all the sensibility of sounds. It is of the essence that they should live in a medium, and in a medium only, since it takes a medium to give them an identity, the intenser the better, and that the medium should subserve them by enjoying in a like degree the luxury of an existence. We need of course scarce expressly note that the play, as distinguished from the novel, lives exclusively on the spoken word—not on the report of the thing said but, directly and audibly, on that very thing; that it thrives by its law on the exercise under which the novel hopelessly collapses when the attempt is made disproportionately to impose it. There is no danger for the play of the cart before the horse, no disaster involved in it; that form being *all* horse and the interest itself mounted and astride, and not, as that of the novel, dependent in the first instance on wheels. The order in which the drama simply says things gives it all its form, while the story told and the picture painted, as the novel at the pass we have brought it to embraces them, reports of an infinite diversity of matters, gathers together and gives out again a hundred sorts, and finds its order and its structure, its unity and its beauty, in the alternation of parts and the adjustment of differences. It is no less apparent that the novel may be fundamentally *organised*—such things as *The Egoist* and *The Awkward Age* are there to prove it; but in this case it adheres unconfusedly to that logic and has nothing to say to any other. Were it not for a second exception, one at this season rather pertinent, *Chance* then, to return to it a moment, would be as happy an example as we might just now put our hand on of the automatic working of a scheme unfavourable to that treatment of the colloquy by endless dangling strings which makes the current 'story' in general so figure to us a porcupine of extravagant yet abnormally relaxed bristles.

110. Robert Lynd, review, *Daily News*

15 January 1914, 4

Clearly referring to Lynd's review, Conrad wrote in his preface to *Chance* in 1920: 'A critic has remarked that if I had selected another method of composition and taken a little more trouble, the tale could have been told in about two hundred pages. . . . No doubt that by selecting a certain method and taking great pains the whole story might have been written out on a cigarette paper.'

As one reads *Chance*, one finds oneself wondering whether Mr. Conrad is after all an extraordinarily patient or a rather indolent writer. He gets his story out in pieces before our eyes. It is as though, instead of showing us an inhabited house, he bade us observe van after van coming up to the door and disgorging the furniture, and the people of the house appearing and disappearing as the pieces were moved in. He certainly contrives in this way to make his people as mysteriously interesting to us as newcomers to the house next door are to the normal decent human being. More than this, he succeeds in bringing along various chance passers-by who have somehow or other—mere chance again—been present at some crisis in the newcomers' lives. And, when we have seen and heard all, we know more about the people than their own mothers do. We have never, as it were, been introduced: our intimacy is indirect. But, just for that reason, we enjoy the added thrill of those who are in other people's secrets.

There is no denying that, if Mr. Conrad had chosen to introduce us to his characters in the ordinary way, he could have told us their story in about 200 pages instead of the 406 pages of the present book. On the other hand, he is not primarily occupied with their story, but with creating an atmosphere of strange motives. It is to some extent an atmosphere of puzzlement. Mr. Conrad enjoys keeping you in doubt as much as any writer of detective stories. But chiefly he enjoys the slow discovery of motives, and the observation of people accidentally goaded by some unusual motive into action. He throws himself into his work with a kind of sinister humour, and immediately every gesture, every intonation, becomes weighted with significance for him. Unlike Mr. Henry James, who scatters about him the bright light of the intellect as he leads us through his maze, Mr. Conrad sheds upon things the romantic and deceptive half-light of tragi-comic poetry. He is more of a poet than Mr. James, and less of a craftsman. Perhaps, too, he is less of a psychologist. He can hardly interest himself, for instance, in the psychology of the ordinary moment. He must have the psychological moment. In other words, he is interested in his men and women, not so much in their complete humanity as in curious and occasional aspects. That is why he hints a portrait rather than paints a portrait.

Probably for this reason many readers will find *Chance* tedious. No one, however, who has the patience to read it to the last word will fail to remember it as one of the most original and fascinating of novels. Like so much of Mr. Conrad's work, it expresses the 'nerves' rather than the passions of a situation. First, we have the 'nerves' of the Fyne household, when Flora de Barral, the financier-convict's daughter, ungratefully elopes with Captain Anthony, Mrs. Fyne's brother. Incidentally to this, we have the 'nerves' of the Brighton household where Flora was brought up by a governess who used her as a bait to keep a hold on an entirely odious young man. Then, after the elopement, we have the 'nerves' of Captain Anthony's ship on which the released convict gets a home with disastrous effects. Flora had perversely written to Mrs. Fyne to say that she did not love the precious captain, though she was marrying him; and, of course, the Fynes had let Captain Anthony know. As a result of this foolish lie, he kept himself apart on the ship, like a perfect knight of self-sacrifice. Flora, not understanding his coldness, was eating her heart out; and the ex-convict, seeing and not understanding, was filled with a monomania of hatred for the son-in-law who was sacrificing everything for him and his daughter.

There you have a fine tissue of misunderstanding—misunderstanding on the heroic scale. The theme only seems to stand out in its heroic proportions, however, on the night on which Captain Anthony's dynamite ship narrowly escapes being run down, and Mrs. Anthony helps Powell the second mate, with the flare that saves them. How beautifully Mr. Conrad describes the final passing of the strange ship!

[quotes part ii, ch. 3: 'The strange ship, a darker shape in the night. . . . "I don't want Mrs. Anthony frightened." ']

In the end, Mr. Conrad, for all his irony is kind. Though the captain's father-in-law tries to poison him, he escapes, and the old madman, drinking the poison himself, clears himself out of the way and leaves room for an understanding between Captain Anthony and Flora. Even so, however, the author can only give them a few years of happiness, and then chance sends the captain untimely to the bottom:

[quotes part ii, ch. 6: 'Mr. Powell gasped at the recollection . . . "I wasn't fit to tie the shoe-strings of the man you have drowned," I screamed at them.']

And that is practically the end, except that the author, recovering his gentleness, leaves us with a clear prophecy of yet other marriage-bells. But it is his study of poisoned atmospheres, not his story of happy marriages, that makes *Chance* a book of magical genius.

111. C. E. Montague, review, *Manchester Guardian*

15 January 1914, 6

The review was signed with the initials C.E.M., and according to the *Guardian*'s librarian is by Charles Edward Montague (1867–1928), novelist and essayist, and on the staff of the *Guardian* 1890–1925.

Chance may not be the finest of all Conrads. It takes more means to its ends than *Lord Jim* and the best of the short yarns did, and the end is not greater than theirs. But it is great, and the book is a true Conrad. If you had found a chapter, out of it, blowing about the Sahara, you would know in five minutes whose writing it was. Nobody else has such divine or demonic visions of the sea. Nobody else, of the first rate, writes, at off times, quite so carelessly. No other tragic writer opens a way for your sight into the burning heart of life with quite that contained, patient bitterness of compassion. Mr. Hardy, the only living writer in English whom one can still place above Mr. Conrad is patient, bitter, contained, and compassionate, yet the two are as unlike as two fruits. Besides, there is Mr. Conrad's unmistakable method of telling a story. In *Chance* he carries it further than ever. He keeps out of sight; he hides behind one man at first and then puts a second in front of the first, and perhaps a third in front of the second. Some shadowy figure of a narrator opens the tale and then melts into the dimness behind it and lets the bulk of it come as a tale told by one of the persons whom he has mentioned, and this second narrator, in turn, hands over the job, for a time, to one of his own creatures. So that the core of the story is, in one sense, like a picture within a frame which itself is painted—it is within a frame too, and that frame within another, again. As the story of Flora de Barral draws to an end this coil is unwound; each discarded narrator comes back to his place—in inverse order, of course,—and the shadowy first narrator puts in a last word. It is like one of those algebraical uses of bracket within bracket, even to three or four brackets of various shapes, or like a child's set of concentric boxes, each with its own colour.

In *Chance* the most obvious gain from this method is that some one or other of all these narrators may be credibly said to have seen or heard whatever needs to be told to the reader on the word of an eye-witness. A much greater gain is that the characters at the centre or heart of the story, the ones who do not narrate, but are narrated about, are shown under the variously searching lights of several observant temperaments, lights thrown upon them from different angles. And yet there is a unity of vision because all these various lights are them-selves only subtly varied versions of one light, which is covered and yet pervasive, like a clouded full moon—the temperament of the author. Mr. Henry James has told of the 'fine little law' by which our interest in an imagined event, character, or emotion is deepened if we get at it not through the direct report of the author but through the perceptions of characters specially equipped by him to do us this ser-vice. The whole affair, is, as he says, 'enriched by the way,' and for this enrichment of the story of Flora's and Anthony's tragic entangle-ment and deliverance Mr. Conrad must have taken an extraordinary amount of thought. You might at first think his corps of narrators, narrating in sections, their narratives inset within one another, an almost clumsy engine. You only come to know how purposeful it is when you have given yourself up freely to the strong charm of this system of interpenetrative lights, or interplaying mirrors, where nothing comes to you as a fact directly and impersonally stated; every new point has a greater reality and thrill than that; for you first see it through the strong emotions of curiosity and sympathy that it raises in somebody else, ostensibly not the author. When this has gone on for some time in *Chance* the whole atmosphere in which the narrative moves acquires a strange and exciting luminousness: you feel that there is a quickened sensitiveness everywhere round you, that all the characters of the book look either movingly clear to one another or else moving by the quality of their mystery. Almost to the end of the book Flora de Barral and Roderick Anthony are involved in a profound, incalculable troubling of the stream of experience, not by their fault. Mr. Hardy likes to show the sufferers, by such tragic embarrassments in their isolation—to show, for instance, how little it mattered to anyone what happened to Tess. Mr. Conrad's temperament or his method, or both, impel him to show how much the fates of Flora and Roderick mattered to many people. And you are worked up, while you read, to a heat of sensibility and curiosity like theirs. Among all these people so intensely aware of one another, so infectiously intent on making one another out, you too put out your feelers, such as they may be, and you are rewarded; you find it immensely worth while, in an air so tingling with communicative quickness.

All the while, too, you are almost apprehensively aware of a master controlling the vision, a Prospero all the more imposing for being almost haughtily unobtruded. No artist's figure looms more formidably behind the thin curtain of authorship than Mr. Conrad's. He is terrifyingly just and austere; his pity itself is only a kind of compunctious sternness, and his scorn is a frozen rage, like a winter wind on top of a mountain. Yet your imagination draws to him. He is tremendously right in any and every choice between two alternatives. If he were given the world to re-make, or at least the heart of man to temper over again, you feel he would do it nobly. Of course he wouldn't. No artist would. It is not his job. . . . But it is a noble impression to leave, without posing. The story ends semi-happily, to one's surprise. For the first 390 pages out of 406 it has been heading for tragedy, clearly—so you have thought. Then it takes a turn, like some patients, when you have given it up—an excellent practice in patients, but not admittedly so in novels or plays. Stevenson said that if they are going to end badly they ought to end badly from the beginning. The happy ending too, it has been thought, ought to grow in the thing from its roots. But rules like this only last until somebody breaks them to good purpose. They merely summarise the practice of the masters up to date. Mr. Conrad is one of the masters, and one hasty reader of *Chance*, at any rate, has not felt that in it a story full of magnificent tragic quality loses by having a close not wholly tragic.

112. Arnold Bennett's opinion

January 1914

(a) Extract from Bennett's Journal, 18 January 1914 (*JAB*, ii, 79):

Conrad's *Chance* came yesterday. Read 150 pp. This is a discouraging book for a writer, because he damn well knows he can't write as well as this. The episode of the arrival of the news of de Barral's bankruptcy at his house in Hove where his daughter and her superb friend of a governess are living is simply sublime. I know nothing better than this, and precious little as good.

(b) Extract from Journal, 24 January 1914 (*JAB*, ii, 80):

I finished Conrad's *Chance* in the middle of the night. It is very fine. The best chapters are 'The Governess' and the last one. The Tea Party chapter, and 'On the Pavement' chapter are too long. The indirect narrative is successfully managed on the whole, even to fourth hand narrative, but here and there recounted dialogue and gesture is so minute as to be unconvincing.

113. Edward Garnett, unsigned review, *Nation*

24 January 1914, 720–2

Garnett was one of the few critics who did not lose his critical vigilance in face of the ecstatic reception of *Chance*. Conrad wrote to Garnett about the review on 28 January 1914, thanking him for 'all the appreciative things' he said, and admitting Garnett's strictures on the work to be just: 'As to the exceptions you take I have always had the feeling that your criticism *must* be right . . . there's no one who can see *inside* my work as you can. And if at the same time you can here and there see *through* it—well I suppose I must put up with being found out in my innocent malpractices' (*LEG*, pp. 243–4).

Chance, though not one of Mr. Conrad's most powerful novels, is very characteristic of his genius for spinning an exquisite, artistic web out of stray bits of experience, odds-and-ends of common, flimsy material, daily oddments and accidents of life, which harmonize under his hands like the colors of an old Oriental carpet. And the design or intellectual pattern which runs through the story—*i.e.*, the infinite permutations out of which chance relations weave people's destinies—is one especially in keeping with the author's gift of philosophic irony. As always with Mr. Conrad's art, it is much less the particular figures of his drama that count than the light that plays on them, and the secret of his power lies in his scheme of human valuations, calling into play the infinite variety of shades and tones that we find, say, in a great stretch of landscape. One may be disappointed occasionally in the speech and gestures of his characters, even in the spontaneity of their thought, but never in the marvellously rich chiaroscuro and poetic magic of the whole picture of life.

The penetrating justness of Mr. Conrad's ironic insight and the breadth of his vision were never more necessary and rarely more triumphant than in *Chance*, where he sardonically brings together on his stage as heterogeneous a collection of types as might be culled in any metropolitan hotel. His method of telling his story through the mouths of three or four people, intermittently assisting in the drama, who unbosom themselves to a chief inquisitor, Marlow, is exceedingly artful, though occasionally a trifle artificial. But the total effect of this method is so fine in its subtle, variegated pattern as to dominate the imagination. The story opens with a chance encounter between Marlow, the retired skipper, and Mr. Powell, a fellow yachtsman, formerly second officer on the *Ferndale*, the late Captain Anthony's ship. The name *Ferndale* leads to the coupling of the two ends of the story. Mr. Marlow holds fast in his memory all the shore-links, so to say, while Mr. Powell is privileged by Fate to unreel all the later sea-links for our delectation. This dovetailing or splicing of the complementary parts of the narrative is most cunningly managed, helping to establish the illusion of the finger of chance having flung the pawns on the board. An important intermediary in the drama is Mrs. Fyne and her husband, little Fyne, 'a good little man in the Civil Service,' who is Captain Anthony's brother-in-law. Mr. Conrad's philosophic derision of all theorists is disclosed in his scathing treatment of the respectable Fynes. Perhaps he over-emphasizes by a shade his ironical derision which plays like sheet lightning round the heads of these self-complacent people, 'common-place, earnest, without smiles and without guile.' Perhaps, in Marlow's dislike of feminism the author's shadow is projected too obtrusively on the curtain, but, anyway, in the portraits of the Fynes, the middle-class mediocre target is riddled with shafts barbed with malicious wit.

Through the Fynes' embarrassed confidences to Marlow we come into touch with the tragic figure of the story—the unfortunate girl, Flora De Barral, the daughter of the 'preposterous' financier, De Barral, of the Orb Bank and Sceptre Trust. It is here, especially, that the magic of Mr. Conrad's vision shows like sunlight lighting up derelict scraps of glass or tin. Strictly speaking, there is nothing in De Barral's personality but an Idea in a frock coat and a tall hat; he himself is a mental vacuum, a mere personal slit, lettered 'Thrift,' into which the imbecile public pour the savings of a lifetime. The story of his rise from clerk to financier, and the sudden, appalling crash of the top-heavy edifice of the Orb and Sceptre Trust, has, of course its counterparts in history; but our author has simplified the type of plausible thimble-rigger into a mere shadow soon to be cast in bankrupt outline on court-house and prison walls. But De Barral serves the artist's purpose of back-ground throwing up his unhappy child's figure of tragedy. Here, again, the critic, admiring, asks himself whether Flora possesses any individual character. For she lives and moves as an embodiment of girlish misery, a poignant feminine spirit of tender youth, deceived, humiliated, and abandoned by the sinister conjunction of evil forces and a sniggering and indifferent world. Flora, in truth, lacks those characteristic traits which might distinguish her from thousands of unfortunate girls; but the author's instinct has not failed him in veiling her lineaments behind a mask of frozen suffering. Abandoned in the hour of the crash by the 'designing horrid people,' her mercenary governess, and the 'graceless scamp,' Charles, who had been scheming to marry her for her money, after a scene of venomous vituperation, poor Flora takes refuge with the good-hearted Fynes. Her bankrupt father soon consigns her to the care of the family of a cousin, a respectable East-end manufacturer, a calculating vulgarian, who 'possessed all the civic virtues in their very meanest form'. But the insolent insults of these odious relatives, eager to be rid of the 'wild-eyed, white-faced girl' when they find that not a penny-piece is left of De Barral's fortune, flay the unhappy Flora alive, and they cast her off again. Through similar vicissitudes, with successive 'protectors', mostly self-seeking or ignoble, is poor Flora dragged by fate, and one can scarcely admire enough the artistic dexterity with which Mr. Conrad intensifies the sombre elements of a tragedy that is only arrested when Captain Anthony appears on the scene. Captain Anthony's arrival at the house of his sister, Mrs. Fyne, while he is ashore for a spell after a long voyage, saves the distraught girl from suicide. Her pitiable state and her secret charm fire the seaman's imagination, and he and we and the corps of narrators, at the close of Part I., are now face to face with the situation first hinted at—viz., that the estimable Fynes are up in arms against the romantic match!

In the foregoing *résumé* we have indicated the tortuous windings of the cunning narrative. But critics more (or less) unscrupulous might do well to decline to follow the twists and loops of its consummate doublings. The tale is a masterpiece of indirect narrative, picked up here and handed on there by Marlow, Mr. Powell, the second officer, or others of Captain Anthony's satellites on board the good ship *Ferndale*. For the marriage does indeed take place between the captain and the unhappy victim of *Chance*. But before it is consummated, and before the ship sails on her new voyage, we assist at some East-End scenes, while the ship is lying in dock. In our opinion, these scenes are the best in the book, done with that intimacy of vision and dexterity of craftsmanship, of which Mr. Conrad is pastmaster. Not so good, not nearly so good, is our last glimpse of little Mr. Fyne, whose outburst against his escaping *protegée*, as against Captain Anthony's 'abominable selfishness' is—well, unnatural. It is curious to note how often the weakest link in the chain of a story is forged with a knowing purpose, and the flaw in *Chance* is the deliberate engineering of the lovers' sustained tragic misunderstanding on their honeymoon voyage. In the conversations at cross-purposes which lead to this situation, due in part to Captain Anthony's over-sensitive chivalry (see pp. 299–312), there is a lack of reality; and it is the same with much of the conversation (see pp. 324–7) between Flora and her father, the released convict, De Barral, when she carries him away from the prison gate to her husband's ship. For the chivalrous Captain Anthony has offered to provide a home for the broken old man, whose term is up just before the ship sails. When the voyage is begun, the situation of Captain Anthony's 'sublimely stupid' self-renunciation is sustained with all the resources of Mr. Conrad's art, and we are held under his spell till the magnificent scene of tragic terror (pp. 370–85) cuts the knot of the threatened tragedy. We will not spoil the reader's enjoyment by hinting at the psychological conflict here disclosed. It focusses and brings to a close the shifting menaces of this tragedy of chances with incomparable skill. But the author's achievement, we must repeat, lies in the magical atmospheric lighting of the whole human landscape. All the instruments of poetic insight, from irony to tragic terror, are used in turn in *Chance* by the artist who is at his highest not when the characters speak, but when he is conjuring up the mirage of their lives in the glass of men's passions.

114. Some opinions of *Chance*

January 1914

Extracts from various reviews praising the novel.

(a) Review by D. S. Meldrun, literary adviser to *Blackwood's Magazine*, *Daily Chronicle*, 15 January 1914, p. 4:

Coming straight from its spell, indeed still in the entrancement, which Mr. Conrad's writing produces, one may well declare the latest to be the best of his books.

(b) Unsigned review, *Standard*, 16 January 1914, p. 10:

Mr. Conrad is a great architect of novels, and this book is wonderfully and ingeniously planned.

(c) Unsigned review, *Spectator*, 17 January 1914, p. 101:

It is a red-letter day in the life of a reviewer when a new novel by Mr. Conrad falls to his lot. It is another matter altogether when he endeavours to fulfil his duties as a critic and render justice to one of the most gifted and original writers of our time.

(d) Review by Sir Sidney Colvin, a friend of Conrad, *Observer*, 18 January 1914, p. 5:

. . . Conrad has been contributing to our literature in the last eighteen years; work which sets before us the fruits of a remarkable experience enriched a hundredfold in the ripening light and head of imagination; work combining, as scarcely any other in our time combines, the three-fold powers of enthralling narrative, magically vital description and an unflagging subtlety and sanity of analytic character study; work finally, distinguished by so resourceful a mastery of English speech and style . . . *Chance* leaves on the mind the impression of a work of genius in the full sense, and helps to confirm its author's position among the very first of living imaginative writers, by all critics and novelists. It is the work of a master from which we may all learn. So much is certain. But we also have an idea that it will appeal more than Mr. Conrad's previous works have done to a wider public. It may prove the means of educating a large number of readers to appreciate the work of one of the most remarkable writers of our generation.

(e) Review by W. L. Courtney, who had not in the past succumbed to Conrad's magic, *Daily Telegraph*, 21 January 1914, p. 15:

Joseph Conrad is one of the marvels of our literature . . . . The interest of the book is wholly independent of the plot. It arises partly out of the literary style, partly out of an acute psychological analysis, partly, again, out of the peculiar technique and workmanship, which this novel, in a superlative degree, exhibits. . . . Probably *Chance* is one of the best works which Mr. Conrad has written comparable with *Lord Jim* and *Nostromo*.

(f) Unsigned review, *Punch*, 28 January 1914, p. 79:

Looking about among the very best *clichés* (my own and others)—'supersubtle analysis,' 'intimate psychology,' 'masterly handling,' 'incomparable artistry'—I found nothing that it didn't seem a sort of impertinence to apply to Joseph Conrad's *Chance*, which *Methuen* has just had the good luck to publish. For the whole thing is much nearer wizardry than workmanship.

5 February 1914, 10

There is some danger that Mr Conrad, by departing from the type of story upon which his great appeal to English readers mostly depends, may find himself sooner or later among that tiny band of artists in fiction whose work is loudly praised but little read, and that would be a pity—a pity for Mr Conrad, for the art of fiction, and for the public. There was always, in Mr Conrad's work, of course, a marked pre-occupation with psychology, unusual in English storytelling, a deliberation of movement, and an interest in souls rather than in bodies, but yet it has been sufficiently concerned with the visible acts of men and women to sustain the interest of that multitude which quite naturally and justifiably demands the traditional elements of the story—elements old as the cave-man, and that hitherto alone have made classics. *Chance*, Mr Conrad's latest work, will no doubt delight Mr Henry James and Mr Ford Madox Hueffer, but they are not the world, and this present reviewer, with the profoundest admiration and respect for the incontestible genius of Conrad, is a little alarmed to find that author deeper than ever before in the slough of introspection. It is hardly necessary to say that of its kind *Chance* is a fine performance; there is work in it that no other living writer in English could do; when you are through with it you realise that you have for a time moved among veritable people in hours and days of great emotional stress and tragedy. But yet somehow *Chance* suggests a formidable scaffolding that people watch being constructed intricately for days, only to find that at the end it was designed for nothing more than the placing of a weather-cock on a steeple. Now we are sure Mr Conrad does not wish merely to interest meteorologists. The story of his new novel can be put in a sentence or two. The daughter of a peculant and convicted financier, a girl whose unusual temperament is the main concern of the author, finds the world very much against her, and is coerced by circumstances into loveless marriage with a sea captain, who takes her and her father on his release from prison to sea. The father, with jealousy for the husband and other plans for himself and his daughter, seeks to poison the husband and fails, but commits suicide himself. The girl learns to love her husband (whose psychology will perplex the average reader, we fear), and the conclusion is not unhappy. But no summary of plot can possibly convey the real and essential nature of the story thus baldly indicated. You may read it with impatience, even skipping here and there, in your eagerness to come to action, or to the knot which ought to be at the centre of all these tangled personalities, but you will not soon, having done with it, forget the Fynes, and Marlow, de Barral and his daughter Flora, though you may wish they had occupied a livelier stage and had more wires jerking at their members. So potent is Mr Conrad's name now that the book has already gone through four or five editions.

VICTORY

24 September 1915

---

116. Robert Lynd, review, *Daily News*

24 September 1915, 6

Mr Conrad can make one's skin feel prickly in a manner all his own. Like Mr Henry James, in 'The Turn of the Screw,' he can fill the air with suggestions of internal horror. He thrills us less by the actions of his characters than by the spiritual background with which he frightens our imaginations. His theme in *Victory*, as in so many of his stories, is the virtuous man in conflict with demons. He gives us the sense all the time of not being very far from the mouth of Hell. His virtuous man is Heyst, a Swede of sensitive and almost egoistic chivalry, who has rescued an English girl from a travelling orchestra of women which makes its living in tropical ports, and who has taken her away out of the reach of a pestering German hotel-keeper to his lonely and volcano-guarded island. *Victory* is the story of the German's scheme of revenge and what came of it.

His hotel for some time past had been the haunt of three of the most terrifying creatures that have appeared in modern fiction. They are murderers, thieves, card-sharpers and most other sorts of bad characters. The German sees a chance at once of getting rid of this incubus from his hotel and of punishing Heyst for running away with the girl. He accordingly leads the three criminals—the two of them at least, who possess human intelligence—to believe that Heyst is a remorseless scoundrel, who has heaped up treasure for himself on his island, and that daring fellows such as they have only to sail thither with their knives and revolvers in order to get hold of an immense swag.

Mr Conrad, it must be confessed, has modified the terrifying aspect of his villains with some fine touches of comedy. He has a way of being ironical at the expense of the virtuous, and he has a way of being ironical at the expense of the devilish; and one part of the present story

285

is like an elaborately ironical study of Satan, Jack the Ripper and Caliban. 'Plain Mr. Jones,' the 'perfect gentleman,' the lean and spectral leader of the gang, is the comic image of Satan. He looked like a corpse, like a spectre, like a pole with a ghost's head on the end of it, and he was as insolent and indolent as an æsthete. Martin Ricardo, the second of the gang, was not at all a gentleman. He was like a cat, in his walk, in his moustaches, and in his voluptuous purrings as he thought about ripping people up with the great knife he carried down his leg. He was the Jack the Ripper of the party. The chapter in which he genially communicates to the horror-stricken German hotel-keeper the bloody incidents of his past life is a good piece of villainous comedy. Laughter is mixed with horror. This cat-like person is essentially a comic exaggeration, like Bluebeard in the pantomimes, and that despicable master of words, Falstaff. 'There ain't much to me,' he explains to the hotel-keeper:

[quotes from Part ii, ch. 6: 'There ain't much to me . . . I don't care what I do.']

The third member of this strange party, a hairy, half-articulate creature, was Pedro, the baboonish servant:

His broad, squat frame denoted great strength. Grasping the gunwales of the launch, he displayed a pair of remarkably long arms, terminating in thick, brown, hairy paws of simian aspect.

After these three children of sin have made their appearance, it is difficult to lay *Victory* down until the last page. They arrive at Heyst's island, parched and half-mad with thirst, one of their bottles having been filled with salt water, and immediately their strange siege of Heyst begins. They do not know whether he is armed; they do not know where his treasure is. As a matter of fact, his only revolver has been stolen by his Chinese servant, who runs away in terror of the newcomers. Here then is virtue helpless, and the demons crawling nearer every minute. Pedro is forced upon Heyst and Lena as a servant, and the cat-like Ricardo wanders about their bungalow, eager to spring, eager to run off with the girl, eager to discover things. He is a figure of shudderings almost to the end, which is brought about by Lena's desperate ruse to save her lover, and by 'plain Mr. Jones's' discovery that his lieutenant is running after a woman.

The curtain seems to me to be rather mechanical. Mr Conrad sweeps the corpses of good and bad alike into the dustbin too much after the manner of an Elizabethan dramatist. Still, that is true to his philosophy. He does not believe in any triumph of the fine over the foul, except in the fact of its being fine. Night swallows both alike. Love, courage, and nobleness, he seems to say, do not survive evil an hour. They perish at the hands of demons. None the less his work is an exaltation of all those beautiful things whose doom is so sure. *Victory* is, compared with *Chance*, an unambitious story, but its sensationalism, its irony, its grotesque and intensely real characters, its atmosphere of the ends of the earth, are likely to make it one of Mr Conrad's most popular stories. Such as it is, it is the true gold of genius.

117. Unsigned review, *Scotsman*

27 September 1915, 2

Mr Conrad seems to have two moods of envisaging humanity. In one he sees them by the white light of imagination as the simple elemental beings they are in the last analysis, and with consummate art he unfolds gradually the inner secrets of their being. In another mood he sees men and women as creatures in a melodramatic world, or perhaps in the absence of a personal vision he merely accepts them from other people's imagined worlds. In this novel these two moods mix and interact with one another. On the one hand we have such personages as Axel Heyst, the hero of the book, an indifferentist, an onlooker on life, preserving an aloofness from the activities and passions of men, because of his conviction of the futility of existence. Over against him there is the girl Lena, as simple in nature as he appears complex, who represents the form that life takes in its struggle with and triumph over his pessimism. The duel between these two, between the personification of unsophisticated and unspoiled humanity and humanity sicklied o'er with the pale cast of thought and repression of the natural emotions, is depicted with an art and psychological insight equal to anything Mr Conrad has yet shown. Side by side with these two intensely visualised characters there is a group of others who are not visualised at all in any real sense, but only seen from the outside. These are the villainous German innkeeper Schomberg, and the two soulless scoundrels, the aristocratic Mr Jones and his 'secretary' Martin Ricardo, who bring the element of physical tragedy into the story. These last two are not real, only figures of melodrama. But it is a testimony to the power of Mr Conrad's method that while the reader recognises at their first appearance that they are merely such figures, they assume before the end of the story a kind of vitality that is at any rate intensely engrossing. This change is wrought by the power which Mr Conrad has, and which he alone perhaps among living novelists has, of creating an atmosphere which is not that of reality as we know it, but seems to penetrate to a more essential and spiritual reality which underlies the ordinary world. It may be an illusion, but the creation of such an illusion is at least no mean artistic achievement. In the closing chapters of *Victory* we appear to be witnessing not a murderous contest between men, but a struggle between the spiritual powers of the universe temporarily incarnate in a little group of human beings on a lonely Pacific island.

118. Walter de la Mare, unsigned review, *The Times Literary Supplement*

30 September 1915, 330

This review was reprinted by de la Mare in *Private View* (1953), pp. 19–22, retaining the title of the review, 'At the World's End'. Two days after this review, de la Mare's second, and different, review of *Victory* appeared in the *Westminster Gazette* (see No. 119).

'Every work of art', said Flaubert, 'contains a particular element proper to the artist's personality, which, quite apart from the execution, seduces or irritates us.' This is certainly true of the art of Mr. Conrad. The particular element is not one that appears and reappears like the shimmer of a precious metal in a fragment of quartz or the vacancy of dream in a quiet eye. It is something which dyes his whole story, every human being in it, scene and word, and seals them as exclusively their author's as do the characters of his own signature. So pervasive and intense is the influence of this personal element that for Mr. Conrad's reader it is not merely a question of liking or disliking his work, certainly not of being just amused or bored by it. Either, when we open the pages of *Victory*, the spell of the old familiar seduction instantly re-envelops us, and we greet it as with the long-drawn sigh a child puffs out at sight of an unutterably rich and bespangled Twelfth Night cake. Either we return to it from time to time as with the half-shudder of expectation with which a young man sallies out to meet the loved and secret (even, maybe, illicit) fair in the profound hush of a world of summer and an ascending moon. Either this; or we are irritated, shocked, repelled.

If fascinated, we acquiesce; if repelled, we criticize. Can the secure life we know and complacently flourish in be *this*? Should the underlying philosophy, mood, obsession of a piece of fiction be almost as intolerable as the stare of a pagan god? Come the faint and tepid airs of our spiritual zone from these exotic, heavy islands menacing with the untranslatable thunder of their surfs? Can such horror dog our

289

secret minds, and we unaware? Are there really and truly men around us of a more deadly and conscious evil than that of the devil we have laughed out of court? And really! are the trivialities of right and wrong, the little cowardices, uncharities, and inhumanities, so vital? How, indeed, shall we ever be able to call our small souls our own if this is the shuddering test to which the Infinite has submitted them?

And here there seems to be a paradox. If it is the solemn and ironic gravity of the scrutiny which Mr. Conrad bends on life in these remote islands, Samburan and Sourabaya, if it is his conversion of the tawdry commonplaceness of existence into a tragedy never more appalling than when he mocks it as grotesque, never more profoundly significant than when so instinctive a creature as Lena risks even ravishment at the hands of the foul and pitiless Ricardo for the sake of her bright and selfless love, if it is this desperate import which Mr. Conrad pours into mortal affairs that may irritate and shock, how can these qualities possibly seduce? 'Life is so hideous', wrote Flaubert, again in one of his letters, 'that the only way of enduring it is to avoid it. And it may be avoided by living in art, in ceaseless search for truth rendered by beauty.'

Of much of Mr. Conrad's truth to 'reality' most of us cannot judge but by his own aid. 'I am not likely', he remarks—how needlessly only his public could assure him!—'to offer pinchbeck wares to my public consciously.' Faced indeed with the expert's little dish of diamonds, even the veriest novice soon realizes that unless all his gems are paste, none can be. It is only by means of Mr. Conrad's imaginative experience that we can be transported to his island of Samburan. It is only his imagination that could body forth for us precisely such a monstrosity as that 'insolent spectre on leave from Hades', that 'merry skeleton', the truly gentlemanly 'Mr. Jones'. And even Mr. Jones, we have to remember—in the eyes of the philosophical dreamer, Axel Heyst (alias 'Mr. Enchanted Heyst', alias 'Hard Facts Heyst', alias 'Mr. Blasted Heyst', himself another 'perfect gentleman', as 'we of the islands' summed him up)—*seemed* to be nothing more awful than an envoy from the outer world, and nothing more substantial than an apparition and chimera. So, too, with Schomberg.

This typical Teuton, the incarnation not of recent animosities, but of 'old, deep-seated, and, as it were, impartial conviction', has appeared twice before in Mr. Conrad's world. Here his 'grotesque psychology is completed at last'. Axel Heyst is a Swede. In a moment of unconsidered compassion he cheats this corpulent hotel-keeper,

Schomberg, of a friendless, drifting young English girl, Lena. And Lena had seemed to Schomberg like a ripe fruit, not only ready to drop into his mouth, but which would prove a delicious antidote to the extremely dry distaste for his battered, fear-besotted wife. His frenzied lust gives him cunning, not courage. When the emaciated Mr. Jones, his pockmarked lieutenant, Ricardo, and their servant, the baboon-like Pedro, storm his respectable veranda, this precious German, torn betwixt wounded vanity and terror of such a trio, hints of other spheres. There is hidden, ill-gotten treasure in solitary Samburan, he leers, where the noxious and eccentric Heyst lives in sin with the girl he has stolen. So the trio take a boat and put to sea. 'Let me undo the button of your shimmy.'

This Schomberg *lives*: and so too Pedro, and so too lives Wang— Heyst's cautious and scrupulous major-domo; not because they exactly resemble any Teuton or alligator-hunter or Chink we may have the fortune to meet. And thus too—with its criss-cross construction, as erratic in its progress as the knight in chess, but as competent wastelessly to cover the board—thus too lives *Victory*, solely by virtue of its having itself been lived in, incident by incident, word by word, by one 'in ceaseless search for truth rendered by beauty'. It is for this reason that such a story may wholly 'seduce' even far less serious, searching, devoted, compassionate souls, because, perhaps, they, more used to the melting mood, have found life not so much hideous as difficult and perplexing, because they also may have been occasionally troubled by a detached view of the universe. 'Suppose the world were a factory and all mankind workmen in it. Well, he discovered that the wages were not good enough. That they were paid in counterfeit money.' It is in these words that Axel (vainly) attempts to explain to Lena the pessimistic views on life of the elder Heyst—the dead and gone philosopher whose heavy, gilt-framed portrait on the flimsy wall of mats broods on in the pregnant heat of Samburan. 'Man alone can give one the disgust of pity' is one of this philosopher's icy aphorisms. And again, 'Of the stratagems of life the most cruel is the consolation of love.' And again—

'Men of a tormented conscience, or of a criminal imagination, are aware of much that minds of a peaceful resigned cast do not even suspect. It is not poets alone who dare descend into the abyss of infernal regions, or even who dream of such a descent. The most inexpressive of human beings must have said to himself at one time or another: "Anything but this!" . . .'

'We all have our instants of clairvoyance'—Mr. Conrad proffers the magic crystal. We peer into it. And we see this familiar life of ours, heightened and deepened, charged with phantasmal terror, carnal disgust, with a thwarted, venomous, and phantasmal evil; and transfigured with humble dutifulness, self-sacrifice, courage, scorn of pain and of death. And confronted with this miracle—whether of verisimilitude or of transformation—those of us who are not irritated are seduced. Our little ceaseless search has also for a moment found rest and solace—'in truth rendered by beauty'.

119. Walter de la Mare, review, *Westminster Gazette*

2 October 1915

A few days ago Mr. Hall Caine[1] took a representative of the Press into his confidence. He confessed with some little wistfulness that if he could have his youth again he would devote its artistic energies to the cinematograph. In a word, he foresees an enviable opportunity for the young and ardent imagination in the Film. That is a curious sigh of regret to come from a writer of fiction, for what, at its lowest, is a novel but an ideal representation of life—feeling, thought, action, in words? What is a Picture Palace but the unsubjective Academy of the deaf mute? When, indeed, such a novel as *Victory* unfolds itself in sound and vision before the imagination, with its rhythms and cadences, music and silences, its unrestricted freedom in time and space, its wisdom and balance and simpleness out of complexity, we begin to realise to what an immeasurable extent life on the world is coloured and quickened by the imagination, how easy it is to recognise, how difficult and unusual to discover.

[1] Mr (later Sir) Hall Caine (1853–1931), immensely popular novelist, a phenomenal best-seller, author of, among many others, *The Eternal City* (1901) and *The Prodigal Son* (1904).

Every reality is something compounded, the outcome of a collusion between the seer and the thing seen. And the simplest work of art—of fiction—is a thing infinitely more abstruse. So that to say that *Victory* is 'true to life' amounts not only almost to ignoring Mr. Conrad altogether, but is an exaggerated compliment to one's everyday consciousness as his reader. For just as form and content in a work of art (or of nature humanly seen) are inseparable, so the originality of a novelist consists not in how he has copied the life we know, but in the life that he has himself created—the life of which, without his witness, we should be ignorant. It is his all of life that is indivisibly his. If Axel Heyst and Lena, if the German hotel-keeper Schomberg ('in a state of rapid moral decomposition'), and that ineffable 'gentleman' and 'brigand' Mr. Jones were handed over to some other practitioner, they would not be merely re-dressed up; they would in themselves cease to exist. And to make a précis of *Victory*, to say that it is the story of the conflict between heart and mind in a man doomed by destiny to the trammels of philosophic doubt and a passionless integrity in the presence of a selfless love and innocence and of an evil as violent and as confined in spiritual space, so to speak, as an atom of radium, is nothing better than to write a name and a date upon a tombstone. We realise sooner or later that Mr. Conrad alone could create *for us* the naïve, fearless, submissive, all-sacrificing Lena, the rancid German, Schomberg, the ivory, silvery philosopher of Despair, Heyst senior, 'silenced destroyer of systems, of hopes, of beliefs,' and that devil of two instincts, lust and violence, Ricardo, just as he alone could float before our eyes Samburan amid its archipelago in the remote waters of an unfamiliar world:

The islands are very quiet. One sees them lying about, clothed in their dark garments of leaves, in a great hush of silver and azure, where the sea without murmurs meets the sky in a ring of magic stillness. A sort of smiling somnolence broods over them; the very voices of their people are soft and subdued, as if afraid to break some protecting spell.

It is an originality that is manifest even in a phrase, as when the peculiar timbre of Lena's voice is described as possessing 'a modulation of audacity and sadness'; or even in just three words for ever individualising Mr. Jones's 'dark sunken stare.'

This is only to insist on a commonplace. It may humble us to realise that Mr. Conrad's Lena could not of herself 'in real life' reveal to us her spiritual loveliness, that we should have discovered most easily in

Heyst what is for ever troubling us in his appearance in his story—those bronze horizontal moustaches, that large white brow, that suave manner and volubility—and probably have missed his tragic, dauntless bearing, his despair, in face of the 'Great Joke'—Life. But in the acceptance of a gift humility does no harm. We may be positively shocked at a plane of consciousness whereon evil is at the same time so hideously substantial and violent and yet so spectral; troubled in face of a beauty so densely mantled with the moods and emotions of sadness, isolation, solemn ecstasy and despair; and remain unsolaced by a presentation of virtue which reaps no reward but that of death. 'Let Heaven look after what has been purified.' But what is this but the recognition of genius? What, indeed, is genius but a power of receptiveness so individual that its revelation in the form of art is the revelation of a new universe?

Mr. Conrad's universe is haunted. The humility of *his* acceptance takes strange disguises of irony and scorn, indignation and laughter. But these are only the clothing of his truth. 'Real bad people get over me somehow,' says Lena. 'I have said to the Earth that bore me: "I am I, and you are a shadow."' 'And by Jove, it is so,' says Heyst. Shadow it may be, but 'It will bite you if you give it a chance.' 'Formerly,' explains the unnamed narrator, 'in solitude and silence, Heyst had been used to think clearly and sometimes even profoundly, seeing life outside the flattering optical delusion of everlasting hope, of conventional self-deceptions, of an ever-expected happiness.' And it is this same victim of blessedest disillusionment who with his last breath cries, 'Ah, Davidson, woe to the man whose heart has not learned while young to hope, to love—and to put its trust in life.'

It is an emptier stage even than that of *Hamlet* on which Mr. Conrad's curtain descends. And yet his story leaves us in the presence of what we long for most just now in the tormented conflict between the chequered good and evil of nations and individuals—for the reassurance of the spirit of love and of life—Victory.

120. Unsigned review, *Nation*

2 October 1915, 25–6

This review might well be the work of Edward Garnett, regular reviewer for the *Nation*, but both treatment and tone suggest some other critic.

The tradition of narrative is as much of a vested interest to Englishmen as lyric poetry. It is a vested interest to all the world, but a positive literary obsession to the unphilosophic, uncurious Englishman. One might also say, indeed, that the predominant genius of these islands leans towards lyric poetry and prose narrative. Satire, too, for that matter, but that, one supposes, is not because it is indigenous, but because it has so many openings. It is the more remarkable, therefore, that narrative, in these modern days, has, somehow or other, lost its balance. The ambitious novelists ignore it, and the mechanical ones batten upon it. Indeed, one of the most striking things about the realists (who absorb the less commercial type of fiction) is their revolt against the narrative form. It is not that they don't tell a story; they cannot very well avoid a certain sequence of events. But they throw the story out of perspective; they put it in the shade, and make it subordinate to the autobiographical purpose. Now, what is the result of this? It is, in a word, to lose that differentiation of identities, which is the supreme justification of the narrative form. The realistic-cum-autobiographical document does not create character; it cannot by its very composition create character. What it does is to issue variations of its author's personality. Even when the central figure in a realistic novel is not an actual projection of the writer's ego, the other characters tend to revolve within his orbit—to express his attitudes, to personify his prejudices, and to be created in his image. The result is a kind of blur—as though certain indefinite figures were to take shape and form out of an insubstantial mist.

Exactly the opposite processes take place by means of the concrete and objective values of first-rate narrative. The characters are not painfully philosophized into being; they create, by their own actions, their philosophies and destinies. They interact with the events and the events with them, and the stronger these characters, the more sharply realized and differentiated, the more likely they are to set vigorously in motion a convincing and significant action. So it is that, from these considerations, we can assert, almost dogmatically, that the best narrative will tend to produce a corresponding intensity, salience, and variety of characterization. The psychological differences may, indeed, be so abrupt as to father the impression of a gallery of grotesques. That does not matter, so long as they do not impair, and as they very seldom do impair, the essential reality.

It has been the peculiar dowry of Mr. Conrad—a Pole—to have restored to England the traditional glories of its narrative. This latest story, *Victory*, a reversion to the *Outcast of the Islands* type, has none of those convolutions and intricacies of psychology by which he gave the lie to those theorists who hold that the narrative form is a stiff and inflexible medium, incapable of squeezing into it any but the less complex manifestations of life. Indeed, the feature of Mr. Conrad's work, in this as in his more elaborate structures, is the equipoise he preserves between his action and his psychology. One is inclined to think that only in *Nostromo* is the one sacrificed to the other, and only in *Nostromo* is the one not a mate and a complement of the other. The issue in *Victory* is as clear as in a Mystery play—the conflict between the forces of darkness and of light; with the difference of actual life that virtue is not triumphant over the enemy. The armies, in fact, are both victims of the convulsion of strife, and it is only in the classical suggestion of καθάρσις, of which Mr. Conrad is so subtle a master, that evil is defrauded of its prey. Nor, by any manner of means, can Mr. Conrad's exploitation of such orthodox material be called a convention. Axel Heyst is a highly sceptical, speculative kind of hero. To the most respectable canons of the world he is, at best a waster and derelict, at worst a parasite. His career is a succession of failures, and at the opening of the book he is living in meditative solitude upon the remote island of Samburan, the ex-manager of the Tropical Belt Coal Company. Nor does Heyst wear his chivalry and active abhorrence of oppression and cruelty upon his coat-sleeve. When he rescues Lena, the English girl, one of a troupe of performing musicians, carried about from island to island, like caged beasts in a menagerie, we are conscious of the acute contrast between the shrinking philosopher and the enterprising Perseus. And in his relations with Lena on his island we are more than ever alive to the delicate shades of his personality—its introspectiveness, semi-futility, mistrust, and lack of recognition of the more unified and elemental devotion of the girl. Heyst is invariably interesting, because of the deprecating cloak in which he wraps his generous temper. With the enemy, on the other hand, Mr. Conrad employs quite a different method. Schomberg, the German hotel-proprietor, who pursues Lena with his half-abject, half-ferocious attentions, and Heyst with his pertinacious hatred, is a combination of formality, timidity, meanness, and brutality. He is, as it were, the interpreter between the enigmatic Heyst and the real extravagant villains of the piece. That these villains —Mr. Jones, the indolent spectre, the ghostly gentleman of evil, Martin Ricardo, his henchman, an amalgam of a Camden Town murderer and a stealthy cat, and Pedro, the hairy simian, with his gigantic strength—are extravagant, grotesque, as the author meant them to be, is true enough. That does not detract from their reality; on the contrary, it gives it a curiously symbolic force. The spectre, the cat, and the gorilla, then come to Schomberg's hotel, for a temporary retirement from business, varied with a little cardsharping. Schomberg, to rid himself of such unloved guests and to satisfy his revenge, induces them, for the price of a hypothetical swag, to sail over to Samburan and dispose of Heyst. The action of the drama from this point, is accelerated and intensified. Heyst is left unarmed, owing to the defection of his Chinese servant, and Mr. Jones is metaphorically disarmed, from Ricardo's savage desire for Lena—women, to Mr. Jones, being the only daunting and unassailable thing in a world of easy conquests. But they all go down to disaster, and the appearance of Captain Davidson, the friend of Heyst, reminds one of the dirge after exhausted combat in an Elizabethan play.

Mr. Conrad does not make much use of that subtle technique, which, as in *Lord Jim* and *Chance*, tosses the narrative, like a ball or loving cup, from hand to hand. That is because the story does not really need it. In *Victory*, the narrative is the thing, and the few elaborations there are are used exclusively for putting the finishing touches upon its speed, its elasticity, and, shall we say, its splendid constitution.

121. Unsigned review, *Atlantic Monthly*

October 1915, 511

Also reviewed were James Lane Allen's *The Sword of Youth* and George Agnew Chamberlain's *Through Stained Glass*.

So we come at last, somewhat heavy-footed, to the finest thing that the season offers. It is Joseph Conrad's *Victory*. Since Henry James has ceased to write novels, Conrad is the ablest exponent of the great method in English fiction. He lays hold of any subject that pleases him —one might almost say, of any subject that happens along. In this case it is the lonely life and tragic death of a man and woman on an inconsiderable isle in the South Seas. To the ordinary observer, Axel Heyst and the girl Lena seem to matter as little in the scheme of things as two human creatures possibly can. One might consider their lives and deaths 'worth' two inches of newspaper space at the most. They are even as the two sparrows sold for a farthing, in their unimportance and obscurity. Conrad takes these negligible folk, their remote beginnings, their horror-smeared end, and soaks himself in the subject till he can give off nothing about them that is not loaded with absorbing interest, with profound significance. He makes a great drama, charged with pity and terror, of these few weeks of their hidden life moving swiftly to its end. He sees them somewhat as one may reverently hope the Creator sees us all. At least, he sees them with crystal clearness, with absolute detachment, yet with a yearning pity, a vast gentleness. To be able to project one's self thus into this or that human situation, to saturate one's self with it, to give it forth again completely, is art indeed, but art at such a marvelous pitch that it deserves some other, some yet greater name.

122. Gerald Gould, review, *New Statesman*

2 October 1915, 622–3

I have been trying to decide what one would think of *Victory* if it came
to one without the glamour of Mr. Conrad's reputation. I suppose that
is at once the fairest and the most difficult form of judgment. No competent critic would deny that Mr. Conrad's work has almost always
come of the quality of greatness, and, at its most unforgettable, is
solidly and unquestionably great: has at once a magnitude and an
intensity—an exactitude and urgency of feeling informing every detail
through which the artistic vision, the intellectual conception, find
expression. His works are not, of course, of the greatest, or anything
like it: but they have a uniqueness, a place in the world of art: they are
themselves: one comes back to the epithet 'solid.' Yet I do not think
that, on its own merits, *Victory* would be credited so much with greatness as with fineness. There is even a rather fatigued air of delicacy, an
evasion, a reticence, in the manner, despite the stark horror of the
matter. I am aware that the most enthusiastic of Mr. Conrad's admirers
will probably tell me that the excellence lies precisely in this union of
horror with delicacy—that Mr. Conrad's special merit is to deal with
battle, murder and sudden death, volcanoes and secret isles and tropical
tempests, as exquisitely as if they were the cultured palpitations of the
drawing-room. I can only say that, here at any rate, he does not quite
bring it off.

Axel Heyst, a detached and wandering Swede, whose father's
philosophy has taught him to wander, to refrain, to form no ties, never
to commit himself to the hurting joys or responsibilities of social life,
is at once the central and the most successful character of the book. His
sensibilities, his strength, his tenderness, his ironies, are all strange
enough, but *right*: and the way in which they entangle him in the ties
he seeks to avoid makes a study in the very ingenuities of psychology.
The girl whom he chivalrously rescues from the persecution of an
unpleasant Teutonic hotel-keeper and takes to live with himself on
what, for most practical purposes, is an uninhabited island, fails, on the
other hand, to give the smallest impression of reality. Not that Mr.

Conrad's psychology is at fault: it is only the wrong kind of psychology. It provides the reactions, the subtleties, that one might expect from the generalisation of laboratory research: each reaction is true enough in isolation from the flesh-and-blood humanity of a particular human being. The rest of the important characters are for the most part fantastic. The springs of their activity are amazingly minute, but a little incoherent. They have all the vividness of falsehood. Indeed (apart from Heyst) Mr. Conrad is here no more a character-delineator (in the sense in which Thackeray is, say, or Meredith) than Turner[1] was a portrait-painter. As in Turner, the human figures are pathetic and fugitive against lurid and fuliginous spaces. The profoundest things in *Victory* are generalisations and descriptions:

Like most dreamers, to whom it is given sometimes to hear the music of the spheres, Heyst, the wanderer of the Archipelago, had a taste for silence which he had been able to gratify for years. The islands are very quiet. One sees them lying about, clothed in their dark garments of leaves, in a great hush of silver and azure, where the sea without murmurs meets the sky in a ring of magic stillness. A sort of smiling somnolence broods over them; the very voices of their people are soft and subdued, as if afraid to break some protecting spell.

The picture is complete. What profundity, too, in such touches as this, concerning the elder Heyst's last book:

In this work, at the end of his life, he claimed for mankind that right to absolute moral and intellectual liberty of which he no longer believed them worthy.

Schomberg, the hotel-keeper, always libellous and poisonous, is maddened against Heyst by a sexual jealousy of which the symptoms are pitilessly recorded. He sends, to violate Heyst's refuge, a pair of highly unconvincing adventurers—a pseudonymous Mr. Jones, whose diabolical traits are accompanied by a morbid fear of women, and his henchman, a sailor, whose fidelity is at last shaken by a violent sudden passion for the girl living with Heyst. This henchman's language is somewhat high-flown on occasion: he talks about being 'as tired as if I had been pouring my life-blood here on these planks for you to dabble your white feet in.'

The story, beginning quietly, colloquially, grows intenser: with admirable if rather obvious art it works up to a climax as bloody as that of *Hamlet*. But *Hamlet*, if melodrama, is melodrama turned tragedy: *Victory* is neither tragic nor melodramatic. None of the

[1] Joseph Mallord William Turner (1775–1851), one of England's greatest masters of water-colour.

characters hold one with any desire for them to go on living: the most touching thing of all is the apathy that descends on Heyst when he realises his helplessness on the island under the designs of the adventurers—and from that apathy death is no change for the worse. A far stronger 'thrill' would, given the same properties, have been attained by many a writer of less genius than Mr. Conrad: but thrills are not what he is after. The many vivid and beautiful pictures—pictures that have emotion as well as colour—are not purple patches: they are an integral part, indeed an efficient symbol, of the philosophy informing the whole. That philosophy has the strength of terrors but the quietness of depth.

123. Unsigned, review, *Glasgow Evening News*

7 October 1915, 8

Up to this time, the *Glasgow Evening News* had been a consistent champion of Conrad.

All art, of course, is symbolic, but if the symbolic intention becomes visible, the art fails; illusion is destroyed and we are confronted merely with a parable, a matter of preaching. This is a danger to which Mr Joseph Conrad is always peculiarly exposed, because there is in him so much of the moralist. He has his eye always on the general, the universal, and great artist as he is, he does not always escape the danger of letting us see that he is thinking about Life, when as an artist he should seem, even to himself, to be thinking only of some particular bit of humanity. Sometimes, even, he drops into sheer melodrama, at which we should laugh were it not for that constant pressure of intellect and impressiveness of mood with which he makes even figures of melodrama vivid, life-like, and sombrely significant.

In this book, which he calls *Victory*, with a subtlety the average fiction reader will assuredly fail to comprehend, Mr Conrad has chosen a theme, entirely characteristic—the union of a man who, though not old, has come to a profound conviction of the worthlessness, treachery, and cruelty of Life with an innocent, simple girl, ardently attached to him both by gratitude and passion. It is an extraordinary study, such as only Conrad, perhaps, could have given us, and it is made the more moving and intense by the setting he gives it of a lonely Eastern island where there is nothing whatever to break or relieve the impact of mind on mind, of mood on mood. How that situation would have been resolved in the absence of change from without, it is hard to guess; possibly Conrad himself found it insoluble, or at any rate insoluble without futility.

His solution, then, had to come from without, and it arrives in the shape of a couple of melodramatic ruffians who have been led by a rascally German hotelkeeper to believe that the mysterious recluse has carried off much plunder as well as the girl, whom the German himself had wanted. These two ruffians—an emaciated, gentlemanly black-guard and his follower, a human jaguar—are stock types of villainy in the lower regions of literary and dramatic art, and even Mr Conrad's masterful skill does not prevent us from becoming a little tired of the constant insistence on Martin's physical and moral resemblance to one of the cat tribe. Their blackguardism is fully justifiable by the artist's original purpose. For here is the baseness and cruelty of Life seeking out the hermit even in the loneliest of refuges no less than its warmth and beauty, offered him by the girl, in spite of his deepest distrust. And in the end, too, it is just that brutal cruelty which gives the girl and Life their triumphant, tragic victory. If only Martin had been a little less like a jaguar and his master a little less reminiscent of the polished villain of the third-rate theatre. Possibly this is to carp unduly. There is no question that *Victory* is a fine book by a great artist. But illusion is such a delicate thing—destroyed by one awkward or miscalculated touch.

124. William Lyon Phelps on *Victory*

1917

Extract from *The Advance of the English Novel* (1917), 217.

The story *Victory* reads as though it were intended to gain for its author a wider audience, as though he had tried to write in a 'popular' manner. Despite many fine passages of description, it is poor stuff, and its author should be ashamed of Mr. Jones, who belongs to cheap melodrama. It is to me inconceivable that Conrad should deliberately lower his ideal, or hoist a white flag to the hostile majority. If that were true, *Victory* would be a defeat. I regard it simply as one of those lapses of which nearly all great writers have shown themselves capable.

THE SHADOW-LINE

19 March 1917

---

125. Unsigned review, *Nation*

24 March 1917

To Garnett, May 1917, Conrad wrote: 'I knew it [the review] was not written by you being under the impression that you ... were not in England' (*LEG*, 250).

To call an artist 'great' nowadays has ceased to be a compliment. There are so many of them, for one thing. And the word has become so much a euphemism of noise, bulk, show, and brag, that to call a mere artist great is something like admiring a mere frog because he has blown himself out to ten times his size. And so when we call Mr. Conrad 'great,' it is in the antiquated sense of the word, in the sense that we speak of 'the great masters.' For that is really the only possible way to look at him; nor is it a labored truism to point it out. Criticism is so delivered over to indiscriminate praise that when a genuine master of literature swims into our ken, there is nothing left but to repeat more hoarsely and more stridently the appreciations we have devoted to not a few of his contemporaries. The utmost we can do is to think of him as a tall man looking over the heads of his fellows. We are unable to conceive him as a pilgrim in the remote and lonely tradition of art, as striding with one step from the past into posterity, and making a brief, towering angle, like Gulliver, over the confused heads of early twentieth-century Englishmen.

But that is how we must try and think of him, because it is his due. It is childish to regard him as a brilliant teller of sea-stories, to point out what an oddity it is for a Pole to use the English language with such rich felicity. Until we recognize once and for all that Mr. Conrad is an artist of creative imagination, one of the great ones, not of the present, but of the world, critical words are wasted upon him. That admitted, criticism can survey him from a new point of vantage, or, as in the example of the Elizabethan attitude towards Shakespeare, throw out a few observations and leave the ultimate valuation to posterity. It is partly on this assumption that we can understand his extraordinary grasp of our language. One might have imagined that Mr. Conrad, a Pole (with a certain occasional likeness to Turgeniev as he has to Henry James in the treatment of character and to Meredith in the treatment of theme) might just as well have chosen to write in French. As a matter of fact, his work has no more affinity to the French genius than an etching has to a pastel. Why? Because he is a romantic, a master of the universal, indefinite, mysterious suggestion (expressed by the utmost delicacy and suppleness of form) which is the highest mark of the true romantic. We may say, therefore, that he chose to embody his genius in English speech, because English literature is the most profoundly romantic of all the art of modern Europe, and because the sheer inspiration of that genius placed in his hands not only the desire but the power of the English tradition. To-day, he is English romance as it is not in contemporary writers and as it ought to be at the artistic bidding of a Pole. So striking, indeed, is this characteristic of Mr. Conrad, that the mind is tempted to dabble in metempsychosis and to see him thrown back three hundred years into the inscrutable person of the old English seaman—Sir Walter Raleigh.

It is no doubt this romantic inheritance that gives Mr. Conrad something of his extraordinary power of narrative—particularly of oblique narrative. He possesses such absolute control of his technique in passing events through a certain period of time and collision, that he is able to discard the mathematics of orderly sequence and to play such tricks with time that the banal progression of past, present, and future lose their rigidity from the compulsion of the artist's vision. In that incomparable study of a romantic psychology, Lord Jim, and a trifle less successfully in Chance, the narrative doubles in and out, as though it had neither end, beginning, nor middle, as though the artist, obeying higher laws imperceptible to all but him, could set natural ones at defiance. It is superfluous to point out how a narrative, directed by such generalship, contributes with perfect spontaneity to the intensity, salience, and variety of the characterization. How can one put a mastery like this beside even the best modern novel, wherein the characters are packed away into a uniform continuity of time, as closely as though

they were in a motor-bus setting out inexorably and without independent deviation from Ealing to the City?

This faculty of combining analysis of character with romantic narrative leads us on to a further point. It is a wrongheadedness of text-book
criticism to associate romance with the subjective. A romantic, it says,
is a man who dramatizes himself in certain experienced or imagined
situations. He projects himself, but he always comes back to himself.
Mr. Conrad's work is a sufficient answer to that. It matters not in the
least that many of the incidents he relates may be autobiographical,
that many of the characters he has described are part of his actual
experience, that his favorite sceptic and philosopher, Marlow, who
plays the interested spectator in *Chance*, in *Lord Jim*, in 'The Heart of
Darkness,' and others is himself. His work is always and inevitably
impersonal, concerned with the abstract and the universal revealed by
the concrete development of incident and the contact of personality
with it. It is this impersonal quality which suggests that Greek and
brooding sense of fate that drives his best art forward as a steady wind
bends the sails of his ships. And it is when that fate is sinister that the
figures of his seamen in conflict with it assume a tragic and heroic
stature. That is the fine end of all great impersonal art, and the failure
to achieve it the limitation of mere personal art.

Before galloping (from lack of space) over *The Shadow-Line*, it
would not be amiss to underline one aspect of Mr. Conrad's treatment
of character. There is a pretty general impression abroad that his
characters are highly complex and evasive—an impression natural
enough, partly because Mr. Conrad is the greatest living psychologist
writing in English, partly because of his method of revealing a personality from every possible angle of vision—as though a number of
searchlights set at different and acutely judged distances apart, directed
and concentrated differently colored beams upon a single object. It
would be truer to say, we think, that on the whole not only are his
characters simple, but that their actions are simple and spring from
simple motives. It is because he sees that actions and motives, simple in
themselves, are tremendously intricate and significant in relation to the
universal into touch with which their very simplicity brings them, and
what tremendous, untoward, and remote consequences are entailed by
these simple motives and actions, that his subtleties seem always to be
imposing themselves upon the reader's perception. 'He complicated
matters by being so simple,' he describes one of his own characters.
And this complexity of foreground must not be confused with his

background of life and character—which, in his grandest work, is as severely simple, elemental, austere, and majestic as the seas which have inspired him.

So lengthy an introduction would be even more tedious were not *The Shadow-Line*, to our mind, written at Mr. Conrad's fullest imaginative stretch. The tale, at first glance, is almost disconcertingly bare and unambitious. The first part is occupied partly in relating how a mate got a captaincy. The second describes his first voyage on his new ship, which the malignity of his dead predecessor drives back to port with all his men except the steward (whose heart is too weak for any but slight exertions) down with fever. But it is a great deal more than that. The first thing that strikes you is Mr. Conrad's elfin power of mingling the natural with the supernatural. All the events that happen upon the voyage that is to say—the first mate's obsession of his former captain's dark intent to destroy the ship, the gradual spreading of tropical fever to all the gallant crew, the constant trifling of the winds with the ship in deceptive breezes, the discovery and remorse of the captain that some noxious drug has been substituted for the quinine, the heroic bearing of the steward, the descent of a darkness and silence at night upon the ship like the darkness of primeval chaos, the sick mate crawling up on deck to cast a last defiance at the dead skipper, the final exorcism of the spell and the sailing of the ship by the captain and the steward back to port—all these suggestions, experiences, and episodes might be ascribed *equally* to natural or supernatural causes. The artist reserves his judgment and we reserve ours. All we can feel and express with assurance is the intolerable weight of evil suggestion, the atmosphere of malevolence as menacing and silent as the darkness, 'which came over me like a foretaste of annihilation.' The whole thing is as far removed as possible from a vulgar occultism on the one hand and a mere dull concatenation of material impact upon the other. Such a power of invoking the insubstantial is in itself a witchcraft of art, quite apart from the way it throws into relief the broad, fate-opposing, Sophoclean outlines of Ransome, the steward, risking every hardship with heroic cheerfulness, and then, when the strain is removed, breaking into a piteous terror over his diseased heart.

There appears, on the face of it, to be a sharp break between the first and second halves of the story. There would be but for the figure of Captain Giles, who gets the mate his ship, and is threaded, with true artistic instinct, into the last few pages of the book. It is impossible to describe Captain Giles. He is a personality drawn in the finest shades

and with that impalpable caress of revelation which is the glory of
Henry James. And how can you describe those figures of Henry James?
All we dare put out is that Captain Giles, so stolid, so heavy, so reputable, even stockish, is so impersonal with it, so intimate with his environment and thereby so extraordinarily acute to it, that he can
perceive anything that distorts or sends a ripple of the unusual across it,
with a ghostly penetration this side second sight—Captain Giles, whose
'watch came up from the deep pocket like solid truth from a well.' If
there were nothing in the book but Captain Giles, it would be a masterpiece. It is impossible to pick out the method of such a psychology.
Such characters seem to happen as a cloud is born instantaneously
into a blue sky. For, let there be no mistake about it, *The Shadow-Line*
is literature—and great literature at that.

126. Extract from unsigned review, *Morning Post*

26 March 1917, 4

This anchorage to actual experiences is an important element in Mr.
Conrad's stories, steadying them against tendencies to soar beyond the
region of visibility. The author yields at times to the romancer's love
of 'ballooning,' and still more he is consumed by his passion for inflating
the material story-structure with spirit. The resulting danger is not a
loss of grip in his psychology, but an elaboration of artistry so determined to buoy his tale in spiritual levels that it strains the cords which
link it to ordinary experience. In *The Shadow-Line* one is conscious of
the self-imposed difficulties in his art which Mr. Conrad has had to
triumph over in order to preserve the relation of the story-structure
and the moral, or perhaps morals, with which he inspires it. It is not
with complete certainty, indeed, that one interprets it as the parable
indicated above; quite possibly a plain parable, the single moral, would
appear to Mr. Conrad to be a negation of that interdependence of

mind on mind—that interweaving of fateful circumstance—in the coil of which man can only find his way by virtue of a strong and faithful heart.

With his passionate consciousness of this Mr. Conrad's method is in perfect accord. Here, for example, the young commander's story, though narrated by himself, never reaches us quite directly, but is seen, as it were, in a mirror that gives back as well oblique reflections of his experience in the mirrors of other men's minds; mirrors set to it at as many individual angles, including the morbid one of Burns's belief in the curse of the earlier ghostly captain. In the extraordinarily concentrated result, the impression left with us, complicated though it be, seems an authentic creation, absolutely self-contained—an incident of experience so isolated as to become related to the universal.

127. Extract from review, *Bookman*

June 1917, 98

The review was signed W.A.L.B.

It had better be at once admitted that *The Shadow-Line* is scarcely one of Mr. Conrad's big achievements. It is not one of those sombre studies of the individual struggling in the meshes of fate in which the author's art is shown in its highest and tensest form, and therefore it cannot be put in the same category with novels like *Chance, The Secret Agent* and *Under Western Eyes,* or with short stories like 'The End of the Tether.' It is the work of Mr. Conrad the sea-captain rather than of Mr. Conrad the psychologist, and being a story of the mischances of the sea, a tale of trials and embarrassments brought about by purely material and accidental circumstances, it may be ranked with 'The Secret Sharer' and with one or two other of those memories in which the writer has embalmed some striking incident of his professional career. Call it what you will, however, a 'confession,' as Mr. Conrad himself christens it, or a yarn, as most readers will be content to regard it, 'The Shadow-Line' is distinguished by that unmistakable air of vraisemblance in narrative and dialogue alike which is one of the most attractive notes of its author's manner.

128. Gerald Gould, review, *New Statesman*

31 March 1917, 618

The Shadow-Line suggests a comparison with *The Ancient Mariner*. There is a ship in it becalmed and bewitched; it is not so much a story as that single episode. It shows us a young man, moved by a sudden inexplicable impulse—'the green sickness of late youth'—to leave his ship, and then suddenly, fortuitously, given command of another ship—a promotion for which in the ordinary course he might have had to wait many years. (When I say 'fortuitously,' I use the word as it should always be used, as a convenient shorthand for inexplicable things: readers of Mr. Conrad will not need to be reminded of how little scope his art usually leaves for any real fortuity—of how persistently he fills his world with the feeling of vague compulsive powers, influences uncomprehended, tragic necessities that urge the hands and snare the feet of men). The new ship lies in harbour at Bankok. Its former captain, whose death at sea has caused the vacancy, was mad; prompted by obscure sentiments of revenge against fate or mankind, he tried to lose his ship with all hands by essaying an impossible course, but he was ill and the first mate overruled him, and his illness ended in death. Bankok is haunted with fever, and the problem for the new captain is to get his ship out to the open sea: there, he believes, his troubles will fall off him and he will be safe. But the fever clings, man after man goes down with it: of wind there is either none at all or one short contradictory puff after another; ultimately, besides the captain himself, only one man is left immune from fever, and *he* has heart-disease. And daily the danger grows that the whole thing, ship and crew, will be lost through the sheer helplessness of a sailing-vessel without wind:

In my endless vigil in the face of the enemy I had been haunted by gruesome images enough. I had had visions of a ship drifting in calms and swinging in light airs, with all her crew dying slowly about her decks. Such things had been known to happen.

To add to the general horror, the first mate is definitely persuaded—and extreme illness intensifies the obsession—that the malignancy of the dead captain has cast a spell on the ship: the sea-buried body lies right across the course the ship should take, and until the spell is broken, the mate thinks, there is no hope of progress or salvation. Mr. Conrad can scarcely commit himself simply to such an explanation; yet he never lets us forget it. In that dim borderground where the mind is sure of nothing, where the subjective illusion seems to change places dancingly with the objective fact, who shall say what is the true explanation of anything? In Mr. Conrad's art the very antithesis of subjective and objective becomes unthinkable. His method here, as always, is psychological. He makes us see his changing pictures as they change in the minds of his characters. *The Shadow-Line* is more bare and simple than his earlier stories in the same vein. The old efficiency of phrase is found (with occasional lapses, such as: 'a perpetual conscious-ness of unpleasant physical sensations in his internal economy,' and 'consigning' so-and-so 'to eternal perdition'). But there is not all the old magic. There is something abrupt, casual, in the treatment. It is as if we were being told: 'This is the fact, whether it moves you or not' —and in consequence we are not moved. There are books, and books by writers much inferior to Mr. Conrad, which one reads with a thrill of excitement. Out of *The Shadow-Line* I, at any rate, can get no excitement whatever. But it is interesting throughout, beautiful in places; there is much of it that no one but Mr. Conrad could have written.

With her anchor at the bow and clothed in canvas to her very trucks, my command seemed to stand as motionless as a model ship set on the gleams and shadows of polished marble. It was impossible to distinguish land from water in the enigmatical tranquillity of the immense forces of the world. A sudden impatience possessed me.

'Won't she answer the helm at all?' I said irritably to the man whose strong brown hands grasping the spokes of the wheel stood out lighted in the darkness; like a symbol of mankind's claim to the direction of its own fate.

That is the beginning of the voyage: the irony of the last sentence is typical of Mr. Conrad's art.

THE ARROW OF GOLD

6 August 1919

129. Extract from review, *New Republic*

10 May 1919, 56

The novel was published by Doubleday in America on 12 April.
This review was signed P.L. Ehrsam (*BJC*, 261) names the reviewer as Philip Littell.

... Captain Blunt is a fantastic figure, to me not quite credible, put
together with patience and knowledge, into whom not even Mr.
Conrad, great creator of men and women, has succeeded in breathing
the breath of life. But Captain Blunt's scruples exist and have their
reason. . . .

Doña Rita remembers her relation to this cousin as having been on
her side a little treacherous, made treacherous by her terror. But in
every other relation of life what most stands out is 'her ineradicable
honesty.' In Mr. Conrad's portrait of Doña Rita his greatest achievement is the absoluteness of our belief in her straightness and sincerity.
But she has many other traits, among which it is a boyish gaiety that
colors the progress of her love for George. She has, I think, too many
traits for Mr. Conrad, whose genius is more apparent in the creation
of simpler and more mysterious characters. As I think of the book, after
finishing it, I find myself wondering whether Mr. Conrad did not
imagine the separate traits more vividly than he did their relation,
whether, in other words, her character, admirably vivid though she is
at many different moments, ever lived quite intensely enough as a
whole in his imagination.

Doña Rita will, I dare say, long divide Mr. Conrad's readers into
those who wholly believe in her, and those who regret, as I do, that
Mr. Conrad's will and intelligence counted for too much in her

making. But about a minor character, Rita's sister Therese, there will never, I am sure, be more than one opinion. Therese is the kind of woman Mr. Conrad calls into existence whenever his genius has its way. She is simple and sinister, not to be forgotten.

The Arrow of Gold is one of Mr. Conrad's few open-faced novels. It is one of his least subtly impleached narratives. In none of his books is inanimate nature less an accessory to the making of destiny. Seldom has his profound knowledge of human nature seemed so little disquieting. Seldom has his moral insight more easily substituted itself for our moral blindness. And the end of the story is a moral surprise. It ends once, and we say 'that is the right ending.' It ends again, and we change our minds.

130. Unsigned review, *Morning Post*

6 August 1919, 3

To Sir Sidney Colvin on 7 August 1919, Conrad wrote that 'the first notices . . . in *Mg. Post, Dly. Mail, Dly. News* are very poor, puzzle-headed, hesitating pronouncements; yet not inimical' (*L&L*, ii, 224).

It would require someone as clever as a bit of Mr. Conrad himself—the bit he here calls Mr. Mills, for example—to say adequately in short review space what is the story in *The Arrow of Gold*. An irritated reader may possibly be found declaring that the whole Conrad assembled has not managed to make it clear in over three hundred pages. And it is no doubt true of many (and not of one only) of those whom the new volume has not irritated, but fascinated, that they were conscious as they read of an additional amused and slightly malicious attraction in observing how carefully and completely the author obscures in it the 'story' elements as these are popularly conceived and contrived.

One might say that it is a story of the Carlist attempt in the 'Seventies; that the heroine Doña Rita, a Basque maid, a goatherd, discovered by Henry Allègre, is an agent, and more, of Don Carlos; and that the hero, a young gentleman of adventurous inclinations, gets involved in the Carlist enterprise (becoming somewhat notorious as 'Monsieur George' in that connection) through love of the lady. It could be continued that he doubtfully wins her and ultimately loses her, following a duel with one Captain Blunt, but directly because of the effect (on her) of certain revelations about her by another—one of many others—the Spaniard Ortega. And it would have to be added possibly that the scene is Marseilles, the Cannebière in particular. All perfectly true about the novel, and as false as any possible statement of a fiction in the terms of fact. True or false, it is also, as will have been observed, very vague. Necessarily so, for definite statements, of the kind found lacking, the author is at infinite pains to avoid. Hence the probable irritation of some readers referred to. And as to obvious opportunities rejected by the author, and possible cause also suggested for a chortle from some readers, an illustration is the tucking away of the 'leading incident' of the duel in one of the two Notes between which, as the sub-title duly advertises, the story proper is sandwiched.

Of course, no one would be so foolish as to rake in this way for dry bones in a story, or at any rate a novel, by Mr. Conrad, or to be surprised at how utterly they have been covered up. His processes of elimination, of glosses and glazes, of presenting his characters at double and treble removes in the reflection of other minds, enriching their individualities by innumerable nuances of parallel and contrast also, are too well known. In the present example Mills, Azzolati, Rita's maid Rose, 'Monsieur George's' man Dominic, Blunt's mother, Mademoiselle Therese, serve this purpose, inextricably and wonderfully blent with the more prominent others in the development of the adventure. An emotional adventure, if ever there was one. (Some early pages illuminating the whole in the light of Rose and Therese, and of Mrs. Blunt, seem to us at high-water mark in Mr. Conrad's peculiar art of ironic exposition. The presence throughout of Allègre, who is yet 'dead and out' before the adventure opens, is a typical achievement.) From strength to strength—one may say—but some may hold by dilution after dilution—the material elements are resolved into a fable of passion, the elemental subtleties of sex caused to emerge in an array of forces calling forth—in the last interpretation of the story—the utmost virtues of courage and endurance. Not that there is any direct moral in justification or condemnation of conduct. 'If anything it is perhaps a little sympathy that the writer ("Monsieur George") expects for his buried youth as he lives it over again at the end of his insignificant course on this earth.' Strange person—yet perhaps not so very different from ourselves.

It is an extraordinarily fascinating work and piece of workmanship —for the consciousness of its craft is seldom entirely absent as one reads. Typical, particularly in its range, and in its concentration upon itself as shown in the extensions of its own researches, the novel has something of the character of an experiment—a testing of how far the author's method can be carried. And the risk involved is part of the fascination.

131. Walter de la Mare, unsigned review, *The Times Literary Supplement*

7 August 1919, 422

There is a word in Mr. Conrad's novels that falls reiteratedly on the ear with a peculiar resonance—the word mysterious. His earth and its humanity seem to lie as if spellbound beneath his regard, the regard of a sombre and mordant magnanimity. Beauty and goodness, amid the perils of a hostile world, are suffused with the light of his compassion. Evil, beyond all ordinary recognition, is held in the pitiless beam of his hatred and contempt. His simple seafaring men pursue their duty, as did the alchemists the philosopher's stone. They stubbornly fight for some last fineness of the conscience which is the narrow brink between their integrity and spiritual shipwreck. The stratagems of circumstance, of 'fatality,' beset them; the passions and appetites of mankind hem them in, cajole, menace, intimidate. But, their duty accomplished, it is left but as a means to an end; and the end is hidden. The rest is silence, a silence wide and mysterious as that of the empty ocean encircling a single ship.

As for the characters by whom they are surrounded, their very humanity has the appearance of an obscure disguise. There is something of the spectral in their appearances. They are possessed. These mummers, unhappy or sinister, beckon, gesticulate, syllable their parts, on the stage of a theatre hung with great cloths of fantasy, omen darkness and disaster. There is no prose in English so sonorous with rumour, invocation, strangeness. In the abstruse music of its words seems the echo of a half-forgotten, barbaric tongue in which the spirit of man communes with destiny in a world whose very loveliness is allied to despair, in whose enormous yet privy solitude we live and die. It is evident that in the heightened condition of consciousness which is induced by such fiction, wherein irony and the sardonic take the place of humour and violence is the antithesis of an intensity of rest, the slightest stumble may mean a serious fall. Everything in it—meaning, value, reference, mere good sense—depends upon its illusion; that illusion is its truth.

But we become fully conscious of the mystery, the 'fatality,' of life only in retrospect, in remembrance; and memory resembles dream. Of its fabric, also, in some inexplicable fashion, the imaginary is composed; and it is out of his memory and imagination that Mr. Conrad weaves his stories. He has *seen* his characters, and to present them to us—'elusively, in vanishing words, in the shifting tones of an unfamiliar voice'—as he sees them, he must bathe them in atmosphere and distance. Direct narration may perhaps be too bare, too crude and close for his purpose. He usually tells his story, therefore, through the consciousness of a shadowy third (and even fourth) figure, in the terms of reminiscence, a reminiscence with the clarity and the quietude of reverie. The faithful Marlowe is one such device. Only thus, in this absorption, can he describe action—that infinite web of intention, motive, effort, frustration; and in action he delights. What other protagonist could he choose, then, than Youth; youth with its unmeasured desires and aspirations, its senses unblunted, heart uncorrupted, hope undismayed, youth that dares and compels, does and endures?

Such youth is the Young Ulysses, Monsieur George, in *The Arrow of Gold*. Such a device of narration is its preliminary 'First Note,' which explains, first, that the pages which follow have been extracted from a pile of manuscript, and next that our Don George spun them out of his recollections to please an old sweetheart of his childhood. She wrote to him:—'I know where life has brought you. You certainly selected your own road. But to us, left behind, it always looked as if you had struck out into a pathless desert. We always regarded you as a person that must be given up as lost.' No devoted reader of Mr. Conrad's will find the echo of these phrases unfamiliar. And George replies:—'If I once start to tell you I would want you to feel that you have been there yourself.' 'There,' in sober fact, we have always been. Last, we are told how George came to be what he is and where he is and in whose company when his story opens, and even what he desired for his reward for the telling of it. 'If anything, it is perhaps a little sympathy that the writer expects for his buried youth, as he lives it over again at the end of his insignificant course on this earth.'

As for mystery; well, is not Doña Rita, Madame de Lastaola, the lovely, the inaccessible, the enigmatic, the half-fabulous, the child of destiny, who 'suffers from a sense of unreality,' whose soul is without a home, is she not, like Helen, like Monna Lisa, like Mother Eve herself, 'as old as the world'? Are not these insatiable lovers of hers—the Royal Pretender, Don Carlos de Bourbon, to whom her purse and person would each be satisfactory in its degree, and Mills, and Captain Blunt, and Henry Allègre, and Azzolati, and the miserable José Ortega, insane with lust, with his black whiskers like a shark's fin, his importunities and imprecations, are not these drones of love, soaring to suicidal ecstasy in pursuit of their queen, mysterious? Assuredly, while Mr. Conrad's incantations have us in thrall; but not in the last resort, we think, mysterious enough.

Don Carlos of them all is the only pretender, and his play in the world's history is here no more than a far background for Doña Rita and Monsieur George. As a lean lanky child, 'shrill as a cicada and as slender as a match' she had tended goats amid the thorns and rocks of the hills of Lastaola 'over there' in Spain. There it was, from her cousin José Ortega—stoning and entreating her in turn—she had first discovered the peculiarities of man; and then she had been sent, from under the eye of her uncle, the village cura, to another and less unworldly uncle in Marseilles. In his warehouse, full of oranges '(mostly in cases),' she dreamed her young 'empty, idle, thoughtless, unperturbed hours away,' until one morning, as 'in her short, black, two-penny frock' she sat in the garden of the neighbouring villa to which she had access, she was 'discovered' by Henry Allègre, 'son of a confounded millionaire soap-boiler,' painter, connoisseur, dilettante, scornful friend of 'Legitimity,' and 'like a severe prince with the face of a tombstone Crusader.' '*Restez donc*,' he murmured; and she 'not even conscious then of her personal existence,' and with her 'terrible gift for familiarity,' was not frightened. For seven years Allègre poured out his culture, his contemptuous affirmations concerning mankind, upon this amazing child of the people; and then he died, leaving his twin masterpieces, 'The Girl in the Hat' and 'The Byzantine Empress,' behind him, and his *protégé* his heiress. His influence, his wealth, his sublime indifference, have given her the entry into a world content, for a considerable fee, to take much on trust. Thus that supple and sleepless Southerner, Captain Blunt, 'Américain, catholique et gentil-homme,' who, as he gallantly asseverates, 'lives by the sword' and is a man of the flesh not unfamiliar with the devil, in the small hours explains the situation to his taciturn acquaintance, the burly and tran-quil Englishman Mills, 'that thick man as fine as a needle,' and to the Young Ulysses, whom they have netted into the service of 'the cause.' And it is then that the latter, whirled round by giddy expectation, meets Doña Rita at lunch.

Thenceforward our Young Ulysses is 'Monsieur George,' the notorious gunrunner. He has already tasted the joys of dubious and romantic adventure in the Gulf of Mexico, and now spends his days and nights between his fast sailing craft and its master, the old Medi-terranean smuggler and sailor Dominic, and Marseilles. Adherent, purely platonic, of Don Carlos, until comes shipwreck, 'this dear, ignorant, flighty, young gentleman' may be; adherent body and soul of Doña Rita, whether shipwreck comes or not, he remains. After lying in close talk one black and gusty night on a bit of dry sand under the lee of a rock on the Spanish coast, Dominic states a case:—

'Speaking with all respect, why should you, and I with you, be here on this lonely spot, barking our shins in the dark on the way to a confounded flickering light where there will be no other supper but a piece of a stale sausage and a draught of leathery wine out of a stinking skin? Pah!'

I had good hold of his arm. Suddenly he dropped the formal French and pronounced in his inflexible voice: 'For a pair of white arms, Señor. *Bueno.*' He could understand.

Here, barely put, is the enigma of *The Arrow of Gold*. Piercing the mist of her rust-coloured hair above the calm brows and carnation of Doña Rita's inscrutable beauty, that arrow threatens and transfixes every poor adorer in turn. Henry Allègre was a philosopher, and died. Don Carlos had a full frying-pan. Azzolati was but a worm, well-nigh incapable of turning. Mills was loyal and phlegmatic, and fled. Captain Blunt, 'Américain, catholique et gentilhomme,' in spite of all his mother's exquisite fence and finesse, is brushed like a pawn from the board, to be momentarily knighted in an epilogue, but only to his further undoing. Señor José Ortega may for a while affright—cursing, whinnying, beating at the doors of the bed-room in which George (a little inanely) and Rita stand rapt in the darkness; but what is his lust but a 'draught ... out of a stinking skin'? Is not his melodrama only saved from being funny by being rather forlornly described as funny? To what paradise, what Nirvana, as old as—older than—the world did that pair of white arms summon our Young Ulysses? Can we, does Mr. Conrad himself, echo Dominic's inflexible '*Bueno*'? Whose where, that 'confounded flickering light'?

Monsieur George, it is true, wins at last to those white arms; but at no excessive expense of mind or spirit; and, for no clear spiritual reason, he is sentenced to, and rather frigidly survives, his renewed banishment. It must be confessed that both as literary device and as explanatory and tidying epilogue, the 'Second Note' is a chilling dissipating douche to the story's illusion, to its romance. Here and there in its telling the power of the magician wanes, though with immense, indescribable relief we find ourselves drifting again—like a ship slipping out of a dull harbour into its own seas—into the charm of his wonderful art. At times his words, his prose, of themselves seduce us; they are incantations and, so being, convince our senses, even when our mind remains dubious and questioning.

Passages abound exemplifying his sense of beauty, his intuition, his grasp of character, his supreme gift of realization. But the colours and shadows of that mystery which veils and yet deepens the ultimate 'meaning' of his fiction seem in the progress, and certainly in the conclusion, of his story to thin, and to leave it in a vital degree fragmentarily and insecurely told. Possibly in so saying we ignore his own warning. 'History has nothing to do with this tale. Neither is the moral justification or condemnation of character aimed at here. If anything it is perhaps a little sympathy that the writer expects for his buried youth.' Sympathy is a rather chilly term for what this author extorts from his reader on behalf of the ghosts out of the region of the mysterious which he has astonishingly evoked in his previous work. So, too, with *The Arrow of Gold*: and yet we have seemed to discern in those other faces an energy, a challenge, a significance that is only precariously present in Doña Rita's and in that of Monsieur George.

132. Unsigned review, *New Statesman*

16 August 1919, 497

Conrad wrote, 21 August 1919, to J. C. Squire, literary editor of the *New Statesman*, and gave an answer to the delicately made criticisms of this reviewer (*L&L*, ii, 228):

Please convey the expression of my profound gratitude to the writer of the *Arrow* review in the *N. S.* It has never been my lot to get recognition so finely expressed as in the opening paragraph of that review.

I am sorry for the disappointment. Nothing would have been more dreary than a record of those adventures. All this gun-running was a very dull, if dangerous business. As to intrigues, if there were any, I didn't know anything of them. But in truth, the Carlist invasion was a very straight forward adventure conducted with inconceivable stupidity and a foredoomed failure from the first. There was indeed nothing great there worthy of anybody's passionate devotion.

But the undeserved appreciation of all those figures, which I have been moved to go and seek in that deep shadow in which from now on they shall rest undisturbed, is what touched me most.

Mr. Conrad's new book, his first full-length novel, unless memory betrays us, since *Victory*, has slipped into the world amid curiously little excitement and with curiously little preliminary heralding. Mr. Conrad in the last few years has stepped into the place left vacant when Mr. Hardy turned his attention away from the composition of novels. He has not only the prestige due to his own gifts, but also the mysterious incalculable prestige which attaches to the man who is admittedly first in any noble pursuit. If it is ever true of any book, then it should be true that a new novel by Mr. Conrad is an 'event'—even if, as in the present case, the new book is something of a disappointment.

For here it is hard to resist the conclusion that Mr. Conrad has exhumed a manuscript of earlier days, has seen in it things which again engaged his fancy and has worked over it enough to give many passages the impress of his finest quality, yet not enough to make it the equal of his latest works. The story is, in itself, a little unfortunate. We are promised gun-running and Carlist intrigues; and, sure enough, we know that Mr. Conrad is the only living man who can make a work of atmosphere and character as exciting as a penny blood. But the gun-running turns out to be the merest and vaguest background. It is, one is inclined to exclaim (certainly without full justice), what Monsieur George goes to do off-stage when the author desires to punctuate his relations with Doña Rita. That is, as we have admitted, not an entirely fair criticism of this device. Monsieur George's expeditions both condition and explain the circumstances of his love affair and the character of his mistress, which are the main concerns of the book. But they are, in themselves, too violent and too important to be touched on so lightly. They should illustrate Monsieur George's character; we ought to know why he was chosen for this work and how he was successful at it. We are obliged to take Mr. Conrad's word for it that he was a brilliant young adventurer when all the materials of proof were at hand. As it is, Mr. Conrad makes his hero speak of his 'luck,' and, for the rest, for all the reader can see, there is Dominic, a brave and resourceful sailor, who apparently has Monsieur George under his wing. Perhaps in that earlier manuscript, whose existence we have surmised, there was more gun-running and less Doña Rita.

But, if the choice for Mr. Conrad really lay between the novel of character and atmosphere and the penny blood, there is no doubt that he chose wisely. It would be ingratitude of the worst sort to allow it to be supposed that this book was one which anyone could think unworthy of inclusion in the canon of its author's works. It is, in fact, in many respects, highly characteristic of him; and it should be admired, if only for the gentle and valuable persistence with which Mr. Conrad continues to teach English writers, who ought to be able to find out for themselves, how to manage their adverbs. But there is more in it than is implied by saying that it is a fresh example of his prose-style. The character of Doña Rita herself is perhaps not a complete success, though it is hard to imagine any other writer succeeding better with this particular task. The woman who has in her 'something of the women of all time' is not precisely an easy figure to portray; and Mr. Conrad's beginning with her, in the marvellous preliminary conversation between Blunt and Mills, is not so well sustained when she appears on the stage. But this conversation, in which the two men, by question and answer and reminiscence, gradually evoke an image of Doña Rita and her career in the slightly muddled consciousness of the young man, who has been drinking too much of Blunt's straw-coloured wine, is one of the supreme examples of Mr. Conrad's virtuosity. There is nothing like it in the book until we reach the scene where Doña Rita and Monsieur George stand in complete silence, he perplexed and she frozen by panic, while her sinister cousin, crazy for her and crazy with jealousy of her supposed lovers, beats on the flimsy locked doors and shouts entreaties and curses through the keyhole. There is, to be sure, another supreme scene, but on a different level, in which Mrs. Blunt, that elderly and exquisitely polished lady from South Carolina, tries to persuade Monsieur George to leave the field, in which Doña Rita's hand is to be contended for, free for her son. This is superb, if somewhat acrid comedy; as the other is superb drama, reaching almost to tragedy.

But the astonishing thing about the book, as with most of Mr. Conrad's books, is the wealth of living, vivid and recognisable persons that fill it. There is, to go no further than the first few pages, Captain Blunt, with his two astonishing declarations, 'I live by my sword' and 'Je suis Américain, catholique et gentilhomme,' with his white teeth, his dark eyes, his insomnia and his endless, consistent, aristocratic meanness. There is José Ortega, Doña Rita's cousin, who engagingly confesses that he would like 'a red revolution everywhere' because 'there are half a dozen people in the world with whom I would like to settle accounts' and 'one could shoot them like partridges and no questions asked.' And there is Mademoiselle Thérèse, Doña Rita's sister, one of Mr. Conrad's finest creations, with her righteousness and rapacity, who acts throughout in obedience to an amazing confusion of motives, and who yet acts so consistently in character that at every stupefying movement the reader is forced to admit the correctness of the author's invention. But these are major characters in the book; and one expects major characters to be lifelike and credible. Mr. Conrad's genius is most evident and most remarkable in the fact that not a single person can walk for a moment across his pages without becoming a distinguished figure, whose personality one feels and whose story one can surmise. It is as though he were able to twist a little dead clay between his fingers, make it into a man with the thumb-print of his surprising gift and throw it down into the world to move and behave of its own interior power. Creatures like the father of the two dancing girls who lodge with Monsieur George in Mademoiselle Thérèse's house, the old uncle, the Cura, puritanically disapproving Rita and blessing her as the servant of the Legitimist King, the Marquis de Villarel, who doubts whether Monsieur George's services to the cause are rendered from the proper religious motives, the banker, Baron H., in whose room there was an 'atmosphere of Royalism, of Legitimacy ... thin as air, intangible, as though no Legitimist of flesh and blood had ever existed to the man's mind, except perhaps myself'—all these, though they occur only once or twice, are living and breathing human beings, so justly sketched that one immediately knows the bare lines are capable of infinite elaboration without alteration. It is hard to think of any other living writer capable of this endless prodigality of creation, which is, if anything can be, the sign and guarantee of artistic greatness. Mr. Conrad may here have failed a little in the construction of his story; but the result is only another proof of his ability to take any theme and so enrich it that it is delightful even while the reader recognises its defects.

133. W. L. Courtney on Conrad's admirers and detractors

29 August 1919, 4

Review entitled 'Mr. Joseph Conrad' in *Daily Telegraph*. This was the second review of *The Arrow of Gold* in the *Telegraph*; the first appeared on 15 August 1919.

The literary public is much concerned at the present moment with Mr. Joseph Conrad and his latest novel, *The Arrow of Gold*, which was reviewed in these columns a fortnight ago. Both his admirers and his detractors—for strange as it may seem there are some people who do not like him—are prepared for a determined battle over the doubtless unconcerned person of the author of *Chance* and *Victory*. We are told by both sides that *The Arrow of Gold* is a test case, the one affirming that for the true Conrad-lover there can be few things more interesting than a novel so unexpected and, at first sight, so disconcerting; the other pointing to the novel in question as the best possible proof that their contentions have been all along right, and that their view of Mr. Conrad is abundantly justified. And what are the contentions of unfriendly critics? In the first place, they say that Mr. Conrad never has been able to tell a story, and is conspicuously unable to do so in the present instance; secondly, that even if we concede to him some portion of the story-teller's gift, he has in *The Arrow of Gold* no particular story to tell; thirdly, that his psychology is not altogether satisfactory neither with the heroine, Doña Rita, nor with the hero, Monsieur George—both of these figures being unconvincing and one enigmatic; and lastly, that in this long-dragged-out romance there is a great deal that is tedious, while some of the conversations do not advance the narrative in the fashion of true and helpful dialogue.

134. Unsigned review, *Nation*

6 September 1919, 680–2

Review entitled 'An Illusory Conrad'.

From more than one point of view, *The Arrow of Gold* is as melancholy a story as any we have read. A certain destined loneliness and even desolation seem to surround all the great figures of Mr. Conrad, but their pose of confrontation is always heroic and classical. Here the rich wool is fleeced away. In *The Arrow of Gold* we are invaded by a double melancholy, the melancholy of a dwarf creation supplanting grandeur and force and thereby laying bare the whole unprofitableness of life and the melancholy of the frustration of the artist's purpose. For *The Arrow of Gold* is Richardson's *Sir Charles Grandison*, Mr. Hardy's *A Pair of Blue Eyes*, and Shakespeare's 'Pericles'.

It is waste of mind to attempt to expound the barometric depressions of genius. The business of the critic is simply to record them. We may say that the material is intractable and confined and upsets the artist's balance and proportion by forcing him into elaborate ingenuities to give it structure and form; or that Mr. Conrad's unique power of externalizing emotional impressions and relating them to the expression of visible nature has very little scope in this book. And so on. But we can no more explain these delicate reactions than we can a wet or tropical summer. They are phenomena, and we have to classify them. In the first place, then, the springs of the action are in marked contrast to the suggestions it is intended to evoke. The story revolves round the Carlist pretension to the throne of Alphonso. The author does his best with Carlos by keeping him strictly out of the way. All the same he presides, like the futile chairman of a working committee, and one cannot help feeling the incongruity of so much nobility and originality of character endowed with such wealth of verbal imagery and description thrown away upon a vulgar, dishonest, and selfish ambition.

Then there is the keystone of the Carlist intrigue, of 'Monsieur George's' affection and of Mr. Conrad's artistic purpose—Doña Rita, daughter of Proteus and Eve, goatherd of the Basque mountains ('shrill as a cicada and slender as a match') and heiress of a millionaire virtuoso of Paris. 'Monsieur George' does all his Carlist gun-running for her, Carlos and Azzolati, the financier, besiege her in vain, Captain Blunt, 'Americain, Catholique, et gentilhomme,' who 'lives by his sword,' as his aristocratic mother by her wits, presents her with his cynical homage, and José Ortega, his brain turned by the agony of his lust, pursues her in a whimpering, threatening fury of desire. She is 'as old as the world,' the aloof and bewitching figure of a legend, mysterious, unfathomable, incomprehensible as the forces and personalities which eddy round her. She is also an English minx and an accomplished Parisian idler. If that adds to her elusiveness, it does not to her romance. There are things, indeed, about her which are both repellent and foolish. Her savage mockery of Ortega when he is rattling the door of her room, raving in an epilepsy of longing, seems partially to change their respective rôles and give him the dignity and her the abasement. No doubt Mr. Conrad intended thus to complicate her, and at his best he could have done it supremely and without too dangerously alienating our sympathies. A goatherd and a fine lady in one demand every ounce of subtlety at his command. But to make her foolish flattens the illusion.

Mr. Conrad introduces and parts with his story in a couple of lengthy

'Notes,' which make, indeed, a very prickly hedge against the reader's entrance to the enchanted castle. In the concluding note, 'Monsieur George,' having won his Rita, fights a duel with Captain Blunt and is severely wounded. What must Rita do but to nurse him back to convalescence and then vanish for ever, presumably upon the motive of self-sacrifice? The whole thing brings us down from our airy craft with a bump. It seems as if Rita were playing some elaborate game of being mysterious and even reflecting that a tame union with her lover would be pushing her over the footlights. So she makes her exit like a goddess into her cloud, but, unfortunately for her, in pantomime dress. When Francis Thompson[1] wrote such phrases as:—

> Ere winter throws
> His slaking snows,
> In thy fasting flagon's impurpurate glows!
> The sopped sun—toper as ever drank hard—
> Stares foolish, hazed,
> Rubicund, dazed,
> Totty with thine October tankard.
> —'Corymbus for Autumn.'

he was crossing the chasm on a razor's edge. None but he could have crossed it, for it is the privilege of genius to employ a special medium of its own impossible to all other men. So it is with Mr. Conrad, with the difference that in *The Arrow of Gold* he is Conrad's shadow and imitator. Thus, in spite of all the splendours of his style and his wonderful gift of analysis and indirect suggestion, his mystery passes into unreality and his spectral into the grotesque. As the celebrants of the ritual disappear in the smoke of their offerings to romance, the observer rubs his eyes in disillusion. Even Ortega and the sinister pietist, Teresa Rita's sister, who are both horribly well-done and stand out in an incisive terror from the shapes and glooms that surround them, are a tenuous compensation for a book in which genius itself seems to become unsubstantial.

1 Francis Thompson (1859–1907), English poet, especially renowned for his 'Hound o' Heaven'.

THE RESCUE

24 June 1920

---

135. Conrad on completing *The Rescue*

1919

Initially called *The Rescuer*, the novel was begun in 1896.

(a) Letter from Conrad to Sir Sidney Colvin, 29 May 1919 (*L&L*, ii, 222):

On the 25th May (Rogation Sunday) I wrote the last words of *The Rescue*, which I began about 22 years ago! On the 28th I finished revising the final chapter, and now I am done with the thing till proofs of book-form begin to come in—next year sometime.

(b) Letter from Conrad to Edward Garnett, 7 July 1919 (*LEG*, 263):

It was the instinct (not the sense—the instinct) of what you have discerned with your unerring eye that kept me off the R[escue] for 20 years or more. That—and nothing else. My instinct was right. But all the same I cannot say I regret the impulse which made me take it up again. I am settling my affairs in this world and I should not have liked to leave behind me this evidence of having bitten off more than I could chew. A very vulgar vanity. Could anything be more legitimate?

136. Unsigned review, *Morning Post*

25 June 1920, 4

The Rescue must take an interesting place in Mr. Conrad's work, of the content of which it is so variously typical and comprehensive. The scenes are those of his earliest books, the thousand islands, big and little, which make up the Malay Archipelago. Its manner is theirs also; and at the same time its rich ornament and its deep and languorous swell pale and fall away in the concluding chapters before the keener directness of his later style. In these concluding chapters significance concentrates on the man and woman, to the urgency of whose story all the circumstance and appearances of the Java seas, with their white and brown civilisations, past and present, are called to witness. Out of the gorgeous ground and intricate pattern of the piece the tragedy of these two at last emerges clear and runs forward to the close in a track of flame. It is difficult to write judiciously of a new novel by Mr. Conrad while still fresh from its magic. We cannot easily clear our eyes and our feet from the mysterious web in which it completely enfolds us. He thrills us, and always the last time he seems to thrill us as never before. Comparative criticism has no chance. It is probably true to say that Mr. Conrad has never more than in *The Rescue* made a determined attempt at this enthralment of our imaginations.

Perhaps—to look at the story as coolly as may be—Mr. Conrad was never more conscious of the difficulty of his effort. Can he so capture our imagination on behalf of Captain Lingard that we shall be established alongside and even inside that sailor adventurer, with understanding of his ideals and passions and, above all, of his reserves, and thus be adequately sensitive to the weight and detail of their frustration, which is the core of this tragedy? That is Mr. Conrad's problem. And, incidentally, he has to work with a set of circumstances extraordinarily intricate, and, therefore, difficult for artistic presentation. There is Tom Lingard's love of his brig, comparatively a simple feeling, yet in its intensity difficult of comprehension for a landsman. Again, there is Lingard's history, which makes possible the adventure to which he has committed himself of restoring their country to young Hassim, the exiled Rajah, and his sister Immada. To us beyond the glamours of the Archipelago the prestige of King Tom, the Rajah Laut, is not easy of comprehension. Lingard's personality is a widespread domination also felt from the Straits to New Guinea. Hassim's kingdom is in Celebes. The Shore of Refuge, the jumping-off place for the expedition, is hundreds of miles to the West, near Carimata. To this vast region Mr. Conrad has to give reality for us who perhaps could find few places in it on the map. And then into it intrudes the schooner-yacht *Hermit*, stranded in the lagoon off the Shore of Refuge, a spoke in the wheel of Lingard's adventure, poised for revolution. We have to be shown the yacht's Western company caught up in the coil of high policy and local policies in these Eastern seas. With all their incongruity there the Travers and their guest and crew must find their level in it, naturally, with the actuality of the mutations of life, while retaining their accidental and local characteristics on which turn life's adventures. Innocently, and with the inevitability of fate, they bring about a devastating catastrophe, in which the adventure and the intrigue of lifetimes are swallowed up. And finally, from all this, in his relations with Edith Travers, the white lady of the yacht, whose presence frustrates his ideals, there issues, traced in a line of vivid flame, the tragedy of the limpid soul of Tom Lingard.

This plot, with all its complications just indicated, is managed by Mr. Conrad beyond admiration. It is sometimes objected to his long stories that they fail in design and structure, especially when, to secure for their characters imaginative reality, he presents them, remote, in their reflections on the minds of others. In *The Rescue* he has adopted the direct narrative, and has sought with wonderful success, to penetrate it with the vibrations and gleams proper to the other method. Anyone can see how elaborately the ground has been wrought, yet the effect of the rich detail—of physical appearances, white adventure, native intrigue, the sailor's craft, the legacies of past civilisations and policies, all the activities of those seas—is only to suggest an infinity of such all about the tragic issue in the author's story. With a few touches he makes the scene historical. With a thousand, he makes it in any case authentic. There is no ingress for doubt. We are drenched in its atmosphere. We could as soon deny our own familiar surroundings as those, unknown to our bodily eye, of Lingard and Mrs. Travers, Hassim, Immada, Jörgenson, D'Alcacer, and the rest.

As has been suggested, we perhaps owe this particular, almost overwhelming triumph of Mr. Conrad's art, of his imagination over our imaginations, to his consciousness that he was to try us rather high in the matter of his hero's emotions in contact with Mrs. Travers. In the matter of the quality of his emotions, that is. For it has still to be asked whether the object is accomplished to which all this beautiful and impressive artistry is bent. Does the captivated imagination leap to an understanding of Lingard? And is it adequately to the means employed, rendered sensitive to what is involved—for his luck, his prestige, his honour, his faithfulness, in fact his soul—by Lingard's surrender to Edith's presence? Of the answer to that we are not sure. Lingard himself, in his inarticulate simplicity, is transparent throughout; it is not certain that with Edith Travers the artist's hand is so steady. The question may be asked whether he has sufficiently simplified her out. It is characteristic, but characteristic of a certain weakness in her story, that over against the Brixham boy, the Rajah Laut, she becomes symbolic of Western civilisation at the expense of her individuality. And yet that symbolism is relevant to the tragedy. Perhaps the most we can be justly conscious of is that when these two figures do emerge clear they make an appeal that is more intellectual, less direct to the senses, than that of the preparations for their appearance. But this does not affect the story's unity. To the refinements of the later psychology the later style beautifully adapts itself, and detection is defied of where the old manner (the old matter probably) merges into the new.

With *The Rescue* Mr. Conrad enriches our literature with still another wonderful romance.

137. Virginia Woolf, unsigned review, *The Times Literary Supplement*

1 July 1920, 419

Review entitled 'A Disillusioned Romantic'.[1]

As it is impossible for any writer to remain stationary, a new book always sets the reader a new problem. When the new book comes late in the list of its author's works we must be ready to grasp some new development wrought out of the stuff of his old achievement. The worst compliment we could pay Mr. Conrad would be to talk of *The Rescue* as if it were an attempt to rewrite *Lord Jim* twenty years later. But in what direction can we expect Mr. Conrad to develop? So we may ask with our finger upon the cover of the new book. It is a difficult question to answer. For Mr. Conrad is a romantic writer. Romantic writers die young. It seems at least harder to preserve the romantic attitude to life against the pressure of continued experience than any other. The romantic writer will either cease to write, or his writing will undergo some violent change. It is true that Mr. Conrad by the greatness of his talent and the good fortune that kept him on the high seas long after most men are tethered to two or three miles of pavement preserved his youthful beliefs far into maturity. By its artistic completeness Mr. Conrad's work satisfied us of his unbroken good faith. Then, as one novel succeeded another, there were signs that the inevitable changes were taking place. He did not relinquish; there were no signs of disillusionment; but it seemed as if what had been before sufficient were now inadequate; and the perfection of the earlier books became broken and confused. There might be something in this to bewilder, but there was nothing to regret; and it could easily be held that in *Chance* and *Victory* Mr. Conrad was advancing, not in the sense of improving, but in the sense of attacking a problem that was different from those magnificently solved before. If Mr. Conrad was ceasing to be romantic, was it not that he surveyed a wider range of human life

[1] According to Dr Henig, this review was by Virginia Woolf.

and therefore attempted to express in his novels a more complicated philosophy? And now we have *The Rescue*.

The first part of the book is called by a name that might stand for much of Mr. Conrad's work—the Man and the Brig. The man and the brig—together they represent a noble and romantic conception of the passions and duties of mankind. The brig lies becalmed off one of the islands of the Eastern Archipelago. Her Captain, Tom Lingard, a man of about thirty-five, is at once her master and her lover. 'To him she was always precious—like old love; always desirable—like a strange woman; always tender—like a mother; always faithful—like a favourite daughter of a man's heart.' Her qualities, 'speed, obedience, trustworthiness, endurance, beauty, capacity to do and to suffer,' inspire corresponding qualities in the man. You accept the fact of them lying there alone at sea with complete satisfaction as if apart from the external beauty there was a deep internal harmony which, however strained, must ultimately result in that concord with which a work of art dies upon the ear whether the event is tragic or joyous. Nowhere has Mr. Conrad indicated more finely than in these opening chapters the outlines of what we have come to accept as his belief. The world rests upon a few very simple ideas, 'so simple that they must be as old as the hills.' Lingard is another of those men of simple nature possessed by the greatness of an idea—a man 'ready for the obvious, no matter how startling, how terrible or menacing, yet defenceless as a child before the shadowy impulses of his own heart.' He was romantic. It matters not how often Mr. Conrad tells the story of the man and the brig. Out of the million stories that life offers the novelist, this one is founded upon truth. And it is only Mr. Conrad who is able to tell it us.

But if the statement of the theme is extremely fine, we have to admit that the working out of the theme is puzzling; we cannot deny that we are left with a feeling of disappointment. Lingard has committed himself and his brig to espouse the cause of the Rajah Hassim and his sister Immada, to reinstate whom he has come in secret supplied with arms. But, before he is able to land, a rowing boat brings word that an English yacht has gone ashore on a sandbank near by. Reluctantly he goes to her help. There, sitting on the deck, toying with a fan, he sees the beautiful Mrs. Travers, the wife of a distinguished English politician travelling in pursuit of useful information. By her stands d'Alcacer, a man of the same world. Their world is altogether the opposite of Lingard's world. Nor could the men of that world have deflected him from his purpose for a moment. But the woman, beautiful, schooled in the training of civilization, is at heart as passionate as Lingard himself. Unlike him, she has as yet found no object worthy of her passion. Her husband, 'enthusiastically devoted to the nursing of his own career,' has ceased to inspire any feeling whatever; and her days went by 'without a glimpse of sincerity or true passion, without a single true emotion—not even that of a great sorrow.' Lingard appeared to her as a relevation not only of manhood, but of life itself. In him almost from the first moment she wakes the same ardour; she is the apotheosis of all that he has felt for his ship, for the natives who trust in him, and for their cause. What could be more romantic, one asks, than the encounter and union of two such natures? Yet here, at the moment when she wakes, when he tells her what he has told no one else, hesitation possesses us. Is it not beautifully told? Of course it is. Is there anything in man or woman, scene or setting, unworthy or jarring upon our senses? If anything, the setting is too flawless in its perfection and the characters too fixed in their nobility. Mr. Conrad has never striven harder to heap up beauty of scene and romance of circumstance until the slightest movement tells like that of an actor upon the stage. Perhaps the reason of our hesitation is to be found in that sentence. In the earlier part of the book beauty has sprung naturally from the rightness of the central conception. Now beauty seems to be sought with effort, as though to bolster up some deficiency in the central idea. It is as if Mr. Conrad's belief in romance had suddenly flagged and he had tried to revive it by artificial stimulants. Mrs. Travers is clothed in beauty from head to foot. Sea, sky, and ship all emphasize the tremendous impressiveness of the spectacle. Mr. Conrad describes her with phrase after phrase of noble and stately eloquence, yet as they accumulate it becomes more and more difficult to refer them to the feelings of a living person. The air is thick with romance like a thunderous sky, and we await almost with fear the lightning flash of passion which is to cleave the dark asunder. And then as the long story winds through the involutions of a complicated plot we give up expecting the lightning. Our disappointment centres in the relationship between Lingard and Mrs. Travers. In him Mrs. Travers was to have found 'the naked truth of life and passion buried under the growth of centuries.' The moment comes, but they cannot take advantage of it. It seems as if they had lived too long to believe implicitly in romance, and can only act their parts with dignity and do their best to conceal the disillusionment which is in their hearts. We are disillusioned also.

The story is both long and elaborate. It need scarcely be said that Mr. Conrad provides out of his great riches all sorts of compensation for what we have called the central deficiency. If he were not Mr. Conrad we should sink all cavil in wonder at the bounty of his gift. Here are scenes of the sea and of the land, portraits of savage chiefs and of English sailors such as no one else can paint. But with Mr. Conrad, as with all writers of first-rate power, we seek that which connects the beauty and brilliancy of detail—that central idea which, gathering the multiplicity of incidents together, produces upon our minds a final effect of unity. When Lingard parts from Mrs. Travers and is left upon the sandbank alone by the grave of the faithful Jaffir, we should upon our showing be left with a conviction that admits no doubt. As it is, our frame of mind is uncomfortably ambiguous. True, the strength of Mrs. Travers's instincts was impaired by civilisation. True, Lingard was drawn from the sphere where his virtues could have their full effect. And if it is tragedy that we demand what could be more tragic than that a man like Lingard should be betrayed and that a woman like Mrs. Travers should have betrayed him? Simplicity has been undone by sophistication, and fidelity and endurance have not availed. The elements of tragedy are present in abundance. If they fail to strike one unmistakable impression upon us, it is, we think, because Mr. Conrad has attempted a romantic theme and in the middle his belief in romance has failed him.

138. Unsigned review, *Punch*

14 July 1920, 39

Rescue is a story in the authentic manner of Mr. Joseph Conrad at his unapproachable best. If it is true, as one has heard, that the book was begun twenty-five years ago and resumed lately, this explains but does nothing to minimize a fact upon which we can all congratulate ourselves. The setting is the shallow seas of the Malay coast, where Lingard, an adventurer (most typically Conrad) whose passion in life is love for his brig, has pledged himself to aid an exiled young Rajah in the recovery of his rights. At the last moment however, when his plans are at point of action, the whole scheme is thwarted by the stranding of a private yacht containing certain persons whose rescue (complicated by his sudden subjection to the woman of the party) eventually involves Lingard in the loss of fortune and credit. Perhaps you can suppose what Mr. Conrad makes of a theme so congenial; how the tale moves under his hand in what was once well called that 'smoky magnificence' of atmosphere, just permitting the reader to observe at any moment so much and no more of its direction. Of the style it would now be superfluous to speak. It has been given to Mr. Conrad, working in what is originally a foreign medium, to use it with a dignity unsurpassed by any of our native craftsmen. Such phrases as (of the prudent mate remonstrating with Lingard): 'What he really wanted was to have his existence left intact, for his own cherishing and pride;' or again, 'The situation was too complicated to be entrusted to a cynical or shameless hope,' give one the quick pleasure of words so delicately and deftly used as to seem newly coined. *Rescue*, in short, is probably the greatest novel of the year, one by which its author has again enriched our literature with work of profound and moving quality.

139. Unsigned review, *Nation*

17 July 1920, 503–4

The tone suggests that the reviewer was Edward Garnett.

Ibsen is a writer with whom one would not in ordinary circumstances think of comparing Mr. Conrad. But in *The Rescue* one is conscious of a weird fascination, such as one feels in *The Master Builder*. One is aware of a mighty conflict of dreams and passions going on behind the brows of men and women of the modern, or at least mid-Victorian, world—a conflict that puts a strain on the prose of common speech and even on the actions of common people. Mr. Conrad is not a realist in the ordinary sense of the word. He can describe real things like a master. But he gets no pleasure, as Mr. Bennett does, merely from seeing a thing as it is. He seeks after the choice and even exotic fruits of experience: he has no interest in the gooseberries of the street market. He likes a scene to be bursting with significance. He compels life, wherever he touches it, into significant and ornamental shapes. He makes his very characters sensitive to the immense significance of the scenes in which they take part. They cry out in comment like a Greek chorus. When Captain Tom Lingard, the 'man of fate' faces Mr. Travers, the spluttering, dry-as-dust, Ibsenite husband, on the deck of a yacht in the seas round the Malay archipelago, Mrs. Travers gasps out: 'No, but this is-such-such a fresh experience for me to bear—to see something—genuine and human. Ah! ah! One would think they had waited all their lives for this opportunity—ah! ah! ah! All their lives—for this—ah! ah! ah!' Again, when the native girl, whose brother's kingdom Captain Tom had promised to recover, sees her hero falling under the spell of Mrs. Travers, she cries: 'O Hassim, have you seen her eyes, shining under her eyebrows like rays of light darting under the arched boughs in a forest? They pierced me. I shuddered at the sound of her voice! I saw her walk behind him—and it seems to me that she does not live on earth—that all this is witch-craft.' By cries and comments such as these—cries and comments in

337

which prose is made to do some of the work of poetry—Mr. Conrad emphasizes and re-emphasizes the meaning of every step in the fatal progress of his drama. He is not merely a narrator but an interpreter.

His love of interpretation, however, is not greater than his love of mystery. His characters are addicted to dark sayings. They do not always explain themselves, but speak in hints and puzzles. When Hassim, the Malay prince of the lost kingdom, is saying farewell to Captain Tom from one boat to another, he shouts:—

'Remember, I promise!'
'And come soon,' he went on, raising his voice, as the brig forged past. 'Come soon—lest what perhaps is written should come to pass!'
The brig shot ahead.
'What?' yelled Lingard in a puzzled tone, 'what's written?'
He listened. And floating on the water came faintly the words:
'No one knows!'

Again, when Captain Tom is pleading with Mr. Travers to take his word that the yachting party is in danger and should come on board his brig, he leaves the reason of his action a mystery:—

'I didn't ask for much,' Lingard began again. 'Did I? Only that you all should come on board my brig for five days. That's all. . . . Do I look like a liar? There are things I could not tell him. I couldn't explain—I couldn't—not to him—to no man—to no man in the world—'
His voice dropped.
'Not to myself,' he ended, as if in a dream.

We are not sure that Mr. Conrad does not at times carry his mystification too far. We feel that Captain Tom might safely have been explanatory regarding the object of his great adventure to a few more people. There is always this to be said, however, that, had he been readier to explain, *The Rescue* would never have been written. At least half the crises in the story are due to the fact that he felt bound to keep his mission a secret. Who, then, will censure Mr. Conrad for his enmity to outspokenness? His love of mystification is a direct result of his sense of the mysterious, and his sense of the mysterious is one of the crowning qualities of his genius.

Life itself, as we see it in *The Rescue*, is a dark dream. The seas are seas of dreamland. The dark shore is the dark shore of dreamland. The figures pass like ghosts, crying out in their anguish or ineffectualness. Captain Tom's 'passion to make a king out of an exile' is a passion from dreamland. The love that blazes up between him and Mrs.

Travers is the love of those who meet and are torn asunder in the chaos of a dream. Mr. Conrad, however, is sufficient of a realist to distinguish dream life from everyday life. He knows that these lovers whom a dream may bind together must be separated by common-place things. They are united by the poetry of their passion; they are sundered by the prose of daily existence. They belong to difficult pageants that meet at a cross-road and then march off under opposite stars. Mr. Conrad has no confidence in love, save as a passing event. He has none of Turgenev's faith in woman as a self-sacrificing re-deemer of man. In *The Rescue*, as in *The Arrow of Gold*, woman passes like a comet, leaving darkness and a memory. Mr. Conrad does not blame her. He does not expect more of her. He feels that she cannot help herself. He probably even feels that she is wise and virtuous to accept the limitations of her nature—to submit to the knowledge that love is but a bay of refuge and not the end of a journey. He endows her with courage equal to a man's, with a heart that jumps in time with noble actions, with a glory of being for which honour itself is well lost. But he does not endow her with a fidelity to her heart. After a brief passion she is wise as a serpent.

It is perhaps chiefly as an interlude in the life of men that Mr. Conrad is interested in women. He does not love them as he loves his heroes. It is not to a woman, but to Captain Tom that he attributes 'a tenderness that could only be satisfied by backing human beings against their own destiny.' That is a remarkable phrase, which suggests one of the finest qualities in the genius of Mr. Conrad as well as in the character of Captain Tom. To Mr. Conrad destiny is a night of storm through which pitiful, brave beasts battle. Pity alone preserves his tragedy from bitterness. It is his pity and his hero-worship that give his work moral as well as imaginative greatness. In *The Rescue* we have the pity of the defeated errand in search of a kingdom, the pity that it should be defeated by the chance intrusion of love, the pity that love cannot last, and then that piteous, terrible ending, as the yacht on which Mrs. Travers is returning to the world passes out of sight.

> 'How was the yacht heading when you lost sight of her?' [Lingard] asked.
> 'South as near as possible,' answered Carter. 'Will you give me a course to steer for the night, sir?'
> Lingard's lip trembled before he spoke, but his voice was calm.
> 'Steer north,' he said.

That is a fable that tells you a great deal of Mr. Conrad's philosophy.

His book is an amazing study of atmosphere, spiritual and physical. It is in construction something of a maze, in which one progresses slowly on with a sense of expectancy, rather than along a direct path with the sense of being given information. Mr. Conrad is luckily a great decorator, and, even when we wonder whether we have lost our bearings, we are willing to pause in amazement at his painted world. We might almost say 'at his painted and haunted world.' Tropical nights have never been described in intimate and imaginative detail as Mr. Conrad has described them. For instance:—

On deck she found a moonless night with a velvety tepid feeling in the air, and in the sky a mass of blurred starlight, like the tarnished tinsel of a worn-out, very old, very tedious firmament.

Then there is his painting of persons. Take the description of the living dead old man, Jörgenson's, native girl:—

She had a wrinkled brown face, a lot of tangled grey hair, a few black stump of teeth, and had been married to him lately by an enterprising young missionary from Bukit Timah. What her appearance might have been once, when Jörgenson gave for her three hundred dollars and several brass guns, it was impossible to say. All that was left of her youth was a pair of eyes, undimmed and mournful, which, when she was alone, seemed to look stonily into the past of two lives.

The Rescue is rich in portraits of this kind—grotesque figures in a tragedy. Grotesque as some of them are, however, they are all enveloped in tragedy and mystery, so that even Jörgenson and his girl share in the beauty of the pageant of which they are a part. At the same time, we are not sure that we like Mr. Conrad best as a novelist of love. It may be that we are subject to a sentimental illusion, but we feel that his philosophy of love walks unnecessarily apart from his philosophy of the heroic life. He has not yet written his 'divine comedy.'

140. W. Douglas Newton, review, *Sketch*

21 July 1920, 428

Do human beings break out into dialogue in the face of a crisis? At the instant of entering upon an action fraught with life and death, do they pause in conversations sometimes irrelevant, sometimes subtle and soul-revealing, always lengthy? I do not know myself; I have no knowledge of the crises that King Tom had to face amid the hushed and tremendous significances of the Malay seas mirrored superbly and ominously in *The Rescue*. But as I read Mr. Conrad's book that question raised itself and refused to be exorcised by an atmosphere so splendid that not merely the human creatures in the story, but even the trees and the glooms of the lagoon and forest on that muted Malay coast had a psychology of their own.

King Tom Lingard, a sailor of real greatness, a man of 'infinite illusions' and 'inexplicable devotions,' is a fellow of superb simplicity and directness. He has resolved to aid Rajah Hassim to regain his throne. In 'one of the secret places of the world' in a silent lagoon on the Shore of Refuge, he secretly gathers men and munitions about the village of a half-willing ally. On this shore, at the critical moment of his plot, a British yacht is stranded. The whites on board form the point of ferment round which the intrigues and suspicions of the natives gather. The white woman with them, Mrs. Travers, is a matter of complication for King Tom's heart and his honour. For though the two leading Englishmen are kidnapped by the natives, King Tom does not actually care a rap about them; it is for the sake of the woman that he 'rescued the white people and lost his own soul in the attempt.'

The story complicates itself in that vast and subtle manner in which Mr. Conrad is master. Really one does not read; one becomes steeped in an atmosphere of tropic silences. Yet, when the situations were poised on the very lip of tragedy, King Tom turns his back on them to talk metaphysics with Mrs. Travers. It tells how powerfully the personality of the woman possesses him; yet, at the same time, it gives one the feeling that one is being needlessly and even artificially held in suspense. And from that one gets the faint sensation that all this is not really the inevitableness of that grimly sardonic Providence which has a hand in Mr. Conrad's as well as Mr. Thomas Hardy's plots, but partly the stage-management of the author. For this reason, the crucial act of the story—when an ignorant mate imperils the lives of everybody by firing on friendly natives—seemed to me to lack the fine force of reality. I felt the hand of the author rather than the hand of destiny. And yet, maybe, it is a small matter; *The Rescue* is a thing so massive, so profound, so beautiful, so masterly, that this faint emotion is entirely submerged in the sense of complete absorption.

141. Unsigned review, *London Mercury*

August 1920, 497–8

The growth of Mr. Conrad's reputation, a plant now a quarter of a century old, has been throughout a curious and impressive subject of study. In the 'nineties *Almayer's Folly* was an immense and exhilarating surprise to those who cared for good letters. There were a number of reasons, which were irrelevant from the literary point of view and need not be recapitulated here, why such an author could not have been expected to write such a book; and these, however irrelevantly, added to the surprise. The author, having displayed a new style in prose, when it was manifestly unlikely that he should be able to write English prose at all, further produced those extraordinary experiments in narrative, *The Nigger of the 'Narcissus'* and *Typhoon*. He also wrote the less experimental but most satisfactory *Lord Jim*, and the brilliant virtuoso piece, *Nostromo*. But in the second decade of this century it seemed that he was doomed to produce masterpieces unacknowledged save by the lip-service of the lettered and the somewhat embarrassing worship of those who like to pay their devotions where they have few rivals. Then, in 1914, came *Chance*, a most remarkable book but probably, on the whole, a mistake from the point of view of form; and in a night the wider reputation was made. A year later *Victory* followed, and was a disappointment. The question began to present itself whether the wider reputation had not come, as it often does, to a writer whose best work was already done. It was true that Mr. Conrad could never degenerate as novelists sometimes do when they have attained late or early popularity. It was true also that his earlier work remained; and here somewhere, it seemed, his masterpiece was to be found, whatever that might be, whether *Lord Jim*, or, as some maintained, the superficially hideous and essentially beautiful *Secret Agent*. Last year the enchanting *Arrow of Gold*, though it was imperfectly constructed, revived hope. Now appears *The Rescue*; and it seems that at the moment when Mr. Conrad is universally recognised as the finest of living English novelists (in succession to Mr. Hardy, retired) he has produced his finest work.

The Rescue is the story of Tom Lingard, whose shadow fell darkly over the first of Mr. Conrad's books. It is the conflict between him, the simple, generous, kingly seaman, and the cramped, suspicious creatures of civilisation who bewilderingly intrude into his remote and dream-like kingdom. The action of the story occupies only a few days. It begins with Lingard preparing the final move which is to restore Hassim and Immada, the exiled prince and princess, to their throne. It ends with the ruin of this enterprise, with the destruction of Lingard's faith in his own luck and in the rightness of the world; and this is accomplished by the intrusion of Mr. and Mrs. Travers. The whole drama is accomplished in the shallows on the Shore of Refuge. There the characters are locked up, isolated from the outer world, lifted, as it were, into a world of their own, while they work out to its conclusion the crisis produced by their meeting.

This is not the place, or perhaps the time, to attempt a decisive or complete estimate of a work constructed on such heroic lines with, as after a first reading it seems, so much success. It is sometimes objected that Mr. Conrad's characters are not living or human. It is perhaps true that they are not human. Certainly they are in this book of more than human proportions: they are all giants, even Mr. Travers in his meanness and narrowness and pettiness. They are the creations of a poet rather than a novelist, as we have generally understood that term. Their passions are intensified, their motives are simplified in a manner that recalls the persons of an epic rather than the characters of prose fiction. The story is, in fact, of an epical nature. Lingard stands in the centre. On the one hand are Hassim and Immada, savages, as Mr. Travers thinks them, simple and noble and untaught, to whom

Lingard is bound by the strongest ties of friendship and honour. On the other hand are the Europeans, who have blundered into this other world, men and a woman of Lingard's own race, though removed by an abysm from his ways of thinking. And as Lingard, to his undoing, stands midway between the civilised and the uncivilised, so Mrs. Travers stands midway between his natural generosity and the cultured meanness of her husband, and is thereby enabled to undo him, perhaps not to her own profit. Lingard is uncultured and noble; Mrs. Travers is noble and cultured. Her duty forces her to use that part of her nature which is foreign to Travers and akin to Lingard to save the former; and as she is forced by her very nobility to betray Lingard, so in the same way he is forced to betray Hassim and Immada,

These are but scanty and inadequate notes on a work the full significance of which is not at all likely to be realised or expressed within a few weeks of its appearance. It is easier perhaps to grasp now the extraordinary sureness and brilliance with which the whole is composed and written. Very few novelists have succeeded in giving to any of their books the consistent texture of writing and intensity of feeling which we expect in a poem. Here we find throughout not only no slack or awkward sentences, but almost no sentences in which the interest of the author does not seem to have been keyed up to the full pitch of intensity which the moment would allow. Mr. Conrad is an acknowledged master of description; but the pictures of which this book is full, exquisite as they are, never once obtrude on the eye. The magnificent passage, describing the brig becalmed with which the story opens, the rolling away of the mist which precedes the blowing up of the hulk— these things, brilliant as they are, take only their necessary place in the story, and no more. It is necessary to make this clear before quoting an example of Mr. Conrad's style, since otherwise it might be thought to be implied that the pleasure this work gives is that which can be given by a succession of beautiful but unrelated details. But it must be understood that this passage has an effect from its place in the story which more than doubles its effect as seen in isolation. It describes the first meeting of Mrs. Travers and the Princess Immada.

Mrs. Travers fixed her eyes on Immada. Fair-haired and white, she asserted herself before the girl of olive face and raven locks with the maturity of perfection, with the superiority of the flower over the leaf, of the phrase that contains a thought over the cry that can only express an emotion. Immense spaces and countless centuries stretched between them: and she looked at her as one looks into one's own heart with absorbed curiosity, with still wonder, with an immense compassion.

This, of course, is, besides the beauty of its feeling and diction, one of the vivid points which give the whole picture shape and composition. And if the fixing of these points and the building round them of the elaborate structure of the book have called forth, as they obviously have called forth, the total of the author's powers, it is clear that the final value of the work cannot be assessed without care and long reflection on the part of the reader.

142. E. M. Forster's criticism of Conrad

1920

Extracted from 'Joseph Conrad: A Note' in *Abinger Harvest* (1942), pp. 134–7. Forster was reviewing Conrad's fugitive material collected together under the title *Notes on Life and Letters*. Forster dated his review 1920 but *Notes on Life and Letters* was not published until 1921.

. . . A proud and formidable character appears rather more clearly here than in the novels; that is all we can say. The character will never be really clear, for one of two reasons. The first reason has already been indicated; the writer's dread of intimacy. He has a rigid conception as to where the rights of the public stop, he has determined we shall not be 'all over' him, and has half contemptuously thrown open this vestibule and invited us to mistake it for the private apartments if we choose. We may not see such a character clearly because he does not wish us to see. But we also may not see it clearly because it is essentially unclear. This possibility must be considered. Behind the smoke screen of his reticence there may be another obscurity, connected with the

345

foreground by wisps of vapour, yet proceeding from another source, from the central chasm of his tremendous genius. This isn't an æsthetic criticism, nor a normal one. Just a suggestion that our difficulties with Mr. Conrad may proceed in part from difficulties of his own.

What is so elusive about him is that he is always promising to make some general philosophic statement about the universe, and then refraining with a gruff disclaimer. Dealing, even in the slightest of these essays, with vast and eternal issues, he won't say whether such issues lead or don't lead to a goal. 'For which may I put you down, Mr. Conrad, for the One or the None?' At such a question Mr. Conrad roughens into a shrewd sailorman promptly. He implies that the One and the None are highly interesting, but that it is more important to distinguish a bulwark from a bollard. Can the reader do that much? If he cannot, may not the interview cease? 'I see, Mr. Conrad. You are a cynic.' By no means:

From a charge of cynicism I have always shrunk instinctively. It is like a charge of being blind in one eye, a moral disablement, a sort of disgraceful calamity that must be carried off with a jaunty bearing—a sort of thing I am not capable of.

And the disclaimers continue each time a general point is raised. He never gives himself away. Our impertinence is rebuked; sentence after sentence discharges its smoke screen into our abashed eyes, yet the problem isn't settled really. Is there not also a central obscurity, something noble, heroic, beautiful, inspiring half a dozen great books; but obscure, obscure? While reading the half-dozen books one doesn't or shouldn't ask such a question, but it occurs, not improperly, when the author professes to be personal, and to take us into that confidence of his. These essays do suggest that he is misty in the middle as well as at the edges, that the secret casket of his genius contains a vapour rather than a jewel; and that we need not try to write him down philosophically, because there is, in this particular direction, nothing to write. No creed, in fact. Only opinions, and the right to throw them overboard when facts make them look absurd. Opinions held under the semblance of eternity, girt with the sea, crowned with the stars, and therefore easily mistaken for a creed.

As the simple sailorman, concerned only with his job, and resenting interference, he is not difficult to understand, and it is this side of him that has given what is most solid, though not what is most splendid, to his books. Nor is he mysterious as a Pole. Seven of these Essays deal with the sea—or rather with ships—for only landsmen would sentimentalize about the sea and think it beautiful or lovable, or a field for adventure. He has no respect for adventure, unless it comes incidentally. If pursued for its own sake it leads to 'red noses and watery eyes,' and 'lays a man under no obligation of faithfulness to an idea.' Work filled the life of the men whom he admired and imitated and whom, more articulate than they, he would express. They had no thoughts of the One or None. And (passing from his profession to his nationality) we find the same quality in his five Essays on Poland, where he voices an oppressed and leaderless people, to whom Russia and Germany are equally loathsome and who can hope for nothing but disaster from the war.

The British Merchant Service and Poland are the local accidents of his life, and his character permits their vehement defence. We need not take him as our guide through the *Titanic* disaster, still less to the Eastern imbroglio. The passions are intelligible and frank: having lived thus, thus he feels, and it is as idle to regret his account of Russians as it would be to regret Dostoievsky's account of Poles in *The Brothers Karamazov*. A philosopher would moderate his transports, or attempt to correlate them. Conrad isn't that type: he claims the right to be unreasonable when he or those whom he respects have suffered.

He does not respect all humanity. Indeed, were he less self-conscious, he would probably be a misanthrope. He has to pull himself up with a reminder that misanthropy wouldn't be quite fair—on himself. Observe (in the quotation given above) why he objected to being charged with cynicism. Cynicism may be undeserved by the poor victims, but that didn't occur to him. He objected because 'it is like a charge of being blind in one eye, a moral disablement, a sort of disgraceful calamity,' because he was touched in his pride. It becomes a point of honour not to be misanthropic, so that even when he hits out there is a fierce restraint that wounds more deeply than the blows. He will not despise men, yet cannot respect them, and consequently our careers seem to him important and unimportant at the same time, and our fates like those of the characters of Alphonse Daudet,[1] 'poignant, intensely interesting, and not of the slightest consequence.'

Now, together with these loyalties and prejudices and personal scruples, he holds another ideal, a universal, the love of Truth. But Truth is a flower in whose neighbourhood others must wither, and Mr. Conrad has no intention that the blossoms he has culled with such

---

[1] Alphonse Daudet (1840–97), celebrated French novelist and humorist.

pains and in so many lands should suffer and be thrown aside. So there are constant discrepancies between his nearer and his further vision, and here would seem to be the cause of his central obscurity. If he lived only in his experiences, never lifting his eyes to what lies beyond them: or if, having seen what lies beyond, he would subordinate his experiences to it—then in either case he would be easier to read. But he is in neither case. He is too much of a seer to restrain his spirit; he is too much Joseph Conrad, too jealous of personal honour, to give any but the fullest value to deeds and dangers he has known. Thus, 'in the whole record of human transactions there have never been performances so brazen and so vile as the manifestoes of the German Emperor and the Grand Duke Nicholas of Russia' to Poland at the beginning of the war; while psychical research, which he affects to examine, is rejected not on the ground that it is false, but because it will not benefit humanity. Anatole France, on the other hand, who runs counter to no prejudice or loyalty, can be judged by the light of Truth alone, by the absolute value of what he has written, and can be given philosophic approval.

Were these essays from a smaller writer, they would not set us worrying. But they are like the snow man that Michelangelo made for young Piero de' Medici at Florence. Every line in them is important because the material differs from the imperishable marble that we know, and may help to interpret the lines of that. Grave historians deplore the snow man, as derogatory to artistic majesty, and Mr. Conrad himself, in his preface, rather doubts whether he has been wise either to write or republish these fugitive articles. Perhaps he has been unwise, but that is his look-out; his readers have an extra volume to treasure. One realizes, more definitely, what a noble artist is here, what an austere character, by whose side most of our contemporary writers appear obsequious. . . .

THE ROVER

3 December 1923

---

143. Unsigned review, *Manchester Guardian*

3 December 1923, 5

The review carries the initials J. B. This is probably James Bone, brother of Muirhead Bone, the artist, who was a friend of Conrad. The title of the review, 'Port after Stormie Seas', is from Edmund Spenser, and part of the quotation given as epigraph to the novel. The same lines were later inscribed on Conrad's tombstone:

> Sleep after toyle, port after stormie seas,
> Ease after warre, death after life, does greatly please.

The air of mystery and of psychological twilight are native to Mr. Conrad. To fling a fluttering curtain over motive and purpose and personality, and then to give to that covering a twitch here and a twitch there until a full radiance of understanding breaks through, is the essence of his narrative method. Life works that way, of course, when we are propelled by destiny into a new social scene; we work on a patchwork of experience, and just so does Mr. Conrad throw patchwork at us in his first chapters and then, elusively but irresistibly, reveal the pattern in the chaos. His new story begins with a nocturne. It is all darkness at that farm on the coast by Toulon to which comes mariner Peyrol in the first years of the nineteenth century. Peyrol is a retired adventurer who has brought triumphantly to port through the British blockade a prize vessel from the Indies. He has shown himself a good son of France thereby, and is old enough to retire from stormy seas and very stormy seafaring. He will settle down and watch the British fleet from the shade of the trees.

But the farm is full of shadows. Who is this Citizen Scevola, the owner, renowned as a great drinker of aristocratic blood? Who Arlette? Who the naval lieutenant? Who Peyrol himself? Not that the place is vulgarly haunted as in some crass story of sensation; men, not ghosts, do the flitting here, men whose minds play on one another as their creator's plays on them. Hints flicker, the light steals in, and then at last the complete illumination comes; the tale races to its close in as fine a piece of direct narrative as Mr. Conrad has ever written. Once again Mr. Conrad has forbidden the jog-trot of the casual reader; it is hard climbing until that noble summit has been reached. One moves with effort at first, with ease later, with delight increasing. Mr. Conrad has been true to his method and his genius.

The end, analysed, is pure romance, rare stuff for a Henty[1] or a Strang. The naval lieutenant is to run the blockade with faked despatches that will put the British fleet on a wrong track. The runner must be captured, but so captured as not to give suspicion. He must ride his vessel as a crooked jockey rides his horse, to lose realistically; only here the reward is death. The lieutenant is going and leaving his Arlette, but Peyrol slips in to save that separation, and by magnificent sailing cheats the English under Vincent. He is shot down on his deck and the English take the despatches. So ends the rover, smiling at his visions. From this romance Mr. Conrad has scoured away all the superfluities on which the romanticist feeds. The narrative is as fast and as bare as the wind, sweeping on with a sting that quickens all the senses. It breeds the violent, almost unbearable excitement with which Mr. Kipling once scourged his readers on.

There are glimpses of 'real people.' Vincent and Nelson, the latter proud, a little pompous, yet utterly compelling and tempering command with comradeship. But the reality of Peyrol dwarfs these men of history. Peyrol is pirate, philosopher, and patriot. Of the English he says:

Don't you know what an Englishman is? One day easy and casual, next day ready to pounce on you like a tiger. Hard in the morning, careless in the afternoon, and only reliable in a fight whether with or against you, but for the rest perfectly fantastic. You might think a little touched in the head, and there again it would not do to trust to that notion either.

A critic of national psychology was Citizen Peyrol. But a sailor before that and a patriot after; he moves unforgettably from the shadow of his farm to the open, engulfing sea.

---

[1] G. A. Henty (1832–1902), author of eighty historical adventure novels including *With Clive in India* (1884).

144. Frederic F. Van de Water, review, *New York Tribune*

4 December 1923, 16

We suppose that, properly, this is a period for weeping. We shouldn't be a bit surprised if by the time this gets into print all those impressively erudite and literary folk who through the years have been bowing the knee in the house of Conrad had forsaken genuflection for sackcloth and ash-sifting.

We have a dark suspicion that Joseph Conrad's latest book is the worst he ever wrote. Probably *The Rover* represents the expiring gasp of a once mighty intellect.

These doubts and premonitions can't be groundless. In our own innermost soul we think it is a grand and powerful story. After years of dragging ourself inch by inch through the works of Mr. Conrad, we have finally come upon something by him that has caught us in a mighty tide and pulled us along with practically no effort on our part whatever.

The Rover, to any one but a benighted Philistine, is probably an awful punk book.

Once, long ago, we almost achieved notoriety. That was when we said in this department that Conrad bored us and that we thought forty minutes of Kipling was worth whole hours of *Chance* or *Lord Jim*. For a week we got almost as much mail as columnists tell their employers they receive. Persons wrote to inform us that we were ignorant, and even more accurate, if mortifying, things.

It would be pleasant to think that since then our literary taste has improved. We don't believe that it has in the least. We still feel a reverent enthusiasm for Kipling, in spite of his latest book of stories, and a resentment toward Conrad for the boredom he has inflicted upon us in the past, despite his new novel. It is only a dull and diminishing resentment, however. We have forgiven him much since reading *The Rover*.

In *The Rover*, as in *The Rescue* and one or two others, Mr. Conrad

351

has been content to tell his story first hand, instead of putting the major part of it into the mouth of some garrulous intermediary, usually Marlow by name. We owe Marlow a lot. It is as well that we can never repay him. Our soul is laden with enough sins of violence as it is.

On the veranda of a clubhouse in Hongkong or Singapore, or some such faraway town, Marlow sits, not by the hour but presumably by the week, recounting a tale and relating what he thought and what he thought some one else thought and what he thought some one else thought a third person thought, until we become as badly tangled up in his narrative as we get while reading *The Arabian Nights*, but much less excited. We have often wondered why some one in the Hongkong or Singapore club didn't complain about Marlow to the house committee.

In *The Rover*, as nowhere else in Conrad, disquisitions on ethics and psychology and metaphysics are conspicuously absent. There seems to be no predestination here, and infinitely more humanity.

Mr. Conrad also has at last become adept in employing the 'cut back.' He has managed to jump the main trail of his story, pick up a minor track and follow it into the highway of his tale again with much more skill and infinitely less confusion than heretofore.

The Rover is far removed from those savage Eastern isles in which Mr. Conrad's earlier heroes have struggled so vainly and verbosely against an inevitable doom. Its scene is laid near Toulon in the time of Napoleon. Its hero is an old freebooter of the Asiatic sea lanes. He is a character that Victor Hugo might have loved, or envied.

The story itself is simple, but, to us, tremendous and Athenian in its power. Even more than the august and masterful fashion in which Mr. Conrad handles his tale we admire the vigorous life he has breathed into the strange and tragic folk who act therein. They are not 'real people,' as one applies the term to the characters of the average novel. They are decidedly inordinary folk, but they live, every one of them.

The story seems to us to be too long. That is the only possible fault we can find with it. In itself it is not stretched out unduly, but it has a final half-dozen pages of anti-climax that detract from and deaden a gorgeous finale. After having got to where he was going Mr. Conrad doesn't shut off his engine soon enough.

It would be rather interesting, some time, to list those books that have been blunted or partly spoiled because the author's brakes wouldn't hold at the obvious place for him to stop; because he insisted on getting all his characters neatly put away in pigeon-holes before he felt he had done his job justice. Owen Wister's *The Virginian* is an example of this.[1] It has always seemed to us that it would be a much better and more perfect yarn if the last chapter were never read. We'd like *The Rover* even better if the last five and three-quarter pages were deleted.

Our enthusiasm expressed above doesn't mean that we have joined the Conrad chorus. Before we can forgive him the past anguish or boredom he has caused us the author of *The Rover* will have to write two more books, equally good. We think that is too much to ask, even of Kipling.

[1] Owen Wister (1860-1938), author of life of Theodore Roosevelt, won fame with his novel of cowboy life in Wyoming, *The Virginian* (1902).

145. Unsigned review, *The Times Literary Supplement*

6 December 1923, 849

Mr. Conrad's story, as a remark on the wrapper assures us, is in no sense historical; and the letter of that statement is quite true. But it is no less true that the author has laid his course for the past, dipping under the horizon line beyond which, for us, lies history. Of the two broad highways which convey the romance of atmosphere the one generally travelled by Mr. Conrad removes us to a distance of place. The other, which he has chosen here, measures its allurement not by mileage but by a journey into time. What has emerged from it is not the full-dress and detail of a historical novel. It is that subtilized past, through the aroma and the intuitive touches, which comes alive in *Rob Roy*, or *The Trumpet-Major*, or even *Treasure Island*. For as Mr. Conrad's sea-rover, Peyrol, settles himself with his big chest and his money-weighted waistcoat at the lonely farmhouse 'in a manner of speaking for ever,' we can scarcely help thinking of Bill Bones arriving as a permanent lodger at the Admiral Benbow. But that is for contrast more than likeness; the two men and the stories are as different as Mr. Conrad is from Stevenson. Mr. Conrad, who can be simpler if he likes than Stevenson, has more complex depths even in those moments; and genial as his creation is, pleasure is not a more decisive element of it than wisdom.

The new story is a straightforward Conrad. The rover's past is more chequered than mysterious, and Mr. Conrad himself tells us all we need know. Perhaps telling is hardly the word for that reconstructed life of the man which floats up so naturally that we are, as it were, inside him. It shows how concrete the art is; we are 'inside' Peyrol because the whole manner and physique of him, and the very ground he treads on, are felt with a tangible vividness. In fact, after being transported there by the book for a few hours on a November day, we begin to share his nostalgia for the sun-baked, salted earth which had been in his bones from childhood. We know, as if we lived there, this lonely swell of ground on the peninsula between Toulon and Hyères, where the scene is fixed, the farm, the rough hillside, the expanse and indentations of the sea. And when, for a minute now and then, the action shifts to the English sloop, outpost of Nelson's squadron, which is hovering off the coast to watch, one still has the sense of viewing it, and imagining the blockading fleet beyond the skyline, from those same few rising acres. The detached, queer group of people at the farm becomes familiar in the same way. There is the miserable Scevola, its nominal owner, once a *buveur de sang* in the Toulon massacres, and now a pitiable but still dangerous neurotic. There is Arlette, daughter of the Royalist couple who had owned the farm and were butchered under her eyes at Toulon, where the child was forced to witness and even share in days of massacre which are still more present to her than actual things. Scevola, who brought her home, has never dared to make her his wife. Her aunt, rigid and silent, bears old tragedy in her handsome face; and even Lieutenant Réal, who comes out there for quiet, and then for service reasons—and other reasons—is a guarded, shadowed character. Peyrol spreads a kind of watchful sanity over all this, while the threads of action and passion meet in the lieutenant.

State designs and private emotions inter-weaving make an honestly thrilling tale of action, with the glint of its time. The sea chase, ending in the destruction of Peyrol and his treasured boat, is a worthy climax; and the glimpse of Nelson which follows is convincing as far as it goes. It was good that the great novelist of sailing ships should have pictured at last, if only in a flash, the greatest sailor. But is the novel, in the main, a mere network of incidents? It is saved from being just that by the creative vision in each trait of the land and sea, and still more by the unfolding traits of human character. Arlette is beautifully drawn. Her change from a shadow-haunted creature to an intensely living person, as she responds first to Peyrol's calm and then comes fully awake in her passion for Réal, is subtly conveyed and brings two fine scenes of revelation. The very least of the characters, down to Peyrol's vague and guileless henchman and a cripple who appears only twice, are individualized. And so are the English, with a stroke or two. But the old rover is the pillar of the book and bears it up, with a humorously sagacious ease, on his broad shoulders.

Mr. Conrad, certainly, has written greater things than this; but among his recent books it stands out for the speed of movement, and not less for the impress of its truth to human nature. Peyrol, you may conceivably think, is idealized, too benignant for his past. But that

sense of the passage and effects of time which Mr. Conrad knows how
to achieve is well applied to the case of the rover. One feels, too, the
rational composure with which he has gone through an amazing life.
He remains sudden and strong of hand; and even in his last self-devotion
there is room for other feelings, such as indifference to mere living and
a grim joke upon the English captain. It would be truer to say that Mr.
Conrad's simplifies, remembering the while those depths under the
firm outline. He shows the ideal not as obscuring the real, but as
inhabiting it. So Peyrol has a classic strength which puts him, like the
old seaman of the *Narcissus*, with the best in Mr. Conrad's gallery of
sailors. It goes deeper than romance and means an unshaken hold upon
reality.

146. Unsigned review, *Glasgow Evening News*

6 December 1923, 2

. . . The people of this tale are perfectly painted. Than Mr. Conrad
there is no writer in English who can make human beings live more
vividly in print. Perhaps the figure of Catherine is a little dim, not so
clearly visualised as the others. Citizen Scevola is complete; a perfect
picture this of a man made a terrorist by his own poltroonery. Arlette
breathes, a figure for pity. Minor but essential figures like Michel
and the friendly cripple people the background. And old Peyrol is as
convincing as a piece of sculpture by Rodin.

The telling of the tale is done according to Mr. Conrad's familiar
manner. It is a simple enough plot, to be sure, but the author weaves
his pattern adroitly. He has a trick of suspense, of delayed explanation,
that is always effective. Bit by bit, a touch of colour here, a shadow
there—so the fabric is built up by one who is, first and foremost, a
teller of tales simply. The end is implicit in the beginning, so to say;
the elaborate lay-out, that is, has a purpose behind it.

Nor does the force of Mr. Conrad's basic philosophy fail to apply here. We have a spacious atmosphere, a sense of the vastness and mystery of the world, and no human figure, however vital to the action of the plot, is anything but a small, struggling figure against that tremendous background. They play the old losing game against a relentless fate, and this version of their struggles is written with a fine pity for that noble but ineffectual effort.

And still *The Rover* is a disappointment. Did we not know by now what to look for in Mr. Conrad's work, perhaps we should fail altogether to discover those excellencies of which I have just written. For most readers would be baffled and disturbed by what seems to be a lack of conviction about the latter half of the book. It is as if the creator's fervour abated at a certain point half-way through, so that not even that magnificent technique could carry the affair off satisfactorily.

Perhaps the fact that the tale is comparatively a short one does not substantiate the point at all, but it can be very clearly indicated where the weak spot in the fabric seems to lie. Chapter xii.—there are sixteen chapters all told—is the crucial point. That is an involved and, I suggest, clumsy chapter. Its matter adds to the distraction and confusion already occasioned in the reader's mind by the apparently excessive amount of attention given to the affair of the seaman from the British sloop. It is not inevitable; it has an almost ingenuous air of artificiality. A tale that has developed slowly and on broad lines suddenly and swiftly loses itself in a sort of theatrical tangle.

Speed of action is no fault, even in the deliberate prose of Mr. Conrad, but in this case, it must be said, Mr. Conrad's gift of sheer good writing seems to have failed him. There are bald spots, lamentably bald spots, and angular transferences of interest; and that right to the end, where a curiously feeble chapter of recapitulation dispels the glamorous memory of the Rover's death. Altogether it is a story to which Mr. Conrad, by some almost incredible accident, has failed to do justice. For once, he appears to have been without a burning intensity of vision and conviction.

These strictures, let us always remember, are made according to comparative standards. One has the right, I think, to judge Mr. Conrad by his own best work. Goodness knows we are grateful for every sentence he cares to write, but while we attempt to assess the values of a single volume and so anticipate posterity, there is no ignoring the precedent of *Victory* or *Nostromo*. One may be wrong—I rather hope I am—but it seems likely that in the eyes of 2024 Jean Peyrol, Master

Gunner, his tale, will not rank in human affections with that of Lena and Heyst or that other loved adventurer of the sea, Lingard of the brig *Lightning*.

147. Raymond Mortimer, review, *New Statesman*

15 December 1923, 306

A novelist's final works (if he does not die prematurely), I suggest, will, in the view of his worshippers, represent the consummation of his art, while to the less fervent—who may not be more right—they will often seem empty stuff supported only by a conjuring trick.

If then Mr. Conrad's new book strikes me as downright bad, it may be because my enjoyment of many of his works, though genuine and great, has not been rapturous, and because contact with his mind does not seem to me a delight in itself. Typically 'late' work, *The Rover* depends less upon the author's invention than upon his personality and the artifices peculiar to himself with which he expresses it. It is possible that those who count Mr. Conrad among their favourite writers and whose love for him is of the heart as well as of the head, may find it a masterpiece; and often an apparently fanatical admiration may prove a better basis for criticism than detachment. *The Rover* is not difficult to read; a boy of twelve might quite enjoy it, though he would probably feel it was a trifle slow. But it is a difficult book to understand, because Mr. Conrad does not make it very clear at what he is aiming; and I perceive that I do not understand it at all when I find Mr. Squire[1] calling its author an 'unflinching realist.' Mr. Leonard Woolf,[2] on the other hand, says, among other very excellent things,

---

[1] (Sir) John Collings Squire (1884–1958), literary editor of *New Statesman* and editor of the *London Mercury*.

[2] Leonard Woolf, husband of Virginia Woolf. He reviewed *The Rover* on 8 December 1923 in the *Nation and Athenaeum* (see Introduction, p. 35).

that 'his characters are melodramatic, for they think, feel, talk, and act melodramatically,' and one feels one's feet again. Accept this view, which is probably just and at any rate comprehensible, and allow Mr. Woolf's demand that we should accept the convention that the world is a melodramatic world just as we are prepared in art to accept other conventions. Will *The Rover* then appear a success? Mr. Woolf evidently thinks so, for comparing it with 'The Secret Sharer', he declares that 'time itself appears to stand still' for Mr. Conrad, and that there is remarkably little change 'in his vision, his thoughts and feelings, and in the form and power of their presentation to the reader.' Now 'The Secret Sharer' is admittedly one of Conrad's best works. *The Rover* is, I suppose, five times as long, and does not contain one fifth as many thrills. Mr. Conrad's vision has not changed, but his power of presentation and his skill in the use of melodramatic conventions seem to me entirely altered. The story of the sham despatches with which *The Rover* ends would have made one fairly good short tale. The rest of the book contains the possibility of another, but only the possibility, overlaid with pages of padding. Mr. Conrad has never been rich in invention, except perhaps in *Nostromo*, and his short stories seem to me, in consequence, his best work. But in *Lord Jim*, for instance, he fairly diverts our attention from this poverty of invention, by the continual psychological soundings which make Captain Marlow's conversation so surprisingly like Henry James's. Conrad's real strength, I believe, lies in the unsurpassed vividness of some of his descriptions, both of persons and scenes, and in the highly charged atmosphere of fatality with which he envelops them. But *The Rover*, for all its Provençal setting, passes in a twilight where nothing is vivid. It contains a few descriptive passages of a carefully varnished beauty, but none, I think, comparable to his best in this sort. The characters are sketched in a summary way that would pass in a short story, but not one is a solid portrait. The young lieutenant is a sort of spectre, and Peyrol himself never appears in the third dimension. These people add nothing to our experience. Arlette is almost a parody of Mr. Conrad's other heroines. He has always tricked in his portraiture of women: making them romantic by folding them in inscrutability instead of by exposing, as other poets have, the riches concealed in the heart. But this woman is not only romantic because she is silent; she is silent because she is half-witted. The reader has to construct for himself all the relations between the characters. Throughout the book Mr. Conrad relies on us to do the work. With some knowledge of his earlier books, we can do it. An image here, a familiar rhythm there, and our memories will lend these faint beings a greater sonority than they possess. But it is doubtful if a critic who had read nothing of Conrad's except *The Rover* would realise that this vague and ill-constructed book was the work of an important writer. Darkness is mysterious, and mystery is romantic. But darkness alone does not make romance. Mr. Conrad's triumphs in the past have been made by skilful contrasts between light and shade. Here there is little but shade.

With *The Arrow of Gold* he entered what we may call the last period of his work. There is nothing left but the style he has created and the values that he has determined. The style seems to have lost much of its attractiveness, but on this point the consideration of the 'late' work of other writers should prevent all dogmatism. The values are too like Kipling's for most of Mr. Conrad's juniors to find them sympathetic, though the greater part given to Fate renders them more acceptable. Any opinion on *The Rover*, I conclude, will be, even more than is usually the case, a matter of taste; but all except Mr. Conrad's fondest devotees may be recommended to put it on one side, and to reread 'Youth' and 'Within the Tides'.

148. Conrad, letter to John Galsworthy

22 February 1924 (*L&L*, ii, 339–40)

. . . I am glad you think well of *The Rover*. I have wanted for a long time to do a seaman's 'return' (before my own departure) and this seemed a possible peg to hang it on. The reception was good,—and so were the sales,—but when the book came out, I was too seedy to care. I had about 10 weeks of a pretty bad time. My recovery was swift,—but my confidence has been badly shaken. However, I have begun to work a little,—on my runaway novel [*Suspense*]. I call it 'runaway' because I've been after it for two years (*The Rover* is a mere 'interlude') without being able to overtake it. The end seems as far as ever! It's like a chase in a nightmare,—weird and exhausting.

149. Desmond MacCarthy on the quality of *The Rover*

1931

Extracted from MacCarthy's *Portraits* (1931), pp. 76–7. Other portions of this essay on Conrad appeared in the *New Statesman*, 9 August 1924, on the occasion of Conrad's death, signed 'Affable Hawk', and in the *Listener*, 4 November 1931, p. 779, entitled 'Biography and Reminiscence' under the author's name.

The last novel published in Conrad's lifetime, *The Rover*, was greatly enjoyed and not a little carped at—respectfully of course. I have no doubt that, had *The Rover* appeared not very long ago, reviewers and readers would have been so occupied with its fine imaginative qualities, that they would have hardly stopped to pick holes. Yet holes can in fairness be picked. I enjoyed it immensely myself; yet when a friend said to me casually, 'I have just finished listening to a performance on the Conrad,' I saw what he meant, and recognized the justice of the criticism. Artistically, it resembles more a voluntary on a powerful organ to show its compass than a musician's constructed masterpiece. All the famous Conrad stops are pulled out one after another. We are given the familiar scene of passion, almost mystically imaginative and supersensual, tinctured perhaps with melodrama but never with a drop of sentiment, in which Conrad's lovers seem to fall together through the crust of ordinary experience into a shadowy grander world, where men and women grow to the stature of gods. We are given the scene of tempted and exalted honour. We are given the familiar contrast between the curt, mild-spoken English sailor and the turbulent, darker, more imaginative highly-strung man. We meet the enigmatic woman. Above all, we are given those descriptions of scene and place which create in us such a strange expectancy; the clean, large, empty room, or the sun-scorched yard of a lonely farm-house, which seem to wait like a stage for something to happen there; and horizons—changing, beckoning, beautiful horizons. This is his master faculty as an imaginative writer; this power of evoking a scene, a gesture, or the confrontation of two people, so that the moment seems charged with all the significance of what is to come, just as scenes vividly re-called by memory are apt to seem to us laden with what was to happen. When we remember how, long ago, someone looked up or turned away, or only, it may be, a hat and pair of gloves on the table, suddenly it may seem to us, that, even then, we must have already understood although we did not know it. Our own memories now and then create these magic moments for ourselves; Conrad could create them for others. It seems to me incomparably his rarest gift. I value such moments in his stories far more than his tremendous set pieces of storms and long breathless tropic nights. I become confused while reading 'Typhoon' and the hurricane in *The Nigger of the 'Narcissus'*; too much, much too much happens. I forget how badly the ship has been already smashed; I forget how overwhelming the last wave but one was com-pared with the one I see coming. The little cup of my imagination was full long ago, but the water-fall goes on pounding down into it.

SUSPENSE, A NAPOLEONIC NOVEL
(unfinished)

16 September 1925

150. Conrad on the reception of *The Rover* and *Suspense*

3 February 1924

Letter to Eric Pinker (*L&L*, ii, 337), son of the famous literary
agent J. B. Pinker. After J. B. Pinker's death on 8 February 1922,
his son became responsible for Conrad's literary affairs.

. . . I am concentrating all my thoughts on the novel, which certainly
by the time it is done will be a biggish thing—I mean in matter and
size. I have been reflecting on certain aspects of criticism provoked by
The Rover. It has dawned upon me that the note of disappointment that
has been perceptible simply means that many people (indeed, I believe
the majority of the critics) took it for the long-talked-of-Mediterranean
novel. And naturally some of them said: 'And is that what it is, then?'
I have no doubt at all about it in my mind. *The Rover* suffered in a
sense from the confounded prenatal publicity that *Suspense* has evoked
simply by being shown about and talked about too much. I too have
been guilty of throwing hints. I shouldn't wonder if on its publication
there was not a certain amount of feeling that, 'Here we've got the
right thing.' The book may profit by it. I must admit that as the
'Napoleonic novel,' the great 'Mediterranean novel,' *The Rover* must
have appeared to some people rather slight. Well, they will find weight
and body enough in what's coming. I can safely promise that.

151. J. C. Squire on the death of Conrad

September 1924

'Editorial Notes', *London Mercury*, September 1924, 449–50.

Seldom has the death of a great artist caused as great a shock as was caused by that of Joseph Conrad. He died suddenly on August 3, and wherever the news penetrated it was received with something like incredulity. It was not that he was very young; he was, in fact, sixty-six. But fame came late to him; the general public had not become accustomed to thinking of him as an elder; he was still in the prime of his powers and known to be preparing a great Napoleonic romance; and even his intimate friends, though they had known for a long time that he was suffering from ill-health, had somehow not contemplated so early a death. That iron will, which had with such resolution made him a sailor, conquered the English language, triumphed over such great difficulties of style and technique, would (they unconsciously assumed) hold death himself at arm's length until all the work Conrad could do had been done. That he is gone is still difficult to believe.

. . . Conrad's position at his death was so high that it is difficult to realise how recently his name became known at all widely. The *succès d'estime* he had enjoyed to the full many times before he knew a more tangible kind of success. Most of his major books—*Lord Jim, Nostromo, The Nigger of the Narcissus*—were welcomed as they deserved by his fellow-artists and by a small public; more than twenty years ago the tour-de-force of *Typhoon* was almost rhapsodised over. Yet the general public, here and in America, still remained unaware of him; and it was not until the publication of *Chance*, in 1913, that the pent-up waters of his reputation burst their dams and spread over the country at large. His latest years saw him no less fertile than before; he was never a rapid, but always a persistent, worker, and since *Chance* we have had *Victory* and *The Arrow of Gold*, *The Rescue*, and *The Rover*, the last of which showed no flagging of his powers.

152. P. C. Kennedy, review, New Statesman

26 September 1925, 666

Christina Alberta's Father by H. G. Wells was reviewed alongside Conrad's Suspense and perhaps it is a measure of Kennedy's importance as a critic that he greatly praised Wells's novel.

It is impossible to speak with quite the same diffuse appreciation—though it is possible, and necessary, to speak with the keenest enthusiasm—of Joseph Conrad's achievement: great as he was, and great in two methods—the philosophical romance, such as Lord Jim, and the sublimated detective story, such as The Secret Agent—he did, towards the end of his life, produce several books which read rather as if they had been written by a student and admirer of the Conrad manner than by the great man himself. He never wrote without distinction, without a certain loftiness and exactness; but it must be admitted that he was sometimes dull. Just at the end, in The Rover, he seemed to be not so much returning to his own grand manner as suddenly developing a new manner; and, since The Rover (we are told) was 'but an interlude suggested by the longer story,' the longer story of which this present fragment is the beginning, it was natural that one should expect great things of Suspense. It is a little difficult to confess that one's expectations have been disappointed. 'This is our master, famous calm and dead': it seems ungracious to belittle his last and incomplete performance. But, whatever we owe the living, to the dead at any rate we owe the truth: let us rewrite de mortuis in that sense. And I am frankly convinced that, if Suspense had been the work of an unknown man, it would not have suggested to most people that it was by an author of genius at all. Nor can it be justly retorted that we ought not to judge by an unfinished work. The fragment is as long as any ordinary complete novel: a novel of genius should come to life on the first page, and must come to life by the time we have been introduced to the main characters and situations. But Suspense does not come to life at all. . . . There is already, in the story as we have it, a beginning of

365

violent action, a swift interweaving of threads; but there is not sufficient for any conjecture as to what will ultimately happen. We have
to be content with a general atmosphere, and with occasional touches—
very occasional touches, but impressive because of what they recall—of
the old Conrad magic. 'Cosmo had a sudden sense of an epical tale
with a doubtful conclusion'—the words, applied as they are to the
Napoleonic campaigns, have yet an almost prophetic and personal
ring; and so has the fragment's noble ending. 'Where is his star now?'
asks Cosmo, about an old man who is dead. 'Signore,' comes the
reply, 'it should be out. But who will miss it from the sky?'

153. Leonard Woolf, review, *Nation and Athenaeum*

3 October 1925, 18

What, I suppose, is the last Conrad novel which we shall read has just
been published. *Suspense* is, like so many posthumous books, uncom-
pleted, but the part which has been completed is so large (running to
300 pages) and seems to have been so carefully written and revised that
it is quite possible to enjoy it as a book and judge it as an achievement.
The posthumous fragments of great writers have a strong and sentimental attraction for many minds, and with *Suspense* I already seem to
notice the not unusual tendency of critics to hail it as the master's
masterpiece. It is, of course, easy to say that *Weir of Hermiston* would
have been the greatest of Stevenson's books if he had finished it, and
one cannot disprove the statement; on the other hand, there is really no
reason at all for believing it. The same applies to *Suspense*, although,
since in this case the completed portion is much larger and there is
much more to go on, it must be harder to delude oneself with the
belief that the portion which was never written would have been better
than *Lord Jim*. As it stands, this fragment, though it shows many of

Conrad's great merits, cannot stand by the side of *Lord Jim* and the best of his earlier works.

Mr. Curle, in a short introduction, says that 'Conrad regarded *Suspense* as, in all probability, his final book' and that he had been writing it for a long time. Apparently, it was begun before *The Rover*, which 'was but an interlude suggested by the longer story.' It is a story of the Napoleonic Wars, the period between the first Peace of Paris and Waterloo, when Napoleon was caged in Elba. The period seems to have had a great attraction for Conrad, and he had obviously made a careful study of its history. It is a 'historical novel' of the classic type, in which major and minor historical persons move somewhat stiffly among imaginary characters. Thus we have a careful portrait of Count Bubna and Lady William Bentinck at the same evening party with the hero. There is much to be said for this convention. Somehow or other, that Count Bubna, whom I remember so well hovering in Paris when fate was closing in on Napoleon in the eighth and last volume of Sorel's great history, the historically insignificant Bubna gives a certain solidity to that imaginary party to which the imaginary Cosmo goes in *Suspense*. And perhaps the story thrills with a little unreal reality when a typical Conradian character, the doctor, tells Cosmo what he heard from Prince Talleyrand through Montrond.

This semi-real atmosphere of the historical novel may be meretricious and artistically indefensible. It depends for its effect, one imagines, upon the possession of some historical knowledge by the reader, who, for instance, must at least know that Count Bubna did exist. Conrad uses it in this book with considerable skill. One can see how, with its help, he has made his book, in the first place, a very good story. It is an exciting story, less psychologically complicated than many of the later Conrads. Indeed, one is so interested in the question of what is going to happen that one's chief regret when it breaks off short is that one will never know. There are many people who will say that this is a proof of the book's merits. It is a proof of one merit which Conrad undoubtedly possessed, that of the storyteller; but it is still more a proof of the book's defects. Suppose we had only three or four hundred pages of *Lord Jim*. Most readers, it is true, would feel a sense of disappointment when they came to the last page at not knowing what happened, how the story ended. But there would have been a far deeper sense of disappointment, a sense of psychological and artistic incompleteness. I am interested not so much in the 'story,' in what *happened*, for instance, at the inquiry into the abandonment of the pilgrim ship, as in the working of Lord Jim's mind, set in a world of other minds. In *Lord Jim*, the moral and psychological problem informs the book; it *is* the book, and that is why, if the book had remained a posthumous fragment, we should have felt disappointment not only that we did not know what happened, but that we had been left with an incomplete work of art.

I have no such feeling with regard to *Suspense*. When I am left on the last page with the hero, Cosmo Latham, obviously on his way to Elba, I am disappointed because I shall never know what happened to him there. I want to know that, but that is practically all I want to know. What happens inside Cosmo Latham's head or inside the heads of the Countess or of the doctor is of no interest. This may be explained by saying that these characters are unreal; they lack that psychological reality which was so startling in Lord Jim or Falk; but the unreality is a symptom rather than a cause of Conrad's failure. Superficially, *Suspense* has all Conrad's merits. It is constructed with immense skill and care; it is solid; it has the grand air; it is the work of an artist or craftsman who has a passion for his work. The characters are wonderfully worked over, typically Conradian. The sentences march until, every now and again, they break into the well-known rhythm:—

He surrendered to the soft and invincible stillness of air and sea and stars enveloping the active desires and the secret fears of men who have the sombre earth for their stage. At every momentary pause in his long and fantastic adventure, it returned with its splendid charm and glorious serenity, resembling the power of a great and unfathomable love whose tenderness like a sacred spell lays to rest all the vividities and all the violences of passionate desire.

And yet, despite its solidity and seriousness, it leaves one with a strong feeling of emptiness and hollowness. I enjoyed reading it, but, as soon as I had finished and began to think critically of it, to look inside it, I had the feeling which one gets on cracking a fine, shining, new walnut, which has just dropped from the tree, only to find that it has nothing inside it. Most of the later Conrads give one this feeling. They are splendid shells, magnificent façades, admirable forms, but there is no life in them. Perhaps to write a great book two things are required: there must be a central, living idea which all through the writing of the book must be giving off radiant emanations like a piece of radium, and the author must also have in his mind the image of a form or shell which can take and hold and mould and restrain this idea. There are some writers—Mr. Wells is, perhaps, one—who have the radiant emanations, but no form or shell in which to enclose them; Mr. Conrad, in some of his early writings, had both, but, in *Suspense* and others of his later novels, he is in the opposite position to Mr. Wells, he has the form, complete and imposing, but the ideas within it have ceased to radiate, ceased to be alive.

154. Garnett's answer to Kennedy's review

10 October 1925

Edward Garnett, in reviewing *Suspense* in the *Weekly Westminster*, took up P. C. Kennedy's attack on Conrad (No. 152). Garnett's reference to 'Dominic' is to Dominic Cervoni, a friend of Conrad's during his early days in Marseilles when both were gun-running for the Carlist cause.

I see that a gentleman named P. C. Kennedy, writing of Conrad's unfinished novel, says:

I am frankly convinced that if *Suspense* had been the work of an unknown man, it would not have suggested to most people that it was by an author of genius at all. . . . *Suspense* does not come to life at all.

In much the same way the younger generation wrote of Turgenev's masterpieces *Fathers and Children* and *Smoke*, 'it does not come to life at all!' But the awkward fact is that the young critics die while the masterpiece remains serenely living. The truth being that the pure work of art transmutes the temporary truth into the essential truth and makes the changing forms and fashions into a thing of beauty. This is what Conrad has done in *Suspense*. He had studied the historical Memoirs of the period deeply, he knew the manners, the outlook, the attitude of Continental society instinctively because he had the tradition in his blood and his nerves in a way no Englishman has, and he

369

proceeded to construct a drama in which the figures, all moving naturally in their own atmosphere, create an organic whole out of their fleeting impact.

I should call *Suspense* myself the most mature of all Conrad's works, mature both in its artistry and philosophy of life. It is indeed not among the most powerful of his creations, but in construction and handling, in variety of scene and in easy mastery of characterisation, *Suspense* is almost faultless. By craftsmanship I do not mean merely technique but spiritual mastery.

The canvas is very large, the background impressive in its range and historical perspective. The drama begins with a twilit scene on a tower on the jetty at Genoa between the young Englishman Cosmo Latham and an Italian sailor. Instantly the Mediterranean atmosphere envelops one, calm like the sea they are watching, but delusively calm. Cosmo by his phlegmatic refusal to take a hint has stumbled into a coil of intrigue, which in the last chapter written, lands him on a felucca's deck with conspirators bound for Elba. But after this Genovan opening, with its hint of the storm cloud from Elba, forty pages of retrospect carry us back to the past life of the Royalist émigré family of the Marquis d'Armand at Latham Hall and in London. These pages give great depth of vista to the whole picture. And they lay the foundations of the plot, for the loveless marriage of Adèle d'Armand with the wealthy adventurer from India, the Count de Montevesso, prepares us for a rapid passionate development, with the future of Adèle, that figure of exquisite womanhood, and of Cosmo, her ingenious English friend, both threatened by the dark intriguing figures in Genoa surrounding them. In these first fifteen chapters Conrad has selected, assembled, and grouped these characters of three nationalities, all emanating the spirit of their time, with the finest instinct for essential values. For while the future of all these characters, including the minor but indispensable figures of Dr. Martel, the Government agent, Cantelucci, the revolutionary innkeeper, and the more important Attilio, the sailor (a second Dominic), is bound by invisible ties to that of the Man of Destiny, the drama will be played out according to their characters.

This is what I mean by Conrad's spiritual mastery, viz., the faculty of the great composer in so carrying out his theme that all the parts are in right relation to each other and to the whole. As an example examine that most original last chapter in which Cosmo escapes the gendarmes and puts to sea in the felucca, and note how exquisitely Italian wiliness is conveyed in the shadowy atmosphere of the scene, in the residence of the Sbirri and in Attilio's adroitness. By mere juxta-position the two men, Cosmo and Attilio, bring out each other's characteristics, while the atmospheric reality of the scene, of night and of dawn, is marvellously exact, and the poetic force of the adventure is enhanced by the death of the old Genoese boatman while still holding the tiller.

'Where is his star now?' said Cosmo, after looking down in silence for a time.

'Signore, it should be out,' said Attilio, with studied intonation. 'But who will miss it from the sky?'

Yes, so far as it goes *Suspense* is a masterpiece, richly mellow in its philosophy of life, with scenes flowing naturally out of one another, a natural drama, stirring, actual and complex. But what would have happened? asks the reader. Nobody knows, and from Conrad's re-mark to Mr. Curle, quoted in the latter's interesting Introduction, about 'five or six different lines of treatment,' it is clear that Conrad was waiting on his instinct. A glance at the map shows that Genoa is equidistant from Elba and Cannes, where Napoleon landed on March 1, 1815, and from Attilio's remark to Cosmo in the last pages about 'his native village on the Riviera di Ponente,' and that 'nothing would be easier than to put him ashore in the course of the next day,' I think it is clear that the next scene of action would have developed on this part of the coast, and that the plot would have hinged on the intrigues of Napoleon's Genoese adherents both by sea and land to bring off the landing, with one flying visit to Elba. All the elements of plot and counter-plot, with their appropriate instruments, are there assembled ready, and the household of Count de Montevesso at the Palazzo Brignoli is itself a mine of intrigue, but how Conrad would have spun the political climax out of the social and domestic threads he had not yet decided himself. It was his habit to refashion things as he went along, recasting chapters and elaborating fresh episodes: he kept the story, so to say, in a sort of stable flux, and by instinct worked towards the inherent solution. There is one chapter he would probably have rewritten, as it follows too closely the Memoirs of a French lady, but in other respects the lines laid down were probably permanent.

Fortunately the novel as it stands is a drama in itself, though un-finished. It is a work of high creative art, one which in its breadth and depth of vision leaves English fiction looking rather pinched and narrow-eyed. I do not expect the insular critic to comprehend this, for *Suspense* is a pure work of art.

155. Unsigned review, *Spectator*

10 October 1925, 613–14

One of the strangest figures in all English literature, Conrad, the foreign sailor who earned a European repute by writing romances in a tongue not his own, made primarily a personal rather than an aesthetic claim on our attention, the more so that he remained mysterious and unknown, took no part in the nation's everyday life, and identified himself with no causes. First and last he was the unexplained stranger who wrote in English and wrote so strikingly and yet was so difficult to read. For a time accepted wholesale as a writer of the first importance, Conrad is now gradually finding his true place. We begin to see that he was an impressive rather than a likeable writer, that he was not the great stylist we fancied, that he has no influence on either the popular imagination or even his fellow-artists, and that he lacked emotional content. Above all, we begin to realize that his characters were not really human beings at all. They were taller and less corporeal than men. This was at once Conrad's triumph and his tragedy; for we can look up to his towering figures and take pleasure in watching their activities, but we cannot love them as we can love the best of Mr. Wells' little human heroes.

In this unfinished tale of the days when Napoleon was in Elba and all Europe was overhung by his gigantic shadow, Conrad's power and inhumanity are very evident. The flaws in his style are also plain; the book begins with a descriptive passage clotted with adjectives:—

A deep red glow flushed the fronts of marble palaces piled up on the slope of an arid mountain, whose barren ridge traced high on the darkening sky a ghostly and glimmering outline. The winter sun was setting over the Gulf of Genoa. Behind the massive shore the sky to the east was like darkening glass. The open water, too, had a glassy look with a purple sheen in which the evening light lingered as if clinging to the water. The sails of a few becalmed feluccas looked rosy and cheerful, motionless in the gathering gloom.

Cosmo Latham, the Englishman-hero, in Italy calls on a childhood's playmate, Adèle, now married to a singularly disagreeable upstart, the

Count of Montevesso. Cosmo does not so much fall in love with Adèle as fall under her enchantment. Conrad's description of the hero's first morning call on the lady is exquisitely done. Their meeting is delayed just long enough to give a bright, quick impression at once of the room itself and of the hero's mood before he discovers Adèle, lovely, competent—and unhappy. With an admirable sense of values Conrad lets us guess her effect on the young Englishman:—

A very small table of ebony inlaid with silver stood between them; her hand rested on it, and Cosmo looked at it with appreciation, as if it had been an object of art. . . .

But there is much more than the psychology of romantic love in *Suspense*. From the moment of his arrival in Genoa, Cosmo has by some hazard or other come up constantly against mysterious figures. There is a sense of Genoa waiting apprehensive for some explosive event, of subterranean intrigue, and—more dimly but very impressively—of Europe becalmed and afraid of a little wind that will come blowing from Elba. Something is on foot and that something—by destiny or accident one hardly knows—draws Cosmo into itself. He falls into a midnight adventure, whose purport he does not understand, is seized by the municipal *sbirri* and astoundingly rescued by his mysterious friends. Here the story ends, most intriguingly and disappointingly, for the last fifty pages of night adventure in the harbour of Genoa are far and away the best part of *Suspense*. Darkness, the water, the dim outlines of empty boats, the excitement and confusion of Cosmo himself are combined magically. Conrad gives little detail, but such detail as he does give is unerringly just what the attentive reader's imagination needs to set the right background against this tale of action.

The epic quality of all Conrad's stories, his heroic projection of the ideal, the Englishman's, character gives to some of his work a coldness which is almost repellent, for his men are composed of concepts of behaviour, not of flesh and blood. They are, that is to say, emanations of Conrad's own world, not flashes of insight into the world of reality. In this he was much more akin to Stendhal than to any other writer: indeed he does not lie in any English tradition at all, nor has he in the least influenced English thought or English writers as other lesser artists have done. His greatest quality is one, perhaps unfortunately, foreign to us: the tasteful restraint which enables him to say as much, and only as much, as he wills. It is not a question of style or diction, though sometimes his choice of words is brilliantly effective in its use of visual stimuli:—

The swaying flames of the candles leaping from one long strip of mirror to another preceded him into the next salon where all the furniture stood ranged expectantly against the walls.

The mariner, with the sculls on his shoulder, followed the group patiently, to where, on the very edge of the quay, the Austrian soldier with his musket shouldered paced to and fro across the streak of reddish light from the garrison door.

Conrad envisaged the development of his stories as a player does a chess-board, shot one beam of light on a precise spot of some dark scene, left an exact amount of speculation. His technique is perfect in its own manner. He had stories to tell. And oddly enough he had nothing to say. In that he was all that is most unlike the great English novelists who have a great deal to say and let their story tell itself at seeming random, making life, the passing of men and women about the humdrum world, seem wonderful and important. Conrad has the great virtue of the magnitude of his conception, of his projection of a heroic world in terms of a familiar, unheroic one. His minor virtue is his constructive ability, the power to select ruthlessly and unemotionally what he would put into his stories. He is never at the mercy of his imagination, and he is always formal, unmoved himself by the vicissitudes he describes. That is why he makes real life seem vapid, because it is unlike the universe of powerful action he describes. Just as his diction lacks tone—no doubt because it was not his own natural diction —so his work as a whole lacks some element of humanity, of wildness and disorder, lacks any continuity of contact with the deepest instincts of his land of adoption. He wrote as an aristocrat, but as a Continental not as a British aristocrat.

156. Milton Waldman, review, *London Mercury*

November 1925, 97-8

Every possible view has already been published concerning the novel upon which Conrad was working at his death, and it is surprising how wide is their range; there is usually closer agreement than this upon books whose authors are admitted, without many dissenting voices, to rank among the great ones of their time. At one end of the critical scale are those who hold that *Suspense* was Conrad's greatest book, at the other those who see in it conclusive evidence that his powers were rapidly failing, and that he was just short of senility. That anyone can subscribe to this latter view is truly surprising, for the very scope of the work would seem to prove how fresh and powerful its author's mind still was. I myself do not put this posthumous book on a level with *Lord Jim*, but I think it not unlikely that Conrad might have made it so; it seems to contain many evidences that it would have been one of the great historical novels of the English language, and even now, I think, remains one of its most splendid literary fragments.

But this view, I grant, presupposes that Conrad had as yet written but a bare introduction to a very long novel which was to employ adequately the rich mass of material gathered together in the existing pages. He had never before set a stage so elaborately, with scores of characters and dozens of possible complications between them, yet all obviously moving under the shadow of the one dominating personality in Europe, Napoleon. In this introductory passage our interest is seized in turn by Cosmo, the hero, Adèle, whom he loves, her father, her brutal husband, the mysterious doctor, the obsequious and intriguing landlord Cantelucci and many others; each leads on to the next, and each, whether consciously or not, is contributing or destined to contribute to the rise or fall of the exiled Emperor. Indisputably the man whose imagination was able to evoke this setting was in the full flower of his imagination, and it seems absurd to doubt that, that man being Conrad, he would have been able to weave these threads into the glowing tapestry which our own imaginations were already prepared to conceive.

We must, certainly, look for a different Conrad here from the one we knew in *Lord Jim* and *Nostromo*. The writing is different, and never, it may be granted, quite of his characteristic beauty. But there is beauty of a different sort, the beauty of language used straightforwardly, economically and significantly. The colour is less, but the form is clearer. Conrad was trying to do a different sort of thing, but that in itself is no sign of a falling off; quite the contrary in fact. And one sure sign that he would have succeeded is that when he is ready to set his plot moving, it develops with whirlwind rapidity; it was almost painful leaving Cosmo at the moment when Fate had snatched him up and moved him, one of many pawns, one square nearer Elba. And, in the matter of actual style, if the gorgeous landscapes are missing, no less an artist was responsible for the lovely indoor scenes, the striking descriptions of rooms and furniture, the light and colour and composition of interiors.

157. W. Somerset Maugham on Conrad's Bornean novels

1933

The discussion in Maugham's story 'Neil MacAdam' is between Neil MacAdam, a recent visitor to the Far East and the Munros, a planter and his wife Darya. Though fictional, I think it can be taken to represent Maugham's own point of view.

'I read a lot of Conrad.'

'For pleasure or to improve your mind?'

'Both. I admire him awfully.'

Darya threw up her arms in an extravagant gesture of protest.

'That Pole,' she cried. 'How can you English ever have let yourselves be taken in by that wordy mountebank? He has all the superficiality of his countrymen. That stream of words, those involved sentences, the showy rhetoric, that affectation of profundity: when you get through all that to the thought at the bottom, what do you find but a trivial commonplace? He was like a second-rate actor who puts on a romantic dress and declaims a play by Victor Hugo. For five minutes you say this is heroic, and then your whole soul revolts and you cry, no, this is false, false, false.'

She spoke with a passion that Neil had never known anyone show when speaking of art or literature. Her cheeks, usually colourless, flushed and her pale eyes glowed.

'There's no one who got atmosphere like Conrad,' said Neil. 'I can smell and see and feel the East when I read him.'

'Nonsense. What do you know about the East? Everyone will tell you that he made the grossest blunders. Ask Angus.'

'Of course he was not always accurate,' said Munro, in his measured, reflective way. 'The Borneo he described is not the Borneo we know. He saw it from the deck of a merchant vessel and he was not an acute observer even of what he saw. But does it matter? I don't know why

377

fiction should be hampered by fact. I don't think it's a mean achievement to have created a country, a dark, sinister, romantic and heroic country of the soul.'

Select Bibliography

Ehrsam, Theodore G., *A Bibliography of Joseph Conrad* (1969): the most complete checklist of writings on Conrad.

Gordan, J. D., *Joseph Conrad: The Making of a Novelist* (1940): particularly chapters v and vi dealing with the reception of Conrad's early stories and his reaction to it.

Lohf, Kenneth A. & Sheehy, Eugene, P., *Joseph Conrad at Mid-Century: Editions and Studies*, 1895–1955 (1957).

Index

The index is divided into three sections: I. Conrad: writings; II. Conrad: characteristics of his work, his personality, and his reception; III. General (includes authors, periodicals, etc.). Characters in Conrad's works are indexed under the stories in which they appear. Works by other authors are indexed by title in section III.

I. JOSEPH CONRAD: WRITINGS

Almayer's Folly, 1, 2, 3, 5–10, 17, 25, 36, 39, 47–61, 63, 65, 66, 68, 69, 72, 73, 75, 79, 80, 82, 83, 92, 98, 148, 206, 342; Abdullah, 58; Ali, 52; Almayer, 47, 48, 49, 52, 53, 54, 55, 57, 58, 59, 60, 61; Babalatchi, 49, 53; Dain Maroola, 49, 52, 53, 61; Nina, 49, 52, 53, 56, 58, 59, 61; the Rajah, 53

'Amy Foster', see *Typhoon, and Other Stories*

'Anarchist, An', see *Set of Six, A*

Arrow of Gold, 29–35, 313–27, 339, 343, 360, 364; Blunt, 313, 315, 318, 319–20, 323, 326; Dominic, 315, 319, 322; Don Carlos, 318, 319, 326; George, 315, 317–18, 319, 320, 322, 325; Mills, 315, 318, 319; Ortega, 315, 318, 320, 323, 326, 327; Rita, 313–14, 315, 318–19, 325, 326; Therese, 314, 315, 323, 327

'Brute, The', see *Set of Six, A*

Chance, 1, 5, 27, 28, 29, 31, 259–84, 262, 287, 297, 305, 306, 309, 332, 342, 351, 364; Anthony, 272, 273, 274, 275, 279; Mr De Barral, 278–9; Flora, 272, 273, 274, 275, 278, 279;

Fyne, 278, 279, 280; Marlow, 278; Powell, 278

'Conde, El', see *Set of Six, A*

'Duel, The', see *Set of Six, A*

'End of the Tether, The', see *Youth: a Narrative, and Two Other Stories*

'Falk', see *Typhoon, and Other Stories*

'Freya of the Seven Isles', see *'Twixt Land and Sea*

'Gaspar Ruiz', see *Set of Six, A*

'Heart of Darkness', see *Youth: a Narrative, and Two Other Stories*

'Idiots, The', see *Tales of Unrest*

'Informer, The', see *Set of Six, A*

Inheritors, The, 15

'Karain, a Memory,' see *Tales of Unrest*

'Lagoon', see *Tales of Unrest*

Lord Jim, 2, 3, 4, 15–19, 25, 28, 31, 38, 41, 94, 111–28, 134, 148, 157, 164, 171, 174, 177, 182, 185, 206, 207,

Lord Jim—contd.
215, 229, 231, 235, 241, 243, 244,
246, 256, 273, 282, 297, 305, 306,
342, 343, 351, 359, 364, 365, 366-7,
367, 368, 375, 376; Brierly, 113,
116; Cornelius, 113, 116; Jim, 111-
112, 114, 115, 116, 119, 121, 122,
123, 125, 126, 127; Marlow, 94,
112, 113, 116, 134, 241, 359; Stein,
113, 116, 124, 207, 241

Marlow, 94, 112, 113, 116, 134, 241,
266-7, 278, 306, 317, 352, 359
Mirror of the Sea, 34, 206, 260-1

Nigger of the 'Narcissus', 3, 10, 11-15,
25, 27, 31, 34-5, 82-100, 106-7, 120,
156, 166-7, 206, 215, 220, 261, 342,
362, 364; Baker, 87, 207, 215;
Donkin, 87, 92; Singleton, 83, 87;
Wait, 83, 87, 89, 91, 92
Nostromo, 15, 19-25, 28, 31, 41, 159-
180, 182, 185, 190, 206, 215, 229,
256, 257, 260, 282, 296, 342, 357,
359, 364, 376; Decoud, 165, 168,
172, 175, 176, 179; Gould, Charles,
172, 176; Gould, Mrs, 168-9, 175,
176, 179; Mitchell, 169, 175, 176,
177, 178, 180; Monygham, 165,
168, 175, 176, 177, 178, 207;
Nostromo, 165, 168, 169, 173, 174,
175, 176, 177, 178-9, 180; Viola,
168, 175, 176, 179

Outcast of the Islands, An, 2, 3, 5-10,
15, 17, 25, 27, 41, 62-81, 73, 83, 92,
98, 107, 206, 236, 296; Aissa, 64, 68,
71, 74, 76, 77, 78, 107; Babalatchi,
64, 70, 76, 107; Lingard, 64, 67, 68,
70, 71, 74, 76, 77, 78, 215; Willems,
64, 67, 68, 70, 71, 74, 76, 77, 78, 80
'Outpost of Progress', *see Tales of
Unrest*

Personal Record, A, 25, 262

Rescue, The, 1, 10, 14, 29-35, 41, 328-
348, 351-2, 364; d'Alcacer, 333;
Jörgenson, 340; Lingard, 329, 331,
333, 334, 335, 336, 337, 338, 339,
341, 343; Travers, Edith, 330, 331,
333, 334, 335, 337, 338-9, 341, 344;
Travers, Mr, 337, 343
'Return, The', *see Tales of Unrest*
Romance, 15, 41, 171
Rover, The, 35, 36, 349-62, 364,
365, 367; Arlette, 355, 356, 359;
Catherine, 356; Peyrol, 349, 350,
352, 354, 355, 356, 357-8, 359

Secret Agent, The, 19-25, 26, 28, 29,
41, 181-209, 222, 229, 244, 256,
258, 309, 343, 365; Heat, 185, 192,
196-7, 207, 215, 244; Ossipon, 192,
193, 198, 200; Professor, 183-4, 185,
187, 192, 198, 199, 200; Stevie, 193,
196, 198, 202, 207; Verloc, Adolf,
182, 183, 185, 186-7, 188, 192-3,
196, 197, 198, 199, 201-2; Verloc,
Mrs, 187-8, 193, 196, 197, 198, 202,
207
'Secret Sharer, The', *see 'Twixt Land
and Sea*
Set of Six, A, 11, 23, 24, 26, 27, 210-
226, 228
'Anarchist, An', 212, 215-16, 219,
222; Gee, 222
'Brute, The', 212, 216, 218, 219, 223
'Conde, Il', 218
'Duel, The', 212, 216, 218, 219, 220,
223, 226, 257; Feraud, 212;
D'Hubert, 212, 223
'Gaspar Ruiz', 211, 215, 216, 218-
219, 220, 223; Gaspar, 211,
212
'Informer, The', 212, 216, 218, 222,
224; Sevrin, 222; X, 222

Shadow-Line, The, 29–35, 304–12;
Burns, 309; Giles, 307–8; Ransome,
307
'Smile of Fortune, A', see 'Twixt Land
and Sea
Suspense, 36, 37, 363–76; Adele, 375;
Attilio, 371; Bubna, 367; Cosmo,
366, 368, 370, 371, 373, 375

Tales of Unrest, 11–15, 25, 101–10, 206
'Idiots, The', 14, 102
'Karain, a Memory', 101, 110, 185,
207; Karain, 101–2
'Lagoon', 107
'Outpost of Progress, An', 14, 102,
107, 229
'Return, The', 103, 107, 207, 229
'Tomorrow', see Typhoon, and Other
Stories
'Twixt Land and Sea, 5, 24, 27, 29–35,
251–8
'Freya of the Seven Isles', 252, 254,
255–6, 257; Freya, 257
'Secret Sharer, The', 30, 36, 41, 251,
253, 254, 255, 257, 309, 359
'Smile of Fortune, A', 30, 253, 254,
255, 256–7
Typhoon, and Other Stories, 15–19, 20,
23, 28, 143–58, 220, 342, 364
'Amy Foster', 144, 146, 154, 156,
157–8
'Falk', 144, 146, 154, 156, 206, 257;
Falk, 144, 146, 154, 157, 244;
Hermann, 146
'Tomorrow', 144, 156, 158, 229;
Bessie, 158; Hagberd, 158
'Typhoon', 143, 146, 153, 156, 164,
206, 251, 256, 257, 362; Jukes,
153, 156, 207; MacWhirr, 143,

146 153, 156, 157, 182, 207,
215

Under Western Eyes, 4, 5, 19, 26, 27,
30, 35, 41, 227–50, 257–8, 309;
Haldin, 227, 233, 238; Haldin,
Natalia, 230, 238; Ivanovitch, 235,
237; Mikulin, 229, 238; Nikita,
235, 237; Professor, 231, 232;
Razumov, 227, 229, 233, 234, 235,
237, 238, 239, 241–2, 243–4, 245

Victory, 4, 29–35, 41, 285–303, 332,
342–3, 357, 364; Davidson, 297;
Heyst, 285, 286, 287, 290–1, 293,
294, 296, 298, 299; Jones, 286, 288,
290, 291, 293, 297, 300, 303; Lena,
286, 287, 290, 291, 293, 294, 298,
299; Pedro, 286, 291, 297; Ricardo,
286, 288, 290, 291, 293, 297, 300,
302; Schomberg, 288, 290, 293, 297,
300; Wang, 291

Within the Tides, 30

Youth: a Narrative, and Two Other
Stories, 15–19, 28, 110, 129–42,
206
'End of the Tether, The', 3, 131,
133, 134, 136–7, 139, 142, 220,
229, 249, 309; Whalley, 136–7,
243
'Heart of Darkness', 3, 37, 129–30,
131–3, 135, 136, 137, 139, 142,
171, 174, 176–7, 200, 229, 238,
254, 306
'Youth', 3, 131, 133, 134, 136, 137,
138–9, 142, 174, 182, 185, 212,
220, 229, 248–9, 254, 256, 257

INDEX

II. JOSEPH CONRAD: CHARACTERISTICS, PERSONALITY AND RECEPTION

action, 246–8, 296, 355; slowness of, 70
aesthetic qualities, 85; *see also* beauty
affectation, 77, 79
Africa, depiction of, 132–3
analytical abilities, 79, 139
anarchism, portrayal of, 196
artificiality, 357
artistic qualities, 82, 106, 141, 203–9, 244–5
atmosphere, creation of, 60, 95, 107, 110, 136, 138, 176, 193, 223, 228–9, 238, 245, 246–8, 251, 271, 273, 275, 280, 287, 288, 307, 317, 322, 324, 330, 336, 340, 341, 354, 357, 366, 367, 370, 377
autobiographical content, 306
awkwardness of style, 52

beauty, 53, 141, 167, 257, 291, 301, 316, 320, 334, 369; in his stories, 108, 139, 209, 255; of style, 58, 78
bravery and courage, 48, 287
breadth, 180
brevity, 113

character analysis, 281
character drawing, 48, 54, 55, 57, 58, 61, 63, 64, 65, 66, 68, 69–70, 71, 76, 77, 78, 79, 83, 86, 87, 88–9, 92, 95, 100, 101, 115, 116, 125, 133, 143, 144, 146, 149, 153, 165, 168, 169–70, 171, 172–3, 175–6, 179, 185, 186, 192, 194, 197, 199, 207–8, 223, 227, 232, 235, 237–8, 252, 254, 255, 271, 272, 274, 277, 278–9, 285–6, 287–8, 293, 296–7, 300, 305–6, 306–8, 313, 315, 317, 322, 323, 330, 334, 340, 343, 352, 355, 356, 359–60, 370, 372, 373; inter-relationships, 275;

relationship with scene, 337, 343, 357
charm, 63
circumlocution, 52
clarity of expression, 122
climax, 355
colloquial language, 90, 96
comedy, 183, 285, 286, 323
complexity of style, 329
Conrad, Joseph
on his autobiography, 262
biography, 40
contemporary response, reaction to, 2
criticism, reaction to, 1–2, 6–7, 13, 66, 83, 88, 94, 97, 104, 120, 131, 145, 197, 203, 210, 219–20, 224–5, 231, 263, 277, 314, 363
his death, critics' reaction to, 364
life story, effect on his work, 72–3
on the literary profession, 62
on newspapers, 1
personality, 162–3, 213, 345–6, 472
Poland, life in, 72–3
on popularity, 261
on publishers, 260–1
on R. L. Stevenson, 261
on style, 10, 261
on his work, 2; *Almayer's Folly*, 7, 159; *Chance*, 259, 263; *Heart of Darkness, The*, 129–30; *Lord Jim*, 259; *Nostromo*, 159–60; *Rescue, The*, 328; *Rover, The*, 360–1, 363; *Secret Agent, The*, 23, 181, 197; *Suspense*, 360–1, 363; *Under Western Eyes*, 236
crudity, 52; of style, 80
cruelty, 224, 302
cynicism, 347

384

degeneration of character, 99, 132, 135, 168, 177

depressive qualities, 93

descriptive abilities, 248-9, 300, 303, 344, 359

destiny, 243, 249-50

detail, attention to, 64, 69, 95, 71, 85-6, 114, 134, 136, 167, 276, 299, 300, 330, 340, 344, 373; see also elaboration

dialogue, 188, 310, 325, 341

diffuseness, 69, 154

discrimination, lack of, 96

discursiveness, 124, 127, 141-2, 153, 167, 171, 178, 179, 189, 305, 352

drama, 177, 298, 323, 371

dullness of his stories, 51, 58, 70, 86, 118, 123, 126, 127, 135, 142, 167, 187, 188, 250, 272, 325, 351, 365; of style, 77, 100

East, Eastern islands, 48, 50, 60, 63, 110, 115, 116, 119, 123, 136, 249, 329, 330, 377; see also tropics

East, life in the, 56, 65; use of knowledge of, 51, 69, 79

effect, building up of, 157; overstraining for, 71; weakened by verbosity, 75

elaboration, 123, 154, 164-5, 250, 335, 345, 375; of style, 109

emotion, treatment of, 110, 315, 326, 331, 334

epic qualities, 124, 131, 139, 204, 343, 373

epithet, use of, 109

events, narration of, 87, 89, 91, 245-6, 305

evil, 290, 292, 293, 294, 296, 316

experience, lack of literary, 54

experience, use of, 158, 206, 214, 226, 237, 277, 306, 308

expression, beauty of, 57

freshness, 90; see also originality

grammar, weakness of, 103

hatred, 236

heroism, 135, 179, 296, 306; lack of, 83

historical elements, 367

honour, 241-3, 361

horror, 102, 137, 143, 219, 235, 285, 289-90, 292, 299, 310-11

human interest, lack of, 100

human nature, knowledge of, 51, 227; treatment of, 192-3, 196, 214, 221, 249, 272, 273-4, 277, 287, 316, 347-348

human sympathy, 58

humour, 53, 90, 112, 134, 135, 144, 172, 173, 182, 183, 184, 189, 194, 195, 199, 212, 216, 221, 223, 226, 271-2, 317

ideals, 356

ideas, 49, 125, 167; subtlety of, 58

illusion, creation of, 311, 317

imaginative qualities, 48, 53, 65, 74, 76, 144, 152, 158, 163, 171, 173, 177, 183, 190, 194, 198, 214, 252, 268, 290, 292, 304-5, 307, 317, 330-1, 375

impartiality, 215, 298, 306; see also character drawing

incidents, description of, 362

influence, literary, on J. C., 85-7, 258; lack of, 79

influence on other authors, 258

insight, 192, 194, 200; into characters, 168, 253

intensity, 77, 157, 210, 231, 252, 255, 299, 300, 344, 357

introspective qualities, 283

irony, 90, 109, 135, 173, 183, 185, 192, 193, 195, 218, 221, 222, 226, 237,

irony—*contd*
238, 273, 277, 278, 280, 285-6, 287, 290, 294, 312, 315, 317
isolation, 74, 132-3; *see also* loneliness

language, command of, 122
literary training, lack of, 103
London, 196, 198
loneliness, 67, 74, 325; *see also* isolation
love, 49, 147, 148-9, 222-3, 287, 293, 339, 340
lucidity of expression, 154

Malay life, 48
maturity, 63
melancholy, 325
melodrama, 301, 303, 358-9
methods of building story, 315-16; unorthodoxy of, 265, 271
middle-class, depiction of, 278
moral theme, 178, 243-5, 301, 308, 314
morality, 79, 81, 113, 183
motives, analysis of, 192, 306
mystery, atmosphere of, 63, 254, 317, 318, 320, 327, 338, 340, 349, 357

narrative, use of, 178, 281, 296, 297, 306, 310, 349-50; ability, 97, 142, 154, 305
narrator, use of, 117, 118, 235, 266, 274-5, 276, 278, 279, 309, 317, 352
nature, 204-5, 214-15, 314

obscurity, 314, 346, 358; of style, 80
observation and perception, 79, 100, 154, 209
originality, 52, 54, 55, 57, 59, 60, 61, 65, 67, 76, 79, 88, 94, 95, 111, 119, 120, 121, 162, 170, 229, 272, 281, 293, 299; of style, 165, 273

parochial spirit, 50
passion, 49, 65, 68, 110, 361
past, romance of, 354
pathos, 48, 65, 74, 78-9, 89, 90, 112, 125, 211-12, 216, 218, 226, 257, 298, 339; lack of, 51
personality, influence on his work, 289, 358
philosophy, 148-9, 191
physical settings, 47, 50, 55, 58, 60, 61, 63, 65, 66-7, 71, 78, 86, 87, 89, 115, 119, 132, 150, 157-8, 161, 170, 175, 248, 252, 302, 334, 354-5, 362, 370, 376
picturesqueness, 58
plot: characteristics, 170, 196, 284, 334, 371; complexity, 341; lack of, 11-15, 83, 95, 97-8, 118, 178, 180, 307, 325; submerged by description, 71; *see also* structure; themes
poetic qualities, 58, 94, 96, 106, 109, 115, 124, 141, 163, 175, 177, 192, 222, 238, 272, 277, 280, 338, 343; atmosphere, 49; of style, 72, 92
popularity, 1, 2, 11, 27, 30, 93, 197, 281-2, 299, 303, 342-3
power of writing, 49, 53, 54, 55, 60, 61, 63, 65, 71, 85, 90, 91, 103, 114, 124, 136, 143, 153, 168, 173, 178, 191, 195, 239, 257, 351, 352, 372; of style, 77, 78, 79
proportion, 167, 326
prose, characteristics of, 254-5, 256
psychological insight, 103, 287
psychology, use of, 120, 132, 153, 190, 227, 229, 230, 232, 233, 237, 238, 253, 272, 281, 284, 290, 296, 300, 305, 308, 311, 325, 331, 349, 359, 367, 368, 373; of action, 158; of characters, 177, 179, 183, 193, 282, 299, 306; of scene, 175, 177, 341

realism, 86, 88, 90, 92, 98, 101, 133, 154, 166, 169, 179, 188, 199, 219, 234, 275, 280, 288, 290, 293, 320, 330, 337, 341; of characters, 297, 299–300, 350

religiousness, 244

repetition for emphasis, 136, 338

restraint, 56, 58, 68, 120, 299, 373–4; lack of, 71

rhetoric, 136, 252

romantic qualities, 50, 57, 63, 75, 76, 78, 116, 135, 151, 156–7, 166, 179, 229, 254, 255, 272, 305, 306, 332, 334, 335, 350, 359, 360

Russian character, 232, 234, 235, 238

sea, 12, 94–5, 99, 133, 143, 145–6, 147, 153, 154, 158, 166, 215, 251, 273; use of knowledge of, 83, 87, 90, 109, 125, 144, 309

seamen, 149–50, 316

sensationalism, 287

sensitivity, 255

sentimentality, 195, 216

ship, human relationship with, 333

simplicity, 194, 292; of plot, 352

sincerity, 195

slavonic qualities, 24, 191, 195–6, 221, 240, 243, 305

slowness of story, 358

sombreness, 14, 48, 53, 55, 60, 65, 101, 102, 109, 119, 221, 279

South American life, 175, 176; see also tropics

spiritual background, 285, 288, 289, 327

storms, 135, 146, 153

strength of presentation, 94

structure of plot, 281, 330, 340, 355, 356; unorthodoxy of, 174, 179, 291

style, 82, 177–8, 188, 206, 258, 327, 331, 360, 372; awkwardness, 52; beauty, 65; complexity, 329;

dignity, 336; haste in, 179; jerkiness, 86, 110; slowness, 58

subtlety, 59, 122, 137, 138, 139, 144, 156, 158, 165, 205, 206, 227, 231, 242, 278; of plot, 127; of style, 77

suggestion, abilities of, 305, 327

supernatural, 307

symbolism, 331

sympathy, 164, 320

temperament, effect of his, 274

themes, 150, 256, 333, 370; beauty of, 57; see also plot

thoroughness, 137–8

time, sense of, 355–6

tragic qualities, 68, 79–80, 113, 124, 154, 164, 212, 238, 254, 275–6, 279, 280, 288, 290, 302, 306, 323, 329, 330, 335, 340, 341

travel experience, use of, 72, 80, 81; see also experience

trivial details, 96; see also detail, attention to; elaboration

tropics, depiction of, 78, 229, 340

tropics, effect on his work, 79

ugliness, 182

unity in his work, 174, 277; of effect, 47; of theme, 123; of vision, 274

universe, vision of, 203–9, 214, 257–258, 301, 306, 346, 357

unorthodoxy of structure, 174, 179, 291

unusual words, 89

vagueness, 142; of story, 86; of style, 74

verbosity, 69, 73–5, 86, 95, 114, 121, 122, 123, 126, 141–2, 164–5, 166, 377

vigour of writing, 167, 170, 184, 216

violence and murder, 188–9, 198, 199, 216, 219, 299, 317

virtue, 285, 296
visual qualities, 94, 124, 198, 206, 231, 256, 268, 280, 287, 292, 374; of events, 78
vitality of characters, 288; of style, 77
vividness, 92, 99, 102, 107, 113, 116, 120, 125, 136, 138, 139, 146, 151, 158, 167, 170, 185, 229, 235, 301,

345, 359; of characters, 300, 313, 354

warfare, 179
wit, 278; see also humour
women, 12, 169, 278, 297, 322, 339, 359
world, knowledge of, 177

III. GENERAL

Abinger Harvest, 345-8
Academy, 4, 11, 12, 17, 18, 27-8, 37, 54, 94-6, 104-8, 109-10, 115-17, 151, 152-5, 162
Academy and Literature, 17, 131-3
Academy award, 14
Advance of the English Novel, The, 38, 303
Ancient Mariner, 32, 251
Antemurale, 40
Armstrong, Martin, 35
Art of Joseph Conrad, The, 40
Athenaeum, 8, 16, 17, 20, 23, 24, 28, 29, 52, 79-80, 137-9
Atlantic Monthly, 38, 298
Awkward Age, 270

Baines, Jocelyn, 40
Balzac, Honoré de, 8, 204-5
Baring, Maurice, 231
Becke, Louis, 8, 13, 52
Bennet, Gordon, 5
Bennett, Arnold, 20, 23, 82, 161, 190, 201, 263, 276; comparison with, 337
Bennett's Journal, 190, 276
Beresford, J. D., 33
Bibliography of Joseph Conrad, A, 41-2
Black and White, 8, 14, 20, 166-7
Blackburn, W., 40
Blackmore, R. D., 89
Blackwood, William, 3, 4, 16, 40, 129

Blackwood's Magazine, 3, 15, 110, 124, 132, 139, 164, 261
Bobrowski, Tadeusz, 40
Bojarski, Edward, 42
Bone, James, 349-50
Bookman, 6-7, 16, 28, 31, 32, 58, 72, 126, 155-7, 225-6, 309-10
Bookman (U.S.A.), 199-200
Bowen, Elizabeth, 39
Bradbrook, M. C., 39
British Weekly, 16, 169-70
Buchan, John, 177
Bullen, Frank, 145
Busza, Andrzej, 40

Caine, Hall, 292
Canby, Henry S., 13
Cannan, Gilbert, 263
Captain Kettle, K.C.B., 152
Captains Courageous, 97
Castles in Spain and other Screeds, 38
Chassé, Charles, 26
Chesson, W. H., 5, 9, 11, 181
Chicago Review, 41
Chwalewik, Witold, 41
Citizen, 8
Clark Russell, William, 83
Clifford, Sir Hugh, 3, 5, 28, 37
Coleridge, S. T., 32
Colvin, Sir Sidney, 30, 33, 281-2
Colvins and their Friends, The, 38

Conrad, Borys, 40
Conrad, Jessie, 10, 20, 26-7, 38
Conrad: A Reassessment, 40
Conrad the Novelist, 40
Conrad: the Psychologist as Artist, 40
Conradiana, 41, 42
Conrad's Eastern World, 40
Conrad's Heart of Darkness and the Critics, 41
Conrad's Models of Mind, 41
Conrad's Polish Background, 40
Conrad's Politics, 40
Conrad's Secret Sharer and the Critics, 41
Conrad's Short Fiction, 41
Conrad's Western World, 40
Country Life, 23, 186-9, 217-19
Courtney, W. L., 17, 23, 36, 85-8, 114-15, 213-17, 219, 224, 282, 324-325
Crane, Stephen, 13, 123; influence on J. C., 85, 86-7
Crankshaw, Edward, 39
Crime and Punishment, 132, 229
Critic, 6, 28, 50-1
Critic (U.S.A.), 16, 127-8
Critical Quarterly, 41
Cumberland, Mr, 1
Cunninghame Graham, R. B., 20, 22, 40, 129-30
Curle, Richard, 20, 26, 27, 30, 33, 34, 37, 228-30, 262
Cutler, F. W., 38

Daily Chronicle, 5, 6, 8, 9, 10, 12, 16, 17, 30, 49, 63-4, 73, 89-91, 181, 281
Daily Mail, 12, 19, 21, 33, 83-4, 103, 145-7
Daily News, 6, 17, 21, 23, 24, 28, 32, 33, 47, 68, 124-5, 210-12, 220, 251-253, 271-3, 285-7
Daily Telegraph, 14, 17, 23, 24, 30, 36, 85-8, 101-2, 114-15, 167-9, 213-17, 282, 324-5

Dana, Richard Henry, 83
Davidson, Donald, 38
de la Mare, Walter, 289-94, 316
Dickens, Charles, 198, 204-5, 256
Doran, Mr, 260
Dostoievsky, Fyodor, 25, 132, 234, 239
Doubleday, Page and Co., 5, 29, 260, 261
Duchess, The, 263
Duchess of Malfi, The, 240

Ebb Tide, The, 122
Edinburgh Review, 22, 201-2
Egoist, The, 270
Ehrsam, Theodore, 41-2
English Review, 240-50
Everyman, 30, 33
Experiment in Autobiography, 38

Fielding, Henry, 218
Flaubert, Gustave, 107-8, 289-80
Fleishman, A., 40
Follett, Wilson, 37
Ford, Ford Madox, 3, 14-15, 21, 38, 171, 240-50
Forster, E. M., 36, 345-8
Fortitude, 263
Fortnightly Review, 37
Forum, 37
France, Anatole, 348
Frederic, Harold, 98-100
Freeman, John, 38

Galsworthy, John, 4, 11, 23, 37, 38, 197, 203-9, 214, 360-1
Garnett, Mrs Constance, 25, 211
Garnett, Edward, 2, 3, 5, 7, 11, 14, 17, 20, 22, 24, 25, 26, 30, 31, 34, 35, 36, 37, 104-8, 131-3, 174-7, 191-3, 197, 221-3, 224-5, 236, 237-9, 277-80, 369-71
George, Jessie, *see* Conrad, Jessie

Gilbert, W. S., and Sullivan, Sir
Arthur, 187
Gissing, George, 140
Glasgow Evening News, 31, 34, 148–50,
301–2, 356–8
Glasgow Herald, 8, 28, 65, 88–9
Glasgow News, 25–6, 195–7, 283–4
Goodenough, Admiral, 34
Gordan, J. D., 39
Gorki, Maxim, 158
Gould, Gerald, 32, 299–301, 310–312
Graham, Anderson, 23, 217–19, 220
Graphic, 17, 18
Graver, Lawrence, 41
Great Tradition, The, 39
Guardian, 7, 8, 35, 57
Guerard, A. J., 39, 40
Guetti, James, 41

Haggard, H. Rider, 35
Hamlet, 300
Harcourt, Sir William, 189
Hardy, Thomas, 33, 195, 274, 275,
321, 325–42
Harkness, Bruce, 41
Harper's Weekly, 260, 262
Harte, Bret, 151
Henley, W. E., 3
Henty, G. A., 35, 350
Hewitt, Douglas, 37, 40
Hitchens, Robert S., 199
Hope, Anthony, 75
Howe, Irving, 40, 199
Hudson, 260
Hueffer, *see* Ford
Hugo, Victor, 9
Hyne, C. J. C. W., 152

Ibsen, Henrik, 337
Illustrated London News, 9, 12, 13, 18,
20, 66–7, 180

Jabłkowska, Róza, 41
James, Henry, 16, 123, 126, 155–6,
207, 229, 258, 263–70, 272, 274, 285,
298, 305, 308, 359
Jean-Aubry, G., 39, 40
Johnson, Bruce, 41
Joseph Conrad: A Critical Biography
(Baines), 40
Joseph Conrad: Poland's English Genius
(Bradbrook), 39
*Joseph Conrad: Some Aspects of the Art
of the Novel* (Crankshaw), 39
Joseph Conrad (Follett), 37
Joseph Conrad: A Personal Remembrance
(Ford), 38
*Joseph Conrad: The Making of a
Novelist* (Gordan), 39
Joseph Conrad (Guerard), 39
*Joseph Conrad: A Psychoanalytical
Biography* (Meyer), 40
Joseph Conrad: Achievement and Decline
(Moser), 40
*Joseph Conrad and the Fiction of Auto-
biography* (Said), 41
Joseph Conrad (Stewart), 40–1
Joseph Conrad (Walpole), 38
Joseph Conrad: A Study, 37
Joseph Conrad and His Circle, 38
Joseph Conrad as I Knew Him, 38
*Joseph Conrad: Letters to William
Blackwood and David S. Meldrum*,
40
Joseph Conrad, Life and Letters, 39
Joseph Conrad's Fiction, 40
*Joseph Conrad's Letters to R. B. Cun-
ninghame Graham*, 40
*Journal of the Discovery of the Source of
the Nile*, 209

Karl, Frederick, 40, 41, 42
Kennedy, P. C., 36, 365–6, 369
King Lear, 34
Kipling, Rudyard, 8–9, 14, 18, 69, 77,

82, 97–8, 136, 142, 143, 145, 151, 152, 252, 258, 350, 351, 360
Kirschner, Paul, 40
Knapp Hay, Eloise, 40
Knopf, Alfred, 5, 29, 260
Koc, Barbara, 41

Lawrence, D. H., 263
Lear of the Steppes, 117, 211, 220
Leavis, F. R., 39
Library of Six Shilling Fiction, 47
Limits of Metaphor, The, 41
Literary News, 5, 59–60
Literary World, 10, 16, 31
Literature, 16
Littell, Philip, 313–14
Littell's Living Age, 28, 33
London Mercury, 1, 5, 34, 342–5, 375–6
Londoners, The, 199
Loti, Pierre, 72
Lucas, E. V., 38
Lynd, Robert, 23, 210–12, 251–3, 271–273, 285–7

Macaulay, Rose, 35
MacCarthy, Desmond, 38, 361–2
Maeterlinck, Maurice, 156
Manchester Guardian, 9, 16, 17, 19, 20, 28, 32, 37, 77, 111–13, 134–5, 171–173, 181–4, 228–30, 254–6, 273–6, 349–50
Marryat, Captain, 85–6, 158
Masefield, John, 141–2, 254–6
Master Builder, The, 337
Maugham, W. Somerset, 377–8
Megroz, R. C., 38
Meldrum, D. S., 15, 16, 26, 111, 281
Melville, Herman, 63, 152
Meredith, George, 90, 111, 120, 256, 300, 305
Methuen, 282
Meyer, Bernard, 40

Michael, Marion C., 42
Milobedzki, Jozef, 41
Mimesis and Metaphor, 41
Moderns, The, 38
Monkhouse, A. N., 32, 37, 181–4
Montague, C. E., 273–6
Morf, Gustav, 39
Morning Post, 16, 18, 19, 21, 22, 24, 32, 33, 34, 143–4, 181, 231–3, 308–9, 314–16, 329–31
Morrell, Lady Ottoline, 38
Mortimer, Raymond, 36, 358–60
Moser, Thomas, 40, 41
Mroczkowski, Przemysław, 41
Murcia, Ugo, 41
My Father: Joseph Conrad, 40
My World as in my Time, 38

Najder, Zdzisław, 40, 42
Nation, 25, 31, 32, 35, 191–3, 221–3, 224–5, 237–9, 277–80, 295–7, 304–8, 325–7, 337–40
Nation (U.S.A.), 7, 80–1
Nation and Athenaeum, 36, 38, 366–369
National Observer, 9, 69–70
Neil MacAdam, 377–8
New Age, 23
New Republic, 313–14
New Review, 3, 11
New Statesman, 32, 33, 34, 36, 38, 299–301, 310–12, 321–4, 358–60, 365–366
New York American, 18, 151
New York Daily Tribune, 16, 22
New York Herald, 5
New York Tribune, 351–3
Newbolt, Sir Henry, 38
Newton, W. Douglas, 34, 341–2
Noble, James Ashcroft, 54
North American Review, 37
Notes on Life and Letters, 36
Notes on Novelists, 263–70

Observer, 22, 23, 30, 33, 281
O'Connor, T. P., 6
On the Eve, 212, 221
Outpost of Progress, 129

Pair of Blue Eyes, A, 325
Pall Mall Gazette, 11, 12, 16, 122–4, 227–8, 261
Pall Mall Magazine, 261
Palmer, John, 40
Paradise of Snakes, 41
Pater, Walter, 252
Pawling, Sidney, 3
Payn, James, 9, 12, 66–7
Pericles, 325
Phelps, William Lyon, 38, 303
Pinker, J. B., 3–4, 21, 33, 36, 259
Poe, Edgar Allan, 235
Polish Heritage of Joseph Conrad, The, 39
Political Novels of Joseph Conrad, The, 40
Politics and the Novel, 40
Poradowska, M., 6
Portraits, 361–2
Prophet of Berkeley Square, 199
Public Opinion, 31, 118
Punch, 30, 34, 282, 336

Quarterly Review, 37
Quiller-Couch, A. T., 11, 12, 13, 114
Quinn, John, 4

Rapin, René, 41
Reader's Guide to Joseph Conrad, A, 40
Red Badge of Courage, The, influence on J. C., 85, 86–7
Resink, G. J., 41
Review of Reviews, 166
Reynolds, Stephen, 37
Rice, David, 3
Richardson, S., 325
Roberts, Morley, 13

Rosenfield, Claire, 41
Rothenstein, William, 38
Russell, Clark, 12, 35, 88, 145

Said, E. W., 41
Sandersons, 34
Saturday Review, 6, 7, 9, 12, 19, 32, 33, 53, 73–6, 97–8, 98–100
Schiller, J. C. F., 71
Schopenhauer, A., 70
Scotsman, 6, 8, 20, 22, 31, 32 48, 65, 287–8
Scott, Michael, 158
Scott-James, R. A., 23, 24
Scrutiny, 39
Sea-Dreamer, The, 40
Sewanee Review, 38, 39, 41
Shakespeare, William, 325
Shaw, George Bernard, 187
Shorter, Clement, 32
Sir Charles Grandison, 325
Sketch, 9, 16, 28, 34, 70–1, 118, 341–2
Smollett, T., 158
Speaker, 5, 6, 12, 13, 16, 18, 55–6, 120–122, 141–2, 157–8, 174–7
Spectator, 8, 9, 10, 14, 16, 22, 27, 28, 30, 31, 32, 35, 36, 39, 61, 78–9, 92–3, 119–20, 177–9, 258, 281, 372–4
Speke, J. H., 209
Sphere, 24, 32
Squire, Sir John C., 358, 364
Stallman, R. W., 40
Standard, 11, 12, 18, 27, 28, 30, 31, 256–8, 281
Star, 30, 198
Stevenson, Robert Louis, 9, 32, 35, 70, 71, 122, 142, 158, 185, 256, 354
Stewart, J. I. M., 40–1
Sunday Times, 23, 29
Swettenham, Frank, 59
Symons, Arthur, 37, 97–8

Tablet, 8

Talk With Joseph Conrad, A, 38
Tanner, Tony, 41
Tarnawski, Wit, 41
Thackeray, W. M., 186, 207, 256, 300
Thomas, Edward, 24, 225–6
Thompson, Francis, 327
Time and Tide, 35
Times, The, 35, 220, 221
Times Literary Supplement, 18, 23, 24, 25, 28, 30, 35, 38, 136–7, 164–5, 184–5, 289–92, 316–20, 332–5, 354–356
Tolstoy, Leo, 158
Tomlinson, H. M., 30
T.P.'s Weekly, 19
Treasure Island, 35
Truth, 21, 32, 194
Turgenev, I., 8, 107–8, 109, 117, 205, 207, 210–11, 220, 223, 234, 239, 305, 339, 369
Turn of the Screw, 285
Turner, J. M. W., 300
Typee, 63

Unwin, Fisher, 2, 3, 5, 10, 47, 51, 82

Van de Water, Frederic, 351–3
Van Marle, Hans, 41
Vidan, Ivo, 41
Virgin Soil, 212, 221
Virginian, The, 353

Waldman, Milton, 375–6
Waliszewski, Kazimierz, 1
Walpole, Hugh, 37, 263
Warren, R. P., 41
Watt, Ian, 41
Watts, C. T., 40
Waugh, Arthur, 6, 50–1
Webster, J., 240
Weekly Sun, 6, 8, 10, 21
Weekly Westminster, 37, 369–71
Weir of Hermiston, 158
Wells, H. G., 7–8, 9–10, 38, 53, 73–6, 181, 368–9, 372
Westminster Gazette, 14, 24, 34, 233–5, 292–4
Weyman, Stanley, 75
'White Man and Brown', 49
White, Stewart Edward, 199–200
Wister, Owen, 353
Woolf, Leonard, 36, 358–9, 366–9
Woolf, Virginia, 38, 332
Wordsworth, W., 64
World, 6, 9, 14, 51
Wrecker, The, 122

Yeats, W. B., 142
Yelton, Donald, 41

Zabel, M. D., 39
Zabierowski, Stefan, 41
Zangwill, I., 94
Zola, Émile, 52, 149, 186